Guns and Rifles of the World

GUNS and RIFLES
of the World

Howard L. Blackmore

CHANCELLOR
PRESS

To the memory of
Cecil Gordon Vokes (1891-1961)
Engineer and Gun Collector

First published in Great Britain by B.T. Batsford Limited

This edition published by Chancellor Press
59 Grosvenor Street
London W1

ISBN 0 907486 01 0 ✓

Printed in Hong Kong

Preface

It would be idle to pretend that one volume, even as large as this, can do more than outline its subject. The number of books which have been devoted to one make of gun alone—the Colt and the Winchester are examples—makes it obvious that only a representative number of models can be illustrated and described within the compass of this book. Nevertheless by gathering together a large variety of firearms and grouping them according to their technical and national features I have endeavoured to provide a convenient visual reference book for the student who, at the moment, is obliged to consult a large assortment of catalogues—not always readily available—in order to locate existing specimens of some particular gun, or to trace examples of some unusual mechanism. At the same time I have written the Introduction so that it follows closely the sections of illustrations, and will, I hope, give both the specialist and the general reader a more comprehensive view of the development of the shoulder-gun from its beginning up to the end of the nineteenth century.

The choice of weapons has raised some problems and has been to some extent governed by the availability of photographs. I must admit also that in some cases I have reduced the number of items on a page rather than sacrifice the detail of a fine photograph. I have not attempted to segregate military from sporting weapons, or to trace the separate development of firearms like the musket, as an adequate range of these models was illustrated by Mr. Claude Blair in his *European and American Arms*. The fully automatic gun which was invented and produced in the last quarter of the nineteenth century I have deliberately omitted, because almost without exception the production models of this period come under the classification of military machine guns, which are another subject on their own.

The task of compiling this book would not have been possible without the co-operation of all those owners or curators of collections who have either supplied photographs or have allowed them to be taken, and who have gone to great trouble to vouchsafe additional information; and it has been considerably lightened by the assistance of my friends of the arms and armour world. I am particularly indebted to Mr. A. R. Dufty, A.R.I.B.A., F.S.A., Master of the Armouries of the Tower of London, and his assistants, Mr. A. N. Kennard, B.A., F.S.A., Mr. W. R. Reid, F.S.A. (Scot) and Mr. H. Russell Robinson, F.S.A., on whose good nature I have trespassed for so long. I am most grateful also to those stalwarts of the Victoria and Albert Museum, Mr. Claude Blair, M.A., F.S.A., Mr. John Hayward, B.A., and Mr. B. W. Robinson, M.A., B.Litt., for their good-natured acceptance of my entry into their highly competent and professional world. Mr. Blair, my long-suffering friend and collaborator in this series, has also been kind enough to read this manuscript and to offer many valuable suggestions. I should also like to acknowledge my debt to the following whose services are far too numerous and varied to be mentioned individually—Mr. C. Bass, B.Sc. (Econ.), Messrs. R. and P. A. Bedford, Mr. F. J. Bubear, Mr. A. C. Carpenter, the late Miss Phyllis Collen, Mr. Mark Dineley, the late Major J. H. W. Gill, Mr. S. B. Haw, Mr. W. Keith Neal, F.S.A. (Scot), Mr. James D. Lavin, Mr. Harold L. Peterson, A.B., M.A., of the United States National Park Service, Mr. A. T. Taylerson, M.A., Mr. J. Bradly Trimmer, B.A., Mr. F. J. Wilkinson, Hon. Secretary of the Arms and Armour Society, Mr. Larry Wilson of the Wadsworth Atheneum, Hartford, and Mr. J. F. R. Winsbury.

Finally I must pay tribute to my wife's encouragement and to her forbearance in my absence from normal domestic duties.

Caterham, February 1965   H.L.B.

Contents

Acknowledgment

Figures 59, 178, 206, 221, 222, 238, 246, 247, 404, 482, 494, 503, 585, 684, 685 and 748 are reproduced by gracious permission of H.M. The Queen.

The Author and Publishers wish to thank the following for permission to reproduce the illustrations appearing in this book:

The Director of the Bernisches Historisches Museum, Bern, for figs. 38, 39, 41, 45, 48, 82, 106, 114, 344–6, 349 and 773.

The Director of the Statens Historiska Museum, Stockholm, for fig. 40.

The Director of the Tøjhusmuseet, Copenhagen, for figs. 42, 52, 98, 115–17, 122, 132, 143, 146, 152, 170, 191, 193, 224, 231, 280, 325, 326, 340, 364, 387, 401, 408, 410, 412, 413, 483, 514, 539, 560, 561, 603, 604, 641–4, 649, 658, 726, 727, 730 and 761.

Mr. William G. Renwick, for fig. 43.

The Director of the Muzeum Wojska Polskiego, Warsaw, for figs. 44, 337 and 533-4.

The Director of the Kunsthistorisches Museum, Vienna, for figs. 46, 93, 124, 229, 356, 357, 424, 520, 763 and 764.

The Director of the Collezione d'Armi Odescalchi and Gabinetto Fotografico Nazionale, for figs. 47, 169, 171, 518, 519 and 831.

The Master of the Armouries, H.M. Tower of London, for figs. 49, 50, 56, 57, 61, 62, 80, 84, 87, 96, 118, 119, 121, 150, 156, 163–8, 177, 179, 180, 188, 197–9, 209, 212–17, 225, 245, 253, 257, 266, 267, 276, 281, 282, 284, 296, 298, 299, 319, 320, 324, 341, 342, 347, 350–3, 358, 359, 363, 370–5, 388, 389, 396, 397, 411, 419, 422, 423, 427, 428, 432, 433, 438, 445–50, 452, 453, 455–7, 477, 481, 489, 490, 496, 497, 500, 508, 515, 531, 532, 545, 548, 551, 559, 569–71, 576, 582, 590, 594–6, 632, 665–7, 669, 670, 673, 674, 713–18, 734, 735, 740–2, 762, 775–7, 793–8, 806–8, 835, 859–61, 865 and 866 (all Ministry of Public Building and Works, Crown Copyright, reproduced by permission of the Controller of H.M. Stationery Office).

The Trustees of the Victoria and Albert Museum, for figs. 51, 68, 79, 92, 97, 145, 151, 172, 203, 223, 226–8, 289, 513, 659, 733, 736, 766, 799 and 864 (Crown Copyright).

The Director of the Kungl. Armémuseum, Stockholm, for figs. 53, 99, 476 and 790.

The Director of the Kungl. Livrustkammaren, Stockholm, for figs. 54, 55, 105, 134, 135, 137, 139–42, 153, 154, 185–7, 189, 190, 192, 194, 285, 286, 512, 538, 579, 650, 651, 724, 725, 728 and 729.

The Director of the Museo e Gallerie Nazionali di Capodimonte and Soprintendenza alle Gallerie, Naples, for figs. 58, 202 and 230.

The Trustees of the Wallace Collection, London, for figs. 60, 65, 66, 88, 102, 103, 109, 112, 218–20, 275, 278, 279, 355, 755, 770, 782, 792, 801, 829, 832 and 833.

The Director of the Musée de l'Armée, Paris, for figs. 63, 517, 540, 556 and 558.

The Trustees of the late C. G. Vokes for, figs. 64, 211, 338, 339, 439–44, 462, 463, 466, 470, 484, 485, 506, 507, 524, 525, 555, 592, 600, 625–7, 634–7, 675, 676, 695, 696, 705, 737–9, 743–5, 747, 749–54, 768, 769, 779, 784 and 802–5.

The Director of The Royal Scottish Museum, Edinburgh, for figs. 67, 550 and 562 (Crown Copyright).

The Trustees of the British Museum, for figs. 69 and 772.

The Metropolitan Museum of Art, New York, for figs. 70–2, 269–71 and 274 (Bequest of George C. Stone, 1936); 104 (Rogers Fund, 1904); 259 and 480 (Gifts of Charles M. Schott, Jr., 1917); 268, 788, 830 and 845 (Gift of William H. Riggs, 1913); 272, 273 and 491 (Collection of Giovanni P. Morosini, presented by his daughter, Giulia, 1932); 277 (Bequest of Edward C. Moore, 1891); 789 (The Bashford Dean Memorial Collection; purchase funds from various donors, 1929).

Mr. A. C. Carpenter, for figs. 74, 75 and 95.

The Keeper of the Royal Armoury, Madrid, for figs. 76, 78, 89, 90, 261–3, 418, 780 and 781 (by permission of Patrimonio Nacional).

The Director of the Bayerisches Nationalmuseum, Munich, for figs. 77, 120, 283, 487, 488, 577, 578 and 774.

The Director of the Museen der Stadt Wien, Vienna, for fig. 81.

Sotheby & Co., London, for figs. 83, 376, 377, 385, 451, 454, 530, 574, 587, 591 and 757.

Museo Nazionale D'Artiglieria, Turin, for figs. 85, 86, 249, 250, 516, 628 and 629.

The Director of the City Art Museum, St. Louis, for figs. 94, 110 and 111.

The Keeper of the Royal Armoury, Turin, for figs. 100, 101, 195, 196, 354, 383, 414, 415, 601, 656, 657, 664 and 679–83.

The Director of the Cleveland Museum of Art, for figs. 107 and 108 (gift of Mr. and Mrs. John L. Severance).

The State Armoury, The Kremlin, Moscow, for figs. 113, 138, 144, 155, 157–62, 416, 417, 537, 564–6 and 573.

Mr. A. R. Dufty, for figs. 123, 175, 200, 201, 204, 205, 254, 746 and 767.

Mr. C. O. Kienbusch, for figs. 125, 128 and 129.

Institut Royal du Patrimonie Artistique and the Director of the Musée Royal d'Armes et d'Armures, Porte de Hal, Brussels, for figs. 126, 127, 130, 131, 522, 523 and 575 (copyright A.C.L. Bruxelles).

The Director of the Norsk Folkemuseum, Oslo, for fig. 136.

Acknowledgment

Baron von Essen, Skokloster, for figs. 139, 141, 142, 185–7 and 189.

The Chief Director of the Germanisches Nationalmuseum, Nuremberg, for fig. 147.

Pitt Rivers Museum, University of Oxford, for figs. 148, 149, 348 and 731.

The Countess of Seafield, for figs. 164–8, 427 and 428.

The Director of the City of Salford Art Gallery and Museums, for fig. 171.

The Committee of Birmingham Museums and Art Gallery, for figs. 173, 425, 426, 671 and 672.

The Director of the State Hermitage Museum, Leningrad, for figs. 176, 288, 521, 557, 648 and 834.

Lord Howard de Walden, for fig. 207.

The Director of Glasgow Art Gallery and Museum, for figs. 208, 297, 362, 365, 378, 429, 492, 493, 580, 655, 677, 678, 732 771 and 809.

The Keeper of Edinburgh Castle, for fig. 210.

The Connoisseur, for figs. 206 and 221.

Mr. B. W. Muir, for figs. 232–4, 236, 237 and 264.

The Curator of The Bucks County Historical Society, for fig. 239.

The Curator of the Winchester Gun Museum, New Haven, for figs. 240–3, 251, 321–3, 327, 328, 334, 335, 366, 367, 381, 382, 434–7, 486, 526, 528, 542–4, 583, 599, 602, 613, 616, 617, 622, 624, 640, 652–4, 689–92, 694, 697, 699–704, 707–12, 848 and 850.

The Smithsonian Institution, Washington, for figs. 244, 248, 336, 400, 552, 553, 588, 589 and 668.

Schloss Schwarzburg, Germany, for fig. 252.

Mr. W. Keith Neal, for figs. 255, 258, 260, 287, 300–5, 361, 407, 495, 572 and 839–43.

Christie, Manson and Woods Ltd., for figs. 256, 384 and 686.

Mr. C. A. Söderlund, for figs. 285 and 286.

Mr. Mark Dineley, for figs. 290, 291, 360, 645–7, 687 and 688.

Mr. F. J. Bubear, for figs. 314–16, 398, 811–20 and 852.

Mr. H. C. Logan, for figs. 329 and 330.

Milwaukee Public Museum, for figs. 331–3, 392–5, 431, 597, 660, 661 and 706.

The Hon. R. H. C. Neville, for fig. 363.

Woolwich Rotunda, for figs. 368, 369, 479, 535 and 783.

The Curator of West Point Museum, New York, for figs. 379, 380, 405 and 406.

Major Noel Corry, for figs. 386, 420, 421 and 546.

The Director of the Nederlands Leger- en Wapenmuseum 'Generaal Hoefer', Leiden, Holland, for figs. 390 and 391.

Morristown National Historical Park, Morristown, New Jersey, for fig. 399.

Mr. Jac Weller, for figs. 403 and 849.

Enfield Small Arms Factory, for fig. 430.

The Curator of the Musée d'Armes de Liège, for figs. 457, 458, 499, 527, 536, 630, 633, 638 and 639 (from photographs by Clément Dessart); 501 and 502 (from photographs by Francis E. Niffle).

Mr. John T. Amber, for figs. 459 and 469.

Mr. James E. Serven, for figs. 460, 461, 464, 465, 467, 468, 471–5, 614, 615, 618–21, 631 and 719–23.

Wallis and Wallis, Lewes, for figs. 498, 505, 593, 598 and 778.

Harolds Club of Reno, for fig. 504.

The Curator of the Royal Ontario Museum, Toronto, for figs. 509 and 510.

The Director of the Musée d'Art et d'Histoire, Geneva, for fig. 511.

The Director of the Dominion Museum, Wellington, New Zealand, for fig. 529.

The Director of the Palazzo Ducale, Venice, for figs. 547, 549 and 765.

Wadsworth Atheneum, Hartford, Conn., for figs. 554, 567, 568, 606, 607 and 609.

Mr. Joe Kindig, Jr., for fig. 581.

The Director of the George F. Harding Museum, Chicago, for figs. 584 and 759.

The Director of the National Museum of Ireland, Dublin, for fig. 586.

The Director of the Kunsthistorisches Museum, Sammlung Schloss Ambras, Innsbruck, for fig. 605.

Mr. William M. Locke, for figs. 608, 611, 612, 662, 663 and 693.

Col. B. R. Lewis, for figs. 610 and 623.

Parke Bernet Galleries Inc., New York, for figs. 756, 758 and 760.

Mr. H. L. Peterson, for figs. 787, 844, 846, 847 and 851.

The Trustees of the late R. Holland-Martin, for fig. 835.

Mr. J. F. R. Winsbury, for figs. 857, 858, 862, 863 and 867–9.

Grateful acknowledgment is also made to George Nicholls, Camera One Ltd., and Ewart Gray for their assistance in the preparation of photographs.

1 The Hand-Gun

In spite of the most intensive research the exact dates of the invention of gunpowder and firearms remain unknown. In the first place there are few original documents on arms of the thirteenth century, which is the crucial period in the history of firearms; and no great reliance can be placed on the accuracy of the later copies of manuscripts which are said to belong to this period. There is also the difficulty in deciding when the various words which now refer to firearms were first used in that context. Just as the English word artillery, before *c.* 1300, described all forms of missile-throwing machinery, e.g., catapults, trebuchets, mangonels, etc., in the same way many foreign words, particularly of the Eastern World, which can now be translated as some form of firearm, had other meanings at that time. The Chinese word *p'ao* (cannon) originally covered all forms of ballistae; the Arabic name *bunduq* at first meant a hazel nut, then a lead bullet, and finally a musket; and the exact meaning of the Mamluk words *naft* and *midfa* in the fourteenth century is still a matter of dispute.

As the employment of incendiary materials was widespread in the thirteenth and fourteenth centuries the last two words are often found in accounts of battles which describe these weapons belching fire and making a noise like thunder. All of which would be quite true if they were machines throwing burning or explosive missiles. Nevertheless it led many of the early translators to believe that they were reading descriptions of the first guns. It is difficult to blame them for then writing the most convincing articles and books proving that firearms were first invented in the country of whose records they were making a particular study. Both India and China have had the most ardent protagonists for this claim.

The legend that gunpowder was invented by the ancient Hindus can be traced to the writings of an Englishman Nathaniel Halhed in 1776 and a Scotsman Quintin Craufurd in 1790, both of whom served in India and became fascinated by the history and religions of this country. They were followed in 1880 by Gustav Oppert,[1] a professor of Sanskrit at Madras, who translated two 'ancient Sanskrit manuscripts' to prove to his own satisfaction, at least, that 'gunpowder and firearms were known in India in the most ancient times'. As many of the statements in his book are palpably absurd—the size of the *Aksauhini* army corps is given as 2,187,000,000 men—and no proper attempt has been made to date his sources, Oppert's theories cannot be accepted.

Manuscripts or printed books which purport to be copies of earlier works have been particularly tempting to Chinese historians. As an example, the military treatise *Wu Ching Tsung Yao* completed in 1040 is available only in a fifteenth-century copy in which later interpolations may have been made. It has been brought forward partly by Goodrich and Fêng[2] to support their opinion that 'there is valid literary evidence for the development, by the thirteenth century, of real firearms in China'. The evidence certainly points to the use of weapons which discharged projectiles by the firing of gunpowder, but whether they can be considered firearms in the modern sense of the word is another matter.

Professor Partington[3] has produced an exhaustive analysis of all available Chinese literature and has come to more acceptable conclusions: that gunpowder of a weak nature was in use at the beginning of

---

[1] *On the Weapons, Army Organisation and Political Maxims of the Ancient Hindus, with Special Reference to Gun-Powder and Firearms*, Madras and London, 1880.

[2] L. Carrington Goodrich and Fêng Chia-Shêng, 'The Early Development of Firearms in China', *Isis*, Cambridge, Mass., U.S.A., 1946. Vol. XXXVI, Pt. 2, pp. 114–23.

[3] J. R. Partington, *A History of Greek Fire and Gunpowder*, Cambridge, England, 1960.

the eleventh century, but only as an explosive of limited powers and not as a propellant, and that about 1130 a long bamboo tube filled with explosive powder (*huo ch'iang*) was utilised as an offensive weapon. In 1233 this tube was made of toughened paper, but in 1259 it was again described as a hollowed piece of bamboo from which solid fragments were expelled by a weak charge of gunpowder—the prototype of a gun.

The *huo ch'iang* is illustrated in the *Wu-Pei-Chih*, an immense compilation on military apparatus published in 1621 but based on earlier sources. Here it is shown as a short hollow tube with its base plugged with a wad of clay and a circular metal plate, just above which was inserted a fuse of slow match. The whole tube was bound with twine to strengthen it and, held in the hand, it was reported to fire 'a nest of pellets'. The illustration given by Partington is taken from J. Amiot's *Art Militaire des Chinois* printed in 1772 in which it is labelled a '*tuyau de feu*'. Amiot's drawings are not accurate, however, and better reproductions of the original illustrations in the *Wu-Pei-Chih* are given in the articles by W. F. Mayer 'On the Introduction and Use of Gunpowder and Firearms among the Chinese'[1] and by T. L. Davis and J. R. Ware on 'Early Chinese Military Pyrotechnics'.[2]

The latter illustrate a number of other interesting firearms described in the *Wu-Pei-Chih*. The 'Lotus' was a reinforced cylindrical container on the end of a wooden stick. It was loaded with all sorts of powder and ejected fire, smoke, poison and iron arrows a foot long. Another gun, without a name, consisted of a copper tube three feet long with a straight wooden handle which shot one arrow at a time a distance of 200–300 paces by means of a small charge of *fa* powder. The ingredients of this powder are worthy of note. They were the chemicals of gunpowder—saltpetre, sulphur, charcoal—plus white arsenic, stone coal, various bitter substances, four kinds of ginger and *human sperm*.

Another historian, S. J. von Romocki, makes the following assessment of these early weapons employing gunpowder in various ways—'some of the incendiary arrows were probably rockets; the "tuyau de feu" was a primitive gun and only required to be made of metal and be properly charged to become a real gun, but if the Chinese had made this step they afterwards forgot.'[3] There is no doubt that the Chinese had the ability to cast in metals, and there are, in fact, in Chinese museums, a number of cast-bronze cannon of small size which bear inscriptions dating them to the fourteenth century. If genuine they are the oldest guns in existence. Unfortunately none can be traced to an archaeologically-dated site and some doubt must remain as to their authenticity. It is interesting to note, however, that J. L. Boots writing on 'Korean Weapons and Armour'[4] reproduces a drawing of an arrow-shooting cannon taken from the Korean book *The Five Ceremonies,* published in 1474. He also gives a photograph of one of the arrows used with such a gun, made of wood with iron tips and feathers, said to be nine feet one inch long.

1 Copper arrow-firing hand-gun. From the *Wu-Pei-Chih*, 1621
2 The arrow-firing *Midfa*. From a reputed fourteenth-century Arabic manuscript. After Oscar Guttmann, *Monumenta Pulveris Pyrii*, London, 1906, fig. 70.

The generally accepted theory that the formula for gunpowder and the knowledge of its propulsive powers were brought to Europe from China by the Arab scholars is supported by the fifteenth-century

[1] *Journal North China Branch Roy. Asiatic Soc.*, Shanghai, 1871, Vol. VI, pp. 73–104.
[2] *Journal of Chemical Education*, Easton, Pa., U.S.A., November, 1947, Vol. XXIV, pp. 522–37.
[3] *Geschichte der Explosivstoffe*, Berlin, 1895–6.
[4] *Trans. Korea Branch Roy. Asiatic Soc.*, Seoul, 1934, Vol. XXIII, Pt. 2.

copy of an earlier Arabic manuscript formerly in the Musée Asiatique in St. Petersburg. The original composition of this manuscript has been dated on no very certain grounds between 1300 and 1350. It contains illustrations of soldiers—some of them with noticeably Mongoloid features—handling a variety of incendiary weapons.

Among these is a weapon very similar to the copper arrow-firing gun of the *Wu-Pei-Chih* (2). The Arabic illustration clearly shows a tube with a charge of powder on which rests a round wad and on top of this an arrow. A second arrow is about to leave the muzzle. Another illustration shows a dumpy cylinder on a stick with a round ball projecting from the mouth—possibly a stylised version of the *huo ch'iang* or the 'Lotus'. The descriptions in the text of the manuscript are unfortunately confusing, and the word *midfa'* is used to describe both these instruments for firing arrows or bullets.

The significance of this word is discussed in full by Prof. D. Ayalon in his book *Gunpowder and Fire-arms in the Mamluk Kingdom* (London, 1956). He has pointed out the ever-increasing frequency with which weapons called *midfa' an-naft* or simply *midfa* or *naft* appear in Mamluk records from the second half of the fourteenth century onwards. Unfortunately *naft*, which can be translated as gun or gunpowder, was also a word for naphtha or other incendiary materials, and it is by no means certain when these words ceased to refer to incendiary-throwing weapons and took on the meaning of gun and gunpowder.

It has been suggested that firearms were first brought to Europe by Arabs when they invaded Spain, but in the earliest accounts of these events the words *naft* or *nafta* again appear to confuse the issue; and Partington in his survey of Spanish sources considers that machines throwing naphtha were involved rather than machines worked by naphtha (i.e. cannon). The Spanish evidence has been re-examined by James Lavin who comes to the conclusion that the earliest reference to firearms occurs in the fourteenth-century *Poema de Alfonso onceno* which describes the use of artillery (signified by the word *trueno*—thunderclap) by the Moors against the Castilians at Algeciras between 1342 and 1344.[1]

If we accept this as the first firm date for the employment of firearms by the Arabs and acknowledge the fact that there is as yet no proof of the manufacture of guns by the Chinese or any other Eastern race before this, then it becomes apparent that the first firearms were manufactured in Europe, for there is irrefutable evidence of this from 1326 onwards. However, when we turn to European sources and try to establish the date of introduction of gunpowder we are faced with the same absence of original documents and the difficulty of deciding whether the existing copies are accurate.

Knowledge of gunpowder in Europe in the thirteenth century can be traced to the works of three authors—Mark the Greek (Marcus Graecus); St. Albert the Great (Albertus Magnus), the German philosopher; and Roger Bacon, the English friar.

To the first is attributed the *Liber Ignium*, a collection of recipes for incendiaries, Greek fires, rockets and Roman candles. The earliest copies of this, prepared in the thirteenth century, contain some formulas which date back to the eighth century when Mark the Greek is traditionally supposed to have lived, but modern research indicates that those recipes which contain saltpetre and gunpowder were inserted late in the thirteenth century. As for the author, he appears to be an entirely imaginary person.

The life of Albertus Magnus, who died in Cologne in 1280, can be traced with some degree of certainty; but whether he was the author of the famous work *De Mirabilibus Mundi* which is attributed to him is questionable as there are no MSS. dated from within his lifetime. Many editions of this Book of Secrets were printed during the fifteenth century, but they vary considerably in content. They include some recipes of a semi-magical nature (one is 'To make men anywhere look as if they have the heads of animals') while others are for gunpowder. Many of the recipes are essentially the same as those in the *Liber Ignium*, but which one is a copy of the other is a matter of conjecture.

Roger Bacon, a student and later a lecturer at Oxford, is credited with three major alchemical works.

[1] 'An examination of some early documents regarding the use of gunpowder in Spain', *Journal of the Arms and Armour Society*, London, Vol. IV, 1964, pp. 163–9.

The most famous of these, *De Secretis Operibus Artis et Naturae et de Nullitate Magiae*, was probably written between 1257 and 1267. The last chapter in a printed version of 1618 contains a supposed anagram which Colonel Hime rearranged to give a formula for gunpowder.[1] If this formula is correct then it would ante-date that of Mark the Greek and St. Albert the Great. Unfortunately this chapter is not included in the only known thirteenth-century copy, and at least one science historian has cast doubt that the cypher was Bacon's.[2] A fifteenth-century manuscript copy of the treatise in the British Museum (Sloane MS. 2156) contains a different version of the anagram which has not yet been solved.

Nevertheless, from passages in his other works written between 1266 and 1268, it is obvious that Bacon knew of gunpowder and its explosive effect at least. One of the passages from the *Opus Tertius* strikes a prophetic note:

> There is a child's toy of sound and fire made in various parts of the world with powder of saltpetre, sulphur and charcoal of hazelwood. The powder is enclosed in an instrument of parchment the size of a finger, and since this can make such a noise that it seriously distresses the ears of men if one is taken unawares, and the terrible flash is also very alarming, if an instrument of large size were used no one could stand the terror of the noise and the flash. If the instrument were made of solid material the violence of the explosion would be much greater.

Up to the last quarter of the thirteenth century, then, we have reasonable evidence that gunpowder was in use in Europe and Asia in a variety of pyrotechnical implements and incendiary materials, and that the Chinese had utilised it in a bamboo contrivance half-way between a firework and a gun. But the propellant powers of exploding gunpowder were still not properly appreciated and it remained to be seen who would first control the explosive powers of the powder in an instrument of 'solid material'.

The credit for the invention of the gun is by a strong tradition dating back to the fifteenth century given to the German or Greek monk Black Berthold (Berthold Schwarz or Bertholdus Niger); and a monument to that effect was erected in his supposed home town of Freiburg, Germany. There are numerous pictures showing the mysterious monk in his workshop with attendant devils and a mortar in which he had been mixing powder, exploding and ejecting the pestle like a bullet.[3] Partington has made a summary of the many accounts of Berthold—it is astonishing how the dates of his life vary—and concludes that he is a purely legendary figure, invented solely for the purpose of providing a German origin for gunpowder and cannon.[4] This comment is perhaps not quite fair as the oldest German accounts of Berthold refer to him as a Greek alchemist. However, we must accept the fact that at present there is no historical proof of the Black monk's existence.

Although there have been several attempts to prove otherwise, the first quarter of the fourteenth century remains barren of any reference to the manufacture of firearms; a passage in the Ghent town records relating to guns, often quoted by earlier historians, has since proved to be a mis-transcription. But in 1326 comes the first firm date in the history of firearms. In that year the Council of Florence passed a decree authorising the appointment of two men to make iron bullets or arrows and metal cannon (*pilas seu palloctas ferreas et canones de metallo*) for the defence of castles and villages in the Republic.

In the same year in England, Walter de Milemete, chaplain to Edward III, prepared two illuminated manuscript treatises for the advice of the young king. The first was a copy of Aristotle's *De Secretis*

---

[1] H. W. L. Hime, *Gunpowder and Ammunition, their Origin and Progress*, London, 1904.

[2] Lynn Thorndike, *A History of Magic and Experimental Science*, New York, 1923, Vol II, pp. 616–91.

[3] See Dorothea W. Singer, 'On a 16th-Century Cartoon Concerning The Devilish Weapon of Gunpowder', *Ambix*, London, February, 1959, pp. 25–33.

[4] Partington, *op. cit.*, Chap. III.

Secretorum[1] and the second he called *De Nobilitatibus, Sapientiis, et Prudentiis Regum*[2] (concerning the nobility, wisdom and prudence of kings). In the decorated borders of each manuscript appear what are generally accepted to be the first pictures of a gun. In the first manuscript, which is slightly earlier in date, the cannon, shaped like a vase, rests on what appears to be a stone table. The other illustration shows the cannon resting on a less stable structure, perhaps of wood, supported by trestles. In both cases a mail-clad soldier is applying a straight rod holding a piece of tinder or match to the touch-hole, and a feathered arrow emerges from the muzzle.

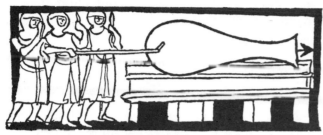

From *De Secretis Secretorum*

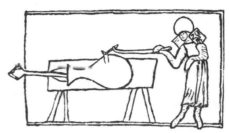

From *De Nobilitatibus, Sapientiis,*
et Prudentiis Regum

3, 4 Walter de Milemete's guns of 1326

These vase-like or pot-shaped guns were by no means the freaks they at first appear. The Italian chronicle of Juliano describes an attack on the frontier town of Cividale in 1331, when amongst the weapons used were '*vasa*' and '*sclopi*'. In the Bibliothèque Nationale, Paris, there is a document of 1338 for the issue of '*un pot de fer a traire garros a feu*' from the marine arsenal at Rouen. This gun was provided with 48 bolts made of iron and feathered. In 1342 the store of artillery in the castle of Rihoult in Artois, France, included 400 arrows '*pour traire de canons*'. These were winged with brass, the wings or feathers being nailed to the wooden hafts. Leather straps were wound round the ends of the hafts to prevent the wings touching the sides of the barrel.[3] An actual example of a pot or vase gun, but so small that it must have been for use in the hand, was excavated at Loshult, Sweden, in 1861. Now in the National Historical Museum, Stockholm, it is just over a foot long and cast in bronze. In outward appearance it is similar to the Milemete guns, but its bore is cylindrical. The touch-hole which is drilled at right angles to the chamber is countersunk to form a priming pan.

From 1340 onwards there are ever-increasing references to guns of all sizes in many of the national archives. German sources have been quoted by General Rathgen.[4] Those of France have been detailed by Colonel Favé[5] and the English examples by Professor Tout.[6]

For the purpose of this book the latter are most valuable. They are taken from the accounts of the Privy Wardrobe, the royal department responsible for the supply of arms to the King's forces. In 1345 appears an entry for the repair of some earlier guns firing arrows and bullets (*gunnis cum saggitis et pellotis*). The following year guns with tillers (*cum telariis*) are mentioned. As the term tiller is normally applied to the stock of a crossbow, it can be assumed that these were guns with a primitive form of gun-stock.

[1] Formerly Holkham MS. 458, now British Museum Add. MS. 47680.

[2] Library of Christ Church, Oxford. MS. 92.

[3] Henry Brackenbury, *Ancient Cannon in Europe*, Royal Artillery Institution, Woolwich, 1865, Pt. I, pp. 6 and 9.

[4] Bernard Rathgen, *Das Geschütz im Mittelalter*, Berlin, 1928.

[5] Col. Ildéfonse Favé, who wrote Vols. III and IV of Napoleon III's *Études sur le Passé et l'Avenir de l'Artillerie*, 1862.

[6] T. F. Tout, 'Firearms in England in the Fourteenth Century', *The English Historical Review*, Vol. XXVI, No. 104, October, 1911, pp. 666–702.

Some of the tiller guns were probably small enough to come within the classification of hand-guns, but although one bill of 1373–5 is for the fitting of handles to guns and hatchets (*pro helvyng viij gunnorum et x hachettorum*) in the manner of pikes (*ad medum pyceys*)—undoubtedly a reference to the socketed hand-guns described below—it is not until 1388 that the term hand-gun appears (*iij canones paruos vocatos handgunnes*).

By this time the gunner had a full complement of accessories, including bullet moulds (*moldes vocata formule*), iron ladles for melting the lead, and iron ramrods (*driuelles ferri*).

The nature of these late fourteenth-century hand-guns is indicated by manuscript illustrations and actual examples still in existence. They may be divided into three main types:

(1) Of cast bronze or wrought iron, bound to the end of a wooden stock with iron bands.
(2) Of iron or bronze with socketed breeches for the insertion of a wooden haft.
(3) Of iron with the breech beaten out into a long handle with a rounded or ring end.

The Loshult gun already mentioned can be placed in the first category as there is no apparent means of fastening it to a stock other than by bands. In the Bern Museum there are several examples of this type of hand-gun with barrels of more cylindrical form. They are in effect miniature editions of the light artillery of the period, examples of which can be seen in the German manuscript *Codex Germ. 600* of *c.* 1400 in the Munich State Library.[1] The method of attaching a gun barrel to its stock by metal bands was retained throughout the fifteenth century, with the barrel becoming steadily longer and the stock of more manageable proportions. An illustration of *c.* 1430 shows a group of crossbowmen and hand-gunners both firing incendiary arrows. Towards the end of the fifteenth century a rudimentary form of shoulder stock was being tried and the military works of Vegetius and Valturius, *c.* 1460–70, show hand-gunners with their guns to their shoulders confidently firing from the tops of ships and the towers of castles.

Of the second type of hand-gun with the socketed breech there are a number of interesting specimens. The most important one was fished out of the sea near Mörkö, Sweden, at the beginning of the nineteenth century and is now in the National Historical Museum, Stockholm (**40**). Cast out of a single piece of bronze and with an overall length of only $7\frac{1}{2}$ inches, its polygonal barrel is inscribed with the inscriptions MARIA PLEA [*Ave Maria gratia plena*] and HIELP. GOT. HELP. UNS. On the top square is a touch-hole and shallow pan guarded by the bust of a man with a bearded, haggard face (Jesus Christ?). Underneath is a pointed projection—the hook which is fitted to many early guns so that they could be rested on a wall or stand and the recoil diminished, and which has caused them to be known as *Hakenbüchse* (hook-guns). From this word came later the English hackbut or hagbut and the French *harquebus*.

Another socketed hand-gun which can be dated to the fourteenth century, also made of bronze and now in the Germanisches Museum, Nuremberg, was excavated from the ruins of the Castle of Tannenberg in Hesse, destroyed in 1399. Although without any decoration, the gun is interesting as its bore is constricted in front of the powder chamber, forming an internal ring on which the lead bullet could be wedged without compressing the powder charge. Another socketed hand-gun, of *c.* 1400, strangely reminiscent of the Chinese *huo ch'iang* (see page 2)—it is of cylindrical shape with a short wooden grip—is illustrated in the Munich Manuscript *Codex Germ. 600* (**5**).

The third variety of hand-gun, of all-metal construction, is represented by examples in the museums at Nuremberg (a hooked gun with a wavy spike handle); at Brussels (with a twisted tail forming a ring at its extremity); at Bern (with a straight iron rod finishing in an oval grip); and at Copenhagen. The last specimen, with a rod handle ending in a convenient knob, has a hook under the barrel which was attached to a ring and then shrunk on to the barrel (**42**). It was dug up on the site of the Castle of Vedelspang in Schleswig, which was destroyed in 1426. W. W. Greener also illustrates one of these guns, with a ring

[1] See A. von Essenwein, *Quellen zur Geschichte der Feuerwaffen*, Leipzig, 1872.

handle and reinforced bands round the barrel, which was small enough to be carried in one hand and used as a club or mace.[1]

There is a drawing dated 1449 which shows a mounted soldier in armour firing a Vedelspang type of gun. Its butt ends in a ring which rests against his breastplate and hangs from a cord tied round his neck, while the barrel lies on a forked stick attached to the saddle. In this fashion the soldier was free to control

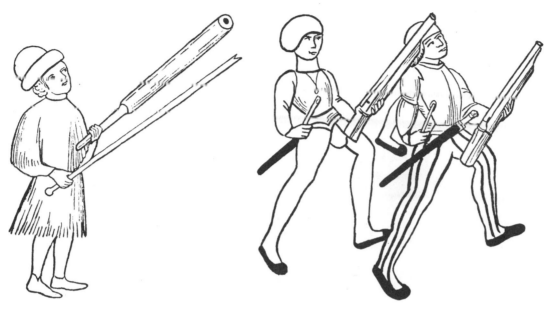

5 Hand-gunner with ramrod, *c.* 1400. From *Codex Germ. 600*, Munich
6 Hand-gunners with tinder firing-sticks, 1502. Detail from a painting in the Germanisches Museum

his horse with one hand and apply a lighted match with the other. There are several versions of this drawing, some of which depict the gun with a hook.[2] A more ambitious outfit is illustrated by Victor Gay in his *Glossaire*.[3] The steed here consists of an ass saddled with an armoured shield armed with three of these guns. It is not clear how the ass escaped decapitation.

This method of holding a hand-gun was of course exceptional. Fifteenth-century illustrations show that there were two main ways of firing the guns. The pole-like stock could be rested on the shoulder like a modern bazooka, or it could be tucked under the arm. In each case the gun could be steadied with one hand and the match applied with the other. Proper aim was out of the question. An interesting illustration of the first method can be seen on a fifteenth-century tapestry in Rheims Cathedral, which celebrates the marriage ceremonies of Charles the Bold, Duke of Burgundy and the English princess, Margaret of York. Two Negro servants are firing a *feu-de-joie* from long tubular hand-guns balanced on their shoulders. Soldiers employing the second method can be seen in many illuminated manuscripts, one of the best examples being *Burney MS. 169* in the British Museum.[4]

With the exception of the mounted knight described above, who has a length of slow-match wound

[1] *The Gun and its Development*, 9th edn. (1910), p. 48.
[2] W. Hassenstein in *Das Feuerwerkbuch von 1420* (Munich, 1941) states that the original drawing was in the Library of Graf Wilczek, Vienna.
[3] *Glossaire Archéologique du Moyen Âge et de la Renaissance*, Paris, 1887, Vol. I, p. 73.
[4] See H. L. Blackmore, *Firearms*, London, 1964, p. 13.

around his waist and holds the lighted end in his hand, it is difficult to judge what the gunners in the other illustrations are using to light their guns. In nearly every case they appear to be holding a straight rod. This has often been described as a red-hot iron, but how could a soldier in the field, even in the limited action of a hand-gunner, keep his iron red-hot? It is more likely that these rods were holders for a small piece of smouldering tinder or match, in style similar to the artillery linstock (6).

2 The Matchlock

The inconvenience of trying to do three things—hold the gun, aim it and light it—with two hands, soon led to the invention of a device known as the matchlock. In its elementary form it was a Z- or S-shaped (depending from which side it is viewed) lever, the so-called 'serpentine'. This was pivoted in its middle either to the outside of the stock or in a slot cut in it. One end formed the trigger and the other held the match in a simple grip, usually of two jaws fastened by a screw. With the aid of this, the gunner could hold the gun with two hands and by pressing the underpart of the lever with his finger-tips bring the match into the priming pan at the required moment. The earliest known evidence of its use is a painting dated 1411 in *Codex MS. 3069*, in the Austrian National Library, Vienna. Another good illustration of it, dated 1468, is the charming vignette in the decoration of a Froissart MS. in the Breslau City Library, which shows a centaur firing this first kind of matchlock. Actual examples of it are extremely rare, the one in the Warsaw Museum being partly a reconstruction (**44**).

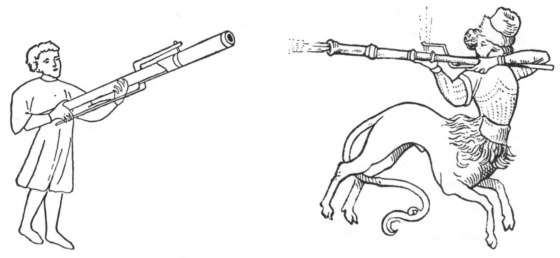

7 Earliest illustration of a matchlock. After a painting dated 1411 in *Codex MS. 3069*, Austrian National Library, Vienna
8 Centaur with matchlock gun, 1468. Vignette from a Froissart MS. in Breslau City Library

Now that the gun could be held with two hands, there was a natural inclination to shape the stock so that it would fit into the shoulder rather than over or under it. During the fifteenth century a flat oblong form of butt was nearly universal. It appears so frequently in contemporary pictures of Landsknecht soldiers that it has become known as the Landsknecht stock (*Landsknecht Kolbe*). There is one variation of it where, to prevent the butt slipping out of position, a niche has been carved out of the base of the butt so that part projects over the shoulder. An improved version of this idea, it may be noted, was to be adopted for target weapons of the late nineteenth century.

Other improvements to the gun were new methods of making the barrel and fitting it to the stock. The old method of manufacturing was to cast or forge the barrel in one piece. Now the barrel was forged into an open tube and its breech end was closed with a screwed plug. The touch-hole was drilled into the side and a separate pan with a pivoted cover attached to it. The narrow bands holding the barrel were replaced by a series of lugs brazed under the barrel which fitted into corresponding recesses in the stock and were fastened by transverse pins.

During the fifteenth century the matchlock mechanism was also the subject of much experimentation, although illustrated manuscripts of *c.* 1520 show that the Emperor Maximilian's soldiers were still carrying Landsknecht guns, some with no lock and others with only a rudimentary form of matchlock, without a trigger extension, screwed to the stock. During the last quarter of the century, however, two improved versions were developed. In both types the old one-piece serpentine was discarded, the matchholder or cock forming a separate part to the rest of the lock mechanism which was let into a recess of the stock and covered by a flat plate.[1]

In the first type, known as the snap-matchlock (*Luntenschnappschloss*) the cock was kept pressed into the pan by the action of a spring. On the inside of the lock-plate a sprung lever was pivoted laterally so that a stud or sear at its end protruded through a hole in the plate. The long thin cock which had a tubular holder designed for the retention of a piece of tinder rather than match, had a projection at its base pointing either backwards (then known as a 'heel') or forwards ('toe'). When the cock was raised out of the pan its heel or toe was caught and held by the sear. This could be withdrawn by pressure on a button release fitted to the rear of the lock-plate or in a recess of the stock behind the lock; the cock with its lighted match then dropped into the priming pan. Examples of this type of snap-matchlock are rare, the best-known examples being military guns at Graz and in the Basle Historical Museum.[2]

Another distinct group of snap-matchlocks, dated specimens of which range from 1570 to 1635,[3] is remarkable for its lock release, which incorporates a spring-actuated intermediary link between trigger and sear—a mechanism later known as a hair-trigger. Nearly all these locks have a long flat rectangular plate. The cock with its tubular tinder holder faces towards the butt. When it is in the cocked position the supplementary trigger is set by pulling or pushing a protruding button. In a few cases the operation is accomplished by pulling a piece of cord. The trigger, which requires little pressure, can in turn take the form of a button, a piece of cord or a conventional shape of slight proportions. The effect of pulling the trigger is to release the secondary spring trigger which hits the sear a smart blow (**957**).

The stock is also of particular interest as no trigger guard is provided, the German type of butt designed to be held against the cheek, being shaped to take the three lower fingers of the right hand. When a conventional type of trigger is provided it is to some extent guarded by the beak-like projection of the under-side of the butt. There is no provision for a ramrod and the fact that the majority of specimens are rifled and are carefully sighted has led to the suggestion that these snap-matchlock guns were intended for target shooting. The decoration on the butt of such a gun in the W. Keith Neal Collection shows a marksman shooting at a circular target.

The second form of matchlock was the most popular, its action being the reverse of the snap type. The main part of its mechanism was a long sear-lever pivoted vertically inside the lock-plate and under pressure from the mainspring. To one end was linked the match-holder, and to the other was screwed an extension lever which hung down under the butt in the fashion of a crossbow. The spring kept the match-holder out of the pan but gentle pressure on the sear-lever was sufficient to bring the match into action. This sear matchlock with its cheap simple mechanism was widely adopted, but in a short while the risk of a premature discharge by an accidental movement of the sear-lever led to the production of an improved model—the trigger lock. The long under-lever was replaced by a modern form of trigger hung separately in a recess under the stock and acting on the right-angled end of the sear-lever. It was protected by a semi-circular piece of metal screwed or nailed to the stock—the trigger guard. Thus not only

[1] Two newly-discovered volumes of Leonardo da Vinci's drawings show that he designed a sophisticated matchlock-mechanism with a automatic pan-cover.

[2] On the Basle guns the lock is placed in front of the pan with the button trigger nearest the muzzle, where it was operated by the fingers of the *left* hand while supporting the barrel.

[3] See Arne Hoff, 'Late Firearms with Snap Matchlocks', *Four Studies on History of Arms*, Tøjhusmuseets Skrifter 7, Copenhagen, 1963.

was a safety measure introduced but the new lock could be more easily removed from the stock for cleaning.

The new lock was introduced in the last quarter of the sixteenth century, but it was some years before the old lock was finally abandoned. In 1631, the gunmakers of London engaged on the repair of government arms were allowed the following rates for conversion work:—

For a Match tricker Locke compleate	1.0*d.*
For a handle or guard of a Tricker	.6*d.*
For furnishing & setting of a Tricker Locke in place of a Seare Locke wth a handle, Tricker and Tricker Pinns	2.6*d.*[1]

In the second half of the seventeenth century the lock-plate of the matchlocks was shaped like that of the flintlock, giving a much neater appearance. The pan and its hinged cover became part of the lock. The last mechanical development in the matchlock was an automatically opening pan-cover. This was a sliding cover which was pushed open when the sear-lever was moved.

The European matchlock, because of its easy and cheap manufacture, was fitted to the majority of military long guns throughout the sixteenth and seventeenth centuries. These long guns varied considerably in size and shape. Nevertheless contemporary writers have divided them into some well-defined classes. Unfortunately different writers often give conflicting information concerning the dimensions of barrel and bore. The largest class in number is that of the arquebus, also spelt harquebus. Derived from *Hakenbüchse*, the word for the original hook-guns, it was transformed into the French *harquebus*, the Italian *archibugio*, the Spanish *arcabuz*, and the English hackbut, hagbut, etc. During the first half of the sixteenth century, the name became generic for all forms of portable firearms.

The larger guns of this period, later designated wall-guns because they were made for use in fortified places, became distinguished as *arquebusses à croc*, 'hagbutis of crocke', etc. In the *Letters and Papers of Henry VIII* there are many references to 'hacbushes with theire frames', 'hagbushes of irone upon trindelles', etc., forming part of the ordnance defending the English towns and castles. They were also used in small carts as a form of light artillery. The name continued into the seventeenth century. Gaya in his *Arms of War* (1678) says 'the Arquebuss a Crock is made of Iron, in the form of a Great Musket. . . . The Bullet of it weighs three ounces'.

At the same time there were small varieties. There were some of half size—the 'half hagis' or 'demihakes'. The official responsible for Henry VIII's personal guns, appointed in 1538, bore the title of Keeper of the King's Handguns and Demy-hawks. In a gunsmith's bill of 1542 appears an item 'for stocking and vernysshing of certain of my Lord's half hawks'. In the same year a report on the French Army describes horsemen with 'hacabuts' at the arson of their saddles. It was not long before the English also provided their cavalry with 'schortte gonnys', and in 1544 a 'Captain of the Demyhakes on Horseback' received his first appointment.

In the second half of the sixteenth century new classes of guns, or at least the names for them, came into use. Edmund Nicholson, in 1559, offered to supply the English Army with a number of weapons including 'Musketts, Basterd Musketts, and Harquebuzes'.[2] The word Harquebus was now being applied to the smallest of the three weapons.

The word musket, from the Italian *Moschetto* (a kind of sparrow-hawk), is an example of the practice of naming classes of firearms after birds of prey, e.g. falcon, saker, etc. Martin du Bellay in his *Mémoires* of 1569 refers to them as '*les arquebouzes qu'on tiroit sur une fourchette*' and states that they were first employed at the Battle of Chiara in Italy in 1521.[3] They were probably the arquebuses which Henry VIII

---

[1] Public Record Office, London, SP. 16/188.

[2] P.R.O., SP. 12/8.

[3] In fact they are mentioned in a Naples inventory of 1499. See A. Gaibi, 'Le Armi da Fuoco', *Storia di Brescia*, Vol. III, Brescia, 1964, p. 826.

was told in 1534 would 'give double the stroke of a handgun'. Lighter than the arquebus à croc, the musket was still heavy enough to require the support of a rest during firing. Sir John Smythe in *Certain Discourses* (1590) bewailed the fate of the musketeers: 'their peeces being so wonderfull heavie, and they troubled with the carrying and use of their rests and loden with their other ordinarie and heavie furniture'.

Muskets also formed part of the equipment of the Navy. In March 1588 Sir Francis Drake at Plymouth wrote to the Council of War in London for supplies for his fleet, putting this P.S. to his letter: 'Forgett not 500 Musketts and at least one thousand arrows for them.'[1] Made by the London fletcher William Reynolds, the latter were apparently short arrows of great penetrative power called sprites, which were used to attack the musket-proof fighting quarters of ships. They were reported to have 'wrought extraordinary disasters' among the Spaniards 'which caused admiration to see themselves wounded with small shott when they thought themselves secure'.[2] As a matter of interest this was not the last recorded use of arrows in guns. As late as 1693 a certain Samuel Pitman notified Viscount Sidney that he had 'found out a new invention of arrows and darts to be shot out of guns with gunpowder'.[3]

9 Musketeer firing an incendiary arrow. From Thomas Smith's *Additions to the Book of Gunnery*, 1643

In the last quarter of the sixteenth century, the barrel of the English musket at least became standardised with a length of four feet. This was confirmed by *Orders for the Generall uniformitie of all Sortes of armies* published in 1630, which also gave the calibre of "12 bulletts in ye pound rowlinge in".[4] The actual bore of the barrel can be better judged by the rates of pay given to gunmakers in 1631,[5] which referred to the difference in size between bullet and barrel (known as the windage) thus: 'the bore according to the Bullett of 10 in the Pound standing and 12 rowling'. There was another type of musket—the bastard musket—which was of the same calibre but had a shorter barrel.

But if the barrel of the musket became fairly standard the shape of the stock did not. Sir Roger Williams in a *Brief Discourse on Warre* (1590) gave his opinion that 'for the recoyling, there is no hurt, if they be straight stocked after the Spanish manner; were they stocked after the French manner, to be discharged on the breast, fewe or none could abide their recoyling, but being discharged from the shoulder after the Spanish manner there is neither danger nor hurts'.

. In 1619 the musketeer was given advice on the two methods of firing: 'If the stock of his piece be crooked, he ought to place the end just before the right papp; if long and straight as the Spaniards use them, then upon the point of his right shoulder using a stately upright pace in discharge'. Yet another

[1] *Calendar of State Papers, Domestic, Elizabeth, 1581–90*, p. 470.
[2] Francis Grose, *Military Antiquities*, London, 1786, Vol. I, pp. 165–6.
[3] *Calendar of State Papers, Domestic, William and Mary, 1693*, pp. 284, 310.
[4] Public Record Office, London, SP. 16/179.
[5] Public Record Office, London, SP. 16/188.

method can be seen in the series of drawings by the artist Stradanus (1523–1605) which show sportsmen stalking game with the curved gun butt resting on top of their shoulders.

The so-called Spanish stocks were not really straight. The butt had to drop slightly to allow the eye to line up comfortably with the sights. At first with the sear matchlock in operation only a rudimentary shaping of the waist of the butt was necessary to make the gun reasonable to hold, the sear-lever being pressed by the ends of the fingers. But towards the end of the sixteenth century the butt began to splay out until a distinct fish-tail appearance was achieved; and with the introduction of the tricker lock a deep recess had to be cut in the upper edge for the thumb, so that the hand could grasp the small of the butt and allow the forefinger to manipulate the trigger (**55–6, 911**).

When the French stock was first introduced the butt had only a slight curve downwards, but this became gradually more pronounced until the stock resembled a hockey stick. With a stock of this exaggerated form, intended to be handled with the butt-plate against the chest, only a light gun or carbine could be used with comfort. They were called petronels from the French word *poitrine* (breast). Although at first this word was applied only to guns with a curved butt, it later became synonymous with any light gun or carbine carried by horsemen. In England, at the time of the Spanish Armada and after, there was a great demand for mobile marksmen ('there should be practised harquebusiers on horseback to repair where danger is imminent'), and in 1585 every Justice of the Peace was detailed to find two 'petronells on horseback'.[1]

Next to the musket in size—apparently taking the place of the bastard musket—was the caliver. The derivation of this word, which is the same as calibre, is explained by Edmund York, an official of the City of London, in Stow's *Survey of London*.[2] He relates how the Governor of Piedmont, *c.* 1555, armed his regiment with harquebuses of the same calibre 'of which Words of Calibre came first this unapt term which we use to call a Harqubuze a Calliver, which is the Height of the Bullet and not the Piece . . .'. In fact the caliver was generally less in length and bore than the musket and so could be fired without a rest. There is disagreement amongst contemporary writers, however, as to how it differed from the harquebuse. Sir John Smythe (1590) affirmed that calivers were 'of a greater length and breadth of bullet and more ranforced than Harquebuzes': but Barwick, in 1594, denied there was any difference 'saving that it [the caliver] is of a greater circuit or Bullet than the other is of'.

Between them these early military writers present a pretty confusing picture. In 1630, however, official English measurements were laid down for all arms then in use. They can be summarised as follows:

	Barrel	Overall length	Bore
Musket	4 ft.	5 ft. 2 in.	12
Caliver	3 ft. 3 in.	4 ft. 6 in.	17
Harquebus	2 ft. 6 in.	3 ft.	17
Carbine or Petronel	2 ft. 6 in.	3 ft.	24[3]

Another gun rarely mentioned, the Currier, is by some writers compared to a musket but by others is said to be of a size and calibre between the musket and the caliver.

At the beginning of the sixteenth century two other forms of ignition which offered many advantages over the matchlock—the wheellock and the flintlock (see Chaps. 3 and 4)—started to appear, and it was to these that the wealthy sportsman turned for the weapon of his choice. The lowly matchlock was left to service the plain and crudely-made arms of the soldier and the peasant huntsman. The finest decoration and workmanship were lavished on the new type of sporting guns. There were exceptions to this, of

[1] *Calendar of State Papers, Domestic, Elizabeth, 1581–90*, p. 249.
[2] 1754 edn., Vol. II, pp. 570–7.
[3] Public Record Office, London, SP.16/179.

course, and if a nobleman conceived a liking for a matchlock gun, then the result was a firearm of elaborate and often bizarre appearance (**63**).

Some of the military muskets made for special troops or the representatives of City Companies were also well decorated with inlays of engraved mother-of-pearl and bone. But the finest examples of decoration are found on the group of snap-matchlocks described on page 10. The example in the Wallace Collection (**60**) is of the highest quality. The pearwood stock, dated 1598, is inlaid with engraved stag's horn in an intricate ornament of foliage and grotesques, while the barrel and lock are engraved with arabesques. A brass foresight and aperture rear sight are provided, and like its companions in the group it has a rifled barrel.

The inner surfaces of these rifled barrels were cut longitudinally with a number of spiral grooves. This may have been an extension of the idea by which the feathers of arrows and crossbow bolts were offset to give a spinning motion to the missile, thus correcting any irregularities in its flight. As the projectile of the gun at this time was a round lead ball often beaten into an irregular shape by the blows of the ramrod, the effect of the rifling cannot have been so profound. There are examples of early guns which have straight rifling, and this has been taken by some writers to indicate that the original purpose of rifling was to afford spaces for the fouling of previous shots to collect in when the bullet was forced down.

By tradition the invention of rifling has been attributed to Gaspard Koller or Kolner, a gunmaker of Vienna in the fifteenth century, or to August Kotter, an armourer of Nuremberg; but no evidence has ever been brought forward to support either of their claims. Colonel Angelucci[1] has suggested that a description of a gun in an inventory of 1476—*sclopetus unus ferri factus a lumaga*—refers to a rifled (twisted) barrel, but this translation is doubtful. Thierbach[2] made an investigation of another early reference. This was an invitation of 1497 to a rifle shooting contest in Leipzig which was supposed to include an event for 'shooting from rifled barrels at targets' but he failed to find any confirmation.

What is considered by some authorities to be the earliest example of a rifle is a hand-gun of 'Landsknecht' type in the former W. G. Renwick collection (**43**). It is illustrated on Plate CXIV of Skelton's *Illustrations of Antient Arms and Armour* from the Meyrick Collection and was the subject of an article by its late owner in which there are photographs showing faint traces of rifling in the muzzle end of the bronze

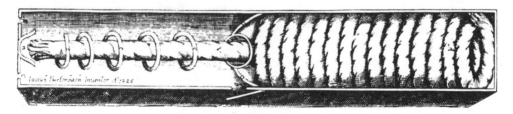

10   Cut-away diagram of a match container for carrying a lighted match in rain.
Marked JOSEPH FURTENBACH. INVENTOR A° 1626. Illustrated in his
Büchsenmeisterey-Schul, Augsburg, 1643

barrel.[3] On the stock is painted the single-headed eagle of the design known to have been used by Maximilian I between 1493 and 1508. The lock, apparently a snap-matchlock with a button trigger, is unfortunately missing.

There is also a German wheellock rifle in the Tøjhusmuseet, Copenhagen (No. B 277), dated 1542; and a rifle barrel, formerly in the Rotunda, Woolwich, was dated 1547. Several rifles in the National

[1] Angelo Angelucci, *Catalogo della Armeria Reale*, Turin, 1890, p. 409.
[2] M. Thierbach, *Die geschichtliche Entwickelung der Handfeuerwaffen*, Dresden, 1886, p. 169.
[3] William G. Renwick, 'The Earliest Known Rifle', *The American Rifleman*, March, 1953, pp. 15–18, 75.

Museum at Zürich are probably of this period. While there is always the possibility that a gun barrel may have been rifled at a date later than that of its manufacture, it is reasonable to assume from the above examples that rifling was known in the 1540s and may well have been introduced at the beginning of the century.

In turning to Oriental countries it will be remembered that the Chinese, at least, appear to have employed gunpowder in what were prototype guns. They may also have succeeded in casting cannon not long after if not before the first European examples. But there does not seem to be any evidence to suggest that any real form of hand-gun was evolved in the Orient until the arrival of the first European explorers early in the sixteenth century.

During the fifteenth century the Portuguese mariners began their voyages down the west coast of Africa in search of a sea-route to India, eventually reaching their destination in 1498. They journeyed on to Ceylon in 1505 and then continued along the coasts of Malaya until, in 1514, a Portuguese diplomatic envoy succeeded in reaching Peking in a Chinese vessel. Trading relations were soon established with Canton and in 1543 three Portuguese traders landed on Tanegashima, a small island south of the four main islands of Japan. They carried with them matchlock guns, and there is little doubt that it was only after sighting these guns that the people of India, China and Japan began to make similar weapons of their own; the type of matchlock depending on that with which they first became acquainted—or so it seems.

The majority of the Indian races adopted the simple sear-lever type with the forward falling cock or serpentine. Unlike the European model, however, the sear-lever itself is cut off near the stock and shaped into a thin-bladed or carved trigger. The whole of the mechanism is contained in a slot cut in the stock, and only the extremities of the action, the trigger and top part of the cock are visible. The barrel is invariably held to the stock by metal bands (*capucines*), and the priming pan, which forms an integral part of the barrel, has a simple hinged cover, or in some cases a rudimentary clip-on lid. No attempt seems to have been made to improve on this simple mechanism, which remained unchanged until modern times. Stone,[1] however, does illustrate an Indian matchlock with an automatically opening pan-cover.

A gadget not found on European guns is the small pricker for cleaning the touch-hole, which is chained to a container fastened to the stock just below the pan. The Indian methods of making gun barrels are recounted in full by Egerton.[2] Apart from his interesting description of the damascening and graining of the surface of the metal, he reveals that some of the longer barrels consist of three or four pieces of cylindrical iron joined together.

The shape of the stock of the Indian matchlock gun, or *toradar* as it was called, varies according to the geographical location of its manufacture. In the north and particularly in the state of Sind, the butt has a very pronounced curve and opens out into a large fish-tail shape. This is known as the Afghan stock as it is modelled after the guns of the neighbouring hill tribes of Afghanistan. But whereas the Afghan gun is usually of crude manufacture the Indian model is often distinguished by a heavy damascened barrel with a muzzle fashioned as a monster's head and a stock ornamented with enamelled plaques rivalling the best productions of Persia.

In the central regions the curve of the butt is less pronounced, but a distinct notch is cut in the top of the butt just behind the breech. The true Indian stock favoured by the Rajputs and the Mahrattàs has a very slim, straight stock of pentagonal section capable of supporting only a light barrel. It is strengthened by iron, brass or silver plates nailed to each side of the lock housing. Although its design is severe in line, the decoration can be magnificent. Even on the plainest of guns the metal side pieces are of watered steel with restrained chiselling. If silver or brass is used the engraving and embossing can be profuse. The wood

---

[1] G. C. Stone, *A Glossary of the Construction, Decoration and Use of Arms and Armor*, Portland, Maine, U.S.A., 1934, fig. 564.

[2] Lord Egerton of Tatton, *A Description of Indian and Oriental Armour*, London, 1896, pp. 60–4.

of the stock is sometimes covered with ivory and ebony plaques. The Indian craftsman delighted in colour and frequently covered the stock with glowing lacquer work or translucent enamels (**65**).

Towards the north-east the metal decoration found on Bhutanese guns shows a strong Tibetan influence (**66**). In southern India the Arab tribes produced slim matchlock guns with rather clumsy rounded butts, often heavily ornamented with silver bands and associated decoration. The type of gun found with the Coorg tribes of the same areas, on the other hand, has an unusual hook-shaped butt with a flat butt plate set at an angle of 45° (**948**). A basket-work reel is often fitted to the top of the butt round which was wound the length of match. In contrast to all these the butt of Cingalese guns is carved into a large flamboyant double-scroll shape which would seem impossible to hold with any comfort (**949**).

On the other side of the Indian Ocean, in Burma, Malaya and Java the simple sear-matchlock of the Indian continent is replaced by a version of the European snap-matchlock. This may have been because the peoples of these countries saw only this type of European matchlock in the formative years. The Malayan word for the matchlock is *istinggar*, perhaps derived from the Portuguese *espingarda*. As one might expect in the humid atmosphere of those countries the lock parts are, as far as possible, made of brass, even the large exterior mainspring. The cock is usually a heavy cast animal's head, with a cluster of rings at the base from which were hung seals, charms or pieces of match (**73**).[1] The butt is short and slightly curved to rest against the cheek and in this position the long heavy barrel has to be supported by a rest.

A very similar shape of butt was adopted by the Japanese, but here the resemblance ends. When in 1543 the Japanese made the acquaintance of the Portuguese matchlocks they were immediately fascinated by the new weapons, and in their own inimitable way began to make copies of them. They were described in a contemporary account which incidentally reveals how little was known of firearms up to then:

> they carried with them one article . . . which was about two or three shaku [feet] in length, straight, heavy and hollow. One end, however, was closed, and near it there was a small hole through which fire was to be lighted. The article was used in the following way—some mysterious medicine was put into it with a small piece of lead and, when one lit the medicine through that hole, the lead piece was discharged and hit everything.[2]

The new Japanese guns were at first called *Tanegashima*, after the island on which the Portuguese first landed. At this time Japan was in the throes of a civil war, and the two earliest specimens still preserved in temples—a barrel claimed to have been made in the first year of the Tensho Era (1573) and a gun dated 1583—are plain fighting weapons.[3]

There is an interesting association between the first Japanese firearms (of the matchlock variety) and Christianity.[4] The earliest Japanese matchlock gun described by J. L. Boots,[5] and preserved in the Kudan Military Museum, Tokyo, had a barrel covered with silver decoration which included the Christian Cross and the head of Christ. Another sixteenth-century matchlock gun in the Victoria and Albert Museum has its barrel decorated with a brass inlay of floral scrolls intermingled with the emblems of the Passion. When one considers the thoroughness with which the Japanese eradicated every trace of Christianity after 1640, it is a miracle that these guns decorated in the Namban style—as the Japanese call 'foreign influence'—have survived.

From 1600, when Japan came under the firm control of the Tokugawa Shogunate, the country was at peace and from 1639 was almost isolated from foreign influence until the arrival of the American force

---

[1] The Malays have always had great faith in the power of charms and the use of magic weapons. See G. B. Gardner, *Keris and other Malay Weapons*, Singapore, 1936.

[2] Robert E. Kimbrough, 'Japanese Firearms', *The Gun Collector*, Madison, Wisconsin, U.S.A., 1950, p. 446.

[3] Ibid., p. 451.

[4] See C. Milward, 'Some Military Relics of the Christian Century in Japan', *Apollo*, March, 1964, pp. 209–13.

[5] 'Korean Weapons and Armour', *Trans. Korea Branch Roy. Asiatic Soc.*, Seoul, 1934, XXIII, Pt. 2, pp. 1–37.

under Commander Perry in 1854. During this period the production of firearms was under strict government supervision. The possession of such arms became a mark of distinction among noblemen, and the gunmakers were encouraged to fashion highly-decorated pieces. The traditional skills of the swordmakers were easily turned to this task. The laborious techniques devoted to the forging of a sword blade were applied to the making of a barrel, the iron being folded and welded many times to temper it. This was similar to the European method, but whereas the Damascus barrel was built up of twisted cords of steel, the Japanese version consisted of laminations, one thin layer of steel being placed over another like an onion skin.

The majority of Japanese matchlock barrels are octagonal in section, but some are round with a flat ridge on top for the rear-sights. The latter is a square piece of metal with a deep transverse cut and a narrow cut parallel to the line of sight. The pointed foresight is usually set on the muzzle ring. A feature of Japanese barrels is the absence of a barrel tang screwed into the stock. The breech plug is invisible, the end of the barrel being held by a brass band round the stock. This is due to the apparent reluctance of the Japanese smiths to make screws. One result of this is that the pan-cover is made double so that a pin could be employed to hold it instead of a screw. Both barrel and lock are pegged to the wooden stock in the same way as the Japanese sword blade is held in its handle.

In the construction of the lock there is the same absence of screws, which are replaced by pins. There are two main types of locks, both of which belong to the snap-matchlock group with the forward-facing match-holder. With the exception of a few minor parts they are made entirely of brass. The first type has a large external U-shaped mainspring, the heel of the cock being held as in its European counterpart by an internal sear protruding through the lock-plate. This is released by a button trigger in a small unobtrusive guard. The second type has two interior spiral springs. One works the cock like a clock spring, while the other activates a sliding sear which engages with a tumbler on the cock spindle. All these brass springs have little power, but the cock is arranged so that little movement is required, and on each lock-plate a stop is fixed so that the cock cannot be pulled back too far (**958**).

The decoration applied to the barrel is usually a rich *nunome* (overlay) of gold and silver in appropriate dragon, wave or scroll motifs. The owner's family badge or *Mon* is given a prominent place near the breech. This badge was sometimes repeated in gilt on the stock. Usually, however, the stock is of plain finish, the only unusual feature being a brass-lined hole through the grip for holding the match. The stock and the barrel often bear groups of Japanese characters which indicate the name of the maker, his locality, the date, and the material used.

A matchlock gun of very similar appearance to the Japanese article was adopted by the Koreans after their country was invaded by the Japanese late in the sixteenth century. In an early Korean description of the making of the matchlock, or bird-gun as it was called, the author observes 'There are no guns like these in China; we got them from the Japanese barbarians'. The Korean matchlock is so close a copy that in some cases it can only be identified by the barrel markings. Instead of a family crest on the barrel there is an inscription in Chinese characters stating the barracks to which the gun belonged.[1]

As we have seen, the Chinese were in contact with the Portuguese at an earlier date than the Japanese, but in spite of this and their much earlier employment of gunpowder they seem to have made no effort to rival their neighbours' prowess in hand-gunmaking. The Chinese military work *Wu-Pei-Chih* of 1621 includes drawings of Japanese- and Indonesian-type matchlock guns which are labelled 'bird beak' guns. But it is quite obvious that even at this date the artist responsible was not clear what the mechanism was or how it worked. When the Chinese did decide to make matchlock guns—and many of them are still in use to-day—they produced the crudest of locks and the poorest finish of all. These guns are easily identified by their long barrels and short curved pistol-grip butts. The lock is a simple serpentine construction. Even simpler is the matchlock found on Formosa. Here the serpentine is pivoted in front of

[1] Boots, 'Korean Weapons and Armour'.

the pan and is attached to the trigger by a piece of string! It is a strange thing that the people who may well have been the originators of the firearm should have taken no further part in its development.

It is an attitude of mind still prevalent. A Chinese junk examined and photographed by *The National Geographical Magazine* in 1946[1] revealed that its armament consisted of muzzle-loading cannon, a crude breechloader of the pattern called *Fo-lang-chi* in the *Wu-Pei-Chih*, and several 'Roman-Candle' guns. The last were bamboo tubes reinforced with bands of rattan and packed with alternating layers of gunpowder and wax-covered tow—a reincarnation of a weapon used as early as the twelfth century.

[1] Robert Cardwell, 'Pirate-fighters of the South China Sea', *The National Geographical Magazine*, Vol. LXXXIX, June, 1946, pp. 787–96.

3 Wheellocks

In the Stone and Bronze Ages one method of producing a spark for making fire was to strike a nodule of iron pyrites with a sharp piece of flint or chalcedony. When man acquired the art of smelting iron he found that this operation could be performed more efficiently by the use of flint and steel. For centuries a piece of steel and flint with a box of dry tinder remained the universal lighter. The soldier and sportsman of the hand-gun and matchlock eras wearily re-kindling their matches with their tinder-boxes must have longed for a similar stone and steel mechanism which could be applied directly to their guns so that the spark fell into the priming pan. But it was to take many years before such a mechanism could be devised.

On the evidence available, it seems that the first of these mechanisms utilised iron pyrites and steel and was what we now call a wheellock. It operated much in the fashion of the modern cigarette lighter, a wheel with a slotted and serrated edge being made to revolve rapidly in contact with a piece of pyrites. The motive power was a powerful V-shaped spring which was connected by a chain to the spindle of the wheel. The outer end of the wheel spindle was squared off to take a box-spanner or key. When the wheel was turned by the key the transmission chain wound itself round the spindle and the spring was compressed; the lug of a horizontally-acting lever, under pressure from its own spring, then engaged in a recess in the back of the wheel and was itself locked in position on the notch of a small sear jutting out at right angles to the lock-plate.

When the sear was pulled out of engagement by the trigger the power of the mainspring overcame that of the sear-lever spring causing the lug of that lever to be forced out of the wheel, which then spun freely. The wheel was positioned so that its rim protruded into the priming pan and the spark was generated in the middle of the priming powder. The pan was protected by a sliding cover which in the fully developed wheellock was controlled by an internal series of levers and springs, which opened it when the wheel was spanned. After the pan had been primed the cover was shut by merely pressing an external button. It was reopened automatically by the action of the wheel as it started to revolve.

The cock of the wheellock, sometimes called a dog-head, was equipped with a pair of screw-controlled jaws which gripped the lump of iron pyrites in a thin piece of lead or leather. Its base was pivoted to the lock-plate so that it could either be held down with the pyrites resting on the wheel ready for firing, or pushed out of the way to lie alongside the barrel. In the latter position the gun could be carried safely, although primed and charged and with its lock wound up ready for action.

By tradition the wheellock is said to have been invented in Nuremberg in 1517, and no less an authority than Moritz Thierbach has given the name of the gunmaker concerned as Johann Kiefuss. The researches of a modern historian,[1] however, have proved that this traditional story and some others that date the invention even earlier are false. There are, however, two manuscripts which provide evidence of the manufacture of the wheellock in c. 1500. They are the military sketches of Leonardo da Vinci contained in the *Codex Atlanticus*, and a volume of drawings done by or for Martin Löffelholz of Nuremberg which are dated 1505.

Unfortunately it is not possible to date Leonardo's drawings precisely, the only definite date being that of his death in 1519. But from 1482 to 1499 he was in the service of Lodovico, *il Moro*, Duke of Milan, and some authorities believe that his military drawings were executed during this period. On

---

[1] Claude Blair, 'A Note on the Early History of the Wheellock', *Journal of the Arms and Armour Society*, London, Vol. III (1959–61), pp. 221–56.

the other hand a study of the artist's handwriting has convinced another expert[1] that the firearms drawings are of later date. Several preliminary sketches of the driving chain of a wheellock and the method of attaching it to the mainspring have been ascribed by him to *c.* 1500–5. A drawing of a wheellock for a hand-gun (**11**) and another for either a tinder-lighter or a piece of artillery, he has dated to *c.* 1508. But whether he is correct or not, the first drawing is the earliest known representation of a gun wheellock. It is an oblique view and the top of the wheel and its housing have been sliced off to give a sectional aspect to this part of the mechanism. In spite of this it has been found possible to make a reconstruction of the lock, which with very little modification has worked satisfactorily (**74–5**).

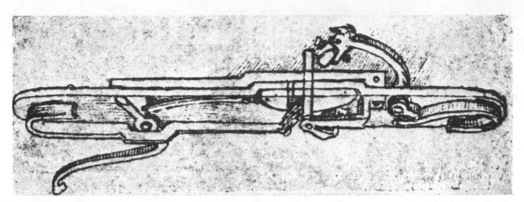

11 Leonardo da Vinci's drawing of a wheellock for a gun. From the *Codex Atlanticus*

It has several features not found on any existing specimen. The method of rotating the wheel is by the usual spring and chain-link attachment, but the spring is shaped like a U instead of the usual V. The sear-lever is attached to the outside of the lock-plate and is pivoted horizontally under the base of the cock. From here it passes across the wheel housing where it is provided with a stud which projects through the lock-plate to engage in the wheel. Its other end terminates in a triangular lug which protrudes through a slot into the interior. The end of a simple lever trigger, like that of a matchlock, is brought to bear against the diagonal surface of the triangular lug, causing it to move its lever sideways and withdraw the sear from the wheel recess.

The head of the cock is shaped roughly like an animal's head, the two jaws being hinged at the rear and closed by a vertical screw. The tinder-lighter drawing on the same folio shows a wheellock mechanism of more substantial design powered by a strong spiral or helical spring. This apparatus has two cocks, both split longitudinally to form jaws which are held by transverse screws with square heads. One holds the pyrites against the wheel and the other is a square-sectioned bar with a step in one face which acts as a sear. There seems little doubt that this wheellock mechanism would also work. What is not so easily decided is whether these drawings are the working plans of the lock's inventor—the preliminary sketches certainly suggest this—or merely the technical notes of an engineer observing existing machines.

The Löffelholz manuscript which contains the other wheellock drawings was formerly in the Staatsbibliothek, Berlin, but its present whereabouts are unknown.[2] It is a volume intended as a record of existing technical devices or secrets. On folio 27v are illustrated two wheellock tinder-lighters (**12, 13**). The first is a comparatively simple pocket instrument consisting of a small L-shaped box in which is mounted a wheel with a long spindle around which can be wound a leather thong. The wheel was set in motion by pulling the thong in the manner of a spinning top. The pyrites was held against the rim of the

[1] C. Pedretti, *Studi Vinciani*, Geneva, 1957, pp. 264–89.

[2] See R. Cederström, 'Ha Gevärslåsen Uppstått ur Elddon', *Livrustkammaren*, Stockholm, Vol. I (1937–9), pp. 65–76.

wheel by a cock with two curved elongated jaws similar to those found on the Baltic type flintlock (see p. 29). It is interesting to note that a similar wheel tinder-lighter was in use in England during the eighteenth century.[1]

The second tinder-lighter is a more complex affair mounted on a rectangular plate. Its design is closely related to the drawings in the *Codex Atlanticus*. The cock is identical to that of Leonardo's tinder-lighter, while the mainspring and chain transmission are the same as those of his gun-lock. A very similar trans-

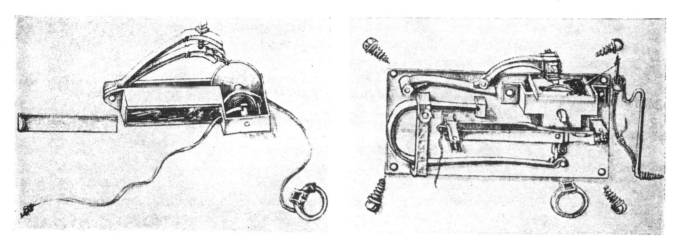

12, 13 Wheellock tinder-lighters, 1505. From the Löffelholz manuscript

verse sear-lever is also employed, but it is released by pulling a thong attached to it. The suggestion has been made that this wheellock tinder-lighter was developed from Leonardo's designs, but the converse could be equally true.

Apart from these two sets of drawings the earliest references to what are presumably wheellocks all point towards a German origin for the lock. In 1507 the steward of Cardinal Ippolite d'Este I, Archbishop of Zagreb, ordered from Germany 'a gun of the type that is kindled by a stone' (*unam piscidem de illis que incenduntur cum lapide*).[2] In 1515 a young man of Augsburg accidentally shot his whore through her neck with a gun which 'ignited itself' (*so schlug es selb feur auff*).[3] Two years later the Emperor Maximilian I issued an edict banning the use of 'self-striking handguns which ignite themselves' (*die selbschlagenden hanndt puchssen, die sich selbe zundten*) in the Hapsburg territories, and the following year extended this embargo to cover the whole of his Empire. The main reason behind this was the realisation that the wheellock made it possible for a gun to be carried concealed but ready for instant use—the ideal assassin's weapon.

The earliest known reference to wheellocks in Italy does not occur until 1522 when the Duke of Ferrara, probably for the same reason, issued an ordinance forbidding the carrying of arms in the streets of Ferrara. These included 'stone or dead fire guns' (*scoppeti . . . da preda o da fuoco morte*).[4] But a group of three wheellock guns combined with crossbows in the Palazzo Ducale at Venice (Nos. A1, 2 and 3) can probably be dated earlier than this. These combination weapons are all made entirely of steel and are of very similar construction. The gun barrel is placed inside the stock with a few inches of the muzzle end

---

[1] Miller Christy, *Catalogue of the Bryant and May Museum of Fire-making Appliances*, London, 1926, figs. 1170–1.
[2] C. Blair, 'A Further Note on the Early History of the Wheellock', *J.A.A.S.*, Vol. IV (1964), pp. 187–8.
[3] Wilhelm Rem, *Cronica newer geschichten 1512–1527*.
[4] A. Angelucci, *Catalogo della Armeria Reale*, Turin, 1890, p. 420.

protruding beyond the bow, and its pan sticks out at the right-hand side. The lock mechanism is suggestive of both Leonardo's gun lock and the Löffelholz tinder-lighter as it employs a large U-shaped mainspring and an external sear-lever. The method of operating the latter is different. The lever is pivoted laterally in the middle, a lug on one end forming the sear and the other end acting as the trigger. Pressure on one end pulls the sear out of the wheel recess at the other end.

This rather primitive form of wheellock with an external mainspring continued to be made in Italy well into the seventeenth century. The mainspring quickly became V-shaped and sometimes it was arranged to act as the cock spring as well. There is also another type of mainspring where the apex of the V has been made circular (**516**). This apparently enabled the length of the spring to be reduced making a small compact lock possible. Examples of this lock are sometimes found on guns of Spanish or Portuguese provenance.[1] Various ingenious ways were found to release the sear. On two combined axes and wheellock guns also at Venice (Q7 and 8), the lever trigger is fitted with a wedge-shaped projection which, when pressed upwards, inserts itself between the sear-lever and lock-plate, forcibly withdrawing the sear from the wheel.

A late sixteenth-century wheellock gun in the National Museum of Artillery, Turin, has an interesting sear mechanism (**86**). When the wheel was wound up the sear-lever had to be pushed into the locked position by a button spigot which can be seen on the outside of the lock in the V of the mainspring. In other wheellocks this manual action was performed by a spring. It will be noticed how the spring and chain of this lock hang down in an uncomfortable position in front of the trigger guard. The same type of lock with a button-operated sear is found on the light birding rifles with curious bent stocks known as Tschinkes (**87–8**).[2]

The word is derived from the Polish form of Teschen, the town on the northern borders of Bohemia, which was the manufacturing centre of these rifles. The majority of Tschinkes can be dated to the seventeenth century, the archaic form of lock with its exterior mainspring being preferred on this type of gun as it enabled the gunmaker to make a light-weight stock. The rear of the mainspring is usually encased in a brass box to protect the shooter's fingers. Although other forms of wheellocks were often signed by the lockmakers there is a complete absence of such identification on Tschinkes.[3]

One of the difficulties in establishing the origin and date of early wheellocks, which rarely bear a signature, is the fact that there was a considerable export trade in both guns and gunmakers. This was particularly so in the case of German gunmakers. Some are known to have gone to Italy where they were employed by the Duke of Mantua. Members of the Marquart family of Augsburg emigrated to Madrid to become royal gunmakers there in *c.* 1575. German characteristics are thus found on the wheellocks of most European countries. One such feature was a distinctive form of lock with a sickle-shaped cock spring.[4]

It occurs first on a combined crossbow and wheellock gun in the Bayerisches Museum, Munich, which bears the coat of arms of the Archduke Ferdinand and can be dated between 1521 and 1526. In spite of its early date the lock is of a quite advanced design with a partially concealed mechanism and such refinements as an automatically sliding pan-cover. There is also a press-button release to the sear. As many of the early wheellock guns are dated it is possible to divide the development of this sickle-shaped spring into three rough stages. From *c.* 1520–35 the spring is of definite sickle shape. The gun with a stag-horn

[1] See W. Keith Neal, *Spanish Guns and Rifles*, London, 1955, figs. 15 and 16.
[2] A. Gaibi, 'Appunti sull'origine e sulla evoluzione meccanica degli apparecchi di accensione delle armi da fuoco portatili', *Armi Antiche*, Turin, 1956, pp. 81–120.
[3] Some of the Stockmakers' initials have been identified. See Viktor Karger, 'Neue Teschner Beiträge zur Herkunftsfrage der Teschinken', *Waffen und Kostümkunde*, 1964, Heft 1, pp. 29–42.
[4] See Arne Hoff, 'Hjullaase med seglformet hanefjer', *Vaabenhistoriske Aarbøger*, Copenhagen, Vol. III (1940), pp. 68–82.

covered stock in the Tower of London (**80**) can be dated to this period. From *c.* 1535–45 the blade of the sickle almost encircles the wheel, and the handle juts out at right-angles. A Spanish-made example in the Royal Armoury, Madrid (**78**), is dated 1546. In the third and last period, which ends *c.* 1560, the handle curves upwards where it is fastened to the circular blade. A representative of this type is the detached lock in the Victoria and Albert Museum (**79**). The last two locks are also interesting as the cock is placed behind the wheel facing the muzzle.

The earliest dated wheellock gun is the carbine in the Royal Armoury, Madrid, whose barrel bears the two sickles mark of Bartholme Marquart of Augsburg, and the date 1530 (**76**). This carbine was probably purchased by the Emperor Charles V when he visited Augsburg in that year. It is also of note as its lock has an unusual form of mainspring. This is V-shaped with a long upper arm and a much shorter lower one. Several early wheellocks bearing the Augsburg mark have this type of spring, which suggests that it may have originated in that city; but other examples are known apparently of Italian origin. From the middle of the sixteenth century either the two arms of the cock spring are of equal length or the lower one is slightly longer.

Another noticeable group of wheellocks, nearly all of French manufacture, were made with a separate mainspring. Instead of being fastened to the lock-plate the mainspring and wheel spindle were housed in the stock, the mainspring being secured by a strong pin which can be seen to the rear of the lock-plate (**96–7**). The wheel spindle passes right through the stock, being supported by a bearing in the side screw-plate. An unusually early example of this lock (*c.* 1540) is found on the carbine K.62 at Madrid,[1] but the majority of this type of gun were made from *c.* 1570 to 1620.[2] The graceful form of lock-plate with its pointed tail was later copied extensively, the mainspring being fitted in the normal way. It was a neat lock which suited the design of carbines for both military and sporting use. The many examples of military arms of this kind made in the Low Countries has led to this later lock being often classified as a Dutch lock, but in fact it was made in nearly every North European country (**98–9**).

While the wheellock itself was being developed, the gun to which it was joined was also undergoing a number of changes, mainly in the shape of the stock. It would be difficult to make out any case for the general development of any one kind of stock, for by the end of the sixteenth century every conceivable form of butt with a trigger guard of appropriate shape seems to have been in use. Probably the most unusual are the carbines (*arcabucillos*) in the Royal Armoury, Madrid, which have a pull-out extension to the butt (**89**). This consists of a convex iron plate on the end of an iron rod known as the *coz de tornillo*. The carbines were convenient weapons for horsemen, taking up little more room on the saddle than a pistol, but still capable of being fired from the shoulder with greater range and accuracy.

Among the many forms of wheellock gun stock (**92, 94**), the large triangular butt of the military musket of the seventeenth century is comparatively rare as it is usually associated with the matchlock. The petronel form of butt (**95**) is found usually on arms of French manufacture, but in this class of guns fired from the chest there is a group of German wheellock guns whose butts terminate in a flat circular scroll (**93**). They were made for the Archduke Matthias, later Holy Roman Emperor (1612–19).

By far the most popular form of butt fitted to wheellock guns is the short thick butt, generally classified as the German butt. This was held to the cheek in the firing position in similar fashion to the Tschinke already mentioned. A round iron knob screwed into the heel of the butt protects the decorated surfaces from contact with the ground. The majority of this type of wheellock gun were rifled and it may be wondered why no injuries were caused to the face by the recoil. In both light and heavy rifles, however, the weight of the barrel was sufficiently heavy to absorb the shock of the explosion. The German butt

---

[1] See Thomas T. Hoopes, 'Drei Beiträge zum Radschloss', *Z.H.W.K.*, Berlin, 1932–4, Bd. 4, pp. 224–9.
[2] A. Norris Kennard, 'Two Sporting Guns in the Scott Collection', *The Scottish Art Review*, Glasgow, 1956, Vol. VI, No. 1, pp. 22–5.

in the middle quarters of the sixteenth century was made in an almost straight line with the barrel and fore-end, and there is only a gentle slope from the breech tang to the butt-plate (109). On the left-hand side the butt was fashioned with a flat, angled surface to act as a cheek-piece. On the other side the space between the lock and butt-plate was occupied by a patch or tool box with a sliding lid. Towards the end of the century the cheek-piece was deepened so that it hung down below the lower edge of the butt. The upper edge developed a distinct drop just behind the breech, after which it continued parallel to the barrel (122).

The decoration used on wheellocks is infinite in variety, and reached some of the highest standards of workmanship. The most popular form of decoration was the use of engraved stag-horn and bone inlays. On the best quality guns, most of the decoration consisted of classical and biblical scenes, sometimes copied from well-known engravings (110–11). The lock itself was frequently the subject of a steel chiseller's and goldsmith's work, the cock being subjected to the most fanciful treatment. The German wheellock is noted for the engraving of its lock-plate. The Italian lock in contrast has a plain plate which acts as a foil for the delicate and profuse carving of the cock and trigger guard (105). Very obviously related to this Italian style of steel-work is the Sardinian gun with its long slim stock covered in metal tracery (107–8).

Apart from these fairly standard national types of wheellocks there were a number of extremely interesting experimental locks. The wheellock is after all a mechanic's delight and presented a challenge to every budding inventor. The ordinary lock in its most advanced stage was complicated enough, and in its double and treble models (521) has enough moving parts to keep any gunmaker busy. But such was the fascination that it exerted that from time to time locks of even more complicated nature were evolved.

One of the very first locks made has a helical spring similar to that drawn by Leonardo da Vinci. It is fitted to the pistol carbine (K. 63) in the Royal Armoury, Madrid. Some gunmakers, perhaps owing to a lack of confidence in their new medium, equipped their wheellocks with a matchlock as well. The mechanism of these was arranged so that the first pressure on the trigger set off the wheellock and sustained pressure brought the matchlock into operation. Such combination locks continued to be made long after the wheellock had proved its reliability and presumably they were in the nature of an insurance against the breaking of a spring, although one cannot help feeling sometimes that the gunmaker could not resist the temptation to fit one more working part (81–4).

Another cause of failure in the wheellock was the possible fracturing of the piece of pyrites. Breakages could be overcome in two ways; the lock could be fitted with two cocks (103), either of which could be brought into play, or the cock could be made with a double set of jaws held by a swivel nut. If one piece of pyrites became useless, the swivel nut was loosened and the other set of jaws was brought into the striking position. This extremely rare kind of wheellock is found on the carbine dated 1531 in Madrid (K. 33).[1] Thierbach (fig. 93) also illustrates a combined matchlock and wheellock with a double-jawed cock.

Mention has been made of the key or spanner (828) used in winding-up the wheellock. The loss of this small item could put the gun out of action, and to avoid this possibility, several wheellocks were constructed with a self-spanning mechanism. The action was achieved by connecting the base of the cock to the wheel spindle by a chain, or by a rack and pinion device, so that when the cock was moved down on to the firing position it automatically wound up the wheel. The most famous example of a self-spanning wheellock is a totally enclosed lock shaped like a stag and signed JACOB ZIMMERMAN 1646, formerly in the Dresden Museum (14). In the same collection was a wheellock which was spanned by pushing down the trigger guard. The latter is hinged in the front to the stock and has a hook-like projection which pulls a chain connected to the wheel spindle. When it was thought necessary, a release catch

[1] See El Conde De Valencia de Don Juan, *Catálogo de la Real Armería de Madrid*, Madrid, 1898, fig. 276.

was fitted to the cock so that the lock could be spanned and the cock then returned to the safe position (**355**).

One essential for the smooth performance of the wheellock was that its many springs and moving parts could be kept clean and free from rust. Several attempts were made to produce enclosed and waterproof locks. In the case of the 'stag' lock quoted, the opportunity was taken to produce an article of ornament as well, and this has also been done with an enclosed wheellock in the Bayerisches National-

14 Front and rear views of a wheellock by Jacob Zimmerman, 1646.
From Thierbach's drawing in *Die geschichtliche Entwickelung der Handfeuerwaffen,* Dresden, 1886, fig. 86

museum, Munich (**120**). The cock is carved into the figure of a philosopher reading an open book, the pages of which can be seen to be engraved with Hebrew characters. The inscription on this lock contains a chronogram of the year 1726.

A much earlier enclosed lock in the Tower of London (**118**) has all its mechanism enclosed and a small pyrites holder forms part of the decorated wheel cover. The wheel spindle goes right through the stock and can be reached by a small opening in the stock on the opposite side to the lock. This may originally have had a disguised plug or cover so that only the owner knew how to load the gun.

One great disadvantage of the wheellock, as with all guns dependent on ignition from priming powder, was the effect of the flash and puff of smoke which were emitted from the priming pan before the main charge took fire. This not only caused discomfort to the sportsman and obscured his aim, but gave a warning to game. Wildfowl were particularly sensitive to this tell-tale signal of an impending shot. It was to remain the bugbear of all shooters until the invention of the percussion cap, and, as we shall see, many ingenious attempts were to be made with flintlocks to overcome the nuisance. In only a few instances does this appear to have been attempted on the wheellock. A rifle made for the Emperor Ferdinand III of Austria (1637–57), now in the Kunsthistorisches Museum, Vienna (**124**), has been fitted with a long tube to take the smoke away from the pan and to cover the flash. Boeheim[1] illustrates a very similar lock with a long tube made by Christian Baier, *c.* 1640. A detached lock in the collection of Mr. A. R. Dufty, Farnham, England, has a much shorter tube built on for the same purpose (**123**). These so-called 'chimney-stack' locks (*Rauchfang Radschloss*) were not quite as clumsy as they appear, for when not in use the tube rested along the barrel.

Another unusual lock, although not strictly in the category of wheellocks, can be mentioned here as there is at least a resemblance between the two. This was the segment lock in which the wheel was

[1] W. Boeheim, *Handbuch der Waffenkunde,* Leipzig, 1890, fig. 539.

replaced by a pivoted segment of steel. No key was necessary with this lock as the segment was simply pulled back until it was held against the pressure of the mainspring by the sear. The mainspring acted on a tumbler fastened to the cock spindle inside the lock in the manner of a flintlock. A cock similar to that of a wheellock was employed to hold the pyrites against the serrated edge of the segment. Thierbach (fig. 56) illustrates a combined segment lock and matchlock in which the cock is connected to the segment by a slotted link and acts as a handle to pull back the segment for cocking.

The invention of the segment lock is attributed by Antonio Petrini in his *Arte Fabrile* of 1642[1] to the Italian gunmaker Rafaelle Verdiani (*c.* 1580–1630). This gunmaker worked for the Medici in Florence and must have been a mechanic of no mean ability; but only one example of his lock is known. It is on a gun in the Tower of London Armouries and is signed and dated inside RAF. VERD. 1619 (**121**).

Another group of locks which come in the scope of this chapter were the 'rasp' locks in which a straight metal rasp is pulled or moved longitudinally against a piece of pyrites or flint. They are based on an early pistol in the Historisches Museum, Dresden, which, because of its traditional association with Berthold Schwarz, is known as the 'Monk's Gun'. It consists of an iron barrel just under a foot long with a long narrow box riveted to one side. Through this box runs a steel rasp of rectangular section, with longitudinal grooving on the upper face, and terminating in a large ring handle. At the front end of the box a curved cock with hinged jaws similar to those of Leonardo's wheellock drawing is pivoted, so that when it is brought down the pyrites rests on the rasp where it runs through the priming pan. The gun is fired by a quick backward pull of the rasp handle. The design of the cock and the use of Gothic lettering in its decoration suggest that this lock is of the first quarter of the sixteenth century.

Other examples of the rasp lock, but of later date, are illustrated by Thierbach (figs. 51–5). They include a brass cannon lock in the Zeughaus, Berlin, with a manual action similar to that of the Monk's Gun, and a gun lock from the Sigmaringen Museum actuated by a spiral spring.

Although much of the interest in the wheellock gun lies in the ingenuity of its mechanism, it must be remembered that it reached the height of its popularity at a time when new ideas in the design of the stock and the barrel were being tried out. Amongst the new types of gun were the blunderbuss, a gun with a wide flared barrel terminating in a flared muzzle and firing a charge of several bullets (**112**); and the hand-mortar gun, designed to propel a hand grenade from a container fastened to its muzzle (**770–2**). More surprising are the wheellock guns with 'off-set' stocks made for right-handed sportsmen who could only use the left eye. The two examples illustrated (**126, 128**) show clearly the difficulties that must have been experienced in bending the stock and lock to this shape.

Even when the wheellock was largely superseded by the flintlock from the middle of the seventeenth century onwards, it still remained popular as the lock of the sporting rifle. Many experimental forms of rifling were made. The number of grooves, their depth and shape, and the degree of twist vary from gun to gun. In the Tøjhusmuseet, Copenhagen, is a wheellock rifle (**115**), the forerunner of a small group of guns whose rifling took the sectional shape of a trefoil, a quatrefoil, a square or a heart. Another interesting form of rifled barrel, which has a detachable liner providing a choice of bores for small or big game, was also developed in the middle of the seventeenth century. The earliest dated examples (1652 and 1653) were made respectively by Sigmund and Cornelius Klett of Salzburg. Others originated in the Breslau district, one by Caspar Sommerfeld being dated 1668 (**113**).

Such was the popularity of the wheellock, which lent itself so readily to superb decoration, that the wealthy patron continued to demand its production until well into the eighteenth century. A German wheellock rifle dated 1726 has been mentioned already. This was no exception. The Austrian gunmaker,

[1] Only MS. copies of this work are known, one being in the Tower of London Armouries, another in the Metropolitan Museum, New York, and the third in the Magliabecchi Library, Florence. See A. Gaibi, 'Un manoscritto del 1660, l'Arte Fabrile, di Antonio Petrini', *Armi Antiche*, Turin, 1962, pp. 111–43.

Joseph Hamerl (1678–1738), who held the title of *Herzoglich Lothringischer Hofbüchsenspanner* (lit. 'winder-up of the wheellocks of the Duke of Lorraine') is known to have made wheellock guns as late as 1735.

The eighteenth-century wheellock is usually of simpler mechanical design, but its lock-plate and external surfaces are heavily engraved or chiselled with sporting scenes (**131**). The cock is equipped with a large decorated plate down its side concealing the jaws and also acting to some extent as a flash container. Towards the middle of the eighteenth century the wheellock was not only fitted to the typical hunting rifle of the period (**132**), but its lock-plate began to look like the flintlock (**133**), an anachronism due to which it was not long to survive.

4 Flintlocks

It is by no means certain that the wheellock was the first of the spark-producing locks, as many of the early references to 'self-igniting guns', etc., could apply as well to flintlocks as to wheellocks. The Italian proclamation of 1522 forbidding the carrying of 'stone guns' or 'dead-fire guns' (see p. 21) could also apply to either type of lock. But it is not without significance that although there are a number of wheel-locks dated between 1530 and 1570, there are no comparable flintlock examples. The flintlock as such is first mentioned in a Florentine ordinance of 1547[1] where there is a reference to *archibusi . . . da fucile*, and in a Swedish royal account of the same year[2] in which the word *snapplås* or snap-lock makes its first appearance. The word *fucile* originally applied to the 'strike-a-light' or tinder-lighter—the piece of steel held in the hand when striking a spark from the lump of flint. Used in conjunction with *archibusi* there can be little doubt that this is a reference to the gun mechanism now known as a flintlock.

The flintlock consists basically of a cock whose jaws hold a piece of flint facing a flat piece of steel, which is pivoted vertically over the priming pan. This cock is pulled back against the pressure of the mainspring until it is held by the sear. When the cock is released by the trigger it snaps back and the flint strikes the top of the steel, sliding down it with a rasping motion and at the same time thrusting it out of the way so that the sparks fall into the pan. It is this abrupt snapping movement which gave it the name *snapplås* in Sweden.

The same action of the cock, so reminiscent of a pecking hen, led to the Dutch or Flemish word *snaphaan* (i.e. snapping hen). The English equivalent was *snaphaunce* or *snaphance* which, by a process of association, also meant an armed robber, a desperate fellow or thief; and it is in this sense that the word is first recorded being used in 1539.[3]

It was a word that obviously puzzled the early firearms historians who were writing when the flint-lock in its fully developed state was still in use. Samuel Meyrick, in his pioneer article of 1829, 'Observations upon the History of Hand Fire-arms',[4] came to the conclusion that during the seventeenth century the word 'fire-lock' meant a flintlock and that 'the Snaphannce was a near approach to the fire-lock but evidently not the same'. Having observed that the earliest flintlocks were of the type in which the steel or hammer was separate to the pan-cover, he gave these the name snaphaunce. Later writers followed suit. W. Grisley in his *Siege of Lichfield* (1840) wrote: 'the snaphaunce differed from the modern fire-lock in the hammer not forming the covering for the pan'. This opinion has since been widely shared, Pollard[5] going so far as to use the phrase 'the true snaphance'. Thus a word which was originally applied to all forms of flintlock mechanisms has now come to mean a particular type of flintlock only. Strictly speaking it is incorrect, but as it is now common usage I have also used the word in the same way.

What is believed to be the earliest example of a flintlock is the snaphance gun now in the Royal Armoury, Stockholm (**134**). It bears a Nuremberg mark on the barrel and is probably one of the 35 Nuremberg harquebuses known to have been fitted with 'snap-locks' in the Swedish royal armoury at Arboga in 1556.[6] This does not necessarily point to a Swedish origin for the flintlock as several German

[1] A. Angelucci, *Catalogo della Armeria Reale*, Turin, 1890, p. 421.
[2] Ake Meyerson, *Stockholms Bössmakerei*, Stockholm, 1936, p. 10, n. 21.
[3] *Oxford English Dictionary*.
[4] *Archaeologia*, London, 1829, Vol. XXII, pp. 59–105.
[5] H. B. C. Pollard, *A History of Firearms*, London, 1926, p. 34.
[6] Ake Meyerson, *Vapenindustriernai Arboga*, Stockholm, 1939, p. 103.

workmen were employed at Arboga at this time, and, as we shall see, there are other indications that German gunmakers were largely concerned if not solely responsible for the development of the first flintlocks. The type of snaphance fitted to this gun appears to be the first of a series of locks which are found mainly in the countries bordering the Baltic Sea, and are known now as Baltic locks.

The early model of the Baltic lock has a cock with a pair of long screw-operated jaws similar to those on the small Löffelholz tinder-lighter (see p. **21**). Its short stem ends in an elongated heel which bears down on the crook of the exterior mainspring. When the cock is pulled right back the heel is caught by the nose of a laterally-acting sear protruding through the lock-plate. The steel is a rectangular plate on a straight stem pivoted to the lock-plate, so that when it is raised it rests vertically in front of the priming pan. The latter has a pivoted cover opened by hand like that of a matchlock.

This form of lock mechanism with an external mainspring sometimes serving both cock and steel had a primitive simplicity, and as late as the early nineteenth century was still being used by the country sportsman. Many of these guns with their crude peasant-type decoration are thus difficult to date. In the early versions of the lock the jaws are set at an angle to the stem of the cock, but from the second half of the seventeenth century the long jaws and short stem are formed in a continuous curve. Although the Baltic lock was later to receive all the improvements of the other European flintlocks, it retained its distinctive curved cock to the end (**145**).

Another group of early flintlock guns is represented by three muskets preserved in the arsenals at Dresden and Veste Coburg, and in the Germanisches Museum, Nuremberg.[1] Dated 1571 or 1572 on the barrels, they are fitted with combined match- and snaphance locks about 12 inches long. The matchlock part has a simple sear-lever action, the long under-lever acting as a trigger guard for the trigger of the snaphance. The latter, considering its date, is of a surprisingly complicated design. The cock is connected by its spindle to a flat piece of metal inside the lock known as the tumbler. The interior mainspring bears on a notch cut in the front of this tumbler, which is held in the cocked position by a laterally-acting sear similar to that of a wheellock. The makers of this lock must have had the wheellock in mind, for the steel is very narrow, only three-eighths of an inch wide; its face is convex and it is cut into four V-shaped grooves with transverse notches.

On the outside of the lock-plate between the cock and the steel is a narrow piece of apparatus controlling the opening and shutting of the pan-cover. This is a sliding cover, pivoted to a sprung lever. When it is closed against the pressure of its spring it is held by the hook on the end of a rocking lever lying horizontally across the lock-plate. The other end of the lever rests just in front of the base of the cock. When the cock is released its specially shaped 'toe' pushes this lever inwards. The other end automatically moves in the opposite direction, thereby releasing the lever of the cover which opens (**147**).

While the provenance of these muskets is unknown it is not unreasonable to suggest that they are German, and indeed, another example of this type of snaphance with the curious pan-cover arrangement is found on a pistol, now in the Tower of London Armouries (**150**), whose barrel is stamped with a Nuremberg mark. This is a snaphance only, and the steel is of a more substantial construction, the stem being joined to the plate by an angular piece of metal. An almost identical lock is fitted to a gun in the Pitt Rivers Collection, Oxford University (**149**). But just to confound the theory of the guns' German origin the lock of this gun is stamped with a gunmaker's mark found also on a group of wheellocks at Capodimonte, Naples, which are believed to be of French manufacture.

The automatic opening of the pan-cover of a flintlock was of some importance. If the pan had to be uncovered manually as in the matchlock, and the contents exposed to the elements for only a short space of time, then much of the advantage of the flintlock was lost. The pan-cover mechanism described above

[1] A detached lock, identical to those on the muskets, and now in a private collection in the U.S.A., was illustrated in the *Gun Collector*, No. 38 (1951), p. 644.

apparently found little favour and was quickly superseded by a much simpler idea. In this the pan-cover arm was placed inside the lock where it was pushed forward by a bar connected to the top of the tumbler. This pan-cover action is found on a type of snaphance lock which is thought to have originated in the Low Countries in the last quarter of the sixteenth century. There was a large export trade in this type of lock from the great manufacturing centres of this area and it was also widely copied in most European countries, so that stylistically it is difficult to tell one country's products from another.

The lock has a flat S-shaped cock, whose heel or tail is caught by a laterally-acting moving sear acting through the lock-plate. In front of the cock is a stop which is positioned so that the movement of the cock is arrested before its jaws hit the pan. A distinctive feature of the lock is a circular or square side guard—known as a 'fence'—fitted at right angles to the outer end of the pan. The steel has a flat arm bent either at a sharp angle or with a pronounced curve.

Some of the most interesting and earliest examples of this lock were made in England. Here the first reference to the snaphance occurs in 1580 when the Dean and Chapter of St. Paul's Cathedral, London, became responsible for the supply of nine light horsemen for military service in Ireland. Amongst their equipment were '9 cases of snaphances at 40s. the peece'.[1] As the snaphances were in 'cases', they were probably pistols. In the accounts of the City Chamberlain of Norwich for 1587–8, the local smith Henry Radoe was paid 12 shillings for making 'one of the old pistols with a snapphance and a new stock for it.'[2] We do not know, of course, whether these snaphances were flintlocks with the steel separate from the pan-cover, but it seems very likely from the two existing English guns of this time.

In the Danish National Museum, Copenhagen, there is a snaphance petronel (**152**) which bears the gun-maker's mark RA and a fleur-de-lis on the barrel, and the stockmaker's initials D.I. and the date 1584 on the stock. This petronel has a lock of well-advanced design, with a graceful long-necked cock and a square fence. It is also one of the few locks of this type to be fitted with a safety catch. This lies behind the cock and is similar to those found on most wheellocks. The whole of the barrel is damascened in gold and silver with martial trophies, whilst the breech bears, appropriately, a representation of St. George and the Dragon. The stock is inlaid with engraved mother-of-pearl in a manner similar to a group of pistols and guns of known English manufacture.[3]

One of these guns is the straight-stocked snaphance musket which has been preserved at Belchamp Hall, Essex, by the Raymond family since the sixteenth century. Although of not so fine a quality as the Copenhagen petronel it was evidently made by the same gunmaker, as the barrel is stamped with the same RA mark and the stock is engraved with two sets of initials R.I. and D.I. The horn butt-plate is engraved with an erotic scene and the date 1588.

It is possible that two snaphance guns in the Livrustkammaren, Stockholm, both unfortunately with broken fore-ends, may be of English manufacture. The barrels of both are octagonal at the breech and round towards the muzzle which is trumpet shaped. One is described in an early inventory of the Armoury as Scottish (**153**), but it is very similar in appearance to the musket shown in the oil painting of Sir Thomas Southwell now in a private collection at Tan-y-Bwlch, North Wales. The second gun (**154**) is a long-barrelled carbine which has a short butt with an extension plate and a belt hook. It also has a Scottish connection, the butt-plate being engraved with the arms of the Scottish family of Spens. The inlaid floral designs on the stock, however, correspond closely with those on a pair of English snaphance pistols in the Bohemian castle of Konopiště. The helmeted warrior engraved on the stock and the fence may also be compared to that engraved on the stock of the Belchamp Hall musket.

One reason for the presence of fine English firearms in foreign princely collections was the pleasant

---

[1] *9th Report of the Historic MSS. Commission*, London, 1883, App. p. 44.

[2] *Extracts from Original Manuscripts*, Norfolk and Norwich Archaeological Society, Norwich, 1846, Pt. 1, p. 16.

[3] J. F. Hayward, 'English Firearms of the 16th Century', *J.A.A.S.*, Vol. III (1959–61), pp. 117–41.

custom of exchanging royal gifts. Amongst these, richly decorated weapons ranked high in prestige. In 1604 James I of England sent Philip III of Spain a number of gifts which included 'Foure fowling pieces with there furniture very richly garnished and inlaid with plates of gold'. Ten years later a more extensive range of presents—horses, hunting dogs and birds, pictures and weapons—was dispatched, and amongst these were 'Fowere fowlinge pieces, two plaine and two with massive gould'.[1]

Of these eight fine guns only a few detached parts remain in the Royal Armoury, Madrid—two barrels, a snaphance lock (**156**) and a trigger guard. Chiselled and gilded with floral decoration, they are sufficient to indicate the high standard of workmanship of which the English gunmakers were capable. The makers of these guns are not known, but one London gunmaker who is known to have received orders for royal guns was Stephen Russell who, in 1613, was paid £190 for 'two rich damasked pieces' and 'two rich white pieces cut and gilded with rich gold'. These were originally ordered by Prince Henry before his death in 1612, but as their number and description fit those of the second Spanish gift of 1614, it may well be inferred that the impecunious James I, faced with having to pay for his dead son's purchases, took the opportunity to make good use of them.

The State Armoury in the Kremlin, Moscow, also contains a number of English firearms of the seventeenth century, relics of similar gestures to the Tsars and their families. Unfortunately the records of these transactions have not been traced. The current catalogue of the Kremlin[2] identifies several pistols of the seventeenth century as English, but there is no mention, for instance, of the splendid array of gifts given by Charles II to the Tsar in 1669. A contemporary account of how the gifts, including vessels of gold and silver, were brought to Moscow on three-score sledges accompanied by 130 men of the Imperial Guard, describes the presentation of the firearms by the Ambassador:

> The first thing that came in was a Gun of King Charles the First, and therefore his Excellencie presented it with this Compliment; This Gun was delivered to me by his Majesties own hand, being excellent in its kind, the same which his Royal Father of blessed and glorious memorie used to shoot in, and which as a Relique of that Renowned Prince he thought could not be better dedicated than to the hands of Your Imperial Majestie.
>
> Next to the Gun came a paire of Pistolets whereupon my Lord spoke again, That pair of Pistolets (saith he) his Majestie delivered me also with his own hand, commanding me to excuse their oldness, which he thought would not make them less acceptable, when You knew they were those with which after so long adversity, He rid in His triumphant Entry into His Metropolitan City of London.[3]

A very interesting snaphance gun (**155**) is said to have been given by the English agent Fabian Smith to Tsar Michael Romanoff in 1625. On the information available it is very difficult to say whether this gun is of English or Dutch manufacture. But its steel and pan-cover mechanism represents an intermediary step between the snaphance and the later flintlock with the combined steel and pan-cover. If the illustration is examined carefully it will be seen that the maker of this gun has introduced a new idea by fitting the base of the steel with a metal extension which in the firing position lay on top of the pan, and formed a cover. But as though not believing this to be an entirely satisfactory cover he has also fitted the old pivoted matchlock type of pan-cover. Presumably the idea was that the gun could be carried primed with the steel pushed forward and the hinged cover drawn over the pan. When it was required to fire the gun the hinged cover was withdrawn and the steel brought down so that its horizontal base covered the priming powder. When the steel was struck by the flint the pan was automatically uncovered.

[1] William Reid, 'The Present of Spain', *The Connoisseur*, August, 1960.

[2] N. V. Gordeev, N. I. Sobelov, V. A. Ermolov, etc., *Gosudarstvennaya Oruzheinaya Palata Moskovskovo Kremlya*, Moscow, 1954.

[3] G. M., *A Relation of Three Embassies from his Sacred Majestie Charles II to the Great Duke of Muscovie, the King of Sweden and the King of Denmark*, London, 1669, p. 182.

Flintlocks

There are a number of guns in the Kremlin with this transitional form of steel and one wonders whether they are copied from the Fabian Smith importation. The Russian gunmakers certainly produced many snaphance locks of Anglo-Dutch design, but usually covered them with chiselled decoration, consisting of rather crude representations of animals and grotesques (**161**). Much of this work is a native form of art, akin to that found in the Balearic Islands and the Mediterranean. The Russian gun stock is nearly always of German form, to be fired from the cheek, but with a longer butt. The decoration is of semi-oriental style, with the lavish use of mother-of-pearl inlaid in geometrical patterns. Another Russian type of snaphance had an exterior mainspring, often of the Baltic type, bearing on the toe of the cock (**158**). Some of these locks also have the steel with an extended base forming a pan-cover (**159**).

While some gunmakers were thus striving to discover a simpler way of coupling the movement of the pan-cover with that of the steel, there was a curious reluctance on the part of others to make any change. From the beginning the snaphance gun attracted the attentions of the steel sculptors and engravers of Italy. The city of Brescia and the villages in its vicinity became the centre for the production of steel work whose quality has never been surpassed (**174**). Barrel-making was the speciality of the village of Gardone, the barrels of such masters as Lazarino Cominazzo and Giovanni Battista Francino being widely sought after. Locks were made mainly at Marcheno, although the finest of all lockmakers, Matteo Acqua Fresca, worked in the mountain village of Bargi, near Bologna.

The feature of the earlier Italian snaphance is the delicate chiselling of the lock which is accompanied by stocks embellished with panels of steel tracery, pierced and engraved with designs of animals, birds, and monsters in a profusion of baroque floral scrollwork. At least one maker, Stefano Sioli or Scioli, made gun stocks entirely of steel, engraved and chiselled in the same fashion (**188**). In the second half of the seventeenth century the Brescian gunmakers in particular achieved an astonishing proficiency for chiselling in deep relief and in the round. This craft was widely distributed, but the work of gunmakers farther south where the Spanish influence was strong lacked the refinement of their Brescian counterparts.

Technically the snaphance, with its separate steel and pan-cover, could not compete with the later-pattern flintlock, but nevertheless it remained in production in Tuscany until the beginning of the nineteenth century. This Tuscan school of gunmakers, headed by Giuseppe Guardiani who worked at Anghiari, were responsible mainly for the manufacture of pistols, but fowling-pieces were also made with floridly carved mounts and snaphance locks *alla fiorentina*, only differing from their seventeenth-century predecessors by the elaborate woodwork of their stocks. An example in the Victoria and Albert Museum (**173**) possessing all these features has in addition a barrel partly sheathed in embossed silver.

Another country which having adopted the snaphance retained it long after it had been discarded elsewhere was Scotland. The locks were probably introduced from England in the last quarter of the sixteenth century, but the Scottish gunmaking trade was essentially a local industry and having adopted its own special style of design and decoration remained unaffected by the trends of European fashion. This is noticeable in the case of Scottish long-guns of the seventeenth century which are among the rarest of collector's pieces; a census conducted in 1961 revealing that only 24 guns are known to be in existence.[1]

The snaphance locks of these slender guns contain the same basic mechanism as the Anglo-Dutch pattern, with an interior mainspring, a laterally-acting sear protruding through the lock-plate, a sliding pan-cover and separate steel, and a circular pan-guard. But the lock-plate is long and narrow with pointed finials at either end. In general design the guns fall into two main classes. There is an early type of which only a few specimens exist whose butt slopes down in a gentle curve. This is provided with a rectangular trigger guard terminating in a scroll or disc. The cock has a flat comb streaming out to the rear like a horse's tail, and its jaws grip the flint with concave surfaces held together by a nut-headed screw. The finest example of this type is the gun dated 1614 formerly in the *cabinet d'armes* of Louis XIII,

---

[1] William Reid, 'Lady Seafield's Scottish Guns', *The Connoisseur*, May, 1961.

in which incidentally it was described as *un petit fusil Irlandois*. It is now in the Tower of London Armouries (**163**).

The later Scottish long-guns with snaphance locks are provided with deep curved butts, which are carved on both sides with three parallel flutes. No trigger guards are fitted, the curve of the butt apparently being considered sufficient protection for the unobtrusive button triggers. Many of the barrels are like those of the pistols, rounded and decorated only on the top surface, the sides being quite plain and flat. All this gives the guns an archaic appearance, and it is strange to find them bearing dates up to the end of the seventeenth century when they look so much earlier. But however tenaciously the Scottish gunmakers clung to the old design, they seem to have dropped it just as abruptly. A fowling-piece in the collection of Mr. R. T. Gwynn, signed by the maker John Stuart and dated 1703, follows the English or French pattern stock and lock of the period. No examples of the old-style gun have been found after this date.

While in some parts of Europe the stately snaphance still had its adherents, the flintlock generally had undergone considerable change. The alteration to the steel of the Fabian Smith gun already mentioned had been anticipated by others as the answer to the pan-cover problem. The long arm of the steel was removed and the right-angled piece of metal was pivoted at the end of its base, forming an L-shaped combined pan-cover and steel. This modification does not seem to have been introduced into England and other northern countries until the first quarter of the seventeenth century. But there is some evidence to suggest that it was in use in Italy before then. A dual-action flintlock and wheellock in the Artillery Museum, Turin, which has the combined pan and steel has been dated by some authorities to the second half of the sixteenth century (**516**).

The new flintlock action was an obvious improvement but it did have its disadvantage. It will be appreciated that with an independent pan-cover the gun could be carried fully loaded with safety. When the pan-cover was made integral with the steel, however, shutting the pan also placed the steel in the firing position, which involved pulling the cock out of the way. In other words the gun could only be carried primed with its lock cocked. Some kind of safety measure, then, had to be devised to prevent an accidental discharge. In one method this was achieved by constructing the combined steel and pan-cover so that when the pan was covered the steel could be swivelled out of the way. For some unknown reason this type of safety steel, apart from isolated examples made as curiosities, is found only on the so-called Baltic lock (**139,145**).

Another method, and the most popular, was to screw a hook, known as a dog or back-catch, to the lock-plate just behind the cock. When the cock was pulled to a half-way position, i.e. before the sear was engaged, it could be held securely by the dog hooking on to the tail of the cock, or, in later patterns, into a notch cut in the rear edge of the cock (**180**). In a few cases this catch or dog was positioned under the cock (**151**). The modern tendency is to group all these locks together under the classification of dog-locks.

Although the combining of the steel and the pan-cover was a great step forward, the flintlock still suffered from a clumsy release system—some form of laterally-acting sear borrowed from the wheellock and suitably modified. The invention of a new type of sear—the final step in the flintlock's development —appears to have been initiated in France between 1600 and 1610. In this the tumbler was shaped roughly like a circular disc. In one side a notch was cut to take the end of the mainspring, and on the other side two parallel notches were cut. Into the latter impinged the sharp edge of a new vertically-acting sear. This simple but far-reaching invention is usually attributed to Marin le Bourgeoys (d. 1634) of Lisieux, an artist and mechanic of the French Court. His name appears on the wonderful flintlock gun in the Hermitage Museum (**176**), which is the earliest recorded French flintlock and was dated by the late Dr. Lenk as probably not later than 1610.[1]

[1] T. Lenk, *Flintlåset*, Stockholm, 1939.

Flintlocks

The new sear mechanism did not receive the immediate recognition that one would have thought, and for some time no change was made in the interior mechanism of many flintlocks, even when the new form of steel was being largely adopted. Thus we have a series of locks with the new-pattern steel and the old-pattern sear. This transitional lock, if it may be called that, was popular in England *c.* 1600–40, and has become known as the 'English' lock (**963**). The earliest examples have a straight lateral sear protruding through the lock-plate and engaging the tail of the cock in the full-cock position. A 'dog' holds the tail in the half-cock or safety position.

Next comes a lock which from the outside appears to be no different, but has a sear with an additional prong inside which comes into operation in the half-cock position, blocking the movement of the tumbler. The gunmakers obviously did not trust this measure entirely and so for the most part retained the outside dog as well. In the 1640s, however, they took this idea one step farther and made both prongs of the sear act on the tumbler, there being no longer a projection through the lock-plate. A pair of pistols with this type of lock, by the London gunmaker William Watson in the Tower of London (XII-1495–6), can be dated to *c.* 1650.[1]

The majority of the 'English' locks are found on military arms and are of comparatively crude construction. The Italian gunmaker Antonio Petrini in his treatise of 1643 wrote '*se ne fanno in gran copia, come anco in Inghilterra, i quali sono lavorati grossamente e malfatti, ma sono pero bonissimi per far fuoco*' (they are made in great quantity, as in England, of rough finish and poor construction, but nevertheless are excellent for giving fire). The musket now in Windsor Castle (**178**), decorated with inlaid bone and mother-of-pearl and engraved with the arms of the Stationers' Company and the date 1619, is an exception.

It would be a mistake, however, to imagine that only snaphances and 'English' locks were being made in England during the first half of the seventeenth century. The fine collection of Civil War guns at Littlecote, Berkshire, the majority of which have London proofmarks, reveals that a wide variety of flintlocks were under construction. Noteworthy are those whose lock-plates imitate the shape of the French type of wheellock (**183–4**). This uncertainty on the part of the gunmakers as to the best means of employing the flintlock is also reflected in the wide variety of stocks. The fish-tail butt of the old matchlock musket, the paddle-shaped butt of the wheellock carbine and, the old favourite, the short German butt were all utilised at first to house the new lock. There was also a heavy flat butt with a straight upper edge and a deep rounded belly underneath (**185–6**).

In the third quarter of the seventeenth century the flintlock was considerably shortened and as the French type of sear gained in popularity the flintlock became a well-functioning compact piece of machinery, with pleasing rounded surfaces—another innovation of French gunmakers which was widely copied. The barrel forgers were also able to produce lighter and stronger barrels and the stockmakers finally evolved a style of stock which gradually superseded all the old-fashioned patterns.

The lower edge of the butt of this swept down in a clean straight line from trigger guard to the toe of the butt-plate. There was a long tubular wrist giving a comfortable grip, and a high comb to support the cheek in the aiming position. The butt-plate itself, no longer a flat heavy strip of metal, was carefully moulded to fit the shoulder, and its tang was extended along the comb for strength. A metal escutcheon or thumb-piece was inserted just behind the barrel tang. An attractive part introduced at the same time was the side-plate—a strip of metal inset in the stock on the opposite side of the lock. Its main function was to prevent the heads of the lock-screws (or nails as they were generally known in the trade) from being drawn into the wood when the lock was screwed up tight, but its decorative possibilities were soon realised.

Artists and engravers began to publish pattern books so that gunmakers were provided with a selection of motifs with which to engrave the metal parts or furniture of their guns. The designs of François

[1] A. N. Kennard, 'A Pair of Seventeenth-Century English Pistols', *J.A.A.S.*, Vol. II (1956–8), pp. 131–5.

Marcou (1657), Jean Berain (1659 and 1667) and Claude Simonin (1685) achieved wide circulation, so that what might be termed an international style developed. The superb decoration on the gun by the obscure gunmaker F. Maddock, whose workshop was in the Castle Yard, Dublin (**197**), is thus little different from that adopted by the most distinguished of Parisian gunmakers Bertrand Piraube. In fact were it not for the signatures on guns it would be sometimes difficult to achieve a satisfactory identification.

Much of this standardisation in both decoration and pattern of lock and stock was due to the movement of gunmakers from one country to another. In 1685 the Revocation of the Edict of Nantes exposed the

15 Design for a flintlock. From De Lacollombe's *Nouveaux desseins d'Arquebuseries*, 1730

French Protestants (Huguenots) to all the brutalities of which religious persecution is capable. Many fled to England. One of the greatest of all gunmakers to come to London, Pierre Monlong, was appointed Gunmaker-in-Ordinary to William III. He was followed by artist mechanics like Jacques Gorgo, who designed some ingenious multi-shot firearms (**581**), and Isaac de la Chaumette, whose breechloading system was eventually to make history (see Chap. 6).

Artists of international repute have always sought the patronage and experience of other countries, and gunmakers were no less disposed to travel. Johann Gottfried Kolbe, the iron chiseller and engraver of Suhl in Thuringia, is known to have worked in London in the 1730s where he produced for George II the magnificent air gun now in the Victoria and Albert Museum (**733**), and the pair of five-barrelled revolvers in Windsor Castle. His finest work was the suite of rifles, fowling-pieces and pistols in the Capodimonte Museum, Naples, which he created for King Charles III of Spain.[1]

By the middle of the eighteenth century, however, certain national characteristics began to assert themselves. The English ideal was a simplicity of design and a mechanical perfection. The gun *par excellence* was a double-barrelled shotgun with the barrels and locks side by side. The clean-cut walnut stocks were devoid of carving except for a slight moulding round the barrel tang and lock; and the barrels and locks carried the minimum of engraving or chiselling. If decoration were needed, restrained

[1] J. F. Hayward, 'Les Collections du Palais de Capodimonte', *Armes Anciennes*, Vol. I (1953–6), Pl. XLI.

Flintlocks

silver mounts and silver wire ornament were applied (**204**). Towards the end of the century a few of the London gunmakers catered for the oriental trade and were able to call on the London goldsmiths for suitably florid ornamentation. Ezekiel Baker, set to replace a pair of gold-inlaid barrels belonging to the Prince Regent which he had broken in proof, found little difficulty in finding a goldsmith capable of the task (**206**).

The carbine and blunderbuss enjoyed the widest popularity in England. Many of the earlier carbines were inspired by the pistols of the period with rifled turn-off barrels. There was a vogue at the end of the seventeenth century for them to be fitted with an extending butt-plate (**208**). The desire for lightness and compactness in these essentially travelling weapons led to a variety of folding, detachable and skeleton butts (**211**). Then in the last quarter of the eighteenth century came the era of the brass-barrelled blunderbuss with folding bayonet, the personal arm of the mailcoach guards.

In France the only restraint ever placed on the decoration of guns was the cost. For most of the eighteenth century the Royal gunmakers with a *logement* in the Louvre gave full scope to the iron chisellers and goldsmiths of Paris. When the Republic was declared and the gunmaking industry was concentrated at Versailles it seemed that there might be a change of policy. But soon the extravagances of the Republicans were as excessive as those of the Court which they had displaced, and, in 1793, the Director of the State factory, Nicolas Nöel Boutet, a former *Arquebusier Ordinaire du Roi*, was allowed to set up a special workshop for the manufacture of *armes de luxe*.

While Boutet was responsible for a number of minor technical improvements to locks, and re-introduced rifled barrels to France—he favoured rifling of the polygroove or micro-groove variety—he is mainly remembered for the wonderful presentation pieces that came from his factory between 1800 and 1818. The hall-mark of his work apart from the lavish use of gold and silver inlays is the precision of finish of both wooden and metal parts. Boutet also emphasised a decorative feature often found on French guns and rarely elsewhere. The lower part of the stock behind the trigger guard is carved with a monster's or animal's head, so that it forms a slight pistol grip (**220**).

Another state factory which was to produce some outstanding firearms was that of Tula, on the river Upa in Central Russia. From the middle of the seventeenth century it was the centre of a region noted for its ironworks and in 1705 an arms factory was founded by Peter the Great with the intention of making it the main source of supply of military weapons. Not long afterwards, however, a number of craftsmen were imported from Germany, Sweden and Denmark for the purpose of making fine quality firearms for the use of the Imperial Court.[1] Some of these firearms, bearing dates from 1720 to the end of the century, are still preserved in the Kremlin.

During the latter part of the seventeenth century the Russians had adopted the French type of flintlock with the vertical sear, but their guns still showed evidence of Scandinavian and oriental influences (**223**). With the establishment of the Tula factory there was a complete break with tradition and both the form and decoration of firearms followed contemporary western European fashion. During the reign of the Empress Elizabeth (1741–62)—probably the most flourishing period—the Tula gunmakers followed rigidly the gunstock designs published by Nicholas Guérard in Paris early in the century. There are in existence three lavishly ornamented guns (one in the Tøjhusmuseet, Copenhagen, one in the Tower of London Armouries, and the third in the Keith Neal Collection) which bear her cypher on the barrels and have almost identical scenes inlaid in silver on the butts (**224**).

Tula was always a centre for silversmiths and iron workers and much of the ornamentation on Tula guns of the first half of the century, which does not come up to the standard of the best German or French artists, is probably the work of local craftsmen. At this time it was customary for only the word Tula and the date to appear on the guns. Catherine the Great, however, encouraged the steel chisellers

[1] J. F. Hayward, 'The Imperial Russian Arms Factory of Tula', *Apollo*, August, 1949, pp. 43–5, September, 1949, pp. 69–71.

36

to perfect their technique, and it is noticeable that guns made during her reign are not only of restrained and first-class execution, but are signed by the maker. Good examples are the pieces at the Hermitage signed by Ivan Lialin, a gun by Ivan Pushkin in the Kremlin, and a most striking gun now in the Victoria and Albert Museum which bears the name of A. LEONTIEW [Archip Leontiev] (**227**).[1]

The flintlock, which had encouraged the development and the popularity of the lightweight fowling-piece, was not received with so much acclaim by the devotees of the rifle. German, Austrian and Bohemian sportsmen still clung faithfully to their wheellock rifles—at least for a time. But it was gradually realised that a better result could be obtained by firing a flintlock rifle from the shoulder than with the old wheellock rifle from the cheek. The gunmakers of Carlsbad, Prague and Vienna began the development of their famous flintlock Jäger rifles. One can see the beginnings of this arm in the seventeenth-century flintlock rifle in the Tøjhusmuseet, Copenhagen (**231**), which has a heavy octagonal barrel, a stout rounded butt with a cavity or box for patches covered by a sliding lid, and double 'set' or 'hair' triggers protected by a large trigger guard. These were to remain the essentials of the European hunting rifle and, with the exception of the special triggers, were to be adopted by the rifle companies of the Prussian and Austrian armies.

The barrels of these hunting rifles, invariably of octagonal section, are rarely decorated, the gunmakers concentrating on their technical performance. The Kuchenreuter family of Regensburg, Court gunmakers to the Princes of Thurn and Taxis, were famed for the accuracy of their rifled barrels. A most unusual form of rifling was used in the barrel of the gun by Walster of Saarbruck in the Windsor Castle Collection (**238**). This has been forged to a heart-shaped bore, and then twisted to form rifling. The locks of the better class rifles were chiselled and engraved with hunting scenes and at least one gunstock maker produced superb stocks of light walnut, inlaid with engraved bone plaques and rococo scrollwork (**235**).

From the beginning of the eighteenth century the American colonies were urgently in need of rifles to kill game and Indian marauders, both of whom presented targets far too elusive for the smoothbore musket or fowling-piece. Unable to obtain rifles from the British authorities who were only concerned with military needs, the colonists were forced to undertake their own manufacture. Many of the settlers in the State of Pennsylvania were Swiss[2] and Germans who had brought the Continental rifles with them. From these short-barrelled rifles developed, strangely enough, a rifle, known now as the Kentucky or Pennsylvanian rifle, with exactly the opposite characteristics.

The American rifle had a long barrel from 3½ to 5 feet in length, of a calibre averaging 0·45 in., supported by a full-length maple stock of slender proportions. The brass patch-box lid was hinged and usually formed part of a decorative plaque on the side of the butt (**244**). The butt-plate had a very pronounced concave curve. All these parts were made by local smiths working in small workshops with the simplest of tools. The locks were another matter. It was not until the first quarter of the nineteenth century that the American gunmakers appear to have achieved any success in the wholesale manufacture of gun-locks. Previous to this they relied mainly on imported German and English locks. The Birmingham firm of Ketland and Co. were the largest suppliers and eventually opened a branch in Philadelphia.

Flintlock guns formed an important part of the European export trade in the eighteenth and nineteenth centuries. Cheap and crudely made guns—often put together with materials rejected for military use—were specially made in the big manufacturing centres at Birmingham and Liège, and also in France, which country monopolised the trade with Turkey and the Middle East. The Dutch East India Company had a factory at Amsterdam which assembled guns from Belgian parts for export to the Dutch colonies. The English East India Company generally purchased complete arms from the London and Birmingham

---

[1] Claude Blair, 'Archip Leontiev's Gun', *The Connoisseur*, February, 1962, pp. 116–17.

[2] J. G. W. Dillin in *The Kentucky Rifle*, p. 12, states that the Swiss gunmaker Peter Leman started making rifles near Lancaster as early as 1721.

makers. The various companies trading with the West African coast exchanged muskets for slaves and then sold slaves to the American colonists.

Many of the early guns sent to the West Indies with long barrels and rectangular sectioned butts were adopted by the buccaneers, who gave their name to a type of trade gun which became known as the Buccaneer gun.[1] '*Fusils boucaniers*' with brass mounts and their stocks painted red were still mentioned in Belgian exporters' lists until quite recently. An intriguing division of this group of guns, for which I

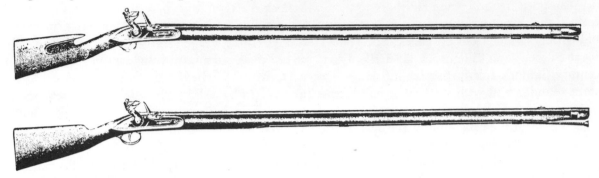

16 Modern flintlock trade guns from the catalogue of Theate Frères of Liège
Top '*Boucanier femelle*', 51 in. barrel, 22 bore. *Bottom* '*Boucanier mâle*', 52 in. barrel, 11 bore

have been unable to advance any anatomical or anthropological explanation, is the naming of those guns with a thumb cavity cut into the butt as '*boucanier femelle*', while those with the normal comb to the butt are '*boucanier mâle*'. They are presumed to have been exchanged respectively for female and male slaves. A gunmaker who unwittingly gave his name to another export gun was Lazarino Comminazzo. The well-known quality of his barrels caused many of the guns made in Spain and Liège for export to South America to be stamped LAZARINO LEGITIMO or some similar inscription.[2] They became known in the trade as 'lazarinos'.

This world-wide movement of firearms commenced early in the seventeenth century when London and Dutch merchants conducted a lucrative trade with the Barbary Coast of Africa, bartering their snaphance locks and long birding guns for the exotic goods of North Africa. A gun with the Anglo-Dutch type of snaphance and a long barrel has continued in use amongst the tribes of Morocco until the present day (268). Few of the original locks and barrels survive, but they have been copied extensively and accurately by the native gunmakers. Rather angular versions of the lock were made in the late 1800s.[3]

This clinging to an outmoded lock, and a North European one at that, is all the more curious when one considers that the Mediterranean countries had from the beginning developed special flintlocks of their own. As we have seen, one of the first mentions of a flintlock occurs in an Italian document and possibly the earliest surviving flintlock is also Italian (516). The latter has been previously noticed as it is an early example of the use of a combined pan-cover and steel. Its mechanism—the flintlock portion—is one of the first of a distinct group of locks known as the Roman Lock or the Italian toe-lock (249). In this lock the mainspring is fashioned with a hook on the end which presses down on the toe of the cock. The base of the cock is also fitted with a heel, and, in the fully cocked position, is caught by the horizon-tally-acting sear protruding through the lock-plate (966).

[1] Other types of flintlock trade guns were Long Dane Guns (with choice of three stock colours—black, brown or red), Fuzees, Birding Guns and Elephant Guns.
[2] J. Alm, 'Handelsgevär', *Livrustkammaren*, Stockholm, Vol. V (1949-52), pp. 73-108.
[3] W. W. Greener in *The Gun and its Development*, 9th edn., 1910, p. 228, illustrates one of these locks made by Moorish gunsmiths in his factory in 1885.

On the earliest examples of the Italian toe-lock the cock is retained in the safety position by a catch which hooks on to the heel. In the later and more sophisticated locks this is replaced by a secondary sear which passes through the lock-plate under the toe of the cock. An offshoot of the first Italian toe-lock is an Arab lock of striking appearance (**272**). This is a large long lock often inlaid with brass or silver in the Eastern style with the external mainspring bearing on the toe of the cock. The sear, which catches in a slot cut in the inner side of the cock, is the double-lever type used on the wheellock. The safety position is achieved by a sprung hook which engages in a notch in the rear of the cock. Nearly all the surviving examples of this lock bear dates in the eighteenth century, but its origins can be traced back to a lock of *c.* 1610 in the W. Keith Neal Collection.[1] The guns which mounted this type of lock have the usual long Arabic barrel set in a straight stock profusely decorated with silver and brass inlay. The narrow triangular butt is usually without a trigger guard.

Another type of Mediterranean lock, referred to in the seventeenth and eighteenth centuries as the Spanish lock (*llave española*), is known to-day as the miquelet lock. This word—never in contemporary use it should be noted—appears to have originated late in the nineteenth century, and is derived from *miquelete*,[2] the term applied in Catalonia to irregular mountain troops who presumably carried guns armed with these locks.

This lock also embodies the L-shaped combined steel and pan-cover together with a horizontally-acting sear, but it has a different mainspring. This has a straight upper leaf which passes under the base of the cock and presses the heel upwards, in the same way as the spring of the early Baltic lock. Unlike the latter, however, the cock of the miquelet lock has a very prominent toe which in its upward movement is caught first by the sear itself in the half-cock position and then by a lug on the sear spring in the full-cock position. The miquelet lock, although frequently of heavy and crude construction, is the most compact of all the flintlocks. The cock has a very short straight stem and faces a small square steel. The flint has only a small striking arc, and to help create a satisfactory spark a strong mainspring is necessary and the face of the steel is cut with vertical grooves. It is significant that one of the first names for the Spanish flintlock gun was *arcabuce de rastrillo* (from *rastrillar*, to comb or rake).

The earliest example of a miquelet lock is found on the lance, mounted with two pistols, in the Royal Armoury, Madrid (**780**). The locks of these pistols, however, are most unusual in having *sliding* steels and pan-covers. The Spanish gunmaker, Alonzo Martinez de Espinar, in his *Arte de Ballesteria i Monteria* published in 1644, states that there were then four types of Spanish locks in use—the *patilla*, the *agujeta*, the *inuencion* and the *calco*. The first, taking its name from *patilla* (foot), referred to the miquelet lock with its pronounced foot or toe on its cock. Espinar does not describe the next two locks properly but says that they were more complicated, with little springs to operate the sear which got out of order. The only sear which answers to this description is the wheellock type with two levers worked by a spring.

There are several Spanish or Mediterranean locks which have this type of sear. There is a rare Spanish type which has an internal mainspring and tumbler, with the double sear acting on the tumbler (**260**). One of the earliest Spanish flintlock guns in the Royal Armoury, Madrid (K. 123), has this kind of lock. The Arab toe-lock already described also has the double sear, so that either of these locks would fit Espinar's description of the *agujeta*. The *inuencion* was said to be easy to disarm, and it therefore seems likely that here Espinar was referring to one of the Italian snaphance locks with a separate steel, which sometimes had a double sear. As *calco* meant a rear sear it can be surmised that this referred to the Roman or Italian toe-lock. On the subject of locks another interesting feature mentioned by Espinar is the *fiel* or retaining pin which was inserted in the screws of the cock and steel to prevent them from coming out of adjustment. These small pins, however, were discarded by the end of the seventeenth century.

---

[1] See W. Keith Neal, *Spanish Guns and Pistols*, London, 1955, Plates 97–100.
[2] The word can be spelt with a 'g' or 'q'.

Flintlocks

The Spanish gun barrels of the eighteenth century were as renowned as those of Italy in the seventeenth century and as much sought after. They are often found mounted by English, French and German gunmakers. In shape the sporting gun barrels are octagonal for one-third of the length from the breech, the remainder being circular. The point of junction is marked by turned rings or chiselled foliage. The three upper flats of the barrel bear the maker's name and mark inlaid with gold (the best quality barrels also being dated and marked with the town of manufacture) (**261**). Few Spanish gun barrels are rifled, but they are of sufficient strength to be used with either ball or shot.

The stocks of Spanish guns fall roughly into two classes. In the 'Catalan' style the lower edge of the butt sweeps down in graceful curves to form a blunt toe (**258**). Both upper and lower edges of the 'Madrid' stock are, in contrast, quite straight, parallel fluting being carved on the sides for decoration (**256**). The wood is usually a fruitwood, the most popular being cherry. While giving an excellent finish, this was not as strong as walnut, which was available only in small quantities. This shortage of good wood for the stock was the cause of most barrels being fastened to the stock with metal bands. It probably accounts for the continued popularity of the miquelet lock which, with its exterior mechanism, needed only a shallow cavity in the stock.

In 1701 the French King Philip V acceded to the Spanish throne and some of the French fashion in gunmaking began to spread to the Spanish gunmakers. A lock developed which was something of a compromise between the Spanish and French types of lock. This is now called the Madrid lock, but was known then as the lock *a la moda* (**264–5**). Apart from two projections on the S-shaped cock it had the smooth outline of the French flintlock, the mainspring being placed inside the lock where it bore on the toe of a tumbler. The sear action, however, was the same as the miquelet lock, except that the cocking positions were different, half-cock being effected on the rear projection of the cock and full-cock on the front. This lock is found both on fine-quality fowling-pieces and on military muskets. The southern part of Italy and Sicily were also for some time under Spanish domination and here again there was some intermingling of gunmaking techniques. It is not unusual to find an Italian-type lock in a Spanish stock (**253**), and many Spanish-type miquelet locks are either decorated in an Italian manner or were actually made in Italy (**518**). Not unnaturally the islands of Corsica and Sardinia, lying between Spain and Italy, were also affected, and the distinctive type of Sardinian gun was fitted with the miquelet lock (**268**). The use of the lock spread along the coasts of the Mediterranean to Albania, Greece, Turkey, Persia, and finally to the Caucasus.

The mechanism of the eastern Mediterranean miquelet lock does not differ materially from the western examples although it has an additional outer plate which stretches from the cock pivot to the screw of the steel, and affords some cover for the latter's small spring. But the lock is noticeably smaller in size—there are no specimens comparable to some of the great jagged Spanish locks—and the way in which the head of the cock is rounded off is quite distinctive.

Albanian guns are noted for their spindly all-metal stocks ending in a fish-tail butt (**274**). By comparison Turkish and Persian guns have a heavy, sometimes massive, stock of pentagonal section with a sharp step behind the barrel tang. Decoration varies from a few simple brass or silver inlays to the complete coverages of ivory, ebony and silver with coral studding (**273**). The barrels range from long light smooth-bores to short heavy rifles of the dimensions of wall-guns (*Shir-Bacha*). Some of the latter barrels taken from former matchlocks are made of fine Damascus steel. A Persian rifle in the Metropolitan Museum, New York, is dated 921 A.H. (A.D. 1515). This rifle has a large ogival backsight with several apertures, one above the other for use at different distances.

Both Turkey and Persia came under strong European influence during the second half of the eighteenth century, and there are a number of guns made in these countries which are direct copies of English and French examples. In nearly every case, however, they are made with a dummy ramrod, the real article being carried separately with the powder-flask (**805**). The blunderbuss was the firearm most copied, many of the Eastern-made barrels being forged with enormous flared muzzles. Even the decoration on these follows closely the French pattern in style and shape—compare the Turkish-made blunderbuss (**279**) with the French rifle (**220**)—and the locks are also modelled closely on English and French patterns. The lock of a beautifully decorated Turkish blunderbuss in the Wallace Collection (**278**) is engraved IONDON WARANTED, the nearest the native gunmaker could get to the inscription 'London Warranted', the recognised mark of quality which was stamped on English export locks.

In the Caucasus and parts of western Persia the miquelet gun is distinguished by narrow tubular stocks with only a slight step between barrel and butt (**275**). The native craftsman covered them with black leather and ornamented them with bands of silver niello work. A piece of ivory usually acts as a butt plate. Farther north the miquelet lock gun loses this Circassian style of decoration and is furnished with roughly-shaped undecorated stocks. The locks themselves, however, are chiselled with very obvious Russian motifs of animal and human representations.

In India, the few flintlocks made by the native gunmakers were also close copies of the European type. One often finds a typical Indian stock and barrel equipped with a good quality London-made lock. In the island of Ceylon, however, a most unusual form of flintlock was developed—a version of the Arab toe-lock, with a hook safety-catch (**276**) usually fitted to the left-hand side of the stock. The unique scroll-shaped Ceylon form of butt carries the most profuse kind of ornament. The butt of the gun in the Metropolitan Museum, New York (**277**), is set with panels of pierced ivory in silver frames. The flintlock gun believed to have been made for the last great warrior King of Ceylon, Raja Sinha, who died in 1687, is an outstanding example of Sinhalese art.[1] Both the barrel and wooden stock are overlaid with sheet silver, parcel gilt and embossed with repoussé designs and filigree work, and inlaid with rubies. The lock of this gun, however, probably of later date than that of the stock, is either of European manufacture or a close copy of one.

East of India the flintlock is rarely found, but mention must be made of an isolated Japanese specimen in the Military Museum, Mexico.[2] This at first sight appears to be a three-barrelled matchlock revolver. But the jaws of the cock have been turned horizontally to take a flint, and the priming pans, although fitted with the usual side-swinging double pan-cover, are also equipped with pivoted steels with ribbed faces. As far as is known this is the only Japanese flintlock gun; but in a volume of Hokusai's drawings in my possession, there is an illustration of Japanese sportsmen dressed in Portuguese fashion with morion-type helmets and bandoleers, firing what appear to be matchlock guns from wooden rests. A closer study of the locks, which are all on the left-hand side of the guns and partly hidden, reveals that they are actually flintlocks. The Japanese characters identify the guns as HI-UCHI DZUTSU (fire-strike guns). Another of Hokusai's drawings in the same series shows a French flintlock pocket pistol in which the word 'fire-strike' is used to describe the steel. The pan is the HI-MON (fire-gate) and the cock the SEKI-GIŌ (stone grip). This seems to indicate that flintlock guns were not unknown in the artist's lifetime, and it is possible that other Japanese flintlock guns may exist.

Another example of an Oriental flintlock is on a gun taken from a Tartar tribe called Meos in North Siam, now in the Royal Scottish Museum, Edinburgh (1894, 292). The short curved butt and long barrel are distinctly Chinese in character, but the lock is evidently copied from an old European tinder-lighter with an external mechanism. The native gunmaker has been unable to make proper screwed jaws to hold the flint and has fashioned instead a rudimentary two-pronged grip into which the stone was jammed.

Returning to Europe, brief mention can be made of the various attempts to perfect the flintlock or to eliminate some of its faults before it was replaced by the percussion lock. When the French type of flintlock with the vertical sear was invented the gunmakers had taken the last major step in the flintlock's

[1] See J. F. Pieris, 'A King of Ceylon's Gun', *The Connoisseur*, September, 1936, pp. 153–5.
[2] Robert E. Kimbrough, 'Japanese Firearms', *The Gun Collector*, September, 1950, p. 458.

development, but many kinds of minor improvements continued to be made. Early in the eighteenth century the bearings of the cock and the steel were strengthened by brackets known as bridles—mention is often made a of single- or double-bridle lock. A roller was later fitted to the steel spring, and the main-spring was connected to the tumbler by a link—both modifications designed to give a smoother action. A pivoted segment, known as the 'detent', was applied to the side of the tumbler, on better quality locks, to prevent the sear from catching in the half-cock notch when the lock was fired. And yet the lock still suffered from three basic faults which prevented its proper use. It could misfire because the flint had broken, or because the priming had become damp; and if it did fire satisfactorily, the flash and smoke from the priming pan either obscured the target or gave a warning to game. Many attempts were made to eliminate these faults.

The most ambitious were the efforts to produce a concealed flintlock. In its elementary form this consisted of a box placed round the lock, but it was a clumsy piece of apparatus necessitating either an outside lever or a dummy cock to work the lock inside (**284**). The Danish gunmaker, M. Kalthoff, made a lock *c.* 1660 in which the cock slid along the top of the lock-plate to strike a combined steel and pan-cover lying almost horizontally over the pan (**280**). This idea was modified by a few gunmakers in the eighteenth century who produced guns in which the flintholder was on the end of a bolt propelled by a spiral spring, and the steel was a hinged part of the barrel. The priming pan of these guns is placed just behind the breech plug which is drilled for the touch-hole. A single-barrel specimen by Stanislas Paczelt of Prague is in the Tower of London Armouries (**282**), but the most remarkable is a double-barrelled fowling-piece now in the Bayerisches Nationalmuseum (**283**). Made around the middle of the century, it has a tortoiseshell-veneered stock decorated with engraved silver inlay.

Guns with the advantage of unobstructed sighting were those with the flintlock placed underneath the breech end of the barrel. The London gunmaker, Joseph Egg, patented such a lock in 1813 (**288**); but several Continental gunmakers had forestalled him. For the most part they favoured concealing the mechanism of the lock in the stock, and to some degree guns of this construction can be said to be more weather-proof than guns with conventional locks on the outside. Although it would seem that when they were fired the priming powder would drop out unignited, actual trials with these guns have proved that they function satisfactorily. Thierbach (fig. 172) illustrates an upside-down flintlock which is also enclosed with a hinged cover. The cock of this is connected to a hinged butt-plate by a series of levers, and is cocked by pulling down the butt-plate.

The problem of ensuring that the flint was properly positioned or shaped to give a good spark does not seem to have attracted the attention of many inventors. Most gunmakers and sportsmen evidently considered it easy enough to fit a fresh flint. But in the heat of a battle or naval action this was not the case. Clip-in flintholders which could be quickly inserted into or withdrawn from the cock were found to work loose and it was the old wheellock cock with two sets of jaws (see p. 24) which was finally resurrected by the English soldier-scientist Sir Howard Douglas in 1817. Author of a *Treatise on Naval Gunnery*, he persuaded the British Board of Ordnance to introduce this lock for use on naval cannon.[1] A few sporting guns were similarly equipped (**297**).

In 1799 Sir Edward Thomason took out a patent for a gun-lock in which the cock could be easily removed for safety when the gun was loaded.[2] Another part of the patent applied to a cock in which the action of cocking gave a slight turn to the flint so that a fresh surface was offered to the steel at each discharge. Previous to this a more complicated lock with a similar purpose was patented by Sir George Bolton in 1795. A single piece of flint was held in jaws which could be swivelled from side to side by a

[1] H. L. Blackmore, 'The Douglas Flintlock 1817', *The Gun Collector*, April, 1953, pp. 818–20.

[2] In his *Memoirs*, published in 1845, this prolific inventor states that the sales of the lock did not cover his expenses. He managed to recuperate his fortunes, however, by patenting a corkscrew which is still being made to-day.

large knurled wheel on the side of the cock (**296**). As the face of the flint wore down it could be adjusted to give a better spark. Bolton's lock, which he described in a book *Remarks on the Present State of Fire-arms, etc.*, published in the same year, had other interesting features. It had an automatic safety bolt which prevented an accidental discharge, and in general design it was one of a number of so-called screwless locks.

The main purpose of the screwless lock (the only screw was that holding the jaws of the cock) was to enable a lock to be quickly taken to pieces for cleaning or for the changing of a broken spring. In the normal way this was a job which could only be tackled by a gunmaker or armourer. The first practical example was designed by Jonathan Hennem, an arms contractor of Lewisham, England, in 1784. His lock was of conventional appearance but the springs and moving parts were held to the lock-plate by means of clips and spigots instead of screws, and could be easily removed by a special tool. An experimental number of these muskets were tried with these locks[1] and they were also fitted to the Egg breechloading carbine of 1786 (see p. 63).

In this year a screwless lock of superior design was invented by the London gunmaker, Henry Nock. This great gunmaker and engineer had, as early as 1775, patented a gun whose lock was placed in a cavity of the stock behind the barrel.[2] In this position it was waterproof and its smoke was carried off by a tube. His screwless lock was also an enclosed one, made like a box, and was the result of a long series of experiments conducted by the Duke of Richmond, Master General of the Ordnance, to produce a new pattern musket for the British Army. The musket was eventually constructed with this lock, but it was so difficult and expensive to make that it was abandoned in favour of an inferior but cheaper gun at the outbreak of

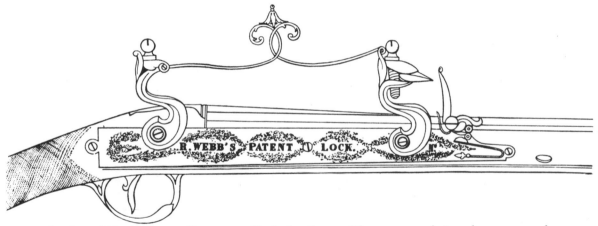

17 Richard Webb's drawing of his patent flintlock of 1795. The gun was designed to protect the user in the event of the barrel bursting

the Napoleonic Wars. Another screwless lock to be given a military trial was that of the Danish gun-maker, C. W. Kyhl. This was introduced into the Danish Army as the Model 1806.

Some of these screwless enclosed locks were tried on sporting guns but the nature of their design made them heavier and clumsier than the normal lock. They certainly could not match the delicacy of the much-vaunted locks of such makers as Joseph Manton. In 1812, Manton patented what was probably the last word in flintlocks (**490**). The pan, its cover with a special lip, and the breech, were all designed to allow water to escape without affecting the powder. A 'gravitating stop' consisting of a weight attached to a

[1] H. L. Blackmore, 'An Eighteenth-Century Musket Trial in Ireland', *The Irish Sword*, Vol. II, No. 7 (winter 1955), pp. 172–6.
[2] Pat. No. 1095 in conjunction with William Jones and John Green. It is illustrated by H. B. C. Pollard, *A History of Firearms*, London, 1926, p. 76, No. 4.

pivoted lever was attached to the lock-plate in front of the cock so that the gun would only fire in a horizontal position—at any other angle the 'stop' prevented the cock from moving. Finally an additional spring was added so that when the lock was cocked 'a pleasant and musical sound' came forth.

For some time after this date other gunmakers sought to perfect a waterproof lock. In some a leather pad covered the pan, and in one lock made by Joseph Egg in 1816, an air-tight slide protected the touch-hole. This lock was fired successfully after numerous immersions in water. In other locks, priming magazines fitted to the steel (**586**) or in mechanically operated containers next to the pan (**294**) sought to solve the problem by delivering a fresh charge of powder to the pan just before firing.

But no amount of inventive genius could disguise the fact that by now the flintlock was an outmoded form of ignition. Early in the nineteenth century the gunmaking industry turned its attention somewhat reluctantly to a new form of priming which was to revolutionise the whole development of firearms.

5 Percussion Locks

During the seventeenth century chemists and gunmakers conducted experiments to find a more powerful explosive than gunpowder. In 1625, the Italian military writer, Giuliano Bossi, described various means of increasing the range and fire-power of arquebuses and muskets.[1] These included fortifying gunpowder with other ingredients such as antimony or mercury precipitated with aqua fortis. One of Bossi's recipes—an additive of two or three grains of powdered gold precipitated with aqua fortis, adulterated with sal ammoniac and congealed with oil of tartar—produced what he called simply, but with feeling, 'The Fart of the Devil'. This kind of formula probably produced what is known now as a fulminating powder—a powder stronger than gunpowder and sensitive enough to be easily exploded by the blow of a hammer. In Bossi's case it was gold fulminate. Another fulminate, that of mercury, is believed to have been discovered by the German alchemist Johann Kunckel (1630–1703). Samuel Pepys in his *Diary* for 11 November 1663 describes the detonation of gold fulminate (*Aurum Fulminans*), a grain of which gave 'a blow like a musquett'. The following year the Royal Society of London indulged in a series of experiments to test the comparative powers of ordinary gunpowder, *aurum fulminans*, *pulvis fulminans* and another powder called 'Prince Rupert's'.[2]

Between 1712 and 1714 the Academy of Sciences in Paris published the results of several experiments with fulminating powders by Nicholas Lemery. Further researches were made by Fourcroy and Vauquelin in 1758, and by Bayen in 1774. In 1786 the great French chemist Claude Berthollet (1749–1822), who also successfully isolated silver fulminate, persuaded the French Government to commence the manufacture of a new explosive powder composed of chlorate of potash, sulphur and charcoal. This proved to be only too easily detonated and a serious explosion in the factory at Essonnes soon brought the whole project to an end.

On 14 June 1794 the newly-formed Society for Philosophical Experiments and Conversations of London gave a demonstration of the known detonating powders.[3] These included not only the fulminates of gold and silver—the latter sensitive enough to be exploded by the touch of a feather—but a powder made of 'three parts of Nitre, two of prepared Kali of the London College and one of Sulphur. Fired by a spark it exploded 'with a loud and shocking report, and with a flash so momentary as to make but little impression on the sight'. It was also demonstrated that oxygenated muriate of potash (or chlorate of potash) could be exploded by mere trituration.

Up to this point mercury fulminate had proved difficult to manufacture, but in 1799 Edward Howard discovered a satisfactory process and immediately began a series of experiments which were published the following year.[4] Like his predecessors his researches were entirely devoted to finding a substitute for gunpowder. Small charges of fulminate were exploded in guns and grenades, but the sole result was to burst the guns without increasing the velocity of the bullet. Howard concluded that 'it was pretty plain that no gun could confine a quantity of the mercurial powder sufficient to project a bullet'. He noted that the fulminate could be set off by the blow of a hammer but somewhat surprisingly asserted that the mercurial powder would not ignite gunpowder. After an explosion in which most of his apparatus was

---

[1] *Breve Trattato d'Alcune Inventioni, etc.*, Antwerp, 1625.
[2] Thomas Birch, *The History of the Royal Society of London*, London, 1756, Vol. I, p. 455 *et seq.*
[3] See *Minutes*, London, 1795.
[4] *Philosophical Transactions of the Royal Society of London*, 1800, Pt. I, pp. 204–38.

destroyed and he himself was badly wounded, he declared himself 'more disposed to prosecute other chemical subjects'.

Another experimenter, however, was to continue the researches on slightly different lines. The Reverend Alexander John Forsyth, the Minister of Belhelvie, Aberdeenshire, was an enthusiastic mechanic and chemist. He showed his interest in the new detonating substances when in July, 1799, he published an article 'On certain useful Properties of the Oxygenated Muriatic Acid' in Nicholson's *Journal of Natural Philosophy*. He was also an enthusiastic shot and well aware of the faults of the flintlock's priming with its time-lag and tell-tale puff of smoke. Undeterred by the results of Howard's experiences, he began experiments to see if he could utilise the detonators not as a substitute for the main charge of gunpowder but as a means of priming which would be practically instantaneous. As the detonators, fulminates or chlorates, were only known in the form of powder, Forsyth had to devise a mechanism which would store the powder safely and deliver a small portion for ignition near the touch-hole. This he succeeded in doing, and in the spring of 1806 he brought a new type of gun-lock to London.

It was an ingenious mechanism (**300**), to which most gun-locks could be converted with little difficulty. The lock-plate and inside mechanism were unchanged; but the cock was replaced by a hammer and the steel with its spring was removed. The priming pan was also cut out and in its place a round plug was screwed into the barrel. The touch-hole ran through this plug ending in a small cavity on its upper surface. A magazine shaped like a vase or scent-bottle revolved round this plug so that in one position it deposited a few grains of powder in the cavity and in the other brought a spring-loaded firing-pin under the hammer. When the trigger was pressed the hammer struck the pin, which in turn detonated the powder in the plug.

Lord Moira, the Master General of the Ordnance, became interested in the military possibilities of this lock and arranged for Forsyth to continue his experiments in the Tower of London. After some difficulties, locks were produced for a carbine and a carronade, but these were declared unsatisfactory after trials at Woolwich under Colonel Thomas Bloomfield in 1807. Exactly what happened at these trials is not known, but it is difficult to see how any military authority of the time could have adopted such a complicated and potentially dangerous lock. Forsyth was paid for his expenses, official support was withdrawn, and he was obliged to seek other markets for his invention.[1]

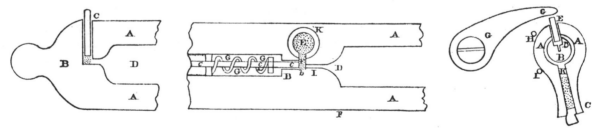

18 Drawings from the 1807 patent of Alexander Forsyth, showing two percussion cannon locks and the 'scent-bottle' lock

On 11 April 1807 he took out a patent (No. 3032) for 'An Advantageous Method of Discharging or Giving Fire to Artillery and all other Firearms, Mines, Chambers, Cavities and Places in which Gunpowder or other combustible Matter is or may be put for the Purpose of Explosion'. No particular type of detonating powder was specified, although with his own researches in mind no doubt, he recommended a mixture containing an oxymuriatic salt. Various means of applying the detonating powders were described in general terms (the drawings to the patent show a simple hammer and pin-fire device, a bolt-

[1] H. L. Blackmore, *British Military Firearms*, London, 1961, pp. 159–62.

action firing-pin and the scent-bottle lock) but the whole thing was so cleverly drafted that throughout its life of 14 years it successfully blocked the efforts of other inventors to publicise new and improved forms of detonating locks. Having founded the gunmaking firm of Alexander Forsyth & Co. at 10 Piccadilly to sell his guns to the sporting public Forsyth appears to have taken no part in the subsequent experiments to find the ideal detonating lock. He remained faithful to his original powder magazine and brought successful legal actions against any competitor.

On the Continent, where the patent held no validity, the Forsyth lock was copied extensively and improved upon. The French patents[1] are our main source of information on events which were to follow. An exact copy of the lock was patented in France on 17 April 1810 by the Paris gunmaker François Prélat. Two months later LePage, *Arquebusier du Roi*, patented several types of magazine locks in which the piston or firing-pin and its housing were separated from the powder container. In September of the same year the Versailles gunmaker, de l'Étrange, brought out improved versions of both the Prélat and LePage locks whereby the movement required to alternate the magazine from its charging to its firing position was reduced. This movement was later made automatic by linking the hammer to a sliding magazine—an improvement patented in 1819 by the Lyons gunmaker Bruneel. It is possible that Forsyth was the originator of this type of magazine as a number of locks of this type made by his firm exist. But they were made in nearly every country, the Austrian gunmaker, Joseph Contriner, being responsible for a number of finely engraved specimens. A most amusing lock on this principle was made by Joseph Gutierez of Seville in 1820 (**305**). In the same year Henri Pottet of Paris patented another version by linking a rocking or swivelling magazine to the hammer.

Although the percussion lock using loose detonating powder was to continue to be the subject of patents for a few more years—the moment the Forsyth patent expired in 1821 both William Webster (No. 4590) and William Westley Richards (No. 4611) patented various improvements in England—its popularity was by this time threatened by a number of other types of detonators. They can be divided into the following classes: (1) pills or pellets, (2) discs or patches, (3) tubes, (4) tapes, and (5) caps.

Pills

The detonating pill consisted of a few grains of powder held together by a suitable coating or binding. Wax-covered pellets were very effective but were susceptible to warmth, and, to use the words of a contemporary writer, they 'suffered from agglomeration'. An analysis of a bottle of pellets made by the London gunmaker, Charles Moore, *c.* 1830 revealed that they were made of mercury fulminate coated with iron oxide (rouge).[2] Each pellet weighed about 20 mg. and was about 2 mm. in diameter. Such small pellets were difficult to handle and either a special form of dispenser or charger had to be used or a magazine with automatic dispenser had to be fitted to the lock.

When the pellet was used singly it was also necessary to construct the lock so that the tiny object was held securely. The earliest of the pellet locks was probably that patented by Joseph Manton in 1816 (**316**). The hammer of this lock held a detachable tube, in the end of which was dropped a pellet. A hollow striking pin was then inserted in the tube, holding the pellet in place and detonating it when the hammer fell. This lock was patented in France by the Paris gunmaker, Étienne Dabat, in 1821. Manton also made a lock which used wooden plugs. These were conical in shape with an iron pin projecting at the top.

---

[1] References to French patents in this book are taken from *Descriptions des Machines et Procédés Spécifiés dans les Brevets d'Invention*, etc., Paris, 1823, and succeeding volumes.

[2] H. L. Blackmore, 'An Early Pellet-Lock Gun', *The American Rifleman*, Washington, D.C., July, 1960, pp. 24–5.

The plugs were placed in a cup-shaped cavity above the touch-hole and the pin detonated a pellet of fulminate in the base of the plug (**999**).

The method most favoured by Continental makers was to place the pellet in a cup near the touch-hole where it was held by a pivoted cover until ready for firing. Charles Moore, the London gunmaker, adapted the Westley Richards patent lock of 1821 (for use with pellets) so that its rocking bar automatically knocked off the cover as the hammer fell (**317**). The '*fusil à capote*' patented by the Paris gunmaker, Alexis Moreau, in 1821 worked in exactly the opposite way. The pellet was placed in the cover which was then pushed down over the nipple. The hammer then hit the cover detonating the pellet underneath.

Many of the early powder magazine locks were constructed so that they could also be used with pellets, but besides these there were numerous magazine locks specially devised for the purpose. One of the first was patented by Joseph Egg of London in 1822 and in Paris in 1827. In the most successful model of this lock the pellets were contained in tubular magazines lying along the top of the barrel and were fed by gravity into the pan. A sliding cover protected the pellet and was withdrawn automatically when the trigger was pulled. Such locks had a considerable vogue and one was patented as late as 1834 by Henry Shrapnel. Another type of pellet lock invented by T. H. Hayward, a Winchester gunmaker, took part in the British Ordnance percussion trials of the same year (**306**). One method was to fashion the hammer so that its head formed a magazine for pellets. William Webster patented a hammer of this kind in 1821. Another one with a circular head turned by hand was marketed by Isaac Riviere (**318**).

In America the pill-lock, or punch-lock as it was generally known there, was made popular by Dr. Samuel Guthrie, one of the discoverers of chloroform. He not only set up in business as a maker of pills of potassium chlorate mixed with gum arabic, but he inveighed against the use of other forms of percussion primers on health grounds. His sales campaign led to the manufacture of a number of pill-lock guns (**614**). One was patented by William A. Hart of New York in 1827, but the most celebrated maker was William Billinghurst of Rochester, New York. He was noted for revolving rifles of good quality and accuracy using this form of primer (**615**).

When other forms of primer had largely superseded the pellet, it still had its strong supporters. In 1852 Joseph M. R. von Winiwarter of Vienna patented in England new detonating compositions composed of mixtures of fulminating mercury or zinc, amorphous phosphorus, chlorate of potash, sulphate of antimony, binoxide of lead and potassium ferro-cyanide. These chemicals were bonded together with collodion (a solution of gun-cotton in ether), which also acted as a waterproof varnish. The explosive mixture could be moulded into any shape of pellet, disc or nail and could be used either as a means of ignition or as a propellant. Improved formulas were patented in 1853 by Joseph's brother George, who in a lecture to the Society of Arts in London made the claim that the pellets were so safe that they could be crushed between the teeth without exploding!

Discs and Patches

The difficulty of handling tiny pills or pellets led some manufacturers to insert the detonating globule in pastilles or discs of paper, paperboard or soft metal. The paper ones resembled those still used in toy pistols. An early disc primer invented by Joshua Shaw (see p. 52) in 1825 consisted of a cardboard disc barely a quarter of an inch in diameter with a small hole punched through it for the fulminate. This was made waterproof by a coating of wax, which also served to hold the disc in position in its cavity on the breech. Another percussion disc made in similar fashion ('*un morceau de carton garni au centre de poudre fulminante, recouverte d'une feuille de cuivre très-mince*') was used in a gun patented by Gosset of Paris in 1820. The disc was placed in a special holder projecting into a touch-hole on the underside of the barrel and was detonated by a hammer also underneath.

In the gun-lock designed by Collinson Hall, the London gunmaker, which was awarded a silver medal by the Society for the Encouragement of Arts, Manufactures and Commerce in 1819,[1] the disc primer was inserted in a countersunk cavity in the hammer where its waxed surface kept it in place. Hall's primer was a paste of oxymuriate of potash, flowers of sulphur, powdered charcoal and gum arabic.

The great advantage of the disc primer as with the pellet was that it could be placed in the touch-hole close to the charge. Another point in its favour was put forward by the English gunmaker, Westley Richards, in 1842 during the British Ordnance percussion trials. His discs were made of pasteboard covered with tin foil and he asserted that they would be less likely to harm the bare feet of sailors when thrown on deck after use than other metallic forms of primers.

Nevertheless, in spite of the apparent advantages of the disc primer, it was adopted by few gunmakers for use in the normal methods of single loading. It did, however, achieve great success in the hands of the American gunmaker Christian Sharps, who patented a magazine disc primer in 1852. His discs, made of copper, were only an eighth of an inch in diameter and were contained in a spring-loaded vertical tube cut in the action just in front of the hammer (311). When the hammer fell a sliding lever or 'driver' connected to it pushed the topmost disc on to a nipple over the touch-hole, where it was caught and detonated by the nose of the hammer. A similar magazine primer for discs was patented by Jesse S. Butterfield and Simeon Marshall in the United States in 1859. In the Butterfield primer the feed mechanism named the 'driver' by Sharps was called a carrier or conductor. It was also employed to cover the vent when the hammer was raised in order to protect the main charge from rain. This primer was patented in England in 1858 by Joseph Lemuel Chester and was applied to a small number of Enfield military rifles (312).

Tubes

This type of primer took the form of a small tube of thin copper less than an inch long, filled with fulminate. There were two ways in which it could be applied to the gun. In the first and most popular, one end of the tube was thrust into the touch-hole while the other end lay on a flat pan or anvil where it was held in position by a snap-cover or a pincer-like spring. This type of tube lock was patented by Joseph Manton in 1818, and a number of fine sporting guns were made with these locks (314). In the English tube lock the hammer hit the tube directly to detonate it, but there was an Austrian Army version invented by Giuseppe Console[2] and modified by General Vincent Augustin (it was known as the System Augustin) in which the priming tube was detonated by a firing-pin running through the protective cover. This method had the advantage of preventing the tube from being blown out of the touch-hole, and also protected the firer if the tube broke into fragments. The hammer of a lock by the London gunmaker George Fuller (315) is fitted with a side shield for the same purpose.

In the other type of tube lock the tube was made with a flanged umbrella-like top. A nipple with a wide hole was screwed into the barrel to act as a touch-hole. The tube was thrust into this and was detonated by the hammer hitting its top. These tube primers were more convenient to handle and were recommended by Colonel Peter Hawker in his *Instructions to Young Sportsmen* (9th edn.). They also formed the subject of an English patent of 1831 by Westley Richards, who designed a special nipple for their use.

---

[1] See *Transactions*, Vol. XXXVI, pp. 80–4.
[2] *Deane's Manual of Fire-arms*, London, 1858, p. 91.

Tapes

Being practically in contact with the charge in the barrel the tube primer was probably the most effective of all the primers but it was almost impossible to devise a magazine form of lock capable of handling it. The primer most easily adapted to multiple firing was the tape primer or, as it was known in France, *l'amorce continué*. The first example of this type of primer was patented in France by Lebœuf de Valdehon on 21 September 1821 (**19**). It was a most ingenious gun. In the first place it was a breechloader with a detachable chamber chamfered at its puzzle so that it fitted into the coned mouth of the barrel and formed an effective seal against the escape of gas. This chamber could be withdrawn for loading after the release of a hinged block at its rear. Underneath the barrel ran a short length of straw filled with fulminate, with one end projecting over a nipple which was screwed into the under-side of the chamber. A sprung hammer with a combined cutting and striking head was also situated underneath, so that when it was released it cut off a piece of the straw and detonated it on the nipple, all in one blow. The piece of straw was then moved along to bring a fresh piece of priming in position for the next shot. At least, that was the idea. But there is no record of any manufacture of the *fusil de Valdehon*, and one suspects that difficulty would arise in a gun dependent on the manipulation of a piece of straw.

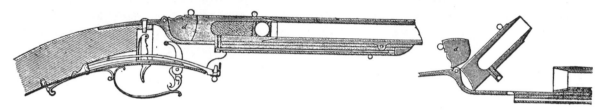

19 Drawing of the breechloader with tape priming patented by Lebœuf de Valdehon in France, 1821

In 1834, however, the distinguished French urologist, Baron Charles Louis Stanislaus Heurteloup,[1] patented a gun in France and England which had a primer described as 'a small pipe or tube made of soft metal[2] or other substance which may be easily divided, containing the priming'. This was housed in the butt of the gun and was automatically fed on to the nipple by a toothed wheel when the cock was pulled back. The lock was the normal side-action type. An example of this action is found on the musket M. 812 in the Musée de l'Armée, Paris. It may be noted in passing that Heurteloup's patent also included designs for a break-action breechloader similar to that developed later on a commercial scale by Lefaucheux.

In 1836 Heurteloup appears to have become aware of the previous Valdehon patent. After ensuring that it did not endanger his own patent, he promptly adopted its under-hammer action which he eulogised in a *Mémoire sur les Fusils de Guerre*, and gave his new gun the name *koptipteur* (derived from the Greek words for to cut and to strike). During 1837 improved models were patented in France and Scotland (the latter under the name of Thomas Theophilus Biggs). The following year a patent was taken out in Belgium in the name of J. Sigrist. Both these gentlemen were presumably agents of Heurteloup.

In the first models of the under-hammer *koptipteurs*, the primer was moved automatically by a cog when the action was cocked, but in later models, patented in 1839, the self-priming mechanism was omitted and the priming tube had to be moved into position by hand. Although the *koptipteur* was re-

[1] See W. Reid, 'The Fire-arms of Baron Heurteloup', *J.A.A.S.*, Vol. III (1959-61), pp. 58-81.
[2] In one patent the composition is given as 10 parts lead, 2 parts zinc and 2 parts tin.

jected by the British Board of Ordnance after trials in 1837 (**308**) it was adopted (in conjunction with the Delvigne Breech, see p. 56) to a limited extent by the French and Belgian armies.

An under-hammer gun very similar to the *koptipteur* was invented by Major Gustaf Erik Fleetwood, the Director of the Swedish State Manufactory at Husquarna, in 1837. It had the same tape primer fed from a magazine in the fore-end, but the firing mechanism was different. The hammer was housed in a cylinder containing a coiled spring attached to the hinged trigger guard. The latter was lowered to move the primer and when it was returned to the butt the trigger caught on a stud projecting through the cylinder and cocked the hammer. The inventor presented three examples of his gun to the Danish King Frederick VI in 1838 but did not succeed in obtaining official orders (**325–6**).

It was inevitable that there should be some prejudice against the unorthodox under-hammer action. In 1839 a conventional type of side-lock was patented in Paris by M. Martin in which a priming tape was coiled into a spiral and held in a container in the lockplate in front of the nipple. It was fed on to the nipple by a trip mechanism operated by the hammer. Heurteloup was obliged to follow suit and in 1841 took out his last British patent for a similar lock. The patent also covered a new method of making the priming, which had suffered some criticism from its tendency to burn right through like a slow match. The primer in this lock was coiled in a box attached to the barrel on top of the lock. Although an ugly and clumsy-looking device it could be adapted to existing military muskets. Heurteloup failed to convince the British experts of this, however, and made a journey to Russia to try and interest the military officials there. While there is no record of any Russian orders for the lock, a musket in the Musée de L'Armée, Paris (M. 1202), with a lock of this design dated 1841 and bearing a Russian inscription suggests that he may not have been entirely unsuccessful.

Heurteloup's box magazine was patented by J. Sigrist in Belgium in 1843. Another coiled primer magazine similar to the Martin lock was patented in Paris by Augustin Thibert in 1842. But the whole idea of a continuous piece of priming necessitating a satisfactory cutting device was open to many objections, and none of the locks had any real success. In 1845, however, an American dentist, Dr. Edward Maynard, patented a tape primer, made of two narrow strips of paper cemented together and enclosing small pellets of fulminate set at regular intervals. This tape was placed in a coil in a small cavity cut in the lock-plate between hammer and nipple. From here it was fed on to the nipple either by a cog-wheel or by prongs or 'fingers'. The Maynard primer was an immediate success. It was used to convert flintlocks to percussion and it was fitted to both muzzleloaders (**309**) and breechloaders. Maynard patented a tip-up barrel breechloader of his own design in 1851, and the first models of this rifle made by the Maynard Arms Co. of Washington were equipped with the tape primer (**310**). The United States Government eventually purchased the rights of the primer and utilised it on a number of military rifles, carbines and pistols (**328**). In a lock patented in America and England by Lieutenant J. N. Ward in 1856 the Maynard tape primer was employed in a magazine fitted into the head of the hammer.

Caps

All the percussion primers so far discussed had their good points but they were all—with the exception of the Maynard tape—outweighed by some disadvantage. From 1820 onwards the military authorities and sportsmen in general sought a primer which could be effective, safe to handle and easy to use. It cannot be said that the primer which finally achieved universal adoption—the percussion cap—really answered to all these requirements, but it was the best of the lot. Unfortunately most of the early percussion cap experiments appear to have taken place in England where Forsyth's patent laid a restraint on the publication of any new idea. As a result it is now difficult to judge who amongst the many claimants was the real inventor of the percussion cap. They included such personalities as Colonel Peter Hawker,

Percussion Locks

Joseph Manton and James Purdey. Joseph Egg, the London gunmaker, went so far as to have the words 'Inventor of the Copper Cap' printed on his trade labels and engraved on his guns. But the man generally accorded this title is Joshua Shaw, the English artist. In 1815 he patented in England a glazier's diamond and, according to a later autobiography[1] and a statement made to Henry Wilkinson who recorded it in his *Engines of War* (1841, p. 79), he also began experimenting with metal primers in the shape of a miniature top hat.

First made of steel and pewter and finally of copper, these caps had a small portion of detonating powder in the crown which was placed over the orifice of a nipple screwed into the barrel. Shaw emigrated to America in 1817, but did not take out a patent for his percussion primers until 1822. There is now no record of this in the American Patent Office, but at a later date an affidavit was made confirming that Shaw was in fact granted a patent for a percussion cap on 19 June 1822.[2] In 1824 a Committee appointed by the Franklin Institute, Philadelphia, to investigate the merits of Shaw's primers reported that one was made of copper, had been patented in the U.S.A. and had been in general use.[3] Thus there seems little doubt that Shaw introduced the copper cap to America. At least he had little difficulty in convincing the American authorities of this. When the American Government adopted the percussion cap, he petitioned for compensation for the use of his invention, and in 1847 Congress passed 'An Act for the relief of Joshua Shaw'. The sum finally awarded to him was 18,000 dollars.

Whether he did make the first percussion cap is another matter. By the time he had been granted his American patent, the cap was well known in Europe and was mentioned in at least two French patents. On 28 July 1820, the French gunmaker Prélat was granted a *certificat d'addition* to his patent of 29 July 1818. The latter was for a percussion lock which utilised a nipple, but the '*foyer d'amorce*' was placed in a recess in the nose of the hammer. In the supplementary patent, however, '*une capsule de cuivre rouge*' containing detonating powder was placed over the nipple. Later in the year, on 22 September, another Parisian gunmaker, Deboubert, was granted a patent for a lock using a percussion cap ('*chapeau en cuivre*') primed with silver fulminate. Little weight can be attached to these patents and certainly Prélat can make no claim to be the originator of the system, as previous patents of his are known to be copies of foreign discoveries.

The copper cap is not mentioned in an English patent until 1823 (John Day of Barnstaple), and it may seem strange that no one hastened to claim its invention immediately after the expiry of Forsyth's patent in 1821. But the copper cap of this period was an uncertain and even dangerous object. The soft metal sometimes jammed the hole in the nipple or split into flying fragments when the hammer fell—an unpleasant occurrence when the shooter's eye was only a few inches away. The detonating powder commonly in use in caps—a mixture of oxymuriate of potash, sulphur, charcoal, etc.—was also found to have a strong corrosive effect on nipple and barrel. All this and the fact that the percussion primer was not always easily obtainable led many gunmakers to offer their clients a combined flintlock and percussion lock with a choice of ignition systems. One lock was patented by Samson Davis in England in 1822.

The percussion cap did not achieve any popularity, in fact, until E. Goode Wright of Hereford published his paper 'On the Substitution of Fulminating Mercury in place of the Detonating Compositions into which Chlorate of Potash enters, as a Priming for Percussion Guns' in *The Philosophical Magazine and Journal* of 1823. The Editor (Thomas Gill) of *The Technical Repository* who reprinted Wright's paper endeavoured to raise the old bogy of the danger of accidental explosion with fulminating mercury ('its energy, close at hand, is most tremendous'). But the manufacturing processes were taken up by the London chemist Frederick Joyce, and the following year both Colonel Hawker[4] in England and the

[1] Joshua Shaw, *A Sketch or History of the Copper Cap*, Bordentown, N.J., 1847.
[2] Lewis Winant, *Early Percussion Firearms*, London, 1961, p. 50.
[3] This report was reprinted in the *Mechanic's Magazine*, 1825, Vol. II, pp. 142-3.
[4] See 1824 edition of *Instructions*, p. 469.

Committee of the Franklin Institute in America commented favourably on the new caps. Soon Joyce was calling himself 'the inventor and sole manufacturer of the anti-corrosive gun cap'.

The work of E. Goode Wright does not seem to have been given proper recognition and it may well be that he played an even bigger part in the development of the percussion cap than is generally supposed. According to *The Temple Anecdotes*[1] he was experimenting with fulminating mercury 'as far back as the year 1805', and actually wrote to the Duke of Wellington, then Master General of the Ordnance (in 1820?), suggesting that his mercury caps should be used on naval cannon as they were waterproof and did not cause rust. The Duke replied that the Government had decided against percussion primers and that 'there are strong objections to the use of the copper-cap'. When the British Government did adopt the percussion cap Wright's son apparently sent the correspondence to Lord Dundonald who observed 'the greatest characters may be led to acquiesce in wrong conclusions (from mental indolence) by trusting to ignorant, jealous, or interested officials'. The Rev. A. J. Forsyth, who had at least started the percussion era if he had had no hand in the development of the percussion cap, also wrote to the authorities in 1840 to claim compensation. He was awarded £200 in 1842, and just after his death in 1843 a further £1,000 was divided among his relatives.

The military powers of Europe and America had very good reason for taking their time in making a change-over from flintlock to percussion. They had to choose a system which was strong enough to stand up to military use and which would be simple and cheap to make. Preferably it could also be adapted to existing stocks of arms. France was first in the field, issuing a few percussion arms as early as 1829; but it waited until 1840 before deciding on complete adoption. The British Government began their percussion trials in 1831, but did not officially adopt the percussion cap until 1838. Sweden began its transition with naval arms in 1833 and completed it in 1840. In the United States a number of guns were converted in 1833, but it was 1841–2 before the percussion cap became standard for all troops.

The general adoption of the percussion cap was not accomplished without some minor difficulties. The tendency of the early caps to splinter has been mentioned, but much of the damage from this kind of accident was prevented by hollowing out the head of the hammer so that the cap was partially covered on detonation. But if the cap contained too strong a charge of fulminate the hammer of the gun was blown back and sometimes fractured. This possibility encouraged the design of a number of enclosed percussion locks. Usually these have the nipples screwed into the centre of the barrel breech in line with the axis of the bore. Concealed hammers or strikers are cocked by external levers or an additional trigger. Access to the nipple for priming purposes is obtained by a sliding or hinged cover. In their efforts to conceal the action the inventors often produced very clumsy-looking guns. The gun of Baron de Berenger with its large cocking trigger is an example (**339**).

Far easier to handle were the fine double-barrelled guns with concealed locks and dummy cocks made by Charles Jones of Birmingham.[2] Others were patented in England by David Laurence and John Crundwell in 1829, and by George Stocker and Joseph Bentley in 1839 (**338**). Another method of lessening the danger of injury to the eyes was to place the hammer and nipple several inches up the barrel and connect them to a dummy cock in the usual position by the breech. This action was patented in France by Barrier of Vernoux in 1845, and by C. C. E. Minié in 1860.

Many gunmakers and sportsmen, however, preferred guns with external locks of the side-hammer or under-hammer type. They offered some protection if the cap blew up and they had the advantage of a much simpler action. Few working parts were necessary. The hammer and mainspring could be combined (**324**) or the mainspring fashioned to form the trigger guard (**330**). One of the first percussion cap patents—that of John Day of 1823—related to a neat under-hammer lock which was used extensively in England on walking-stick guns. A military musket was invented by Colonel Whitelock, aide-de-camp

[1] R. and C. Temple, *The Temple Anecdotes*, London, 1865, pp. 93–5.
[2] Nearly identical locks were patented in France by Joshua Sholefield in 1834, and by R. B. Cooper in 1839.
   A very similar gun in Eastnor Castle is signed: COLOMBO IN MILANO INVENTO ANNO 1834.

to the King of Sweden, in 1835, and this was copied by Henry Wilkinson who patented it in 1839, and by Jean Joseph Guérin who was granted a patent in France in 1840. The under-hammer gun reached the height of popularity in America, where an astonishing variety of long guns, carbines (**321**) and pistols (**329**) carried these locks.[1]

Another fault of the percussion cap was the difficulty of handling it, particularly in cold weather. For sportsmen there were a number of magazines or cappers which could be slipped in the pocket and which would feed one cap at a time from their nozzles (**842**). Soldiers were normally issued with a leather bag or purse, although the French Army experimented with the idea of tying a cap to each paper cartridge.

Great efforts were also made to fit a magazine cap primer to the lock of the gun. The primer patented in 1838 by William Westley Richards (in London under his own name and in Paris under the name of Miles-Berry) consisted of a tubular magazine fixed on top of the lock. A sliding conveyor moved by the thumb brought a cap to the open end of the magazine where it was pressed down over the nipple. Other magazines worked automatically when the gun was cocked. The snag that all had to overcome was the awkward angle at which the nipple was set on the barrel. In the capper patented by Della Noce and Bianchi of Turin (in France in 1854 and in England in 1865) a carrier working in an arc transported the cap from a tubular magazine to the nipple (**313**). A simpler solution was advanced by Thomas Motte-Falisse of Paris in his patent of 1832. He constructed the nipple so that it swivelled to pick up the cap and then turned to meet the hammer.

The neatest designs were those which concealed the magazine of caps in the stock. One patented by Alonzo Perry in the United States in 1855 had a tubular magazine running through the butt from the butt-plate to the nipple. In the English patent of Alexander Rousseau of 1842 the tube from the butt ended in a swivelling nozzle which turned to the nipple when the hammer was drawn back and then moved out of the way as the hammer fell. Even the old *koptipteur* was revived briefly by Frederick Prince who, in 1859, patented a modification so that its under-hammer action would work with the copper cap (**442**).

When the percussion cap became firmly established, the gunmakers were faced with the task of converting existing flintlock guns to the new primer. This applied to military guns where it was an economic necessity and to the fowling-pieces and rifles of sportsmen loath to discard their favourite pieces. The gun-lock presented little difficulty. A percussion hammer was substituted for the cock and the steel and spring were removed. The real problem was to fix the nipple on the barrel so that it could be properly hit by the hammer and convey the flash from the cap to the barrel by the most direct path. The easiest way of doing this was to screw the nipple directly into the barrel, but in any position other than underneath or on the side, this entailed bending the hammer sideways or offsetting the nipple. At first many gunmakers simply screwed a cylindrical plug into the touch-hole and placed the nipple at a suitable angle on this. This device was found to work loose. The most secure method, and that generally adopted, was to braze a lump on the barrel by the breech to take the nipple and then to bore a touch-hole through this (**337**). This was known in America as a 'bolster alteration'.

Gunmakers designing new percussion guns soon found that they could produce much neater and more unobtrusive locks and actions than with the flintlock. The box-lock form of flintlock was re-introduced in simplified fashion. In the lock patented by Isaac Riviere, the London gunmaker, in 1825, the mainspring was fastened to the underside of the false breech, the hammer and tumbler were in one piece, and only the upper portion of the hammer was visible. A similar lock was patented in France in 1837 by Philipe Guillemin-Lambert, a gunmaker of Autun (Dept. de Saône-et-Loire).

The side-locks with the mainspring in front of the hammer (**342**) remained most popular, and many of these also had enclosed hammers (**340**). But a new type of lock known as the back-action, with its

---

[1] See Herschel C. Logan, *Underhammer Guns*, Harrisburg, Pa., 1960.

mainspring lying behind the hammer and sometimes operating both hammer and trigger, brought with it changes in the shape of the stock. In the traditional straight English stock this lock served to strengthen the narrow wrist of the butt where it was most weak. It could be turned almost vertical to reinforce the pistol grip which was to become increasingly prevalent on Continental and American stocks (**341**). Gustav Delvigne of Paris patented a cavalry carbine of this design in 1841.

Although the American gunmakers retained their traditional shaped butt for many percussion guns

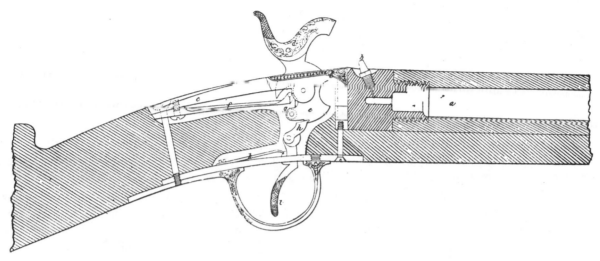

20 Isaac Riviere's gun-lock. From the English patent of 1825

(**334**), they also developed rifles with fancifully-shaped butts designed for target shooting (**332**). These were copied from the German and Swiss rifles brought to America by emigrants in the nineteenth century. They came from countries where shooting was a national sport and shooting festivals (*Schuetzenfest*) were important social events. Firing was conducted almost invariably from the standing off-hand position, and the calibre, weight and length of barrel of the rifle were not restricted as long as the man could fire it from his shoulder. In order to support the heavy weight of the barrel an upright stance was adopted with the left elbow resting on the hip and the fore-end of the rifle supported on the tips of the fingers or by a palm rest (**333**). To bring the sights comfortably up to the eye there is a very pronounced angle or drop between the line of the butt and that of the barrel. Heavy iron butt-plates (known as Schuetzen butts), with elongated prongs to keep the butt firmly in the shoulder, and double set-triggers completed the equipment of these specialised rifles.

Inspired by the widespread Romantic movement (e.g. the novels of Sir Walter Scott) the gunmakers of France, Belgium, Germany and Spain brought to the decoration of the percussion gun all the fantasies of Victorian Gothic and a style which can only be described as neo-Renaissance. Both the wooden and metal parts of the gun were deeply carved with mythological, hunting or heroic figures, after the designs published by Charles Claessen.[1] The International Exhibition held in London in 1862 included some of the most elaborate examples. The butt of a gun by Claudin was, as one commentator put it, 'perforated' by carvings of dragons. The cock of another lock was shaped as a Crusader casting a Saracen head against the nipple. Another exhibitor, Le Page Moutier of Paris, made the ebony and chiselled steel shotgun later presented by the President of France to the President of Mexico (**504**). Deeply sculptured with flowers, leaves, animals, etc., it is an example of the nature style known as '*genre végétal*'.

The percussion era saw the heyday of the muzzleloader and the introduction of the precision rifle. At the

[1] *Recueil d'Ornements et de Sujets pour être appliqués à l'Ornementation des Armes*, Liège, 1857.

beginning of the nineteenth century there were two main types of flintlock rifles—the heavy short-barrelled rifles used by European hunters and by the rifle companies of most armies, and the long-barrelled Pennsylvanian rifles of the American colonists. Each gunmaker had his own ideas as to the number of grooves in the rifling, the shape and depth of the grooves, and the degree of twist. In some barrels the rifling was progressive—the spiral increasing in its degree of twist or the grooves of the rifling increasing in their depth towards the muzzle. But the science of ballistics being in its infancy no one could prove that one particular form of rifling was superior to the rest.

The main bugbear of the muzzleloading rifle was the business of loading. Everything depended on how carefully the lead ball was wrapped in its patch and rammed down the barrel. Any deformity in its shape or in the way it gripped the rifling would deflect it from its true course. A form of oval boring was introduced into the Hanoverian and Brunswick armies in 1834 in the hope of making loading easy, and this was developed by the British into the two-groove rifling of the Brunswick rifle which fired a belted ball. This idea was taken a step further by General John Jacob in India who produced in 1858 a double-barrelled four-groove rifle capable of firing a conical studded bullet up to 2,000 yards. But it was not a rifle which could be placed in the hands of the ordinary soldier. When towards the middle of the nineteenth century it became obvious that the soldier's smooth-bore musket would have to be replaced by a rifle, intensive efforts were made to overcome the loading problem.

It had been known that for quick firing the rammer could be dispensed with and the lead ball dropped down the barrel, where it was held by a ring or chamber inserted in the breech end. This idea had been put forward by the French engineer, Deschamps, in 1718, and an experimental number of muskets were made for the British Army in 1811.[1] In 1826 Captain Gustav Delvigne resurrected the idea for another purpose. The chamber breech was fitted to a rifled barrel and a bullet which just cleared the rifling was pushed down and hammered on the rim of the chamber. This expanded the bullet into the grooves of the rifling. The system was adopted by the French Army in 1842. Experience soon showed that the final shape of the bullet varied considerably and so did the accuracy.

Delvigne began experimenting with cylindrically-shaped bullets with a flat base which could be expanded with more consistent results. In 1840 he patented an explosive bullet of this shape ('*balle-obus*') (**1054**). This needed a rammer with a cup-shaped head and a lot of confidence on the part of the loader. The following year Delvigne patented his cavalry carbine which utilised his special chambered breech. With this he now suggested the use of cylindrically-shaped bullets with pointed noses and hollowed-out bases ('*balles cylindro-coniques evidées*').[2]

The significance of the latter does not seem to have been appreciated at first, for another type of breech submitted by Colonel Louis Thouvenin was chosen for trial by the French Army in 1846. This was simply a short steel pillar ('*tige*') jutting out from the breech plug, on which the bullet was hammered for expansion. The difficulty of keeping the powder chamber clear round the pillar made this gun unpopular, but nevertheless the *carabine à tige* was employed with great effect by the French Chasseurs d'Orleans in the Algerian War.

Inventors had in the meantime turned to the idea of the self-expanding bullet. The English artillery officer, Captain John Norton, began experimenting with these in 1818[3] and approached the Board of Ordnance unsuccessfully in 1823. The gunmaker William Greener brought out the first practical version—an oval-shaped bullet with a conical plug—in 1836,[4] but this was rejected by the Board

[1] H. L. Blackmore, 'Gardner's Musket 1811', *J.A.A.S.*, Vol. I (1953-5), pp. 25-33.

[2] Leonardo da Vinci drew such a bullet in 1508. See *Arundel MS. 263, f. 54* in the British Museum.

[3] He made this claim in a letter to the *Volunteer Service Gazette*, 15.6.1861.

[4] Greener illustrated his bullet in his book *The Science of Gunnery* in 1841. When the expanding bullet was officially adopted, he started a campaign for compensation and was awarded £1,000 in 1857.

of Ordnance on the grounds that a 'compound' bullet was not considered suitable for military service (**1049**).

Following the introduction of the Thouvenin breech into the French service, another officer, Captain Claude Étienne Minié, began experiments with the old Delvigne bullet. In 1849 he patented a series of hollowed-out bullets with plugs of zinc, wood, iron, copper or lead set in their bases. The theory was that the explosion would drive the plug into the softer bullet, expanding it and forcing it into the rifling. In practice it sometimes drove the plug right through the bullet. The plug chosen by the British for their version of the Minié rifle was an iron cup. Both the Minié and its successor the Enfield rifle proved their worth in the Crimean War, and *The Times* Correspondent at the Battle of Inkerman wrote of the enemy 'the volleys of the Minié cleft them like the hand of the Destroying Angel'.

In a few years the Minié rifle was adopted by most European countries in some form or other. At the same time in the United States experimenters at Harper's Ferry Armoury had reached the same conclusions. The Assistant Master Armourer there, James Henry Burton, also designed a hollow bullet which needed no plug, and this was officially adopted. Neither Burton nor Delvigne, who had first noted the possibilities of the expanding hollow-based bullet, received their due credit, for all types of self-expanding bullets were popularly labelled the 'Minnie'. The bullet was subjected to many modifications—each country had its own ideas as to the external shape of the bullet and the number (if any) of cannelures cut in its surface—but it continued in use until the establishment of the modern metallic cartridge.

In the space of a few years the rifle, which had rarely been fired over 200 yards, was being used with confidence at ranges up to 1,000 yards. The activities of the Volunteer Associations and numerous rifle clubs were a major contribution to the increase in accuracy of long-range shooting. The oval bore was revived by N. S. Jessen in Denmark and Charles Lancaster in England, and a unique hexagonal rifling and bullet were invented by the engineer Joseph Whitworth. Whitworth, with his experience of working to fine limits, was originally called in by the British Government to increase the standards of manufacture of the Enfield rifle. He was provided with an enclosed range of 500 yards where his experiments led him to the design of a polygonally-grooved barrel. He was not the first in this field, as such a barrel had been suggested to the British Ordnance Board by a Sergeant-Major Robert Moore in 1843, and the civil engineer Isambard Brunel had had a rifle of this kind made by Westley Richards. It is not without significance that Whitworth asked for this gunmaker's help in the construction of his own rifle. Whitworth's experiments were rivalled by those of W. E. Metford and Alexander Henry with more conventional forms of rifling. The trend was now towards longer bullets of smaller calibre. The Enfield bullet with a length of 1·81 diameters of the bore could not compete with the Whitworth (3 diameters) and the Metford (3·02 diameters) at ranges of over 1,000 yards.

Much of the success of the Whitworth was due to the accuracy with which it was made, and its corresponding high cost ruled out any adoption by the Army. But while military and civilian experts engaged in heated arguments over the relative merits of the other muzzleloaders, the rival claims of the breechloader suddenly asserted themselves.

6 Breechloaders

Although it is sometimes difficult in the early records to distinguish guns with movable breeches from those with more than one barrel, there seems little doubt that the first breechloaders made their appearance during the first half of the fourteenth century. In 1342 the arrow-firing cannon in the castle of Rihoult in Artois, France (see p. 5) was made in two parts; a tube to receive the arrow and a cylindrical chamber for the powder charge. When loaded the latter was placed in the breech end of the barrel where a wedge called a '*laichet*' kept it in position. In this fashion a gun could be provided with more than one chamber for quicker loading. A brass gun with three of these 'pots' (*uno gonne de latone, cum iij potz*) was sent to Calais in 1372. Other cannon are spoken of as having two or more *capita* or *testes*.[1]

In another early form of breechloader the barrel was also made in two parts, the breech end screwing into the main barrel. In the second half of the fifteenth century both forms of construction were applied to hand-guns. Like the cannon founders the makers of hand-guns were faced with the task of constructing a barrel whose breech could be opened and loaded easily and then be shut so that there was no leak of explosive gases from the joint. This, the problem of obturation, was not solved until the invention of the metallic cartridge in the middle of the nineteenth century. Until then a considerable number of breeches of infinite variety were devised. They can be divided into four main groups which will be discussed in turn.

Guns with Movable Barrels

The collection of drawings of Leonardo da Vinci known as the *Codex Atlanticus, c.* 1500–10, contains many drawings of cannon with breeches which unscrew for loading. One drawing of particular interest shows a light breechloading field-gun on a wheeled carriage which fires a metal arrow with offset

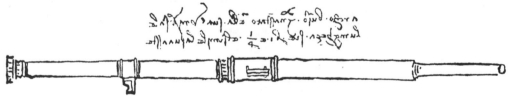

21 Breechloading *Hakenbüchse* with turn-off barrel, drawn by Leonardo da Vinci
From the *Codex Atlanticus*

feathers. Leonardo also envisaged this kind of breech being used on hand-guns, for another drawing depicts a *Hakenbüchse* which has a breech attached to a short pole instead of the usual stock. This form of stock made it possible to unscrew the breech from the barrel. At the same time, however, it did not provide a comfortable grip. Leonardo's theories do not seem to have found any support at the time and the earliest guns with barrels which can be unscrewed from the breech appear to date from the first half of the seventeenth century.

[1] T. F. Tout, 'Firearms in England in the Fourteenth Century', *The English Historical Review*, Vol. XXVI (Oct. 1911), pp. 666–702.

A unique example is the wheellock gun of *c.* 1650 made by Michael Gull of Vienna (**356–7**). All the mechanism of the wheellock including the cock and its spring has been mounted behind the wheel so that the barrel can be unscrewed (probably with a suitable wrench) without hindrance. This type of barrel was most popular in England in the seventeenth century where it was known as the 'turn-off' barrel. The advantage of this was that the diameter of the chamber and ball could be made slightly bigger than that of the bore of the barrel, so that when the ball was fired it would grip the rifling, without the help of a wad or patch. Rifling was thus a more practicable proposition on these guns than on the muzzle-loader. The breechloaders which were rifled were said to have 'screwed turn-off' barrels. The earlier models are fully stocked and the fore-end is arranged so that it unscrews with the barrel (**362**). On the later models the stock finishes at the breech end and the barrel has a running ring round it linked by a hinged rod to the body (**365**). This prevented loss of the barrel when loading on horseback.

The business of unscrewing a barrel, loading the chamber with ball and powder, and then making sure that it was properly replaced, was not always easy or quick, and during the eighteenth century gun-smiths adopting the movable-barrel principle for breechloaders sought means other than by a simple screw thread for joining barrel to breech. The London gunmakers, Thomas Wright and Charles Byrne, took out a patent in 1772 for a variety of breeches involving the use of quick threads, interlocking studs, bayonet and spring catches, all of which could be opened by a quick turn of the barrel or by the release of a catch. The patent also included a number of different types of priming magazines and a method of preventing 'the disagreeable effects of recoiling' by a sprung butt-plate.

Breechloaders on the lines of the specification of the Wright and Byrne patent are the French gun in the Tower of London (**359**) with a pull-out barrel and spring catch, and the more complicated Spanish sporting gun by F. Castano, *c.* 1800, in the W. Keith Neal Collection (**361**).

The action which was, as the late J. N. George described it,[1] 'as nearly perfect as any which could be devised for a breechloading flint rifle, which must necessarily be loaded with loose powder and ball', was invented by Durs Egg and incorporated in a handsome rifle made for George IV when Prince of Wales (**360**). The barrel is rotated by a folding lever, one turn being sufficient to move the barrel forward and disclose a loading aperture on top, just forward of the lock. When closed this hole in the barrel is sealed internally by the screwed portion of the breech and is covered on the outside by a silver sleeve.

One of the last of the flintlock moving-barrel breechloaders was patented by the French gunmaker Pottet in 1818. The barrel was joined to the false breech by a quick screw thread and rested in a collar attached by a hinge to the fore-end. Just beyond this was a handle, which on being turned drew the barrel forward when it could be tipped up for loading.

Two percussion breechloaders using the moving-barrel principle were given a limited trial by the British Army. One invented by the London gunmaker, Frederick Prince, was operated by a handle moving in a slot which unlocked the barrel and drew it forward (**447**). Similar actions, but with different methods of locking the barrels, were produced by T. Murcott of London (**448**), Henlein of Germany, and Ghaye of Belgium. The other breechloader, a carbine patented in America in 1854 by Lt.-Col. J. Durrell Greene, had a massive 18-inch barrel which swivelled sideways for loading (**438**).

Guns with Movable Breech Plugs

The use of a moving barrel in a breech action placed a restriction on the size and the weight of the gun barrel—one could not manipulate the barrel of a wall gun, for instance, in this way—and there was al-ways the danger of the barrel working loose in its housing. In the majority of breechloaders, therefore,

---

[1] *English Guns and Rifles*, Plantersville, South Carolina, U.S.A., 1947, pp. 181–3.

the barrel was firmly held and the gunmaker sought to open and close the breech by the simplest and safest of mechanisms. The simplest method, if not the safest or the most efficient, was a screw plug let into the barrel on top (**398**), at the side (**396**), or underneath (**392**). With the plug removed the barrel was tilted upwards and first powder and then ball was dropped in; that is if the chamber was behind the opening. If the screw plug was next to the breech plug, then the operations were reversed. Again, as with the turn-off barrel guns, the bore of the chamber could be machined slightly larger than the barrel, making the ball fit tight to the bore or rifling. The snag with these simple screw-plug breechloaders was the difficulty often experienced in replacing the plug once the threads had become fouled with burnt powder.

They were amongst the first breechloaders tried and, although the indefatigable Leonardo da Vinci does not seem to have recorded his version of one, there are at least two specimens in existence dating to the sixteenth century. In the Bayerisches Nationalmuseum, Munich, there is a gun barrel with a screw-plug breech made by Freiherr von Sprinzentstein of Munich (1593); and in the Royal Armoury, Madrid, there is another breechloader said to be the work of Cristobal Frisleva (1565–95?). The plug of this gun is recessed on top to form a priming pan and is drilled with a touch-hole communicating with the chamber.

Late in the seventeenth century a plug screwed right through the barrel with a handle underneath was utilised by Daniel Lagatz of Danzig in a flintlock magazine gun. Its main purpose was to isolate the magazine channel in the butt after it had delivered a charge to the barrel, but in its lowered position it

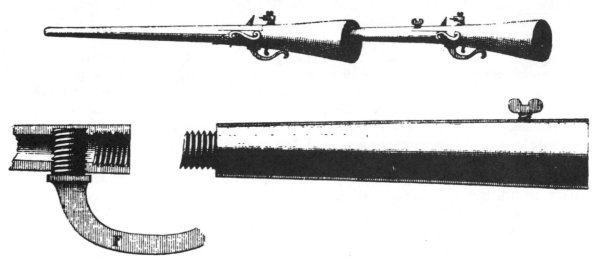

22 De la Chaumette's '*Pistolets d'arcon dont on peut faire une Carabine*' of 1700
From *Machine set Inventions Approuvées par l'Académie Royale des Sciences*, Paris

left an aperture on top of the barrel which could be used for single loading. In 1700 the French engineer, Isaac de la Chaumette, published the first of a series of inventions relating to guns and accessories.[1] This was a pair of saddle pistols which could be converted into a carbine (*Pistolets d'arcon dont on peut faire une Carabine*). To do this the barrel of one pistol screwed into the rear of the other. A vertical screw plug connected to the trigger guard of the front pistol was then lowered out of the way. It did not pierce the top of the barrel. La Chaumette soon realised the possibilities of this action and in 1704 he produced his first proper breechloader. In this the screwed plug ran right through the barrel which could be opened for loading by two or three turns of the trigger guard.

[1] See *Machines et Inventions Approuvées par l'Académie Royale des Sciences*, Paris, 1735, Vol. I, p. 201.

The following year he produced two more breechloaders, one with a screw plug let into one side of the barrel and the other with a pull-down conical plug held in place by the pressure of a spring-loaded trigger guard. Neither of these, however, was to achieve the fame of his first gun.

La Chaumette then transferred his business to London and took out a patent in 1721 to cover all his inventions. The gun having been given a public demonstration on the Artillery Ground, London, attracted a number of customers—enough to incur the displeasure of the Gunmakers' Company, who disliked foreign interlopers as much as any modern trade union. A compatriot of the inventor called Bidet was responsible for some of the finest examples. The decorated rifle which he made for George I of England (**388**) is actually engraved with a poem praising La Chaumette for inventing a gun which would end all wars and 'establish the Golden Age'.[1] Other examples of his breechloaders are in Windsor Castle (No. 175), at Leiden (**390–1**), and at Frauenberg Castle in Czechoslovakia.

The principle of the movable plug was being applied elsewhere in Europe at the same time. The Danish gunmakers, who developed a successful magazine system (see p. 85), also experimented with single-shot breechloaders. Heinrich Kappel designed the gun whose trigger guard rotates, moving a breech block in a horizontal direction so that the barrel can be loaded from the rear (**408**). His pupil, Johan Merckel of Copenhagen, who became a master gunsmith in 1706, made a screw-plug breechloader in which the operating handle is separate to the trigger guard (**387**). It is amusing to note that the Norwegian gunmaker, Erik Larsen Svørsdal (1762–1825), in 1810, as master gunmaker of the Bergenhus infantry regiment, made a copy of the La Chaumette breechloader and proudly presented it as his invention to his king, Frederick VI (**410**).

This type of breechloader also had its supporters in France. Brion of Paris was an early maker (**409**). The system was adopted, on paper at any rate, by the French leader, Marshal Saxe. In his military exposition *Mes Rêveries*, published in 1757, he advocated its use for carbines and for a wall gun or light field-piece which he named the *Amusette*. One of these guns was actually tried in Dublin in 1761 at a range of 800 yards.

It was in England that the breechloader was to achieve its greatest success. Bidet the gunmaker appears to have improved on La Chaumette's original design by cutting a quick thread on the plug which enabled it to be opened by one turn only of the trigger guard. Even so the screw plug still suffered from the fault of its kind—that of jamming after a few rounds. In 1776 the British officer, Captain Patrick Ferguson, made several minor but important modifications to the action which he patented. They consisted of a smooth recess cut into the plug where it formed the breech end of the barrel and a number of vertical grooves cut across the screw threads. These successfully cleared the threads of fouling as the plug moved up and down. After a most convincing demonstration of his breechloading rifle, in which he maintained a rate of fire of four shots a minute in spite of heavy rain and high wind, Ferguson persuaded the Ordnance to give his rifle an official trial. One hundred rifles were specially made and a company of Riflemen trained in their use. Under Ferguson's leadership the Riflemen fought with distinction in the Battle of Brandywine Creek in 1777, but when Ferguson was severely wounded the whole project was abandoned. Ferguson took up his military career again in 1778 to be eventually killed at the head of a loyalist army in the Battle of King's Mountain in 1780.

The fate of his rifles, the first military breechloaders, remains a mystery, only one being known to survive (**399**). No more were commissioned by the Army but a small number were made for the East India Company (**402**), and several Volunteer companies also adopted them (**403**). Durs Egg, the London gunmaker, who made Ferguson's own rifles, produced some outstanding sporting rifles including two identical models with sliding bayonets (one in Glasgow and the other in the West Point Museum (**405**).

---

[1] Another poem to 'L'illustre et fameux La Chaumette, Géomètre, artilleur, poëte, etc.' was published in *Archives de l'Art Français*, Series 2, Tom. 2, Paris, 1862.

The magnificent silver-mounted and gold-inlaid rifle in Windsor Castle (No. 420), which bears the crest of the Prince of Wales, was also made by him in 1782 (**404**).

In spite of the success of the Ferguson rifle, the screw-plug breechloader was destined to failure, for it was essentially a gun to be used with loose powder and ball. The beginning of the nineteenth century witnessed a brief resurrection, but the increasing emphasis on the use of the cartridge brought its final eclipse. It is interesting to note, however, that the principle of the screw plug with the quick thread formed the basis of a cartridge breechloader patented by Charles Reeves in 1860.

Another type of breechloader which may be brought into this group is the kind with the revolving breech plug or 'faucet' as it was called in America. This breech was the main part of the so-called Lorenzoni magazine action (see p. 86) invented in the seventeenth century. In the magazine guns the revolving block was used as a conveyor of bullet and powder from butt-magazine to barrel before acting as a solid breech plug. It was adapted to a single-shot action by cutting a loading aperture in the top of its housing. The cavity in the block then became a chamber, being turned upwards for loading and then horizontally for firing through the barrel. A carbine with this action submitted by a man called Hulme was given a brief trial by the British Army in 1807 (**397**). The revolving-block breech was also patented in America by O. Stith in 1819 and was subsequently used in a number of patents for cartridge arms.

In this group also come breechloaders, like that of William Jenks, patented in 1835 in America and in France (under the name of Adolphe Nuglisch), which were the forerunners of the bolt action. To load the Jenks gun, a lever placed along the top of the small of the stock was raised and swung back, bringing with it a sliding breech plug or bolt, which left the breech open. Because of the position of the breech mechanism a side-hammer lock was necessary (**327**). The same principle of using a moving plug to thrust the cartridge into the breech was used in the breechloader of Westley Richards (the so-called 'monkey-tail') (**440**), and that of Calisher and Terry (**441**).

One of the first true bolt-action breechloaders was patented by Lt.-Col. J. Durrell Greene in 1857. It was ingenious but complicated. The bolt was pulled back and a hollow-based Minié bullet was first pushed into the breech by the bolt. It was then withdrawn and a paper cartridge containing powder with another bullet in its base was pushed up behind the first bullet. When the gun was fired the second bullet acted as a gas-check. It was then moved forward so that it was ready for the next shot. Two other unusual features of this rifle were its oval-bored barrel and under-hammer lock.

Guns with Pivoted Chambers

This kind of breech was essentially the rear end of the barrel detached and hinged at the rear, at the front, or on the side, so that it either tipped up or opened sideways for loading. Two interesting guns show that it was known at least as early as the seventeenth century. The first gun, by Peter Duringer of Mainz, *c.* 1680, has several noteworthy features (**368–9**). It has a combined match and flintlock; a long knife bayonet is hinged to the barrel; the butt is hollowed out to give a better grip for bayonet fighting; and finally, the barrel has a chamber hinged to the breech at the rear and is joined to it by an interrupted screw thread. To open the breech the barrel and fore-end are given a twist and pulled forward, and the chamber can then be tilted up for loading.

The second gun, *c.* 1660, made by John Bicknell of London, who was gunsmith to Charles II, has a much simpler action. The rear end of the chamber is connected underneath to a long trigger guard. Downward pressure on the end of this raises the mouth of the chamber, which joins the barrel by a butt joint (**370–1**). This action may be that described in the English patent of Abraham Hill of 1664—'a new way of makeing of a gun or pistoll, the breech whereof rises upon an hindge by a contrivance of a motion from under it, by wich it is alsoe let downe againe and bolted fast by one and the same motion'. In this action there was no seal between barrel and chamber and, however well the gun was made, after a little use the joint was bound to start leaking gas, with unpleasant consequences.

Perhaps for this reason the pivoted chamber breech was neglected for many years. But it was revived by Giuseppe Crespi of Milan in 1770. His carbine with a tip-up chamber was brought into use by the Austrian cavalry (375). An exact copy of the gun was then made by Durs Egg, fitted with Hennem's screwless lock and armed with a long spear bayonet (372). Thirty of the carbines with barrels of three different lengths were given a trial by the British Army in 1788. In the Crespi and the Egg breechloaders, although the front of the chamber and the rear of the barrel were simply butted together, the joint was a sloping one and the two pieces were pressed together by a hinged locking lever which engaged under two lugs on the breech casing. But there was still an escape of gas and some of the Austrian models still in existence show that this leak was enough to singe the wood of the stock. It was also enough to stop the British Army adopting it.

Nevertheless the system was patented in America by John H. Hall and William Thornton in 1811. Their breechloader, which was officially adopted by the United States Army in 1817, differed from its European counterpart in that the lock mechanism with its trigger, and the chamber with its spring catch,

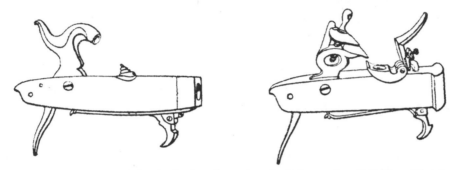

23 Percussion and flintlock chambers detached from the Hall breechloader
Drawings from the French patent taken out by Veuve Gerin et Cie of St. Étienne in 1832

were built as one self-contained unit (379). One would have expected this Hall breechloader to have failed for the same reasons as its predecessors, but in spite of an acknowledged leak at the joint the gun continued to be made until 1850. Many were converted to percussion and soldiers using this model found that the chamber could, if necessary, be removed from the gun and used as a pistol. For some unknown reason the Hall breechloader was patented in Paris in 1832 by Madame Veuve Gerin and Company of St. Étienne (23).

Attempts were made to improve the obturation of the tip-up breech gun. In 1817 Urbanus Sartoris, a merchant of Paris, patented in France, England and Scotland a breechloader whose barrel was linked to the chamber by an interrupted screw thread like that of Peter Duringer's. A folding lever was usually hinged to the barrel so that it could be turned and moved forward to enable the chamber to open. No government arms were made with this breech, but there is evidence that some carbines and rifles were made in England for Volunteer units (384–5). A well-made double-barrelled sporting gun is also in the Royal Armoury of Turin (383). In the Winchester Gun Museum there is a flintlock breechloading carbine of rather doubtful vintage. It has the appearance of an Austrian Jäeger rifle but bears the name of the London gunmaker Ezekiel Baker on its barrel and lock (382). The join between chamber and barrel is closed by an ingenious slotted collar. This device appears identical to that patented in America in 1859 by Edward Lindner.

Breechloaders

The main advantage of the tip-up chamber was its suitability for use with the paper cartridge containing ball and powder then in universal military use. The introduction of the percussion system made it relatively simple to construct guns of this type. A very early example was the '*fusil de Valdehon*' of 1821 (**19**), in which the nipple was placed underneath the chamber. It was also much easier to construct a gas-tight joint by making the mouth of the chamber fit into the barrel, as in the Valdehon, or vice versa. In a percussion breechloader patented by François Vallet of St. Étienne in 1837, the barrel was connected to a coiled spring which forced the mouth of the barrel over the chamfered edge of the chamber when it was closed.

In 1833 the Danish gunmaker, N. J. Løbnitz, invented a breechloading system with a hinged chamber which was moved backwards and then upwards by means of a side lever with an eccentric stud on its axis. Although it was never introduced into the Danish Army, a number of civilian models were made (**444**). In 1839 Løbnitz offered the British Government, without success, a breechloading musket and pistol on this principle, with the added refinement of a copper tape primer *à la Heurteloup*. His breech action did, however, form the basis of the breechloader constructed by Captain F. W. Scheel and adopted as the standard arm of the Norwegian Army in 1842. This also incorporated an under-hammer lock.

In 1831 the French Army introduced a breechloading percussion wall piece (**432**). Based on the '*fusil de Valdehon*', it had a locking block to the rear of the chamber which, when lifted, allowed the chamber to be pulled out of the barrel and raised for loading. An experimental copy of this was made for the British Army by the Inspector of Small Arms, George Lovell, in 1840 (**433**). It was designed for use with the Brunswick two-groove rifling.

Another percussion breechloader with a tip-up chamber considered by the British Army was that of William Mont Storm, awarded a silver medal in the International Exhibition of 1862. The chamber of this was hinged in the front and had a recess for a locking bolt in the rear. Advantages claimed for it by its inventor were that it could be used with a paper or skin cartridge or with loose powder and ball, and that a soft metal ring round the mouth of the chamber sealed the joint from an escape of gas.

One of the few successful breechloaders to employ a chamber block which was hinged sideways was that of James Leetch of 1861. By this date, however, the hinged chamber was being replaced by a breech block to operate a metal cartridge.

Guns with Separate Chambers

These guns employed one or more reloadable steel chambers, consisting of a piece of tube of smaller calibre than the barrel, which could be pushed into the breech like a modern cartridge. The first of these guns, however, was copied from the cannon whose chamber was, in effect, a detachable section of the barrel. One of these is illustrated in a manuscript, *c.* 1460–80, in the University Library at Erlangen (**24**). Its chamber lies in a trough at the breech end of the barrel and is held by a pin running through a lug which projects underneath. It is doubtful whether any of this kind of breechloader were made later than the second half of the sixteenth century.

The same manuscript shows an example of a gun whose chamber was inserted into the barrel (**24**). The chambers illustrated are of a most unusual construction, the rear end or base being bent round at right angles. The centre of this base is pierced to act as a vent for the match and is protected by a hinged cover. How this chamber was locked in the barrel (if it was not so locked it would be blown out by the explosion) is not clear, and there is no known specimen of its kind.

There are several drawings of breechloading guns in Leonardo da Vinci's *Codex Atlanticus*. They include two breeches with reloadable chambers of a type which were to be utilised intermittently until the nineteenth century. These have projecting lugs at the base which carry the vent and also fit into a slot cut into the top of the barrel. A strong metal peg is inserted through the breech behind the lug and prevents it from moving. This lug also served as a means for knocking out the cartridge if it became jammed.

The earliest examples of these breechloaders appear to be the two guns made for Henry VIII, now in the Tower of London. In these a different method of locking the chamber in position was used. Both guns

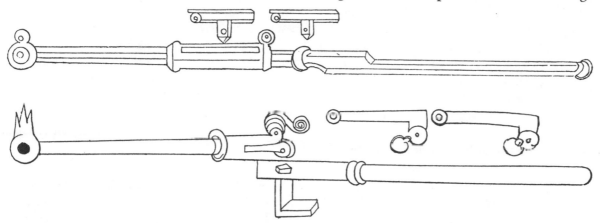

24 Breechloading hand-guns with reloadable metal cartridges, *c.* 1460–80
From *Codex MS. 1390*, University Library at Erlangen

have a hinged lid at the breech which opens to reveal a cut-away section of the barrel into which is dropped a loaded iron chamber with a projection sticking out at the base. The chamber was slid into the barrel, the projection fitting into a slot cut in the top lip of the barrel. The lid was then shut down behind. A vent in the barrel casing communicated the fire from the pan to the touch-hole of the chamber. The original locks, probably wheellocks, are missing from both guns. A matchlock with an automatic sliding pan-cover has been fitted to the smaller gun at a later date.

The latter gun (350–1), which has a barrel 26 inches long, was formerly covered with velvet and was probably used as a saddle carbine. The initials HR and the date 1537 appear on the barrel, which is finely chased and gilt. The stock bears a brass shield engraved with the figures of St. George and the Dragon. On the breech block is stamped the maker's mark of WH over a fleur-de-lis. This may be the mark of William Hunt, appointed Keeper of the King's Handguns and Demi-Hawks in 1538. In the same year he was 'emplo'd about the makeing and furnishing of the King's Highnesses' devices of certain pieces of artillery'.[1]

The larger gun (352), which has a 43½-inch barrel and weighs 18 lb., is described in a seventeenth-century inventory as 'King Henry Eights fowling piece', but its heavy barrel and tubular rear-sight suggest that it was used for bigger game or for target shooting.

There are several examples of wheellock guns with similar breeches in existence but they are all of later date. Finely decorated specimens are represented by the rifle in the Wallace Collection (355) and the small carbine in the Royal Armoury, Turin (354).

Few matchlock guns were considered worthy of such ingenuity, but the matchlock *Hakenbüchse* in the Historical Museum, Bern (349), provides an example of an entirely different method of loading. The iron chamber in this case has been forged on the end of a substantial plug and handle. This is thrust into the open breech end of the barrel and is held by a flat vertical peg which passes through a slot in the barrel and a corresponding one in the rear of the chamber plug.

[1] *Letters and Papers of Henry VIII*, Vol. XIII, Pt. 2, pp. 193 and 533.

Breechloaders

During the flintlock era sporting guns continued to be made with reloadable chambers or cartridges. Although some retained the old-style tube with its projecting lug (**417**) and at least one, a seventeenth-century piece by Michael Gull (**424**), employed the hinged-lid chamber of the Henry VIII guns, the majority now had metal cartridges each with its own priming pan and steel (**420**). This increased the weight of the spares, but it did away with the need for ensuring that the touch-hole in the chamber was in correct alignment with the corresponding hole in the barrel.

Many of these flintlock breechloaders were made with a hinged barrel which dropped down for loading in the fashion of the modern shotgun. Others were arranged to break open sideways—a fine example of this being the chiselled steel gun by Acqua Fresca, dated 1694 (**426**). A few guns broke upwards (**421**), while one seventeenth-century gun by I. Fullick of Salisbury was made to swivel sideways for the insertion of the cartridge (**428**). Perhaps the finest decorated example of all these breechloaders is that made by Joseph Cano of Madrid in 1736, now in the Royal Armoury, Madrid (**418**). It bears the coat of arms of Philip V in gold set with diamonds. The action is of the drop-down type and the gun has a set of a dozen spare cartridges.

In terms of efficiency the outstanding breechloader was devised by Henry Nock during a series of experiments in 1786. Two examples of his breechloader exist; one in a private collection in America and the other in the Tower of London (**423**). The reloadable cartridge is pivoted to a slide and when inserted in the barrel is held by a vertical peg. A quick upward and backward pull of this peg unlocks the breech and extracts the cartridge into an upright position for loading. The musket is also fitted with one of the early models of Nock's screwless locks.

Shortly after the introduction of the percussion system the self-contained expendable cartridge gradually gained precedence over all other forms of breechloaders, but not before a variety of reloadable metal chambers complete with a percussion nipple had been given a full trial, especially in France (**458**). The revolving shotgun patented by S. H. Roper in America in 1866 (**704**) used this type of reloadable cartridge as did a number of large-bore game and punt guns, where they were an economical proposition.

Cartridge Guns

The word cartridge means a case containing the charge for a gun. Leonardo da Vinci was familiar with cartridges and made some reference to them in his notebooks. In one note he advised that carabineers should carry 'pouches full of rolls of plain paper filled powder'. Another of his notes reads 'see that they are well supplied with guns with a thin single fold of paper with the ball within so that they have only to put it in and set alight'.[1]

Up to the second half of the seventeenth century it was customary for the powder charges of sporting guns to be carried in paper cartridges kept in a decorated belt box (**787–9**). Soldiers using the matchlock gun were issued with bandoleers (**790**)—belts from which hung a dozen or so of wooden tubes containing powder—and the loose balls were carried in a separate bag. But by the end of the seventeenth century the military were also using paper cartridges with the ball tied in one end. When loading, one end of the cartridge was bitten open, a little of the powder poured into the priming pan and the rest down the barrel. Then the ball, still wrapped in its paper covering, was rammed down on top of the charge, the paper acting as a wad.

Many of the breechloading guns described so far used paper or skin cartridges in their chambers; the separate chambers discussed in the last section could also be considered as cartridges; but, for the purpose

[1] E. MacCurdy, *The Notebooks of Leonardo da Vinci*, London, 1938, Vol. II, pp. 194–5.

of this chapter, the term 'cartridge gun' is confined to one using a self-igniting cartridge containing its own priming.

The credit for the invention of such a cartridge is generally accorded to the Swiss inventor and balloonist, Samuel Johannes Pauly (1766–1819?).[1] In 1809 he is recorded working in Paris, where one of his workmen was a journeyman lock-maker called Von Dreyse who was to become the inventor of the needle-gun (see p. 68). While in Paris in 1812, Pauly took out a patent for a revolutionary form of breech-loader which employed a centre-fire self-obturating cartridge. Two kinds of breeches are described in this patent, one a drop-barrel break-action and the other a lifting-block action. An interesting example of the first action is the seven-barrelled gun now in the Tower of London (451–2). Its charges are inserted in a seven-chambered breech piece and are simultaneously fired by a percussion pellet placed in its base. The second action was fully enclosed and was divided into two halves. The top hinged portion containing the striking pins was opened by a lever lying on the small of the butt, which lifted it up, leaving the breech end of the barrel exposed for the cartridge (453). The lower section housed the mainspring and cocking mechanism which had an outside cock.

The cartridge was an entirely new concept, somewhat similar to the modern shotgun cartridge. The base was made of soft metal or hard wood and around it was glued a paper case for the charge and shot. In the centre of the base was a 'rosette' containing the detonating compound, with a short tube leading into the powder. The base had a bevelled rim which was pressed into the chamber of the barrel when the breech was closed, forming an effective seal. A rare cased Pauly gun (455) contains a number of these cartridge bases made of turned brass with cartridge papers in two colours (green and yellow), one for ball and the other for shot. Amongst the accessories are a brass 'former', for making the cartridge case, a cartridge extractor, a bullet mould and various measures.

Pauly's gun was brought to the attention of Napoleon, but both he and a group of army experts agreed that while the gun offered great advantages to the sportsman it was not suitable for military use. When Paris fell to the Allies in 1814, Pauly came to London, where after a few months he was granted another patent (No. 3833); this time for an 'Apparatus for Discharging Fire-arms by means of Compressed Air'. This was not, as might be expected, an air-gun, but a means of igniting the powder of a gun. It worked on the principle that when air is compressed through a small opening great heat is generated.

In this Pauly was undoubtedly drawing on the previous 1807 patent of Richard Lorentz which applied to a walking-stick tinder-lighter working on this principle. To adapt his breech loader to this form of ignition, Pauly replaced the strikers and detonators with pistons and cylinders, and the hot blast of air was directed through an orifice in the breech on to the rosette, which now contained gunpowder covered by paper. A second compressed-air patent was lodged by Pauly in 1816 containing some slight improvements, but two years later another French gun-designer Urbanus Sartoris patented a similar action.[2] He was followed in 1826 by Benjamin Newmark of Cheltenham. There are, however, no examples of compressed-air guns by either Sartoris or Newmark.

All Pauly's projects, including one with Durs Egg to construct a large navigable balloon known as the Dolphin, came to naught, but the success of his breechloaders fired the imagination of the French gun-makers. At first they concentrated, understandably, on improvements to Pauly's action with its lift-up hinged breech. The main faults were not so much in the action, which was to be copied for many years, as in the excessive wear of the rosette of the cartridge, and also the tendency of one cartridge to set off the other (in double-barrelled guns). The first modifications made to his action therefore were mainly aimed at altering it to percussion cap and nipple.

[1] See W. Reid, 'Pauly, Gun Designer', *J.A.A.S.*, Vol. II (1956–8), pp. 181–210.
[2] When in financial difficulties, Pauly is known to have worked for Sartoris, and he may well have sold his patent to him.

This could be done either by using a reloadable iron cartridge with its own nipple, or by directing the fire from a stationary nipple through the breech on to a paper cartridge. Improvements on these lines were lodged at the Paris Patent Office by Henri Roux, who took over Pauly's factory at 4 Rue des Trois Frères, in 1816, 1818, and 1823; by his *cessionnaire*, Eugène Pichereau, in 1825; and finally by their joint *cessionnaire*, Casimir Lefaucheux, in 1828. The gunmakers Cessier and Delebourse also patented similar improvements or modifications in 1826 and 1828 respectively.

The first indication that better systems might develop was given in the French patent taken out in 1826 by Antoine Galy-Cazalat, a Professor of Mathematics at Perpignan.[1] Of its kind it was just as revolutionary as that of Pauly's, for it was not only a revolving-block breechloader using a centre-fire cartridge, but it was set off by a long striking-pin powered by a spiral spring—an early form of 'bolt-action'.

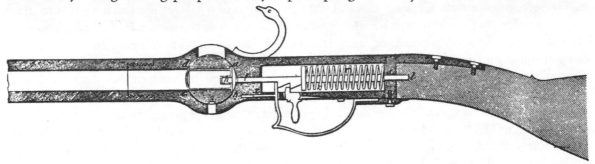

25 French patent drawing of the Galy-Cazalat centre-fire cartridge gun of 1826

Then came the patents of Clement Pottet (1829) for a metal and paper cartridge which had a percussion nipple set in its base,[2] and that of Joseph Alexandre Robert (1831, with additions in 1835), which included a metal-based cartridge with priming in the rim. These were the forerunners of the modern centre-fire and rim-fire cartridges (**1013, 1035**).

A break with the Pauly type of breech was made in 1832 when Casimir Lefaucheux patented a drop-down break-action breechloader with a locking action consisting of a lever with an eccentric stud which fitted into a cut-out lug brazed under the barrel. This under-lever action continued in use until the end of the century. It brought forth a number of other French patents covering drop-down actions, and a variety of cartridges with wood and metal bases holding cap and tube primers. In 1835 Lefaucheux again took the lead in design by obtaining a *certificat d'addition* to his 1832 patent, for a paper cartridge with a brass base, out of which stuck at right angles a short peg or pin. When the cartridge was inserted in the barrel this pin projected through a slot cut in the top of the breech. Here it was hit by the hammer and it detonated a percussion pellet or cap placed inside the base. This was the first pin-fire cartridge (**1007**).

In the meantime Pauly's former workman, Johann Nikolaus von Dreyse, who had returned to his native Prussia, had produced in 1827 a bullet with a cavity in its base containing a small charge of fulminate. It was used in a modified flintlock muzzleloader, and was detonated by a needle, connected to the cock, which passed through the centre of the breech plug. As the fulminate charge proved dangerous (his right arm was damaged in a premature explosion) Dreyse altered the breech in 1828 so that the needle passed through a spigot (*Nadelrohr*) which protruded into the chamber. A wadded bullet was positioned over the spigot so that the needle detonated a percussion cap set in its base and ignited a charge of powder in the chamber. This action was patented in England in 1831 by Dreyse's agent, A. A.

[1] The same action was patented by W. Golden and J. Hanson in England in 1841, but the cartridge advocated by them was a fulminated bullet (**1037–8**).

[2] This base was screwed into the cardboard case. An almost identical cartridge was patented in America in 1868 by T. Cullen.

Moser (**1027**). Dreyse then began experimenting with various breechloading actions until in 1835 he produced a bolt-action needle-fire rifle which, after a successful experimental issue, was adopted by the Prussian Army in 1840 (**26**).

Immediately there were a number of German and foreign inventors like Schilling, Borse and von Baumgarten,[1] who sought to imitate or improve on the von Dreyse system. There were also the detractors of the needle-fire gun who pointed out that its needle was subjected to the full force of the

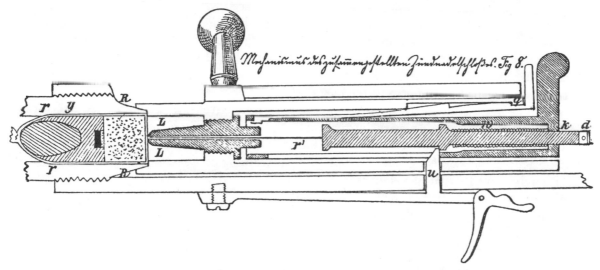

26 Drawing of von Dreyse's needle-fire breech and cartridge
From A. Mattenheimer, *Die Rückladungs-Gewehr*, 1876

explosion and would soon burn out. To some extent this was true, of course, and some so-called needle-fire guns (that of Spangenberg and Sauer of Suhl is an example) used cartridges with the detonator placed in front of the powder, becoming in effect a centre-fire cartridge. The Prussian Army answered all criticisms of its arm by using it with deadly effect in their short war against Denmark in 1864, and in the Seven Weeks War with Austria in 1866.

In France the gunmakers continued the development of their own cartridges. From 1847 to 1849 Lefaucheux patented improved versions of his own pin-fire cartridge and also a centre-fire cartridge designed for a breech with a separate diagonally-striking firing-pin. The Paris gunmaker Houllier also patented various cartridges between 1847 and 1850. These were mainly of pin-fire ignition but one was for rim-fire ('*capsule annulaire*').

In 1847 Bourcier brought the modern shotgun one step nearer with a patent for a centre-fire breech-loader with a diagonally-striking pin and an automatic ejector. Finally in 1855 Pottet patented in France the centre-fire cartridge as used to-day. This has a separate anvil set into the base of the cartridge on which the primer is detonated. François Eugène Schneider patented another in 1858 with a slightly different anvil and base. All Schneider's designs were bought by the London gunmaker George Daw, who sought to protect them by patents in his name in England and America. The Schneider-Daw cartridge was largely copied by Colonel Edward Mounier Boxer, Superintendent of the Royal Laboratory, for his centre-fire cartridge patented in 1866[2] and adopted by the British Army in the same year. One new feature introduced was the coiled brass cartridge case which expanded on being fired, but here again it had been anticipated by Joseph Needham's patent cartridge of 1852 (**1040**).

[1] See A. Mattenheimer, *Die Rückladungs-Gewehr*, Darmstadt and Leipzig, 1876.

[2] Boxer's patent was challenged unsuccessfully by George Daw. See his *The Central-Fire Cartridge before the Law-Courts, the Government and Public, etc.*, London, 1867.

Breechloaders

In the 1860s cartridges of all kinds were available to the gunmaker. Apart from the four main classes—pin-fire, centre-fire, rim-fire and needle-fire—there were other curiously primed items like the teat-fire, the lip-fire, the annular rim, and the inside pin-fire. The teat-fire (**1026**) and the lip-fire (**1025**) were metallic versions of some of the early attempts to attach the priming to a teat in the centre of the base of the cartridge or to a lip projecting from the rim. Both they and the annular rim-fire, in which the primed rim was placed round the side of the cartridge, were intended mainly for revolvers; but the inside pin-fire cartridge was designed for a rifle firing a Minié bullet. Faced with this wonderfully-varied material the inventors and gunmakers by the hundred rose to the challenge. Between them they produced a number and variety of breech actions which defy even simple listing. There were breech locks hinged at the rear, on the side, or in the front; breech blocks which rose and fell, or rolled backwards, or to one side; and bolt-actions with needles and striking pins of all kinds.

In France the pin-fire cartridge breechloader retained its popularity for sporting guns. For indoor gallery shooting an interesting group of low-power guns were developed which utilised either a bullet with a primer in the base acting as the propellent—as patented by Gastinne-Renette in 1847—or the power of the percussion cap alone to eject the bullet. The latter idea was patented by Louis Flobert and Antoine Regnier in 1846[1] and an under-hammer gun working on the same principle was patented by Cusson-Pourcher and Rossignol-Lefebvre in 1850. The French Army, however, seeking a rival to the German needle-fire rifle, adopted the bolt-action centre-fire gun patented by M. Chassepot in 1866.

In England, although a muzzleloading needle-fire gun had been patented by Abraham Adolphe Moser as early as 1831 (it was rejected by the Board of Ordnance in 1834), and some fine sporting breech-loaders using this cartridge were later made by Joseph Needham and George Kufahl, the military viewed them with suspicion. During the Crimean War, experimental issues of the Westley Richards, Greene, Terry and Sharps breechloading carbines were made, but it was not until 1866 that a breechloading conversion of the existing Enfield muzzleloading rifle was approved. This was the breech of Jacob Snider, consisting of a hinged breech block, with a firing-pin passing through it, which opened sideways for loading (**439**). It was a stop-gap measure only and after a nationally-advertised competition, in which over a hundred breechloaders took part, the falling-block breech of Friedrich von Martini, used in conjunction with rifling designed by Alexander Henry, was chosen in 1869. The Martini action with an interior striking pin was a modification of an earlier action patented in America by Henry O. Peabody in 1862. The Providence Tool Company of Rhode Island, U.S.A., who marketed the Peabody, once described the 'so-called' Martini as an illegitimate offspring made for amateurs. A similar action, the Werder, was adopted by the Austrian Army.

If the English gunmakers had lagged behind their European rivals in the development of the breech-loader, with the introduction of the Daw and Boxer central-fire cartridges they speedily began the perfection of their particular *métier*, the double-barrelled shotgun. Competition was sharpened by the series of gun trials instituted by the *Field* newspaper. In the last quarter of the century came the perfection of the hammerless lock and the automatic cartridge ejector.

The American Civil War, with both sides desperate for arms, produced a host of breechloaders. The outstanding gun of them all was the breechloader first patented by Christian Sharps in 1848. It was made famous by John Brown in his raid on Harper's Ferry and was nicknamed 'Beecher's Bible', because the famous American preacher asserted that one Sharps rifle carried more moral weight than a hundred bibles. Its action was simple but immensely strong. The breech block moved vertically up and down in a mortice cut in the frame, with the trigger guard acting as a lever. In its early models paper, skin or linen cartridges with a separate primer (Maynard's tape or Sharps's discs) were used, and the breech block was designed to cut open the base of the cartridge as it closed.

[1] The Flobert-Regnier percussion primer was more in the nature of a plug than a cap and fitted *into* the hole of the nipple.

70

After the Civil War, during which thousands of Sharps's rifles and carbines were supplied to the Union forces, the action was successfully converted to the metallic cartridge. Its great strength now made it suitable for heavy bullets and powder charges and the result was a series of rifles made specially for buffalo hunters and long-range target shooters. Armed with a Sharps's target rifle the American rifle team first won the International Match at Creedmoor, Long Island, in 1877. The model most sought after to-day by collectors, however, is the Civil War model with a coffee grinder in its butt (**436**).

Another strong but simple breech was developed at the close of the Civil War by the Remington Arms Company. Known as a rolling-block breech, it was opened by cocking the hammer and rolling the breech block back with the thumb. Hammer and breech block were locked together at the moment of explosion and it was almost impossible to blow it out. At the Imperial Exhibition held in Paris in 1867 the Remington rifle was awarded the highest prize in its class. As a military rifle it was adopted by Denmark, Norway, Spain, Egypt and several South American countries. In its own country it did not achieve much official recognition, however, and it was a hinged block action constructed by Erskine S. Allin, Master Armourer at the Springfield Armoury, which was finally chosen as the official conversion unit for the large stocks of American muzzleloading rifles. The Springfield breech block, with a firing pin running through it, was hinged in the front and was flipped up like a trapdoor for loading.

Two English breechloading rifles which made a name in the sporting field were those of William Soper, in which the depression of a side lever throws up a hinged breech block (**462**), and John Farquharson, patented in 1872. The latter has a falling-block breech pulled down by a hinged under-lever and is cocked by another lever on the side. In spite of its involved action, the Farquharson rifle, made mainly by the Bristol gunmaker George Gibbs, is regarded by many collectors as the finest single-shot rifle ever made.

Single-shot cartridge breechloaders of great accuracy and speed were now being made in Europe and America, but the latter quality was beginning to be the main desideratum, at least in the minds of the military. The problem which the gunmakers now had to face was how to adapt their new cartridges to the multi-shot or repeating form of gun.

7 Multi-Shot Guns

In the second half of the fourteenth century the gunmakers began their long struggle to produce a satisfactory repeating gun. In the English Wardrobe Accounts of 1382–6 the London cannon-founder William Wodeward was paid for an 11-barrelled gun weighing 665 lb. It had one barrel firing a large stone, and ten smaller ones for the discharge of lead bullets or quarrels.[1] The first account of a multi-barrelled hand-gun—a rather large one it must be admitted—appears in 1435, when an inventory of the Bastille, Paris, included an entry for '*Ung canon a 7 troux sans chambre, estant en la basse court, d'un espan de long ou environ*'.[2] This is also the first mention of a seven-barrelled gun, a combination of barrels which was to prove popular at a later date.

Manuscripts of the late fourteenth and early fifteenth century show how these groups of barrels were usually mounted on stands with a rudimentary form of elevating gear. By the beginning of the sixteenth century these batteries of barrels firing lead balls of approximate musket size had been brought into common use on wheeled carriages as a form of light artillery. Mounted in flat tiers, in square boxes or in complicated swivelling-frames which allowed different sizes of barrels to be brought into action, these multi-barrel guns were known variously as *ribaldes*, *ribaudequins*, or, from their resemblance to the pipes of the musical organ, as *orgues* and *Orgelgeschütze*. In 1523 the Ordnance Train of Henry VIII's army employed 167 carters for the guns called 'organs'.

Because of the great weight, and the difficulties of loading and igniting a number of barrels, this form of construction was not popular at first when applied to hand-guns. Nevertheless the idea was beginning

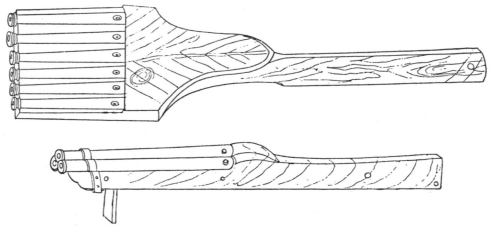

27 Three- and six-barrelled *Ladenbüchsen* made for the Emperor Maximilian I, *c.* 1500–10
From *Codex icon. 222*, Munich State Library

to be tried out. A manuscript of *c.* 1500–10 in the Munich State Library shows several examples of the hand-gun with groups of from three to a dozen barrels (**27**). Leonardo da Vinci's *Codex Atlanticus* also shows a four-barrelled hand-gun. It is doubtful whether any of these guns had any practical value.

[1] T. F. Tout, 'Firearms in England in the Fourteenth Century', *The English Historical Review*, Vol. XXVI, No. 104, October, 1911, pp. 687 and 698.
[2] Victor Gay, *Glossaire Archéologique du Moyen Âge et de la Renaissance*, Paris, 1887 and 1928, Vol. I, p. 273.

A certain amount of prestige value could be attached to the so-called 'holy water sprinklers'—two-handed spiked maces with groups of three barrels set in the head. One in the Tower of London, probably made in the reign of Henry VIII, appears in seventeenth-century inventories as 'King Henry ye 8ths walking staff' (**477**). This combination weapon has a swivelling muzzle cover to protect the barrels from rain, and originally had sliding pan-covers, but these are now missing. A similar weapon in the Metropolitan Museum of Art, New York, is fitted with snap-matchlocks (**480**).

There are a number of three- and four-barrelled hand-guns in existence which are often mistaken for European fourteenth-century hand-guns. They have a socketed breech for mounting on a pole and are of crude construction with open pans (**478**). J. L. Boots,[1] however, writing on 'Korean Weapons and Armour', reveals their oriental origin and states that the small guns were actually used as signal guns. He reproduces a drawing taken from a Korean military instruction book of 1791, which shows a mounted warrior standing on his saddle and holding a three-barrelled gun in one hand. The caption to this precarious position reads: 'First they ride standing up on the horse firing the three-barrelled gun'.

There were other Chinese multi-barrelled hand-guns which undoubtedly had an offensive purpose. A gun in the Rotunda, Woolwich (**479**), has two flat banks of five barrels mounted on a long pole. It is the type of gun referred to in the *Wu-Pei-Chih* (see p. 2), which has a gun barrel $1\frac{1}{2}$ feet long surrounded by ten barrels $\frac{1}{2}$ foot long mounted on a long pole. A man of great strength, it was stated, was required to present it in the face of the enemy.

The great weight of the multi-barrelled gun was always its main disadvantage, and during the second half of the sixteenth century any references to multi-shot guns are nearly all to 'engines' of war, which come under the classification of artillery rather than of hand-guns. The *Calendar of State Papers, Domestic* mentions some of these. Emery Molyneux's invention of 1570 was reputed to discharge 'a thousand musket shot; with wild fire not to be quenched'. In 1575 there was another engine of war 'whereby 24 bullets can be discharged from 1 piece at a time'. These were outdone by William Engelbert's engine of 1579 which 'could discharge every way round about, above 2,000 musket shots'.

By the first quarter of the seventeenth century, however, gunmakers had managed to construct guns with more than one barrel light enough to be carried and fired from the shoulder with comfort. A seven-barrelled sporting gun in the Tower of London (XII-470), probably restocked in the eighteenth century, has barrels bored out of a single piece of steel dated 1612. The gunmakers had also contrived to find several ways in which to fire more than one shot from a single barrel. For the purpose of this book multi-shot guns can be divided into four main groups: (1) Multi-barrelled guns; (2) Superimposed charge guns; (3) Revolving guns; (4) Magazine guns.

Multi-Barrelled Guns

This group of guns can also be divided into those in which all the barrels were arranged to fire together (volley guns) and those in which only one barrel could be fired at a time. In the latter case this usually meant one lock for each barrel with its attendant increase of weight. The earliest firearms of this sort ignited by wheellock or matchlock rarely exceeded two barrels. The German double-barrelled wheellock rifle dated 1588 in Windsor Castle (**482**) shows that even with two barrels the gunmaker had to display some ingenuity to construct the necessary lock mechanism. This rifle is an example of the 'over-and-under' method of mounting barrels as opposed to the more common 'side-by-side' method.

When the flintlock became fully operative in the second half of the seventeenth century, the double-barrelled sporting gun with light barrels and a slender stock enabled sportsmen to shoot birds on the wing with some degree of success for the first time. The over-and-under gun in the Tøjhusmuseet,

[1] *Trans. Korea Branch, Roy. Asiatic Soc.*, Seoul, 1934, XXIII, Pt. 2, pp. 1-37. In Malaysia, known as the *Sampa-tjin*, it was used for firing *feu de joie* in religious processions. See *Z.H.W.K*, v (1909-11), p. 25.

Copenhagen, *c.* 1650, by Abraham Munier of Geneva (**483**) is a particularly interesting example, as the two side-by-side locks are operated by a single trigger. An interesting mechanism often found on multi-barrel pistols—a sliding or rotating cut-off on the priming pan which enables one lock to serve several barrels—is rarely encountered on long guns. It can be seen on the double-barrelled rifle in the C. G. Vokes Collection, Alton (**485**). This has only one lock, but is fitted with a revolving plug in the pan (the operating lever can be seen in front of the cock) which directs the priming flash to either barrel as required. A most unusual construction was adopted by the London gunmaker, Jacques Gorgo. The two chambers of a double-charged gun are placed side by side and are fired by two locks; but each chamber discharges its ball through a funnel-shaped passage into a single barrel. The latter unscrews so that the chambers can be properly loaded (**363**).

The most common form of double-barrelled shotgun is the side-by-side gun with double locks. This first achieved popularity in the second quarter of the eighteenth century and has remained the standard construction, at least in England, to the present day. The English gunmakers were content to concentrate on the mechanical excellence and performance of their guns, vying with each other over the range and pattern of the shot. Plain walnut stocks with the minimum of engraving on metal parts distinguished the London-made gun. One rarely finds a profusely decorated gun from this source. The Continental gun-maker suffered from no such inhibitions and delighted in the most lavish of ornamentation (**503**).

With the principle of one lock for each barrel there was obviously a limit to the number of barrels it was possible to handle in the flintlock range, and this seems to have been reached in an interesting group of four-barrelled four-lock shotguns made by French gunmakers. They are discussed by Magné de Marolles in *La Chasse au Fusil* (1788), who points out that the number of occasions when a sportsman needs to fire four shots in quick succession are so rare that the four-barrelled guns must have been intended in the first place for a collector's cabinet rather than for sport. Of the five examples known of this group (**491–5**) four have their triggers grouped in one guard. It must have been very easy in this design to choose the wrong trigger. The other gun in the Windsor Castle Collection has a double row of triggers, but this was just as clumsy an arrangement, it being very difficult to reach the bottom row of triggers. Apart from those illustrated the remaining gun in this group is in the Musée de l'Armée, Paris, a hand-some piece with blued barrels and gold decoration made by Regnier of Saumur (1757–1825).

With volley guns using a single lock there was no reason why the gunmaker should not exceed four barrels, and indeed the only limit to the number was the overall weight of the gun. The most popular number of barrels, however, was seven. Whether this was because it was a convenient number from the constructional point of view, or whether the significance of the number seven in mythological superstition governed the choice, is not clear. The need for firing a volley of bullets (not to be confused with a charge of shots) could only arise in certain situations. For close quarter work against a mob the blunder-buss with its multiple charge was normally sufficient. But in 1779 the British Admiralty decided to adopt a seven-barrelled gun invented by Captain James Wilson (Royal Marines) for the purpose of arming their snipers in the 'tops' of sailing vessels. These guns were about three feet long and weighed 12 pounds. The 20-inch barrels were brazed together in a six-round-one formation. The touch-hole from the priming pan led into the chamber of the central barrel and from this channels drilled in radial fashion led to the chambers of the other barrels. Altogether 655 of the guns were made for the Royal Navy by Henry Nock between 1780 and 1788, at a cost of £13 each.[1] Apart from the first two prototype models, which were rifled, the barrels were smooth-bore. There is no evidence that they made any major contribution to naval warfare and their only known service was with Lord Howe's fleet at the relief of Gibraltar.[2]

[1] H. L. Blackmore, 'The Seven-Barrel Guns', *J.A.A.S.*, Vol. 1 (1953–5), No. 10 (June, 1955), pp. 165–182.
[2] In 1805 Wilson suggested that the guns should be re-introduced for the use of the Sea Fencibles and boat crews, but the Admiralty replied that they had been 'long considered obsolete'.

Their novelty did not escape the notice of the sportsmen, and for some time after their introduction into the Navy, a number of sporting volley guns were made for deer and wild-fowl shooting. Their greatest exponent was Colonel Thomas Thornton, who had his portrait painted holding a 12-barrelled rifle. His *pièce de résistance* was a double seven-barrelled gun which could be used with one or two sets of barrels (**499**). Thornton, in his book *A Sporting Tour through Various Parts of France*, tells an amusing story how Joe Manton, not to be outdone by this impressive armament, endeavoured to fire a double-barrelled rifle with seven bullets in each barrel—with dire results to the rifle.

When the percussion lock with its simpler construction was introduced, gunmakers had an easier task in designing a multi-barrelled gun. A few seven-barrelled guns were made (**500**)—tradition dies hard —but there was a decided preference for four-barrel groups, made to fire either in volleys or singly. The latter effect could be obtained with either one or two locks. With two locks it was a matter of arranging the heads of the hammers so that they could be swivelled to hit either the top or bottom nipple of their particular pair of barrels (**505–6**). The Irish gunmakers, William and John Rigby, devised an ingenious lock (used mainly on pistols), which had a hammer with a revolving turret head arranged over a group of four nipples so that as the hammer was cocked the striker moved round to each nipple in turn (**507**). A similar lock mechanism was used by the Canadian gunsmith, J. Gurd, on two carbines, one with three barrels and the other with five; but with the difference that the nipples were arranged in line instead of in a circle (**509–10**).

When the breechloader and cartridge appeared the double-barrelled gun sufficed for most needs. But the seven-barrelled Pauly gun (**451**) shows how the multi-barrelled gun was quickly converted to cartridges. The Belgian gunmaker, Pieper of Liège, produced several seven-barrelled rifles with a Remington rolling-block action modified to fire a cluster of 0·22 rim-fire cartridges. The centre-fire cartridge was

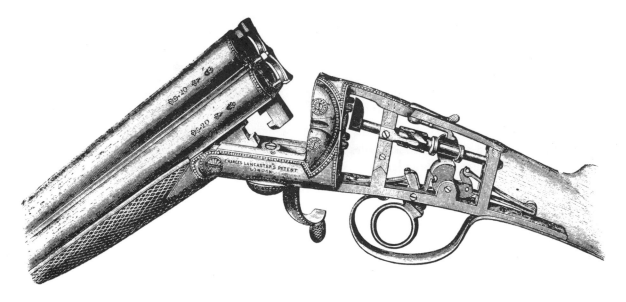

28 Charles Lancaster's four-barrelled gun. Original model

used on a group of four-barrelled pistols with enclosed actions and a revolving striker. They include the Martin-Marres-Braendlin 'Mitrailleuse' pistol, the pistols of John Bland and Charles Lancaster. The advantages claimed for this design over the revolver were the absence of any projections to catch in the clothing and no loss of gas. Of the three makes, only the Lancaster appears to have been made in shotgun and rifle sizes (**28**).

It can be mentioned briefly that the multi-barrelled gun had a brief resurgence of power between 1860 and 1890, during the infancy of the machine-gun. Volley guns like that of General Vandenburgh, the Billinghurst Requa Battery gun, the French Mitrailleuse, and the Gardner gun, consisted of groups of barrels automatically fired and reloaded by the turning of a hand crank.

Superimposed Charge Guns

The Roman Candle firework, in which a tube is loaded with alternate layers of gunpowder and pellets so that when the front is lit the flame feeds back, setting off the charges behind one after the other, formed the basis of many of the early military pyrotechnical devices. The *Wu-Pei-Chih* includes such weapons as the 'upset horse fire-serpent divine staff'—a wrought iron tube loaded with spattering fire and lead bullets; and the 'toxic fire spouter', a bamboo tube bound with wire and filled with noxious substances. Both of these worked on the Roman Candle principle. The great disadvantage of this idea was that once the front charge had been lit nothing could stop the remainder from being ignited.

More control could be exercised over the 20- and three-shot repeaters also illustrated in the *Wu-Pei-Chih* (**29**). The first gun was made of wrought iron with solid middle portion. The two ends consisted

29 Guns with superimposed charges. *Left* 20-shot, *right* three-shot
From the *Wu-Pei-Chih*, 1621

of hollow tubes drilled with ten touch-holes evenly spaced. The sections between were loaded with individual charges of bullet and powder divided by paper partitions and were fired consecutively by the application of a match. The second gun had a short barrel with a slot cut along the top. Three paper cartridges complete with ball and a protruding fuse were loaded into the tube so that their fuses projected above for firing.[1] Again only one shot at a time could be fired.

In Europe the superimposed charge principle was also known at an early date. A printed version edition (1529) of the German *Feuerwerkbuch*,[2] of which there are manuscript examples dating back to the first half of the fifteenth century, refers to a straight gun barrel containing alternate charges of powder and iron or lead bullets (*Klötzen*); the latter being bored through and filled with powder to facilitate the passage of the flame as it travelled backward from the muzzle towards the breech. A so-called *Klotzbüchse* is illustrated in an early fifteenth-century manuscript (*Codex* 3060) in the Stadts Bibliothek, Vienna.[3] Like the Chinese 20-shot repeater it is divided into sections each with its own touch-hole.

[1] T. L. Davis and J. R. Ware, 'Early Chinese Military Pyrotechnics', *Journal of Chemical Education*, Vol. 24, No. 11 (November, 1947), pp. 522–37.
[2] W. Hassenstein, *Das Feuerwerkbuch von 1420*, Munchen, 1941.
[3] P. Sixl, 'Entwicklung und Gebrauch der Handfeuerwaffen', *Z.H.W.K.*, Dresden, 1897–9, Vol. 1, p. 139.

In the sixteenth century appeared the first of many books and patents devoted to the subject of super-imposed charges and it was only the introduction of the metal cartridge that finally doused the enthusiasm of the inventive minded for the Roman Candle idea and its associated devices. Porta's *Natural Magick* (English edition of 1658) gave the following instructions for loading such a gun ('a great brass-gun'):

> First put in a certain measure of Gunpowder, that being put in, may discharge the Ball, then put in the Ball, but a small one, that it may go in loosely, and that the powder put in upon it may come to touch the gunpowder; then pour in the dark powder[1] two or three fingers depth; then put in your Gun powder, and your bullet; and thus in order, one after the other, until the Gun seems to be full to the very mouth.

In 1546 a Cremonese merchant sent to England for the King's service was said to have made 'a hand-gun with which (having but one charge) he shot iiij pellets the one immediately after the other'.[2] John the Almain, writing to Walsingham about 1580 (?), recommended one of his countrymen who could made an harquebus 'that shall containe ten balls or pellets of lead, out which shall goe ot, one after the another, havinge once given fire so that with one harquebuse one may kill ten theeves or other enemies without re-charging'.[3]

Edward, Marquis of Worcester, took out a patent in 1661 for a number of inventions including multi-shot firearms, but neither in the patent nor in his *Century of Inventions* (1663) did he give any specification. But another patent granted to Charles Cardiffe in 1682, which refers to 'severall and distincte shotts in a singell barrell and locke, with one priming and with double locks oftener, reserving one or more shotts till occasion offer', shows that gunmakers were finding more elaborate methods of using the super-imposed charges.

In fact they had been known for some years previous to this. Giuliano Bossi made a special study of the use of superimposed charges and at the time he wrote his *Breve Trattato d'Alcune Inventioni* in 1625, nearly all the methods which were to be employed at later dates with varying degrees of success had been investigated by him. He describes guns of the simple Roman Candle principle in which the bullets were pierced and filled with powder. The touch-hole of the foremost charge was connected to the priming pan by an iron tube filled with powder. This tube could be used in an ingenious fashion to give the firer a reserve shot. The lock was constructed with a double pan, one above the other, and the priming tube led from the top pan only. The lower pan had a touch-hole in the normal position. The first charge loaded down the barrel had a solid bullet with a firm wad over it. Then came the superimposed charges with the bored-out bullets. The first flash of the lock ignited the top pan which set off the multiple charges. When these had finished discharging the rear charge was left awaiting the flash of the lower pan.[4] Another method of accomplishing this, as indicated in the Cardiffe patent, was to employ two locks, one in the usual position and the other farther up the barrel next to the foremost charge (**530**).

Bossi had also seen the gun with a sliding matchlock igniting each touch-hole in turn (**540**), but he dismissed this action with the contemptuous remark: 'Those who attempt to put this idea into practice are optimists rather than persons of long practice and experience.' One wonders what he would have said of the guns in which this procedure was reversed, the barrel being moved forward charge by charge past a stationary lock. A gun in the Kremlin with this action could fire ten consecutive shots (**537**). Unfortunately Bossi does not describe his own solution of the problem, other than to indicate his preference for

[1] This was a rocket mixture composed of 'Turpentine-Rosin, liquid Pitch, Vernish, Frankincense and Camphire, equal parts; quick Brimstone a third part and half; two parts of Salt-Peter refined; three parts of Aqua Fortis, as much of Oyl of Peter and Gun-Powder'.

[2] *Letters and Papers Henry VIII*, Vol. 21, p. 227.

[3] *Calendar of State Papers, Domestic, 1547-80*, p. 696.

[4] The same principle was used by Andrew Dolep in the double-shot fowling-piece made for the Medici family *c*. 1680 (**195**).

the use of two shots only; the reader was advised to await the publication of his next book for the facts.

But one of Bossi's guns in the Mark Dineley Collection, inscribed JULIANUS BOSSIUS INVENTOR 1631 AD DESTRUCTIONEM INFIDELIUM IN BELLO, leaves little doubt that the inventor preferred a double-lock gun firing superimposed charges. Bossi speaks of experiments with these and how he had discovered that when the first charge exploded, the powder behind was first compressed, and then as the front bullet left the barrel a suction effect was created drawing the second bullet a short distance away from its powder charge. When the latter was set off an abnormal pressure built up in the barrel and the result was a burst breech. As far as one can tell Bossi got over this by placing a tube in the breech end of the barrel. The first ball was then firmly seated on the mouth of the tube to prevent any movement.

Other gunmakers obviously agreed with Bossi's findings, for the most common of the superimposed charge guns are those with two adjacent locks (**511**). There were, of course, the gunmakers who had to go one (or two) better. Three- and four-lock guns with matchlocks, wheellocks or flintlocks are known, but they are extremely rare (**521–5**).

One system of superimposed charges which Bossi did not foresee utilised a group of four or five barrels. In the former the four barrels are grouped in square section and mounted with one barrel underneath. One of the side barrels is loaded and fired in the usual way. But when the flame of the discharge reaches the muzzle it is partly diverted through an internal channel to the muzzle end of the other side barrel, which is filled with powder and acts as a powder train. As the flame burns its way down this barrel it is directed through internal holes to alternate charges set in the top and bottom barrels.

A wheellock pistol of this type in the A. C. Carpenter Collection with barrels only nine inches long is designed to fire 15 shots.[1] Other pistols of this type are in Windsor Castle (No. 340) and the Museum of Military History, Vienna.[2] There are four flintlock carbines built on the same principle, two in the Museum of the Polish Army, Warsaw, one in the W. G. Renwick Collection, and one in the Tower of London (**531**). The last is designed to fire 29 shots and is signed FRANCISCO MAMBACH. One of the Polish carbines has five barrels, with the centre barrel acting as the powder train (**534**).

Nothing is known of the use of any of the guns so far described, which all relate to the seventeenth century or earlier. In the last quarter of the eighteenth century, however, we have the first record of the superimposed guns in action. In 1777 Joseph Belton of Philadelphia offered the Continental Congress a superimposed charge musket which could fire eight shots and then be 'loaded and fir'd with cartridge as usual'. He was authorised to make 100 guns, but the British invasion prevented any further development. Belton then went to London in 1784, where he tried to interest the British authorities in his weapon. Failing in this he entered into partnership with the London gunmaker, William Jover, who made a number of guns with detachable chambers and sliding flintlocks for the East India Company (**541**). In doing this they were apparently contravening the 1780 English patent of John Aitken, a Fellow of the Royal College of Surgeons, which covered a sliding-lock repeater. Aitken described the wads separating the charges as 'intermedia or colfings'.

The greatest success was achieved by Joseph G. Chambers, also a Pennsylvanian, who was granted an American patent for 'repeating gunnery' in 1813. The United States Navy and the Commonwealth of Pennsylvania ordered 850 of his muskets, rifles and pistols together with a small number of seven-barrelled swivel guns which could fire the impressive total of 224 shots each. Some of these Chambers guns saw service in the War of 1812.

To-day only one of the original Chambers guns, a swivel gun, survives (**536**). There is, however, a musket in the Tower of London, which was an interesting connection (**535**), and indicates

---

[1] A. C. Carpenter, 'A Fifteen shot Wheellock Repeating Pistol of circa 1650', *J.A.A.S.*, Vol. IV (1963), pp. 93–100.

[2] E. Wettendorfer, 'A Wheellock Automatic', *The American Rifleman*, March, 1954, p. 49.

the nature of the Chambers gun. In 1815 John Bland, 'a Black and Whitesmith' of Philadelphia who claimed to have taken part in the manufacture of the Chambers gun, came to London to try and sell the secret. Under the direction of the Board of Ordnance an India pattern musket was converted by the addition of a pistol lock placed about ten inches in front of the normal lock. Bland then demonstrated that 11 consecutive shots could be fired and one held in reserve, but the Ordnance were unimpressed.

In spite of this publicity other inventors continued to lay their claims. In America Isaiah Jennings patented a rifle with a sliding flintlock in 1821, and a contract for 520 rifles for the New York Militia was obtained by Reuben Ellis. Another American maker was Simeon North (**542**). In England a similar patent was granted to Jacob Mould in 1825, both flintlock and percussion locks being included in the specification. This patent apparently changed hands, for a gun in the Tower of London with a percussion sliding lock is marked 'CAPT. RITSO'S PATENT' (**545**). No patent is registered either in this gentleman's name or in that of Boyce & Co., which appears on other guns of similar construction. An idea which was patented but was never brought into use was John Macintosh's 'Roman Candle' gun of 1852. This used the old-style perforated bullets brought up-to-date by making them self-expanding in the fashion of the Minié bullet.

In Denmark the sixteenth-century 'organ' gun was revived as a vehicle for superimposed charges by Nicolaj Johan Løbnitz. In October, 1850, he demonstrated a 20-barrelled model which fired 300 shots at a time. It also required three-quarters of an hour to be loaded. This gun, known as the *orgelespingole*,[1] was for a short time adopted by the Danish Army and Navy.

French inventors also made their contribution to the designs of the superimposed charge gun. In 1824 Claudius Ramel patented in Paris a breechloader with a metal cartridge containing four charges. De Lancry and Charoy of Paris followed in 1831 with a patent for a muzzleloader with two charges and one lock, various means being adopted to prime the nipples. The most ambitious of these guns were those with a sliding series of sprung-hammers and nipples underneath the barrel, tripped off by a sliding lever and stud. In Auguste Robert's patent of 1838, the trip mechanism was pulled back by the trigger, but in the following year an improvement was registered by Gardon, Aubry and Robert of Rheims in which the lever was moved automatically by a pull-out clock spring.

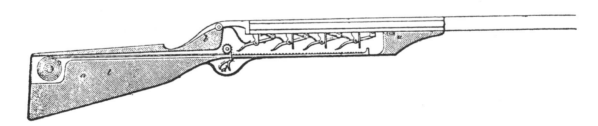

30 Superimposed charge gun patented by Gardon, Aubry and Robert in France, 1839

It was the simplest of the French patents, however, a two-charge barrel fired by side-by-side locks, patented by Jean Luzier in 1827, which was eventually to score most success. It was taken up by John P. Lindsay, of New Haven, Conn., U.S.A., who constructed a musket with a double, side-by-side hammer and a single trigger which fired two superimposed charges (**528**). The construction of the breech was exactly like that recommended by Bossi in 1625. The rear bullet was seated on the edge of the chamber which communicated directly with one nipple. The vent from the second nipple passed through a

[1] Egon Eriksen, *Danische Orgelespingolen mit Einheitspatronen 1850–77*, Tøjhusmuseet Skrifter 3, Copenhagen, 1945.

passage in the metal of the barrel to reach the front charge. When the two hammers were cocked, the trigger automatically set off the front charge, but so strong was the gun that if the hammer of the rear charge only was cocked and fired, both charges went off without any damage to the soldier. In 1863 Lindsay received a contract for 1,000 of the muskets at 25 dollars each which were delivered the following year.

Revolving Guns

Hand-guns with either chambers or barrels which revolve to bring one charge at a time into line for firing cannot claim such an early origin as other forms of multi-shot firearms. But the genesis of the action can be seen in the illustrations in early fifteenth-century military manuscripts, which show groups of small guns mounted on a circular platform like the spokes of a wheel (**31**).

From the outset the gunmaker had the choice either of making the barrels of a gun revolve, in which

31 Revolving guns, *c.* 1400. From *Codex Germanicus 600*, Munich State Library

case he might produce a gun of excessive weight, or of fitting the breech of the barrel with a revolving cylinder containing a number of charges. In the latter case he had the difficulty of trying to prevent the escape of gas from the gap between barrel and cylinder. This fault, while bearable in a revolver held in the hand, could be dangerous in a gun held to the shoulder with the eye only a few inches from the gap.

It is doubtful whether the first hand-guns with revolver actions appeared before the second quarter of the sixteenth century. In Venice there is a matchlock pistol with three revolving barrels which is almost certainly the '*schioppo da serpa con tre cane*' listed in an inventory of that city in 1548. This seems to be the earliest known example. The *Wu-Pei-Chih* of 1621 illustrates what appears to be a Japanese type of matchlock revolver. This type of multi-shot gun appears to have been quite common, but the majority of existing specimens (and those of other oriental countries) are of later date (**550–5**).

European matchlock revolvers, on the other hand, are rare. The *cabinet d'armes* formed by Louis XIII (1610–43) includes several (**556**), and there is a fine decorated specimen in the Hermitage, Leningrad (**557**). Even rarer are the wheellock revolvers (**559**). The reason for this is that the wheellock had to be primed and spanned for each shot, so that much of the advantage of the revolver—its speed of shot—was lost. It was much easier to apply the matchlock or, for that matter, the flintlock.

The snaphance came into use on the revolver at a very early date and the earliest dated revolver is, in fact, the German snaphance rifle dated 1597 now in the Tøjhusmuseet, Copenhagen (**560**). It is one of a group of revolvers made in Nuremberg, all with similar mechanisms (**561–2**). A small flat steel is positioned over the touch-hole on a long flat arm. The pans are protected by sliding covers held by a spring catch. Another spring fastened to the barrel prevents the chambers from moving out of alignment with the barrel as the lock fires—an important point. Both the chamber and the pan-covers have to be moved manually, but on a long-barrelled pistol-carbine in the Kremlin (**563**) the cock has been fitted with a lever which knocks the pan-cover open as the gun is fired. This was an adaptation of the methods used on the ordinary snaphance for uncovering the pan.

The snaphance revolver appears to have been made in most countries of Northern Europe. Apart from the German revolvers already mentioned there are examples from Russia (**564**), France (**567**), and England (**568**). The maker of the last gun, John Dafte of London, is believed to have made the all-brass snaphance revolver pistol now in the Tower of London. On this, the action of cocking also revolves the cylinder, a small pawl attached to the front of the cock engaging in a ratchet cut in the rear of the cylinder. This mechanism was far in advance of its time and was not to be successfully developed until the second quarter of the nineteenth century.

At the beginning of the eighteenth century an attempt was made to construct a revolver in which there was no escape of gas between barrel and chamber. In 1718 James Puckle, a notary public of London, patented a revolver the size of a wall-gun (**548**). This was mounted on a tripod and was intended for the defence of ships and fortified positions. The project was launched with a great deal of publicity and the public were allowed to purchase shares in a company which was to market the gun. In the first place the gun was remarkable for its ability to fire round bullets against Christians and square ones against the Turks, a square-bored set of chambers being provided for the latter. More important from the mechanical point of view, the mouths of the chambers were cone-shaped, and before the gun was fired a handle at the rear of the cylinder was revolved, pushing the cylinder forward so that the end of the chamber entered the counter-sunk breech-end of the barrel. The gun was given a successful trial on the Artillery Ground, London, and was reported to have fired 63 times in seven minutes. But the inventor could not obtain any Government orders and eventually the shareholders lost their money.[1]

With the introduction of the combined steel and pan-cover the revolver became a more feasible proposition, and an immediate development was the three- and four-chambered revolver with a pan and steel on each chamber. These and the other revolvers were in the main luxury arms. They are usually well made and often superbly decorated. Two of the finest specimens are the five-chambered sporting gun by the Russian gunmaker, B. Kalesnikow, in the Bayerisches Nationalmuseum, Munich (**577–8**), and the double-barrelled gun by Le Conte of Paris in the Livrustkammaren, Stockholm (**579**). Both guns are profusely ornamented with gold and silver inlay. The latter is an example of the turn-over gun known in Germany as the *Wender* gun. A modified version of this action can be seen on the single-barrelled guns with two long turn-over chambers made by the Huguenot gunmaker, Jacques Gorgo, and some of his compatriots in London during the last decade of the seventeenth century (**580–1**).

The turn-over gun was a very popular weapon and in its flintlock models was made in combinations of up to four barrels (**583–5**). Over this figure the full-size gun became too weighty for normal use. Small carbines, however, with seven revolving barrels were made by Henry Nock, obviously inspired by his famous volley guns. A seven-barrelled revolver in the National Museum of Ireland, made by William Rigby of Dublin, is only two feet long and has the refinements of a magazine primer and a folding bayonet (**586**). Such revolvers with clusters of short barrels were appropriately nicknamed 'pepperboxes'.

The first revolvers to be produced in any quantity were those invented by Captain Artemus Wheeler of Concord, Massachusetts. In 1818 he was granted an American patent for a 'Gun to discharge 7 or more times'. This was a flintlock revolver with a special priming magazine. Two specimens survive in the U.S. National Museum (**588–9**), one being a 'pepperbox' type and the other having a seven-chambered cylinder. Both revolvers had to be turned by hand. Wheeler failed to gain any financial support for his revolvers, and after the Navy had turned them down in 1821 he appears to have relinquished his interest in them.[2]

Two Boston men, however, Cornelius Coolidge and Elisha Collier, took the revolver to Europe and patented it, Coolidge in France in 1819, and Collier in England in 1818. In his English patent Collier introduced several improvements of his own and the result was a very complicated mechanism. The

[1] H. L. Blackmore, *British Military Firearms*, London, 1961, pp. 237–40.
[2] Lt.-Col. B. R. Lewis, 'Capt. Wheeler's Revolving Guns', *The American Rifleman*, April, 1953, pp. 38–40.

rotation of the cylinder was controlled by a spiral spring which was wound up like a clock spring. The mouths of the chambers were coned and another spring gave the cylinder a backwards and forwards movement, locking it on to the end of the barrel for the shot and then releasing it when the next chamber was required. A priming magazine was combined with the steel so that in theory all that was required to make the gun ready was to close the pan and pull back the cock. In practice the internal mechanism frequently broke down, and when the revolver was submitted to the Ordnance in 1819 it was rejected for this reason.

Collier subsequently simplified the action and in 1824 produced a percussion revolving rifle for trial, but this was merely a conversion of the original model and was also rejected (**618**). From 1824 to 1827 he had a retail shop in London and later claimed to have sold over £10,000-worth of rifles, shotguns and pistols. But in 1836 he patented a steam boiler and turned his attention to engineering matters.

All over Europe different types of percussion revolvers were now making their appearance. In 1826 Jacques-Philippe Le Lyon, a gunmaker of Versailles, patented in Paris a simple four-shot percussion revolver (**595**). This had a hand-turned cylinder. In 1829, at Venice, Cesare Rosaglio was awarded a medal for a percussion revolver in which the cylinder was revolved by a large handle-grip underneath the action.[1] The cylinder also locked on to the barrel in the manner of the Collier. The Rosaglio revolvers were made at Cremona under licence by Giacomo Verno. An unmarked model at Schloss Ambras, Innsbruck, may be an early prototype (**605**).

In Denmark, Peder Rasmussen, town clerk of Rudkøbing, began designing revolving guns of the pepperbox type in 1827. In 1834 he demonstrated a gun which fired ten shots in as many seconds before King Frederick VI, but it was not until 1843 that he succeeded in gaining the interests of the Danish Army and Navy in his gun. A number of experimental models were made (**603**), including a wall-gun (**604**), but eventually the whole project was abandoned. The Rasmussen gun was both revolved and fired by the movement of a lever under the thumbgrip.[2] Another highly original revolver was patented by Jonas Offrell of Sweden in 1839.

The question of which was the best way of rotating the cylinder of a revolver was to become the bone of contention among gunmakers and their supporters for many years. In the Mariette system patented in Belgium in 1837, a ring trigger drew back a partly-concealed under-hammer and revolved the pepperbox barrels, so that when the hammer was released it hit the next loaded nipple. In 1840 Joseph Prélat patented in Paris another self-cocking revolver with a bar-hammer lying across the top of the action. Many of the Mariette-type revolvers were made by the Birmingham gunmaker, Joseph Rock Cooper, who took out a similar patent in England in 1840. Three years later he was granted a Registered Design for another self-cocking revolver. Swivel guns made to this design have a curled lever instead of a trigger to work the gun, and a bar-hammer of the Prélat type.

In America the cult of the revolver had started even earlier. A pepperbox mechanism was patented by Benjamin and Barton Darling in 1836, but in this the hammer was cocked to turn the barrels. The following year Ethan Allen patented a pepperbox revolver whose barrels were revolved and fired by the trigger. All these self-cocking and turning revolvers had a very fast action, but little accuracy. Even with carbines fired from the shoulder (**600**) it was difficult to take aim with a moving barrel. This did not matter with a pistol held in the hand when it was necessary to fire a number of shots quickly at close quarters, but for shoulder guns and rifles where accuracy was the overriding consideration many sportsmen preferred the older hand-revolved turn-over guns (**596–7**).[3]

It was on the point of accuracy that the American Samuel Colt was to build much of his success. He

[1] T. T. Hoopes, 'Two Early Revolvers', *The American Rifleman*, February, 1947, pp. 16–18.

[2] Arne Hoff, *The Rasmussen Revolving Guns*, Tøjhusmuseets Skrifter 4, Copenhagen, 1946.

[3] As late as 1858 a gun of this type with up to four barrels, which would be smooth bore or rifled, was patented in Canada by Michael Mater.

began experimenting with revolvers in 1830 at the age of 16. In 1835 he patented his first revolver in England and France. An American patent was obtained the following year. After an initial setback when his first factory at Paterson, New Jersey, was obliged to close down, Colt managed to interest first the Texas Rangers and then the United States Army in his revolving pistols, and from then on his success was assured, or rather one should say the success of his pistols.

The Colt revolver was a single-action design in which the hammer had to be thumbed back to revolve the cylinder and to cock it. Although it was not so fast as the self-cocking pistols of Colt's English rivals, Robert Adams and James Webley, it could be aimed properly and it was superior in range and accuracy. The carbines and rifles had similar actions and qualities.

The first revolving rifles were made for the youthful inventor by Anson Chase and W. H. Rowe of Hartford in 1832 (606). During 1833 the gunsmiths True, Davis and Samuel Gibson of Albany also made models from Colt's designs. When he moved to Baltimore in 1834 this work was taken over by John Pearson (607). At first a lever next to the trigger was used to rotate the cylinder, but this was soon replaced by a ring in front of the trigger guard. This ring appears on the models made at the Paterson factory from 1835. Nearly all the ring-lever rifles were made with eight chambers, but they vary in calibre, length, and details of the mechanism. In 1839 Colt introduced carbines and rifles with an exposed hammer which could be used for cocking and rotating the cylinder. The majority of these have only six chambers, including the shotgun model (611).

With the closure of his Paterson factory in 1842, Colt concentrated his resources on the sales of his pistol, and when he opened a new factory at Hartford in 1847, he continued on this line of production. In 1855, however, he brought out his side-hammer pistols, the so-called Root model based on the designs of Elisha K. Root, the factory superintendent. At the same time he put into production a number of carbines and rifles with a similar action (612). They were made in different calibres and barrel lengths, and many were of military or semi-military design. When the Civil War began in 1861, Colt had expectations of large orders for his revolving rifles. But the military authorities never forgot an incident in an early official trial when two of the chambers in a Colt revolver went off together, and they never ordered more than small trial batches of the weapons.

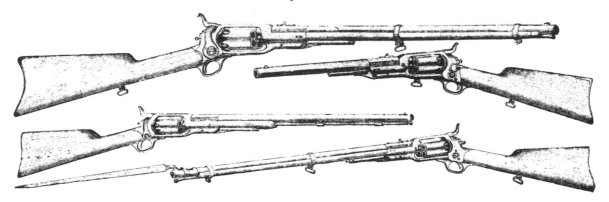

32 Colt's side-hammer revolving guns. An advertisement drawing showing military and sporting rifles, a carbine and a shotgun

The Civil War, however, encouraged the invention of many other types of revolvers. Some were designed originally to circumvent Colt's patents. The most original of these were the 'turret' guns in which the chambers were positioned like the spokes of a wheel. Examples of these were the Cochran gun of 1837–8 with an under-hammer (622), the Porter gun of 1851 with a side hammer (621), and the Graham gun with a concealed front hammer (620). Ingenious as these were they had the disadvantage of possessing loaded chambers pointing towards the user.

Another imaginative and more practical revolver was patented by Dr. Jean Alexander François Le Mat of New Orleans in 1856. It had a cylinder bored with nine chambers which fired through a rifled barrel in the usual way. Underneath this barrel was a large but shorter barrel of smooth bore which could be loaded with grape-shot. This was fired by turning down the nose of the hammer (**626**). A number of these revolving pistols were made for the Confederate Army and Navy, many being shipped from a factory in France. The Civil War also saw the beginnings of the machine-gun. There was a large revolving Confederate cannon like the Puckle gun; a radial turret gun invented by General Josiah Gorgas, and the revolving machine-gun of Dr. Richard Jordan Gatling, patented in 1862.

This need for a large number of shots was reflected in a group of shoulder guns known as the 'chain-guns' in which a number of chambers were suspended from a continuous chain passing through the breech. The earliest of them was patented in the United States by E. A. Bennett and P. F. Haviland in 1838. Their chain consisted of 12 rectangular blocks bored out as chambers on a linked belt moving in a horizontal plane (**623**). The chain was turned by a disc with four spindles hanging down under the gun. A very neat French design with a chain of up to 100 shots was based on the patents by P. Gay and H. Guenot of 1879 and E. Fabre and A. Tronche of 1888. A British design was patented by Thomas Wright Gardener Treeby, a London engineer, in 1855. The chain in this gun revolved in a vertical plane, but the outstanding feature of the gun was the method used to join the barrel and chamber together to effect a gas-tight seal. This was a threaded collar which when turned by a lever moved the barrel against the mouth of the chamber and locked it in this position. It actually formed part of a patent taken out by James Thomson in 1814. Although it improved the performance of the gun it also slowed down the rate of firing. At an official trial of the gun in 1859, a belt of 30 chambers took 1 min. 30 secs. to be discharged.

Another method of increasing the firepower of the revolver was to fit more than one cylinder. In 1855 Joseph Enouy patented a revolver in which two or more cylinders were connected in a frame so that when the charges of one cylinder were exhausted another loaded cylinder could be moved into its place. A pistol with eight cylinders has been recorded,[1] but the extra weight involved can be imagined. In long guns the inventor does not seem to have had them made with more than two cylinders (**628**).

In 1854 Edward Lindner of New York patented a revolving gun with a six-shot cylinder which was fed with cartridges from a tubular magazine under the barrel (**633**). This gun was dependent on the effectiveness of its paper cartridges and according to the patent was designed for needle-fire or tape primer. Other designs for needle-fire revolvers were patented by Kufahl and Tranter in England but few working models were ever produced.

With the introduction of the metallic cartridge there was a spate of rim-fire (**636**), pin-fire (**635**) and centre-fire (**634**) revolvers. But there was no remedy for the ever-present danger from the escape of gas from the gap between barrel and chamber, and as far as long guns were concerned the revolver never succeeded in rivalling the magazine gun. The last effective revolving rifles were probably those made by the American firm, Smith & Wesson, between 1879 and 1887. They were made because of repeated requests received from satisfied users of their pistols and they were really long-barrelled pistols fitted with shoulder stocks (**640**). The rifles were not guaranteed accurate beyond 200 yards and when complaints began to come in of gas escape, production ceased.[2]

Magazine Guns

If one can believe the *Wu-Pei-Chih* of 1621, the first magazine gun was the 'string of-100-bullets' gun (**34**). This was a small cannon about four feet long made of cast copper. Its chamber was filled with the

---

[1] H. L. Blackmore, *Firearms*, London, 1964, p. 138.

[2] John E. Parsons, *Smith & Wesson Revolvers*, New York, 1957, pp. 156–64. The Belgian firm of Pieper-Nagart subsequently made a small number of nine-shot revolving carbines with a barrel-sealing device.

nauseating *fa* powder (see p. 2). Half-way along the barrel a vertical magazine or hopper was arranged so that the bullets could be fed into the barrel. When the charge was ignited the explosive gas roared up the barrel taking a stream of bullets with it.

It is doubtful whether such a simple piece of apparatus ever worked and a much more complicated mechanism was necessary to convert the single-shot hand-gun to a gun firing several shots from its own

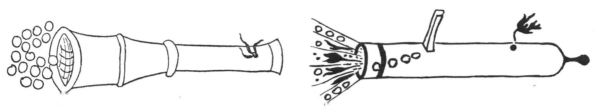

33 Multiple-shot gun firing *Hagelschütz, c.* 1410. From *Codex 51*, Ambraser Collection, Vienna
34 The 'string-of-100-bullets' gun. From the *Wu-Pei-Chih*, 1621

store of powder and ball. It was not until the second quarter of the seventeenth century, well after the appearance of the other multi-shot guns, that a German family of gunmakers, the Kalthoffs, introduced such a weapon. At any rate, Bossi, who in his treatise of 1625 describes multi-barrel guns, revolvers and different kinds of super-imposed charge guns, makes no mention of the magazine gun then.

The first reference to this family occurs in 1640 when Wilhelm Kalthoff was granted a monopoly for the manufacture of repeating guns in France. A similar monopoly was granted to a Peter Kalthoff by the States General of the Netherlands in 1641. No more is heard of Wilhelm, but Peter moved to Denmark where he began making these guns for Duke Frederick (later King Frederick III).[1] A wheellock magazine gun by him dated 1645 is marked 'DAS ERSTE' (the first) (**641**). Another gun by him dated a year later is a flintlock. As far as is known these are the first examples of this kind of gun.

The Kalthoff repeater has two magazines, one for balls, a tubular cavity under the barrel, and another for powder hollowed out of the butt. The pivoted trigger guard has a carrier large enough for a charge of powder plus priming which, when the guard is turned, transports the powder from the butt to the front of the lock where a passage leads to the breech block. The latter is a box-shaped block with three holes, which is moved horizontally across the breech by the trigger guard. One hole takes a ball from the magazine and deposits it in the barrel. Another one is filled with powder and acts as the breech chamber, while the third moves the residue of powder from the carrier into the priming pan.

Other members of the Kalthoff family to be concerned with the manufacture of these guns were Mathias, who joined his brother Peter in Copenhagen, and Caspar, who went to England. Caspar's son of the same name later worked in Moscow.[2] Two identical magazine guns signed C. KALTHOFF are in existence, one in the Tøjhusmuseet, Copenhagen (**649**), and the other at Windsor Castle (No. 226). The mechanism of these guns is slightly different from that of the first models, the breech block being cylindrical and turning on a vertical axis.

The Kalthoff family's monopoly does not seem to have been rigidly enforced, for there are a number of guns made on the system by other gunmakers. Wheellock guns which are contemporary with the first Kalthoff guns were made in Germany by the so-called 'Master from Gottorp' (probably Heinrich Habrecht)[3] (**642**). The latter's guns have a cylindrical or quarter-cylindrical breech with an axis parallel to the barrel. Flintlock varieties with the vertical cylinder breech block were made by Jan Flock of Utrecht (**650**), and by the Dutchman, Harman Barne, who worked in London (**645-7**).

[1] Arne Hoff, *Aeldre Dansk Bøssemageri*, Copenhagen, 1951.
[2] One of his guns is preserved in the Kremlin (No. 7538) and is signed *K. Kalthoff Fecit Moscova 1665*.
[3] See Arne Hoff, 'Gottorpmesteren', *Svenska Vapenhistoriska Sällskapets Skrifter*, Stockholm, N.S. Vol. V, 1957, pp. 53-74.

An improved version of the Kalthoff system appears to have been invented by Sigmund Klett of Salzburg, three of the surviving examples being inscribed SIGMUND KLETT INFENIERT MICH, HANS PAUL MACHT MICH, and two being dated 1652. This system also depended on a powder magazine in the butt and a bullet container in the stock under the barrel, but *two* vertical cylinders worked by the trigger guard were used to place the charges in position.[1] According to the memoirs of Prince Raimund Montecuccoli, Queen Christina of Sweden, in 1653, ordered a Klettner (i.e. Klett) carbine that could fire 30 or 40 shots one after the other.

The Kalthoff guns were capable of firing up to 30 shots, but their complicated structure made them generally unsuitable for military service. Nevertheless 100 were issued to picked marksmen of the Royal Danish Foot Guards and are believed to have been used during the siege of Copenhagen, 1658–9, and in the Scandinavian War of 1675–9.

Although we know that Caspar Kalthoff worked for the Marquis of Worcester for many years in London and that Harman Barne was active there between 1650 and 1661, there is no record of the guns' employment in England. There is of course the intriguing report of the meeting of the Royal Society of London held on 2 March 1664 which contains what appears to be the first mention of an automatic gun:

> [Sir Robert Moray] mentioned that there was to come to Prince Rupert a rare mechanician who pretended . . . to make a pistol, shooting as fast as it could be presented, and yet to be stopped at pleasure; and wherein the motion of the fire and bullet within was made to charge the piece with powder and bullet, to prime it, and to bend the cock.[2]

Books such as Worcester's *Century of Inventions* of 1663 and the firearms patents of that period do not give sufficient detail for us to identify the repeating devices mentioned. In the patent of Abraham Hill (No. 143 of 1664) there is a reference to 'A gun or pistol for small shott, carrying seven or eight charges of the same in the stock of the gun'. This could refer to a Kalthoff gun, but it is more likely to have been a reference to another form of magazine breechloader which appears to have come into operation just after the middle of the century.

In this type of repeater the powder and ball were carried in two tubular magazines running through the butt. Between the magazines and the barrel was a circular breech block. With the gun held muzzle downwards this breech block was revolved by means of a lever on the left-hand side, and first a ball and then a charge of powder was collected from the magazines. The ball was transferred to the barrel and the powder chamber then acted as the breech. At the same time the flash pan was primed from a small magazine on the lock and the lock was cocked.

This system is often named after the Italian gunmaker, Michele Lorenzoni of Florence, who made several magnificent guns of this type (**656**). But the earliest reference to Lorenzoni is in 1684 when a repeating gun was purchased from him by the Elector Johann Georg of Saxony.[3] Another Italian gunmaker, Giacomo Berselli, is considered by some authorities to have prior claim to the invention.[4] An example of his work in the Museé de l'Armée, Paris, appears to be earlier than any of the known guns by Lorenzoni. It will be noticed how similar the breech of his gun in the Royal Armoury, Turin (**664**), is to that of Lorenzoni in the same collection (**667**). A carbine with this type of action in the collection of Joe Kindig, York, Pennsylvania, is signed by another maker, Bartolomeo Cotel, with the proud inscription CARABINO CHE TIRA PIEU VOLTE, NO. UNO. (Carbine that fires many times, Number one). Another specimen of this gunmaker's work is in the Tower of London (**670**).

The fluted decoration and general shape of the barrel of the last gun is remarkably like that of two guns made by a gunmaker, presumed to be English, about whose life nothing is known at present, but who

[1] Arne Hoff, 'Quelques Inventions de la Famille Klett à Salzburg', *Armes Anciennes*, No. 13 (1959), pp. 133–9.

[2] Thomas Birch, *History of the Royal Society of London*, London, 1756, Vol. I, p. 376.

[3] W. von Seidlitz, *Die Kunst in Dresden*, Dresden, 1920–2, Vol. IV, p. 503.

[4] J. F. Hayward, *The Art of the Gunmaker*, London, 1963, Vol. II, p. 142.

signed his guns JOHN COOKSON FECIT (663). One gun is in the Victoria and Albert Museum (659) and the other in the Milwaukee Museum, Wisconsin (660). Another repeating gun by him without the fluted decoration on the barrel but with a very similarly shaped butt and lock is in the William M. Locke Collection, Cincinnati (662). Another John Cookson, perhaps a descendant, who lived in Boston, U.S.A., from 1701 to 1762, advertised a nine-shot weapon of this type in the *Boston Gazette* for April, 1756.

There were many other makers of this type of repeater. The Augsburg gunmaker Wetschzi produced a pair of them, now in the Musée de l'Armée, which he signed WETSCHZI AUGUSTAE INVENIT ET FECIT. A unique example, because of its decoration, in the C. G. Vokes Collection, Havant, Hampshire (675), is unfortunately not signed. Stylistically it is of the same date as the Cookson guns and is probably of Dutch manufacture. The ebonised butt is decorated in gilt, on one side with a painting of a port and on the other with a hunting scene. A hundred years later guns with almost identical actions were still being made, mainly in England (677–8).

Another type of magazine gun, which has also been attributed to Lorenzoni, because fine examples bearing his name are in the Bargello, Florence, and the Royal Armoury, Turin (679), has the tubular magazines positioned under the barrel. The breech chamber is fixed, but the barrel assembly revolves on its axis so that with the muzzle upwards, first powder and then ball are dropped into the breech (682). The earliest example known, in the W. G. Renwick Collection, Tuscon, Arizona, is signed T. LEFER A VALENZA DEL PO. 1668. Another in the Royal Armoury, Turin, is signed GIO PIETRO CALLIN A GENOVA 1685 (681).

This type of turn-over magazine action is often called the Chelembron system after the French gunmaker of that name who produced several of the guns at the arsenal of Pondicherry, India, during the latter part of the eighteenth century. A fine example which bears his signature is in the Windsor Castle Collection (684). In the same collection is a very similar gun of Indian manufacture (685). Another Chelembron gun, in the Mark Dineley Collection, Shaftesbury, is dated 1781 (687).[1] In 1779 Claude Martin, a former French soldier who deserted to the British forces and was eventually raised to the rank of Major-General in the army of the East India Company, was appointed Superintendent of Artillery and Arsenals to the Nawab of Oudh. Under his aegis a number of fine sporting and military firearms were made at the Lucknow Arsenal. They are all signed with his name and that of the arsenal. These firearms are now scattered among many collections. In that of Joe Kindig is a Chelembron-type magazine gun, silver mounted and bearing the inscription LUCKNOW ARSENAL, MAJOR CLAUDE MARTIN.

These various magazine actions continued to attract the interest of inventors. In 1837 François Antoine Henry, a mechanic of Paris, patented a 14-shot flintlock musket which had tubular magazines for powder and ball fastened to the top of the barrel, being fed into the breech by a lever-operated cylindrical block. But no real progress could be made in the design of magazine guns while loose powder and shot or paper cartridges were the only ammunition available.

In 1847, however, on both sides of the Atlantic the magazine cartridge arm was suddenly launched. In England Stephen Taylor, acting on behalf of a 'foreigner', patented a conical-shaped bullet with a hollow interior filled with powder and closed by a perforated metal base. This bullet was designed for use in a tubular magazine attached to the barrel of a gun, with a mechanism for feeding the bullets into the breech. In America Walter Hunt, an inventor of many devices including a safety-pin, and presumably the 'foreigner' mentioned by Taylor, filed a patent (it was not granted until 1849) for a 12-shot repeating rifle on similar lines (689). In 1848 he was granted a separate patent for a bullet like that of the English patent.

Hunt's 'Volitional repeater', as he called it, contained the basic principles of many later arms but in itself it was too complicated to be successful. A skilled mechanic, Lewis Jennings, then took out a patent in 1848 for an improved version of the gun with a rack-and-pinion breech-action. Both the Hunt and Jennings patents were acquired by Courtlandt Palmer, a New York financier, who promptly took out a

---

[1] In the Musée de l'Armée, Paris are two of these guns. One (No. M666) is signed FAIT PAR CHELEMBRON PONDICHERY 1785; the other (No. M665) which was acquired by Louis XV in 1765, is engraved FAIT ET INVENTE PAR JEAN BOUILLET A ST. ETIENNE.

Multi-Shot Guns

French patent covering the Jennings action in the same year. The repeating rifle was then put into production by the manufacturing firm of Robbins & Lawrence of Windsor, Vermont.

In 1854 Horace Smith and Daniel B. Wesson patented a much-improved loading mechanism—a toggle-link lever action—which was to form the basic part of all later designs (**690**). They were taken into partnership by Palmer and in 1855 formed the Volcanic Repeating Arms Company. When this failed in 1857 one of the shareholders, a shirt manufacturer of New Haven called Oliver F. Winchester, took control.[1] He organised the New Haven Arms Company to continue production of the Volcanic Rifles (**691**), which were advertised to shoot 30 shots in less than a minute. But at first they found no better market than their predecessor.

In 1860, however, the factory superintendent, B. Tyler Henry, patented an improved design for a metallic rim-fire cartridge, instead of a loaded projectile. The new gun was marketed and advertised as the 'Henry Rifle'. With a magazine holding fifteen ·44 cal. bullets which could be discharged in ten seconds, the Henry rifle was introduced in time to take part in the Civil War. Some remarkable feats were performed with it and it became known as the gun that you could 'load up on Sunday and shoot all the rest of the week'. Some of the first production were made with iron bodies, but the rest are distinguished by their handsome brass frames (**692**).

The Henry rifle had certain defects and a new superintendent, Nelson King, eliminated them in a patent taken out in 1866. He also introduced a loading gate in the side of the action (**694**). With the birth of a new rifle, named the Model 1866, the firm's name was also changed to the Winchester Repeating Arms Company. Their advertisements now claimed that their rifle could fire two shots a second without loss of aim. Thus began a long line of distinguished lever-action repeating guns, the most famous of which were those marked ONE OF ONE THOUSAND (**698–9**). This designation was engraved on those barrels of the 1873 and 1876 Models which were found on test to shoot with outstanding accuracy. They were then made up into guns with set triggers and extra finish. A few guns were also inscribed ONE OF ONE HUNDRED to indicate a lesser standard of quality.

The Winchester was not without its rivals. A seven-shot repeater patented by Christopher M. Spencer of Connecticut in 1860 also had a lever action which extracted cartridges from a tubular magazine in the butt. The action was not self-cocking as in the Henry and the Winchester, and the hammer had to be thumbed back for each shot. But it was simpler, stronger and cheaper. At the beginning of the Civil War it had the unusual honour of being personally tried by Abraham Lincoln. Over 100,000 carbines and rifles were bought by the United States Government, whose troops nicknamed them 'the Horizontal Shot-Towers'. The Spencer used a heavy ·56 cal. cartridge and after the War the lighter cartridge of the Winchester and its larger magazine capacity gained preference among sportsmen, so that in 1869 the Spencer Repeating Arms Company was forced into liquidation (**703**).

A repeater of somewhat similar design to the Spencer, but firing the ·44 cal. rim-fire cartridge and holding 34 cartridges in its butt magazine, was patented by Warren R. Evans in 1869 (**702**). Manufacture of this arm, which often had trouble with its ammunition feed, was discontinued in 1880. Other kinds of magazine actions were brought out in competition with the lever actions. The so-called 'harmonica' guns (**705**) with a straight magazine moving transversely across the breech like a mouth organ, were based on the 1873 French patent of A. E. and P. H. Jarre.

Another group of guns with a tubular magazine under the barrel were known as pump guns, from the action of a handle which moved up and down the barrel to convey the cartridge into the breech. One of the earliest of these guns was patented in England in 1866 by W. Krutzsch (**707**).[2] They found favour mainly as shotguns and sporting rifles. The Colt Lightning pump-action rifle (**711**) was made in calibres

---

[1] H. F. Williamson, *Winchester—The Gun That Won The West*, Washington, 1952.

[2] The first British patent for a pump-action breech was granted in 1854 to Alexander Bain, but his percussion gun with a vertical 'mouth organ' type magazine does not appear to have been made.

ranging from ·22 to ·50. One model used the ·44 cal. cartridge of the Colt Frontier pistol. A combination of these two guns made a formidable armament, for a feature of the Lightning rifle—and the reason for its name—was that with the trigger held back the gun could be fired by the pump action alone with a speed approaching that of a machine-gun.

While all these developments were taking place in America, the European gunmakers were experimenting with a variety of magazines adapted to the bolt-action breech, which had been adopted by most countries for their military arms. One of the first bolt-action repeaters was invented by Frederick Vetterli of Switzerland and was adopted by his country in 1874. It incorporated a loading gate like that of the Winchester (**721**). Other countries to try tubular magazines were France (Kropatschek and Lebel), Austria (Fruwirth) and Germany (Mauser). In order to improve the firepower, in some designs the tubular magazine was transferred to the butt where various means were taken to increase the number of bullets available. Examples of these are the Schulhof, with compartments of 28 bullets and the Mannlicher treble-tube magazine (**978**).

One defect of the tubular magazine was that the centre of gravity altered as the ammunition was expended; another was that the magazine had to be replenished by single cartridges one after the other. For this reason some guns, like the American Spencer, were provided with cases of spare loaded tubes for quick reloading. The balance of the gun was better preserved by placing the magazine in the middle and constructing it with either a box-like or circular shape. An English patent of 1862 in the name of M. Mennons shows cartridges being fed into the breech from a spiral container under the bolt.

A most unusual shotgun was made by the Roper Repeating Rifle Company (based on the patent of S. H. Roper of 1867). This had a revolving star-sectioned carrier to hold the cartridges, which were reloadable steel shells with a percussion nipple in the base. The bolt passed through the carrier pushing the cartridge into the breech. On the retraction of the bolt the carrier or magazine was automatically rotated by a spring. This shotgun is also notable for its detachable muzzle choke (**704**). One of the most successful circular magazines to be put into production was the Spitalsky rotary magazine of 1879 developed at the Steyr factory in Austria (**715**).

The box-type magazine was first patented in England by a consortium of M. Walker, G. A. Money and F. Little in 1867, but its first practical application was by James Lee in America in 1879. Both these magazines were located under the bolt, the cartridge being forced upwards by a Z-shaped spring. Unsuccessful attempts were also made to introduce vertical hoppers or magazines with a gravity feed, but these interfered with the sighting and manipulation of the rifle (**717**). In England belated efforts were made to convert the Martini-Henry action to a magazine feed (**714**), but in 1888 the British Government also decided to adopt the bolt-action magazine rifle of James Lee (**718**). The final step in the perfection of the box magazine was the invention of the cartridge clip by Ferdinand Mannlicher in 1885. Instead of being burdened by heavy spare magazines, the soldier could now carry several spare clips of bullets, if not in comfort at least with forbearance.

Perhaps the ultimate in magazine guns was reached in the 1886 English patent of E. H. Salvator. A belt magazine containing a considerable number of rounds was strapped to the marksman. The cartridges were fed into the breech by a lever-operated feed-wheel and breech block. As the inventor anticipated that the complicated mechanism would work and get hot, he thoughtfully provided the barrel with a water jacket. In between belts, fresh cold water could be pumped into this from a reservoir in the butt.

In this, of course, the inventor was anticipating the needs of the fully automatic gun, invented by Hiram S. Maxim in 1883. For the first time[1] the power of the cartridge was used to perform all the operations of extraction, loading and firing; and to quote the words of the patent, 'if the trigger be forcibly held back, the whole of the cartridges in the magazine will be fired successively and automatically'. But, as I pointed out in the preface, that forms part of another story.

[1] Perhaps not the first time. To some extent Maxim was anticipated by the English patents of Edward Lindner (No. 1415 of 1856) and W. J. Curtis (No. 1810 of 1866).

8 Air, Steam and Electric Guns

An air-gun is one in which the force of compressed air is used to expel the missile. In its simplest form, the blow-pipe—still in use amongst certain tribes of Borneo and South America—the compressed air is supplied by the human lungs. The primitive blow gun, a wooden tube from 10 to 15 feet long firing a small dart, can be surprisingly accurate and deadly up to a range of 50 feet. Known also in Europe as early as the fifteenth century, it was revived in the second half of the nineteenth century when certain London walking-stick makers and gunmakers advertised them as the best means of killing small birds and vermin up to a range of 50 yards.[1]

Knowledge of a mechanical means of compressing air can be traced back to the pneumatical experiments of Ktesibos of Alexandria (300–230 B.C.). The invention of the air-gun proper is by tradition accorded to Guter of Nuremberg, c. 1430, but there is no evidence to support this. The often repeated story that an imperfect specimen of an air-gun dated 1474 was at one time in the armoury of Count von Schmettau[2] has also proved impossible to substantiate.

By the time of Leonardo da Vinci, however, the air-gun must have been well known, and he gives a casual reference in his notebooks to the construction of a barrel.

> To make an air-gun which shoots with marvellous force you should proceed as follows: stretch a steel wire the width of a finger on a wire-drawing machine by means of a windlass, then temper it, and bend it round two plates of fine copper which you stretch on the wire-drawing machine. Then half to half solder them together with silver, wind thin copper wire about it and then smooth it with a hammer, but make [the air-gun] two bracia long and make it so that it can shoot a dart of a third of a braccio which is of steel.[3]

These constructional details could refer to the barrel of a blow-pipe, and we do not know whether Leonardo had in mind some form of mechanism to supply it with compressed air.

In the sixteenth-century editions of *Magiae Naturalis*, J. B. Porta describes an air-gun which has a brazen cylinder for the compression of the air, but exactly how it worked is not clear.[4] The 1607 edition of *Les Élémens de l'Artillerie*, by Rivault de Flurance, contains an illustration of an air-gun made by Marin le Bourgeoys of Lisieux (35). In this the air reservoir and the valve and release mechanism are clearly shown. Antonio Petrini in his manuscript *l'Arte Fabrile* also gives clear diagrams of the mechanism of both spring and reservoir air-guns.

In 1625[5] an English traveller in Rome reported that he had seen an all-brass air-gun, one of three

---

[1] Eldon G. Wolff, *Air Guns*, Milwaukee Public Museum Publications in History, No. 1, 1958, p. 44.

[2] Petro van Musschenbroek, *Introductio ad Philosophiam Naturalem*, Lugduni Batavorum, 1762, Vol. II, p. 860.

[3] E. MacCurdy, *The Notebooks of Leonardo da Vinci*, London, 1938, Vol. II, p. 188.

[4] The English edition of 1658 makes no mention of a cylinder, the air being compressed by the bullet being forced down the barrel.

[5] Public Record Office, London, SP. 14/185. This document is undated and may be later than the year ascribed to it by the Public Record Office.

made at a price of 40 crowns each by 'an Ingenier of Fountaines, native of Urbins'. This gun had an air reservoir in the stock which retained its pressure for 24 hours, after which he found that 'the aire or winde doth passe and vanish by insensible pores'. He saw this gun put a ball through a wooden board and knock a sparrow out of a high tree.

The three-foot barrel of Marin's gun was stated to be able to shoot a dart or ball 400 paces. This was probably an exaggeration and the range of 150 paces given for an air-gun purchased in Utrecht in 1655

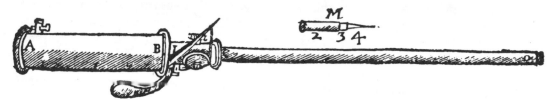

35 Air-gun and dart by Marin le Bourgeoys. From Rivault de Flurance, *Les Élémens de l'Artillerie*, 1607

for the purpose of assassinating Cromwell is more likely. This gun had the advantage of being able to fire seven shots 'with one charging with wynde'.[1]

In 1663 the Royal Society of London began experimenting with a compressing engine and a 'wind gun'. By 1664 it was able to report to its members with some satisfaction that 'a bullet shot a distance of about twenty yards made a very considerable dent in a door, sufficient to have killed a man'.[2] It is interesting to note that M. B. Valentini[3] in 1688 examined in the Gresham College Collection of the Royal Society what he believed to be the most ancient air-gun known. This was presented to the Royal Society by one of their founder members and was in turn given by them to the British Museum in 1781. Its present whereabouts are unknown. Valentini gives a diagrammatic illustration which shows a barrel reservoir gun with a butt pump.

Robert Boyle, the scientist, made some experiments with air-guns in 1674 and devised a gun in which the barrel also acted as the casing for a separate pump. A diagonally-mounted non-return valve of the plunger and poppet type served for both the inlet and discharge of air.[4]

By the end of the seventeenth century it can be seen that several kinds of air-guns were well known, although they were still in the category of high-priced curiosities. Johann Georg Güntner (1646–1726), who worked in Basle from 1686 to 1707, is reported to have charged 100 gold pistoles for his magnificent repeating air-guns.[5]

Whether single-shot or repeating, air-guns can be divided into three main classes.

Spring-Guns[6]

In this type of air-gun a spring-propelled piston or bellows-plunger forces sufficient air into the breech to discharge the ball or dart. The oldest existing specimens of air-guns are in this class. There are the two

[1] Thurloe's *State Papers*, London, 1742.

[2] Thomas Birch, *The History of the Royal Society*, London, 1756, Vol. I, p. 367.

[3] *Museum Museorum*, Frankfurt, 1704–14, Vol. III, Plate XX.

[4] *The Philosophical Works of Robert Boyle*, London, 1725, Vol. II, pp. 562–4.

[5] E. Major, 'Ein Luftgewehr des Basler Erfinders Johann Georg Güntner (1646–1726)', *Historisches Museum Basel Jahresberichte und Rechnungen*, Basle, 1933, pp. 43–7.

[6] Strictly speaking this term should be applied only to guns where the spring is in contact with the bullet and throws it out by its own momentum and not that of compressed air. Some of the cheaper models of modern air-guns work on this principle.

sixteenth-century guns in the Kunsthistorisches Museum, Vienna (Nos. D. 159 and D. 326), and the sixteenth-century gun in the Livrustkammaren, Stockholm (**728**). The last is completely covered in fine woollen velvet and has mounts of engraved and gilded copper. When the collection of guns at Ettersburg Castle, Saxony, was sold in 1927 an air-gun (No. 38) was catalogued as having a barrel dated 1580, but it has not been possible to confirm this. The earliest dated specimen otherwise is the spring air-gun in the Brahe-Bielke armoury at Skokloster, Sweden. This has a barrel dated 1637.

In spite of this early appearance in Europe, the spring air-gun seems to have quickly gone out of fashion and it did not return to popularity until the middle of the nineteenth century, and then in America. Here they were used mainly on indoor shooting ranges. They are nearly all smooth-bores and breechloaders, and they have the same basic mechanism of a short compression cylinder placed between the barrel and lock, powered by a double volute spring piston. This piston could be wound up in three ways: by a detachable crank inserted in the side of the action (**744**); by a folding trigger guard; or by a cocking lever attached to the stock.[1]

Some of the last type were also fitted with a hand-revolved bullet cylinder. One of the best-known makers, Charles Bunge of Geneva, N.Y., secured a patent in 1869 for a 'Revolving Spring Toy Gun'. This patent shows a drawing of a 55-shot gun, but actual examples rarely have more than 12-shot cylinders.

In 1876 Henry Quackenbush of Herkimer, N.Y., patented the first of a number of cheap mass-made spring air-guns. These had simple mechanisms, forged iron or pressed steel frames, and were quickly cocked by pushing in the barrel or, when it was hinged to the action, by bending it. With their arrival the expensive hand-made gallery gun disappeared.

Bellows Guns

As the name suggests, in these guns the air is pumped into the barrel by the sudden closing of a pair of bellows concealed in the butt. Power is obtained from one or two powerful V-shaped springs. A strong key or crank is inserted in the side of the butt to open the bellows. In outward appearance the bellows gun is remarkably like the later type of wheellock gun, with the same full stock, heavy butt and finger looped trigger guard. Existing specimens, however, nearly all date to the eighteenth and early nineteenth century. The bellows gun is the weakest of all the air-guns and was probably used mainly for indoor use. In the absence of fire and high chamber pressure the makers have in nearly every case been able to construct a simple butt joint breech, the barrel in its wooden fore-stock being flexed open for loading. Many barrels are fitted with a brass liner, another indication of their low power. Signed specimens show that there was a limited area of production in an oval bounded by Nuremberg, Prague, Munich and Vienna.

Pump-up Air-Guns

This class of air-guns differs from the previous two in that the charge of compressed air for each shot is taken from a reservoir or receiver on the gun which has been previously pumped up to the required pressure. The air reservoir can be a tube placed concentrically round the barrel, a container in the butt, or a metal sphere screwed on to the barrel.

[1] Eldon G. Wolff, *op. cit.*, divides American spring-guns into five classes according to their geographical location, e.g. Primary New York City, Upstate New York, etc.

The earliest examples of these guns are the two preserved in the Royal Armoury, Stockholm, signed on the barrels HANS KOHLER VON KITZING ANNO 1644 (**724**).[1] The air reservoir on these guns is built round the barrel and is charged by a pump in the butt. When the trigger is pressed the valve of the reservoir is opened and all the air is expelled. Another early group of air-guns consists of two guns (**726–7**) and a pair of pistols made by George Fehr of Dresden, a regimental gunsmith in the service of the Elector of Saxony. The barrels of the guns are dated 1653 and 1655. The same type of reservoir and pump is incorporated in these guns, but a more complicated lock is arranged so that when the gun is fired the valve is only opened momentarily to release sufficient air for one shot, and it is then closed. Once the reservoir is pumped up it can be used for several shots. A common feature of the Fehr guns is a brass cock shaped like a lion. The lock-plate of an air-gun in the Brahe-Bielke armoury at Skokloster (**729**) is engraved with a hunting scene which shows a man pumping up his gun. His foot is placed on the pump handle while he lifts the gun up and down, bringing the weight of the gun to add power to his stroke.

The barrel reservoir guns remained popular during the first half of the eighteenth century, the only difference being that the lock was shaped externally to look like a flintlock. The outstanding maker of this period was Johann Gottfried Kolbe, who worked in London *c.* 1730–40, and then at Suhl. During his stay in London he made the remarkable air-gun now in the Victoria and Albert Museum (**733**). It is not only a fine example of an air-gun with a barrel reservoir and a butt pump (access to this is obtained by a hinged flat in the butt-plate) but its superb decoration makes it one of the finest silver-mounted arms in existence. Other guns of this type by Kolbe are in the W. Keith Neal Collection and the Glasgow Art Gallery and Museum (**732**).

J. T. Desaguliers, describing one of these guns in 1744, wrote 'an ingenious Workman called L. Colbe has very much improv'd it, by making it a Magazine Wind-gun'.[2] The illustration shows a tube under the barrel containing ten bullets which are fed into the breech by a round conveyor block attached to and revolved by the steel of the lock, which resembles a flintlock. This illustration is found in encyclopaedias of much later date, but no actual specimen by Kolbe is recorded. Another ingenious idea was reported by de la Condamine in 1757.[3] On an air-gun made by Mathi of Turin he found that the air reservoir was filled not by an air pump but by the gas generated by exploding two ounces of gunpowder in a strong closed cylinder of bronze. This produced sufficient energy to discharge 18 successive shots at 60 paces.

The repeating air-gun was to be brought to perfection on another type of air-gun which appears to have originated in Austria in the middle of the century. This has a metal butt reservoir shaped like an elongated cone with a convex base cap. It is unscrewed from the barrel and charged by a separate pump of the syringe type. The lock is all enclosed except for an outside S-shaped cocking lever similar to that used by Pauly on his breechloaders. This type of air-gun may be loaded (1) via the muzzle, (2) by a turn-up breech, or (3) by means of a special magazine and chamber. The latter consists of a transverse block bored with a bullet cavity which by a sideways movement transports the bullet from a tubular magazine alongside the barrel to the breech.

This action was invented or, at least, made practical by B. Girardoni, a gunmaker of Cortina d'Ampezzo in the Southern Tirol. He fitted it to a powerful rifle which after trials in 1779 was approved by the Emperor Joseph II. A factory was set up for the production of 500 rifles by workmen sworn to secrecy, at a contract price of 33 guilders per rifle. The official name for the rifle was the *Repetier-Windbüchse M. 1780*. In 1784 the order was increased to 1,000 rifles at a revised cost of 35 florins each, plus five florins

[1] See Arne Hoff, 'Luftbøsser fra 1600-Årene', *Svenska Vapenhistoriska Sällskapets Skrifter*, Stockholm, N.S. Vol. IV, 1955, pp. 35–56.

[2] *A Course of Experimental Philosophy*, London, 1744, Vol. 2, pp. 398–402.

[3] Charles-Marie de la Condamine, *An Extract from the Observations made in a Tour to Italy*, London, 1768, pp. 174–6.

for an extra receiver and three florins for a hand pump. The first rifles were not issued until 1787 when 200 rifles, each with a pair of spare reservoirs, were sent to the Hungarian frontier for use by sharpshooters. Orders were increased and eventually nearly all battalions received their quota. In 1790, on the accession of the Emperor Leopold, a Tirolese Corps of Sharpshooters of 1,313 men was formed. From 1793 to 1796 the Air Rifle Corps took part in many engagements in the Low Countries and on the Rhine. Difficulties were experienced in servicing the air-rifles, however, and in 1801 only 1,091 were reported still in serviceable condition. They were withdrawn from service in 1815. During the 1848–9 revolt of the Czechs and Hungarians the rifles were re-issued for their last employment.[1]

The few surviving examples show that a serial number was stamped on the action and on the butt reservoir. Some degree of interchangeability is indicated by the specimen in the C. G. Vokes Collection (**737**) which is numbered G.1223 on the action and G.1239 on the butt.

These unique military rifles had a calibre of 13 mm. and the magazine held 20 bullets which could be discharged in less than half a minute. To obtain the necessary air power for this, however, the butt reservoir needed a prolonged and strenuous pumping. Estimates of this vary but it seems likely that at least 500–600 strokes of the light hand pump were required for a full charge of 30–40 atmospheres. This operation might take anything from five to ten minutes, allowing for the pump to cool. It was usual for two men to take part, assisted by a foot treader bar. When fully charged in this manner the rifle was capable of 30 effective shots from one reservoir: ten at 150 yards, ten at 120 yards and ten at 100 yards. The pressure and range then dropped rapidly.

The effect of these shots can be judged by the report of an air-gun maker, E. M. Reilly, in 1850.[2] He found that an air pressure of 500 lb. per sq. in. (34 atmospheres) was sufficient to shoot 12 balls through a one-inch board at 50 yards range.

The air-gun with its minimum of recoil and noise was also popular in the sporting field. Ludwig VIII, Landgrave of Hesse (1691–1768), was one sportsman who preferred to use air-guns rather than firearms, and in 1747 is reported to have shot many large deer including a stag of 22 points weighing 480 lb. and a large number of wild boar.[3] His collection of air-guns in the armoury at Kranichstein[4] included large-bore seven-grooved rifles of 14 mm. (0·55 in.) for big game, and some with smooth brass barrels averaging only 9·7 mm. (0·382 in.) for small birds or indoor targets. Both barrel and butt reservoir types were included, and three guns with flintlocks could be used either for air or for gunpowder.

The Austrian butt reservoir type of air-rifle with or without a magazine was the strongest of the air-guns and it is not surprising that it was made in many European countries. Fine decorated examples were the speciality of Joseph Contriner of Vienna (**739**). It was introduced to England by S. H. Staudenmayer who worked in London *c.* 1800–30. Many later examples have a simplified external form of lock mechanism (**749–50**). The only disadvantage of this type of air-gun was its rather awkward shape, and for this reason many sportsmen preferred the conventional shape gun with an air reservoir in the form of a metal sphere (**743**). These ball reservoirs were made of copper, cast iron and steel, but gained an unfortunate reputation for bursting. Enthusiastic shots, having witnessed the maiming or death of a servant while blowing up one of these spheres, followed the action of Captain Lacy who, to use his own words, 'bid a sempiternal adieu to air-guns'.[5]

Another great advocate of the air-gun was the English sportsman, Colonel Thomas Thornton. On a visit to the arms factory at Versailles he hit the mark at 93 yards with his air-gun.[6] It was here that the

[1] August Haller, *Organ der Militärwissenschaftlichen Vereine*, Vienna, 1891, Vol. 42, Pt. I.
[2] E. M. Reilly, Junr., *A Treatise on Airguns*, London, [1850 ?].
[3] E. H. K. Maleyka, *Windbüchsen des 17. und 18. Jahrhunderts als Jagd- und Kriegswaffen*, Berlin, 1905.
[4] See the Catalogue by Karl Hummelsbach in *Der Deutsche Jäger*, 1936.
[5] *The Modern Shooter*, London, 1842, p. 301.
[6] *A Sporting Tour Through Various Parts of France in the Year 1802*, London, 1806.

French general Mortier told him of the deadly effect of the air-rifles in the hands of Austrian snipers, whom the French refused to treat as soldiers and hanged at once when captured.

Such acts of discrimination are typical of the whole history of air-guns, which abounds in instances where some form of prohibition was laid on them. Hans Friedrich von Fleming, writing in 1724, noted that no one was allowed to carry air-rifles unless they were in the service, and that they were completely prohibited in some countries. In 1773 an Edict was passed in Liège banning the manufacture '*de toute sorte de fusils à vent*'.[1] Another Imperial Edict was promulgated from Schönbrunn in 1805 prohibiting the use of air-guns and pistols in France.[2] In 1819 the *Encyclopédie Méthodique* noted that they were still forbidden except in arms collections or in exhibitions of physics apparatus. A Firearms Bill was published in Germany in 1828 prohibiting the use of air-guns of over 7 mm. (0·275 in.) calibre without a licence. It is ironical that in modern England air-guns are exempt from the restrictions of the Firearms Act.

Gas Guns

In 1834 Peder Rasmussen, the inventive town clerk of Rudkøbing, Denmark, was working on a series of percussion revolving arms. A report on his experiments mentioned that he was also working on a gun different from the rest. 'Instead of gunpowder for this gun he intends to use a sort of steam or gas to be generated from a special substance, without the use of fire by the temperature of the atmosphere alone. He hoped to be able to load into the gun, at a time, so large quantities of the substance in question as to suffice for several hundred shots and regularly to fire 20 to 30 rounds a minute. Furthermore the gun has only one barrel but an iron butt like that of an air-gun.'.[3]

The gun was never completed and it has never been established what Rasmussen's special substance was, but it is not beyond the bounds of possibility that it was carbon dioxide, or as it is known to-day dry ice, which was discovered in 1834.

The next inventor to explore the possibilities of carbon dioxide gas as a propellant was more successful. Paul Giffard of Paris (1837–97) was one of two brothers who were responsible for many inventions, including a refrigerator, a steam engine injector, a 'pneumatic telegraph' and other machines for compressing and liquefying air. In 1862 Paul patented in England an air-gun with a pump cylinder under the barrel and an improved type of valve release.

Ten years later he patented in England a breechloading rifle powered by cartridges of compressed or liquefied gas, one of which was needed for each shot. The only example of this patent is the military rifle in the Milwaukee Public Museum. In 1873, however, Giffard patented in America an improved version of his compressed gas gun which had a long cylinder reservoir screwed under the barrel. The final version of this was patented in England in 1889. The reservoir contained sufficient liquefied carbonic acid gas for a large number of shots—one advertisement claimed 300—and could be sent back to the makers for refilling at a small charge. This gun was powerful enough to kill a rook or rabbit at 60 yards, which was the maximum recommended distance. For shorter ranges a different firing pin was used and an increased number of shots was obtained from one reservoir. A special counter on the frame indicated the number of shots left. The guns were made in two bore sizes (both smooth-bore and rifled); in France by the Manufacture Française d'Armes de Saint-Étienne in 6 mm. and 8 mm. calibre, and in London by the Giffard Gun & Ordnance Co. Ltd. in calibres of 0·220 in. and 0·295 in.

Guns powered by small cylinders of liquefied carbon dioxide gas are still being made.

---

[1] Alphonse Polain, *Recherches Historiques sur l'Épreuve des Armes à Feu*, Liège, 1863.
[2] Marquis de Jouffroy, *Dictionnaire des Inventions*, Paris, 1852.
[3] Arne Hoff, *The Rasmussen Revolving Guns*, Tøjhusmuseets Skrifter 4, Copenhagen, 1946, p. 25.

Steam Guns

One of the strongest propulsive powers known to man, steam, was never successfully applied to guns, although efforts to do so were made from an early date. Leonardo da Vinci has left us a drawing of a steam gun (**36**) about which he made the following notes:

> The *architronito* is a machine of fine copper, an invention of Archimedes, and it throws iron balls with a great noise and fury. It is used in this manner: the third part of the instrument stands within a great quantity of burning coals and when it has been thoroughly heated by these it tightens the screw *d* which is above the cistern of water *abc* and as the screw above becomes tightened it will cause that below to become loosened. And when consequently the water has fallen out it will descend into the heated part of the machine, and then it will instantly become charged with so much steam that it will seem marvellous, and especially when one sees its fury and hears its roar. This machine has driven a ball weighing one talent six stadia [about 80 pounds approx. ¾ mile].[1]

36 The *architronito* steam gun by Leonardo da Vinci

It is not until late in the eighteenth century when the first steps towards the exploitation of steam were being made that the next references to steam guns are found. In the Fitch Papers in the Library of Congress, Washington, there is a document describing experiments made on 18 April 1797 with a steam-operated musket by three Philadelphians, G. Turner, Richard Wells and R. Storkton. In 1819 another American, Captain Samuel Money of Orford, New Hampshire, obtained a patent for 'shooting by steam'.

According to the *Annales des Sciences Militaires* of 1824, however, he was forestalled by General Girard of France, who in 1814 constructed a boiler on wheels which supplied steam to a group of six musket barrels. These were fed from a hopper with balls at the rate of 180 per minute.

Very little is known about any of these guns and the only steam gun to be properly demonstrated was the Perkins Steam Gun. Jacob Perkins (1766–1894), a native of Newport, Mass., U.S.A., began his experiments in London in 1824[2] in a building by Water Lane. Here a musket barrel six feet long was connected through the wall to a steam generator. The tremendous power of steam was vividly illustrated when under a pressure of 45 atmospheres a lead ball liquefied when it hit the iron target. This machine was said to be capable of firing 240 shots per minute.

Perkins then took out a British patent (No. 4952) for 'an improved mode of throwing shells'. These shells were really cylindrical rockets filled with water and closed at the rear end with a fusible metal plug. They were heated in a suitable barrel or discharge tube until the plug melted. The water was then converted to steam in the manner of the *architronito* and the shell was driven out of the barrel. Next Perkins

[1] E. MacCurdy, *The Notebooks of Leonardo da Vinci*, London, 1938, Vol. II, p. 188.
[2] See *Annual Register*.

took over a factory near Regents Park and here on 6 December 1825 he demonstrated an improved model of his steam machine-gun before the officials of the Office of Ordnance, including the Duke of Wellington.

Although the British Government could not be convinced of the gun's utility a rifled 4-pdr. gun which fired 28–30 rounds per minute was ordered by the French Government.

This was tested successfully at Blackheath in 1828 but when it was fired over a longer range it did not possess the necessary power.[1]

The original Perkins machine-gun was exhibited as a curiosity at the Adelaide Gallery of Practical Science, Strand, in 1832 and at the Salford Mechanical Institute in 1840.[2] Perkins's son, Angier, and grandson, Loftus, carried on the experiments and adopted Henry Giffard's steam injector in an endeavour to increase the gun's performance. It was exhibited again at the Great Exhibition of 1851. In 1861 the Perkinses reported the last trial of a gun with an improved rifled barrel using Minié bullets of $1\frac{1}{2}$ oz., which they affirmed had been in operation for ten consecutive hours and had fired 60 balls per minute.[3]

Having noted the apparatus needed for this—the furnace, the generator and a complicated array of pipes and valves—and the fact that the gun used water at the rate of 100 gallons per hour, the military powers perhaps rightly refused to have anything to do with it.

A further instance of the use of steam was in the breechloading gun patented by Henry Bessemer in 1854. Here the power of steam was added to that of the recoil to produce an automatic firing and reloading action.

Electric Guns

Although electricity itself as far as one knows was never used to power guns within the period covered by this book, it is of interest to note the affair of the 'Electric Gun' demonstrated by Thomas Beningfield before an Ordnance Committee in London in 1845. According to a printed pamphlet issued by the

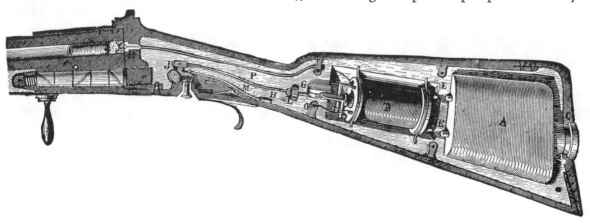

37 Electric-spark gun of Le Baron and Delmas, patented in France, 1866

inventor and labelled '*SIVA or the Destroying Power*', it was capable of firing 1,000 to 1,200 shots per minute.[4] The Committee actually saw it firing lead balls of 48 to the lb. on a 35-yards range. All who

[1] G. and D. Bathe, *Jacob Perkins*, The Historical Society of Philadelphia, 1943, p. 110.
[2] See *Historical Account & Description of Perkins' Patent Steam Gun*, Manchester, 1840.
[3] A. N. and L. Perkins, *Perkins Steam Gun*, London, 1861.
[4] Public Record Office, London, WO. 44/620.

watched its performance were impressed by it, including the Duke of Wellington. Unfortunately the inventor would not tell the Ordnance how the gun worked or let them examine it and they in their turn would have nothing to do with it until he did. Beningfield never patented his gun and never gave a proper explanation of how it worked. A report which appeared in the *Illustrated London News* for 21 June 1845 stated that propulsion was effected by 'the application of gases exploded by galvanic electricity'. William Greener the gunmaker asserted that the gases (presumably a mixture of hydrogen and oxygen) were generated by the decomposition of water by means of powerful galvanic batteries.[1]

Electricity was also used as a means of ignition. An electric discharging device for ordnance and other firearms was patented in England by W. E. Newton in 1863 (No. 30), and, in 1866, Le Baron and Delmas patented in France a gun with a special cartridge with negative and positive connections fired by an electric spark. This was generated by a bichromate of potash battery and an induction coil housed in the butt (**37**). A less weighty and simplified apparatus was used in another electric gun patented by H. Pieper in England in 1883. No advantage seems to have been gained by either of these guns and W. W. Greener reported that the first one was liable to unpleasant vibrations.[2]

Mention can also be made here of the gun patented in England in 1888 by A. Mühle and E. Franke which used an ingenious electrical device as a substitute for normal sights. The trigger was connected to the armature of an electro-magnet housed in the butt, and could only be released when the gun was at the proper elevation for the required range. This effect was achieved by a drop of mercury moving in an adjustable glass tube and completing the electric circuit when the pre-set angle was reached.

Elastic Guns

Having described how the mighty forces of nature were harnessed to the needs of the gun barrel it is perhaps appropriate to end with a note on the humble qualities of elastic. Working much on the principle of the crossbow, a few guns were made which were powered by strong strands of elastic and can be better described as catapult guns.

In 1849 Richard Edwards Hodges was granted an English patent for 'Improvements in mechanical purchases, which are also applicable in whole or part to projectiles'. Guns made under this patent are often well decorated with moulded brass muzzles and German silver locks (**768–9**).

India-rubber was also used to power the air-gun of J. Shaw of Glossop, patented in 1849 (No. 12728) and exhibited at the Great Exhibition of 1851. The following explanation of it appeared in the *Official Catalogue* (Vol. I, p. 357):

> Without any previous pumping, the requisite pressure of air for discharge is procured instantly at the pull of the trigger, by a single stroke of a condensing syringe, actuated by a previously extended India-rubber spring.

[1] William Greener, *The Science of Gunnery*, 2nd edn., London, 1846, p. 298.
[2] *The Gun and Its Development*, London, 1910, pp. 511–12.

HAND CANNON   **38** Iron hand cannon. Early 15th century. *Historisches Museum, Bern* (No. 2195). *L. 25·6 in.*   **39** Hand cannon with hook (*Hakenbüchse*). Late 14th century. *Historisches Museum, Bern* (No. 2193). *B. 7·3 in.*   **40** Bronze hand cannon with hook found in the sea near Mörkö, Sweden. *German (?)*, late 14th century. *National Historical Museum, Stockholm* (No. 23136). *L. 7·6 in. Cal. 0·65 in.*   **41** Bronze hand cannon. Late 15th century. Found near Frankenburg. *Historisches Museum, Bern* (No. 2200). *B. 34·3 in. Cal. 1·2 in.*   **42** Iron hand cannon found at Vedelspang, S. Schleswig, on the site of a castle destroyed in 1426. *German* or *Danish, c.* 1400. *Tøjhusmuseet, Copenhagen* (No. B. 1). *B. 8·3 in. Cal. 0·6 in.*

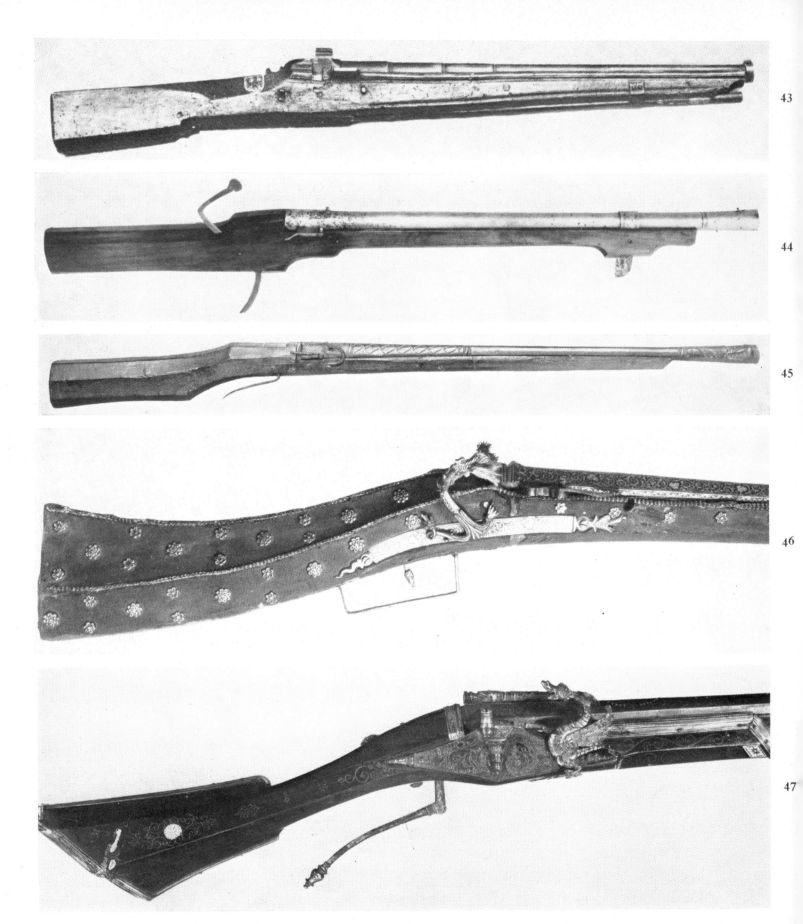

MATCHLOCK GUNS **43** Bronze barrel rifled with 12–14 grooves. Snap-matchlock missing. Coat of arms painted on stock indicates made for Maximilian I between 1493 and 1508. *German, c.* 1500. *W. G. Renwick Collection.* **44** Serpentine lock with one-piece cock and trigger. Stock a reconstruction. *German, late 16th century. Muzeum Wojska Polskiego, Warsaw* (No. 299x). *B.* 38·8 in. *Cal.* 0·9 in. **45** Sear lock. Stock reconstructed. Iron barrel with muzzle carved as dragon's head. *Swiss or N. Italian, mid 16th century. Historisches Museum, Bern* (No. 2206). *B.* 46·2 in. *Cal.* 0·65 in. **46** Lock and barrel damascened in gold. Stock covered with black velvet studded with silver rosettes. *Italian, c.* 1530. *Kunsthistorisches Museum, Vienna* (No. D. 156). **47** Sear lock, with cock chiselled in the form of a dragon. Lock and barrel gilded and encrusted with silver. Ebony stock inlaid with brass wire and stag-horn. *French, early 17th century. Odescalchi Collection, Rome.*

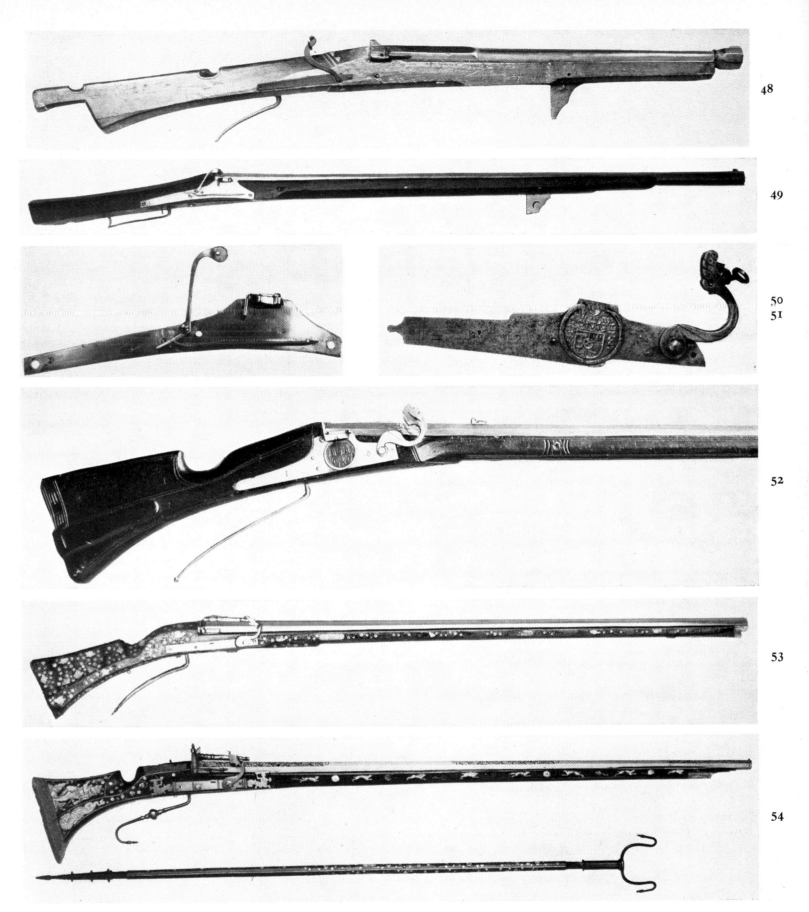

MATCHLOCK GUNS **48** Sear lock. Bronze barrel with hook. *Swiss, late 16th century. Historisches Museum, Bern* (No. 2209). *B.* 35·6 in. *Cal.* 0·79 in. **49** Wall piece with snap-matchlock. *German, barrel dated 1562. Tower of London Armouries* (No. XII–5). *B.* 53¾ in. *Cal.* 0·85 in. **50** Close-up of the lock of **49**. **51** Detached tricker lock. Brass medallion with coat of arms. *Austrian, c. 1600. Victoria and Albert Museum* (No. M57–1912). **52** Sear-lock musket. *German (Suhl), lock dated 1607. Tøjhusmuseet, Copenhagen* (No. B 412). *B.* 41·9 in. *Cal.* 0·55 in. **53** Sear lock. Stock inlaid with mother-of-pearl and brass wire. *German* (?), *late 16th century. Royal Army Museum, Stockholm* (No. AM 25569). *B.* 42·7 in. *Cal.* 0·6 in. **54** Musket with rest. Sear lock bears Amsterdam mark. *Dutch, late 16th century. Livrustkammaren, Stockholm* (No. 1197 a & b). *B.* 49·5 in. *Cal.* 0·74 in.

55

56

57

58

MATCHLOCK GUNS **55** Musket with tricker lock and copper barrel. *Swedish, c. 1625. Livrustkammaren, Stockholm* (No. 1228). *B. 34 in. Cal. 1·6 in.* **56** Musket with tricker lock. Barrel bears proof mark of Blacksmith's Company and maker's mark IW (John Watson?). *English, c. 1640. Tower of London* (No number). *B. 48 in. Cal. 0·75 in.* **57** Musket with tricker lock. *English, c. 1690. Tower of London* (No. XII–36). *B. 46 in. Cal. 0·75 in.* **58** Sporting gun with tricker lock. Stock inlaid with steel tracery. *N. Italian (Brescia), late 17th century. Capodimonte Museum, Naples.*

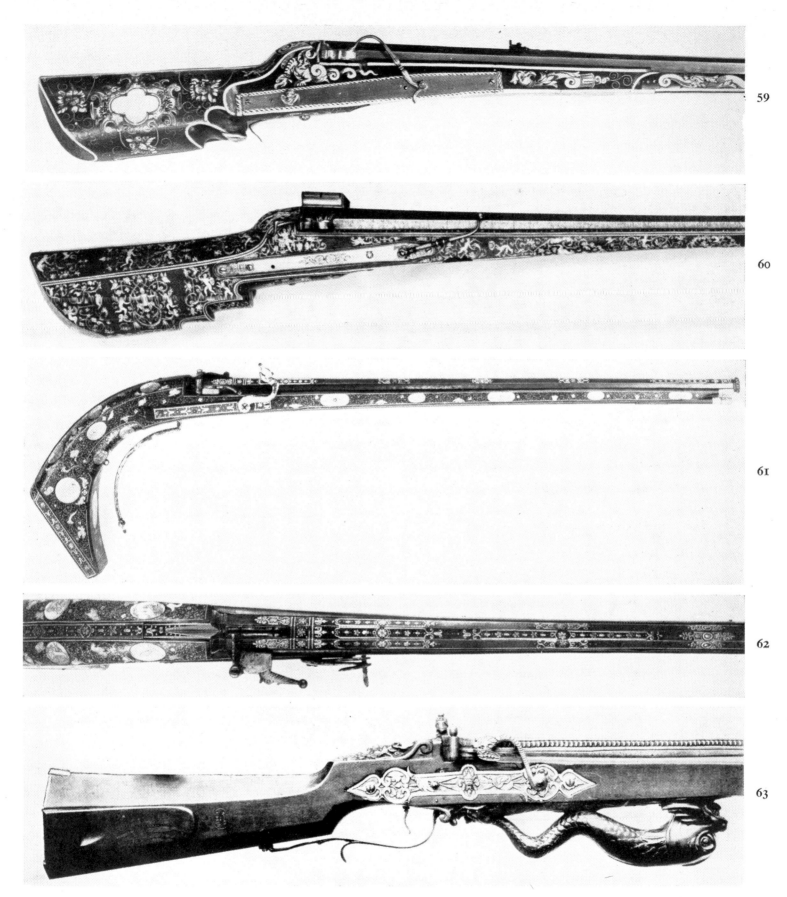

59

60

61

62

63

DECORATED MATCHLOCK GUNS **59** Snap-matchlock. Chestnut-wood stock inlaid with engraved stag-horn. *German, c.* 1600. *Windsor Castle* (No. 351). *B.* 44¼ in. *Cal.* 0·61 in. **60** Snap-matchlock. Pear-wood stock inlaid with engraved stag-horn. Barrel rifled with 12 grooves. *German* (possibly *Nuremberg*), dated 1598. *Wallace Collection* (No. A. 1072). *B.* 38½ in. *Cal.* 0·55 in. **61** Petronel with sear lock. Stock inlaid with mother-of-pearl and brass. *French,* late 16th century. *Tower of London* (No. XII–1548). *B.* 25½ in. *Cal.* 0·44 in. **62** Top view of breech of **61** showing gold decoration on barrel. **63** Musket from the *Cabinet d'Armes* of Louis XIII. Stock bears arms of Cardinal Richelieu. Barrel chiselled and gilt. *French, c.* 1625. *Army Museum, Paris* (No. M. 37). *B.* 49·1 in. *Cal.* 0·5 in.

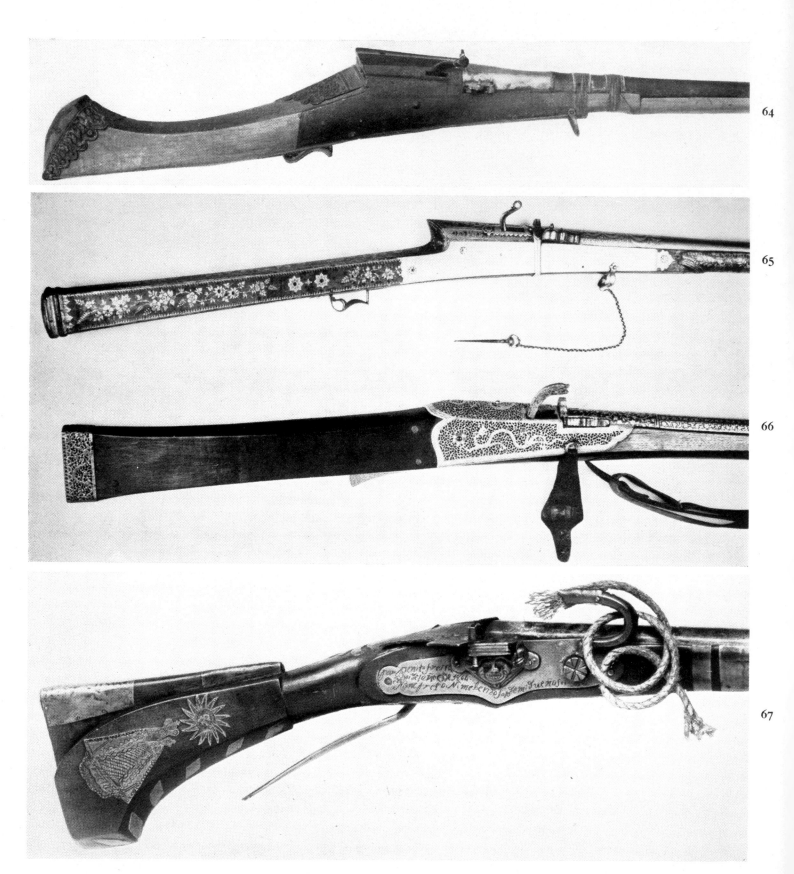

INDIAN AND SPANISH MATCHLOCKS **64** Stock with brass-gilt mounts. *Indian*, 18th century. *C. G. Vokes Collection*. **65** Silver lock-plates. Stock lacquered a brilliant green and painted with silver and gilt flowers. Barrel decorated with gold *koftgari* work. *Indian (Deccan)*, late 18th century. *Wallace Collection* (No. 1983). *B.* 47 in. **66** Mahogany stock. Lock and heel-plates of gilded iron, pierced with dragon and clouds design. *Bhutanese*, mid 18th century. *Wallace Collection* (No. 2003). **67** Iron barrel with flaring brass muzzle. Brass inlay on stock. *Spanish American*, dated 1844. *Royal Scottish Museum, Edinburgh* (No. 1894. 133). *L.* 41½ in. *Cal.* 0.62 in. (*See p. 99.*)

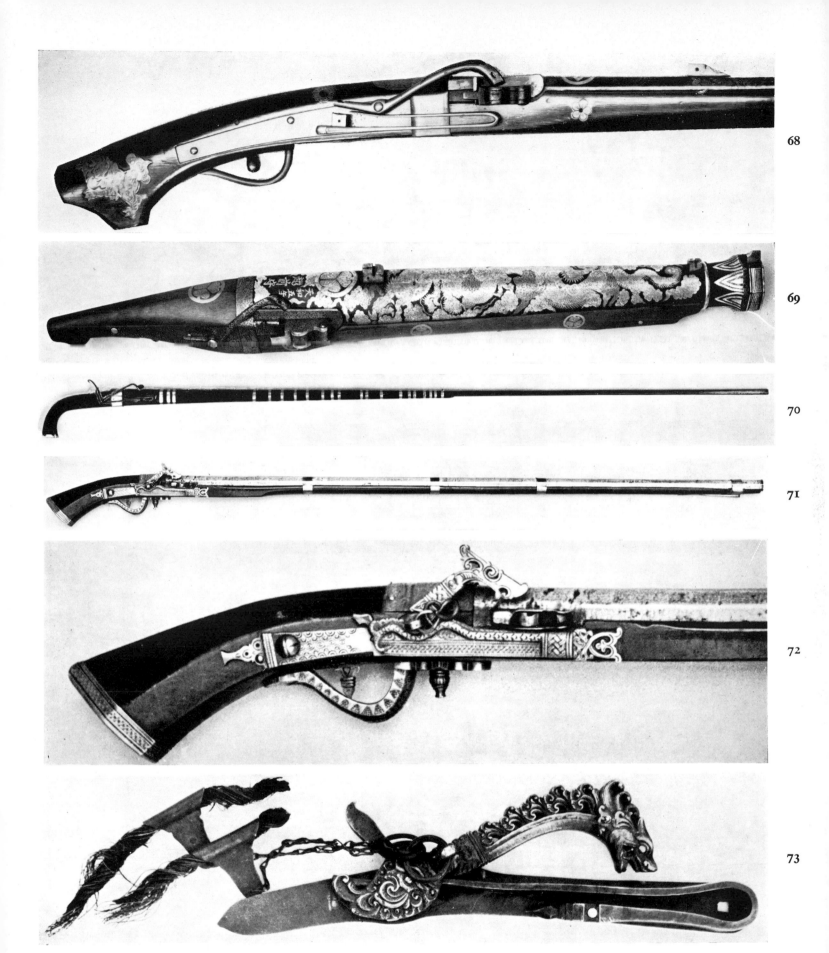

ORIENTAL MATCHLOCK GUNS   **68** Brass lock. Barrel inlaid with badge of the Ii family. Made by Tanaka Nihei of Settsu province. *Japanese, 18th century, Victoria and Albert Museum* (No. M. 969–1928). B. 28·7 in.   **69** Wall gun. Barrel and lock richly decorated in silver and gold. *Japanese, dated 1685 (barrel) and 1852 (stock). British Museum,* L. 40·3 in. *Cal.* 1·4 in. (*See p.* 99.)   **70** Black stock. Silver barrel bands. *Chinese (Mi'ao Chiang), 19th century. Metropolitan Museum, New York* (No. 36.25.2145). *L.* 78 in.   **71** Polished black stock. Lock and mounts of heavy chased brass. *Malayan, 18th century. Metropolitan Museum, New York* (No. 36.25.2187). *L.* 59 in.   **72** Close-up of butt and lock of **71**.   **73** Detached lock of heavy cast brass with two pieces of match attached. *Javanese, 18th century. Private Collection.*

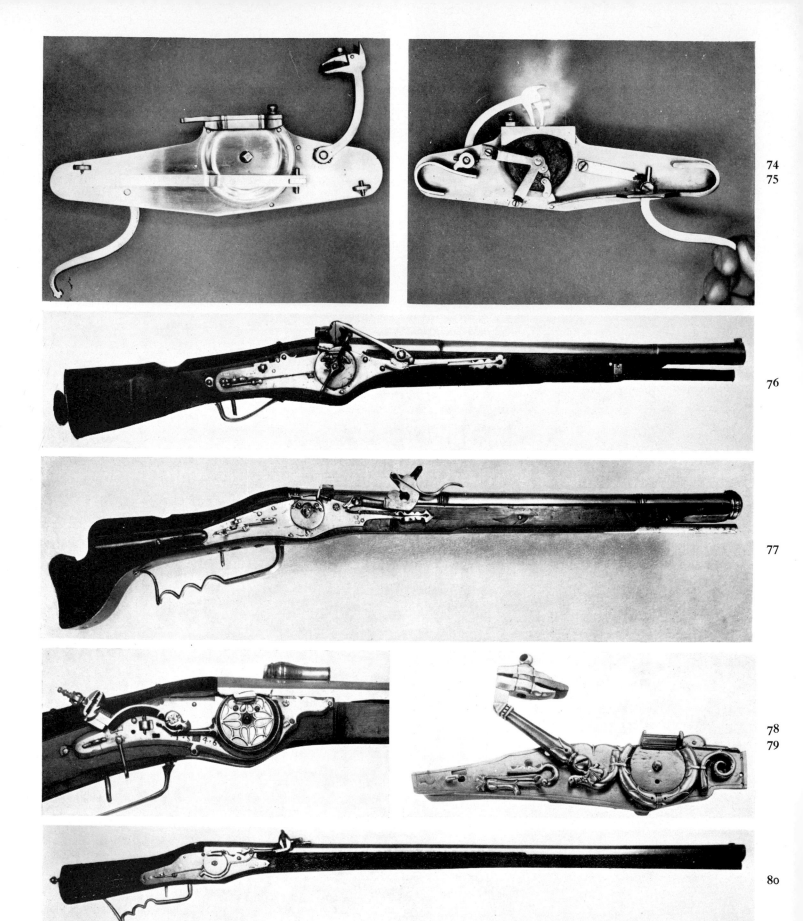

74
75
76
77
78
79
80

EARLY WHEELLOCK GUNS **74** Modern reconstruction of the Leonardo da Vinci wheellock. *A. C. Carpenter Collection.* **75** Rear view of the same lock being fired. **76** The earliest dated wheellock. Carbine of Emperor Charles V. Bears the mark of Bartholme Marquart of Augsburg. *S. German, dated 1530. Royal Armoury, Madrid* (No. K. 32). **77** Stock bears the arms and initials of Otto Heinrich, Count Palatine of the Rhine (d. 1559). *S. German (Augsburg), dated 1533. Bayerisches Nationalmuseum, Munich. B. 21·8 in. Cal. 0·75 in.* **78** Lock with sickle-shaped cock-spring marked with the arms of the monastery of Monserrat, Spain. *S. German, dated 1546. Royal Armoury, Madrid* (No. K. 7). *L. 40·5 in. Cal. 0·75 in.* **79** Detached lock with sickle-shaped cock-spring and self-spanning gear. *S. German, c. 1550. Victoria and Albert Museum* (No. 701-1927). **80** Stock veneered with stag-horn. *German, c. 1535. Tower of London* (No. XII-1566). *B. 37 in. Cal. 0·72 in.*

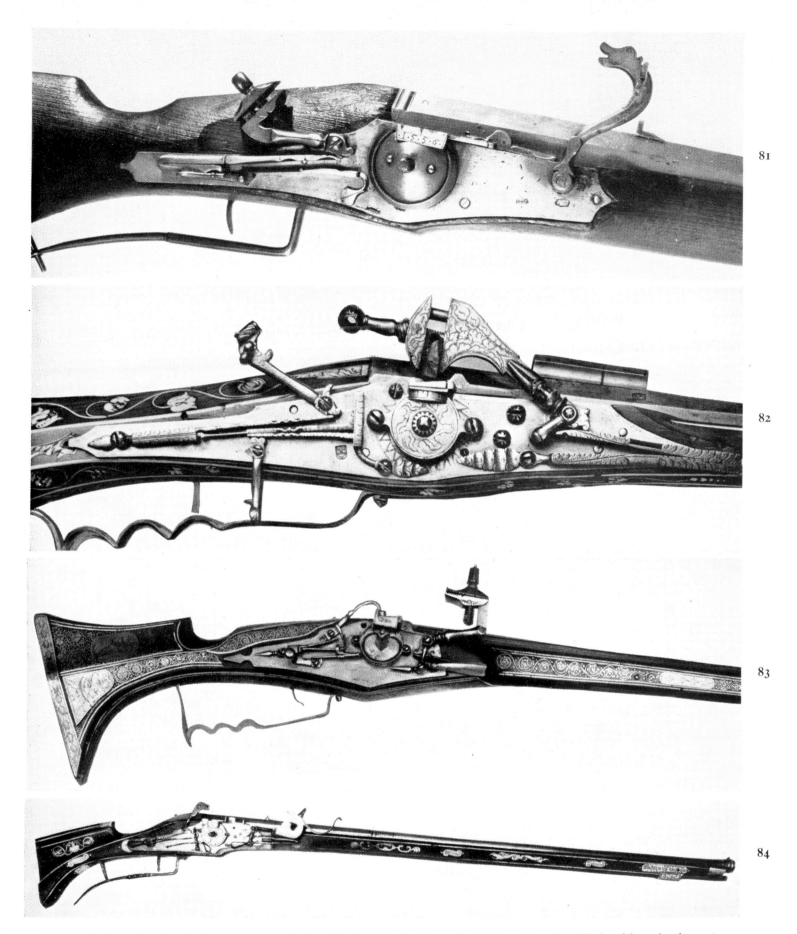

COMBINED WHEELLOCK AND MATCHLOCK GUNS **81** One of 148 Nuremberg '*Halbhakens*' bought through the merchant Georg Liebenauer for Turkish campaign of 1556. Barrel made in Suhl (?). New stock fitted *c.* 1600 during Thirty Years War. *German, dated* 1556. *Historisches Museum, Vienna. B.* 46·97 in. *Cal.* 0·43 in. **82** Lock of gun bearing proof marks of Bern and maker's mark of Vyt Läberli. *Swiss, dated* 1564. *Historisches Museum, Bern* (No. 2225). *B.* 42·5 in. *Cal.* 0·51 in. **83** Stock inlaid with stag-horn plaques and brass scroll-work. Barrel bears maker's mark PL. *Dutch, mid 16th century. Formerly W. R. Hearst Collection. L.* 61 in. **84** Stock inlaid with stag-horn. Brass over cover wheel of lock. *German, dated* 1603. *Tower of London* (No. XII–52). *B.* 39 in. *Cal.* 0·63 in.

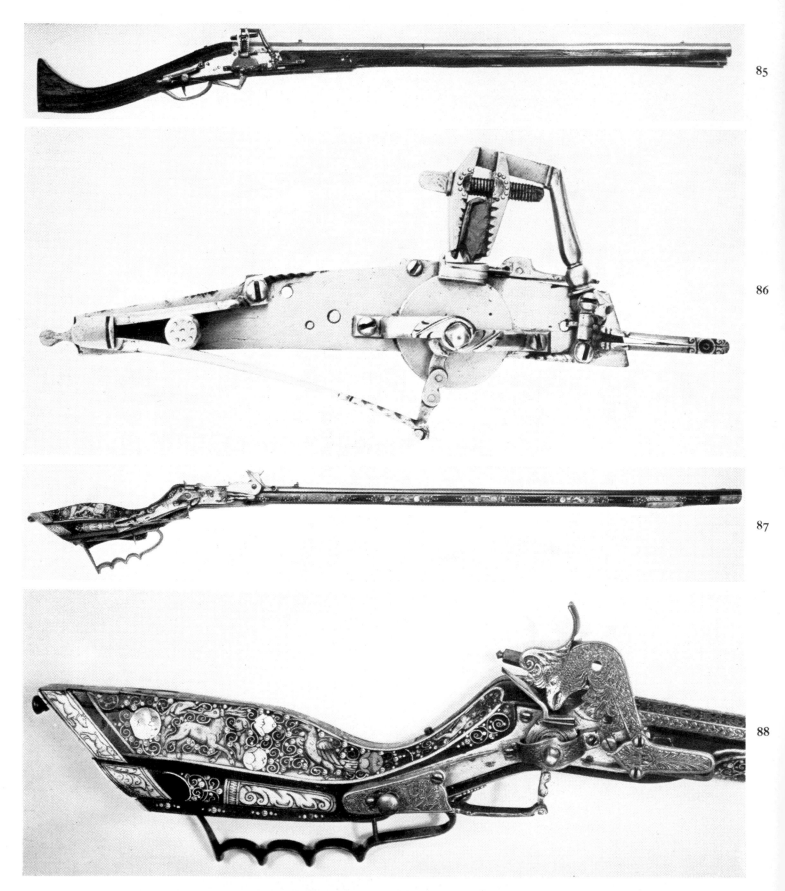

WHEELLOCKS WITH EXTERIOR MAINSPRINGS **85** Gun with plain stock. *Italian, 16th century. National Museum of Artillery, Turin* (No. 2716–M. 5). **86** Close-up of lock of **85.** Button in the V of the mainspring is used to push sear into engagement. **87** Rifle (*Tschinke*). Barrel mark TR. *Silesian, c. 1620. Tower of London* (No. XII–1216). *B.* 37¼ in. *Cal.* 0·3 in.
88 Rifle (*Tschinke*). Chiselled and gilt lock. Walnut stock inlaid with engraved stag-horn and mother-of-pearl. Cheekpiece carries representation of St. George and Dragon. *Silesian, c. 1630. Wallace Collection* (No. A. 1105). *B.* 35 in. *Cal.* 0·3 in.

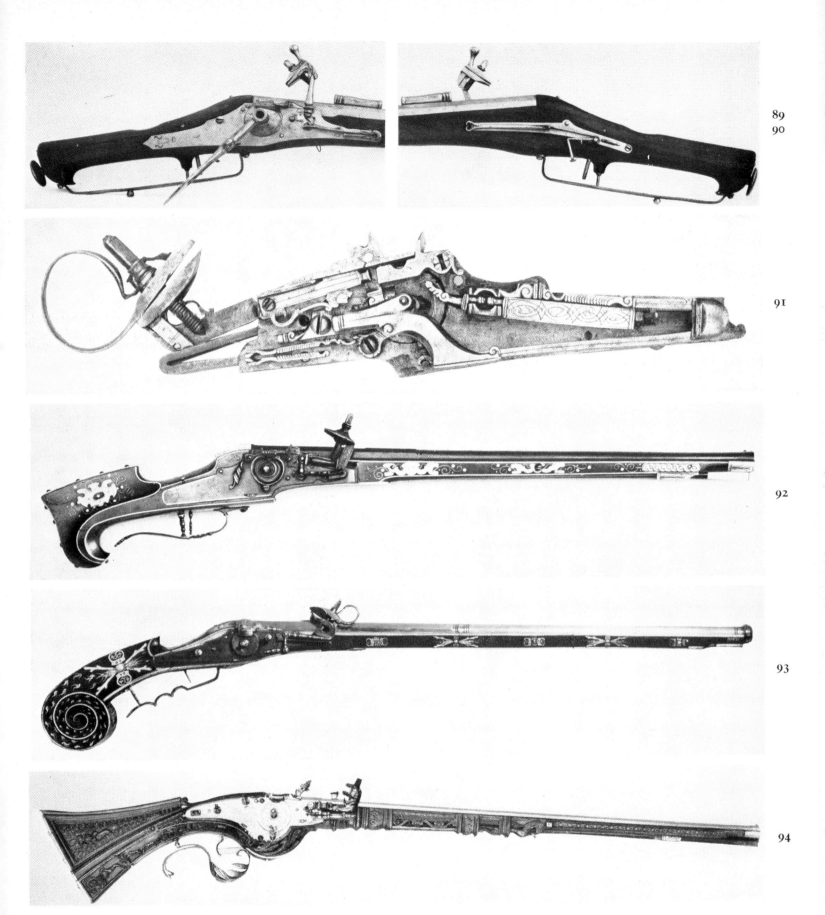

WHEELLOCK GUNS **89–90** Pair of pistol-carbines (*arcabucillos*) of King Philip II. *Spanish, c. 1570. Royal Armoury, Madrid* (Nos. K. 38–9). **91** Interior view of detached wheellock. *German, c. 1580. Author's Collection.* **92** Carbine with sling attachment (on reverse side). Stock inlaid with stag-horn. Later barrel dated 1667. *German, early 17th century. Formerly Victoria and Albert Museum* (No. M. 616–1927). **93** Stock inlaid in stag-horn with the Golden Fleece and the cypher of the Archduke Matthias, later Holy Roman Emperor (1612–19). *German, c. 1600. Kunsthistorisches Museum, Vienna* (No. M. 90). **94** Rifle with deeply carved stock, signed CLAUDE THOMAS A ESPINAL 1623. *French, dated 1623. City Art Museum, St. Louis, U.S.A.* (No. 70.39). *L. 47·6 in.*

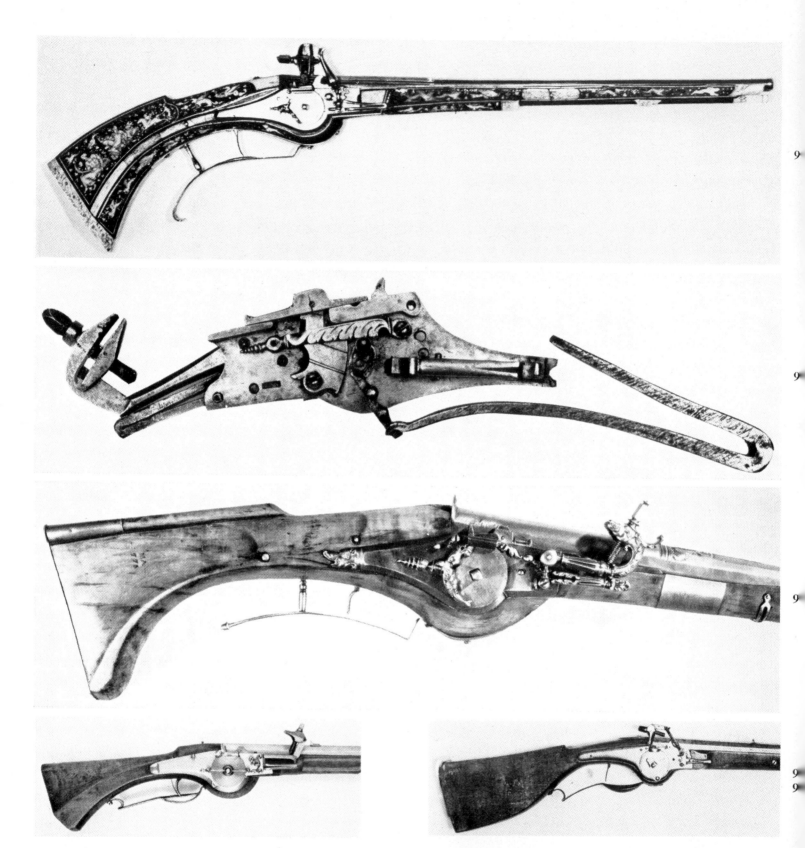

WHEELLOCK GUNS **95** Petronel with French-type wheellock. Lock and barrel restored. *French, c. 1600. A. C. Carpenter Collection. B. 21½ in. Cal. 0·38 in.* **96** Detached French-type wheellock. Interior view showing separate mainspring. *French, c. 1570. Tower of London (No. XII–1068).* **97** French-type wheellock mounted with Turkish barrel. From the *Cabinet d'Armes* of Louis XIII of France (1610–43). *French, early 17th century. Victoria and Albert Museum (No. M. 12–1949). L. 72 in. Cal. 0·75 in.* **98** Musket. *German, c. 1620. Tøjhusmuseet, Copenhagen (No. B. 390). B. 30 in. Cal. 0·92 in.* **99** Carbine. *German, mid 17th century. Royal Army Museum, Stockholm (No. AM. 4071). B. 25·2 in. Cal. 0·67 in.*

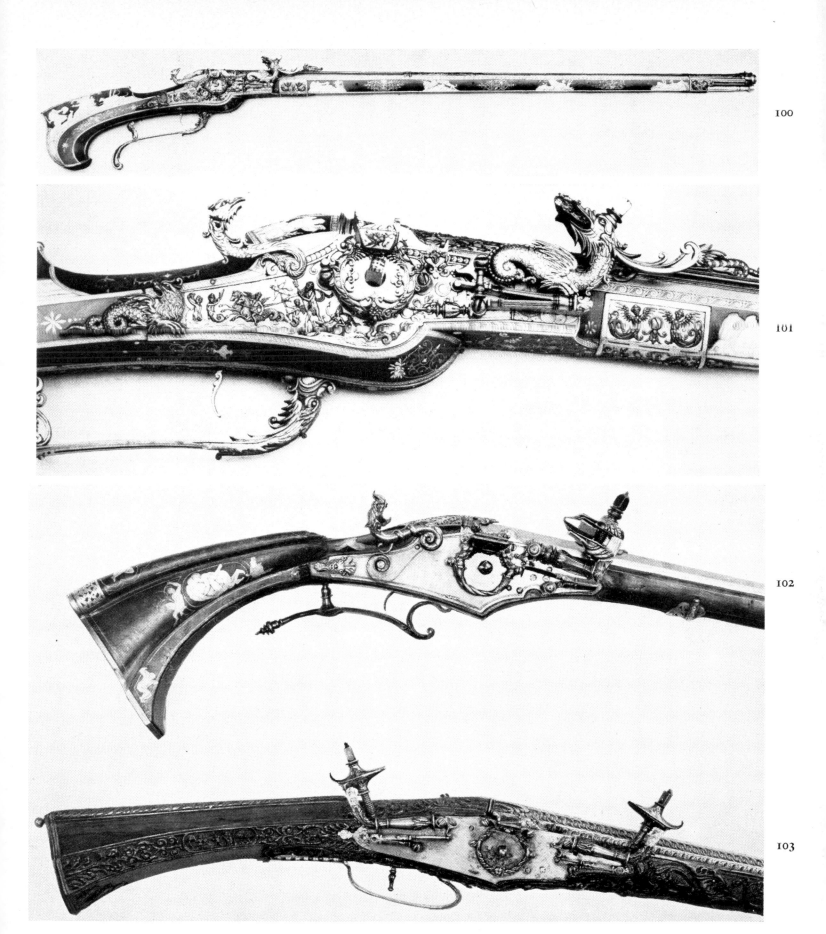

100

101

102

103

DECORATED WHEELLOCK GUNS **100** Combined wheellock and matchlock gun. Lock and barrel elaborately chiselled and blued against a gold-plated background, by Emanuel Sadeler of Munich. Stock inlaid with engraved horn, gold and silver, signed AV [Adam Vischer of Munich]. Made for Duke Maximilian of Bavaria. *German, c. 1600. Royal Armoury, Turin* (No. M. 12). *B.* 50·4 in. *Cal.* 0·71 in. **101** Lock of **100**. **102** Combined wheellock and matchlock gun. Chiselled lock with silver appliqué ornament. Rear-sight in form of reclining female nude. Stock of Italian walnut decorated with silver plaques engraved with erotic scenes. *Italian, c. 1620. Wallace Collection* (No. A. 1074). *B.* 32½ in. *Cal.* 0·5 in. **103** Lock with two cocks serving the same pan. Walnut stock richly carved in relief with foliage and acanthus decoration. *Italian (Brescia), c. 1640. Wallace Collection* (No. A. 1113). *B.* 33½ in. *Cal.* 0·6 in.

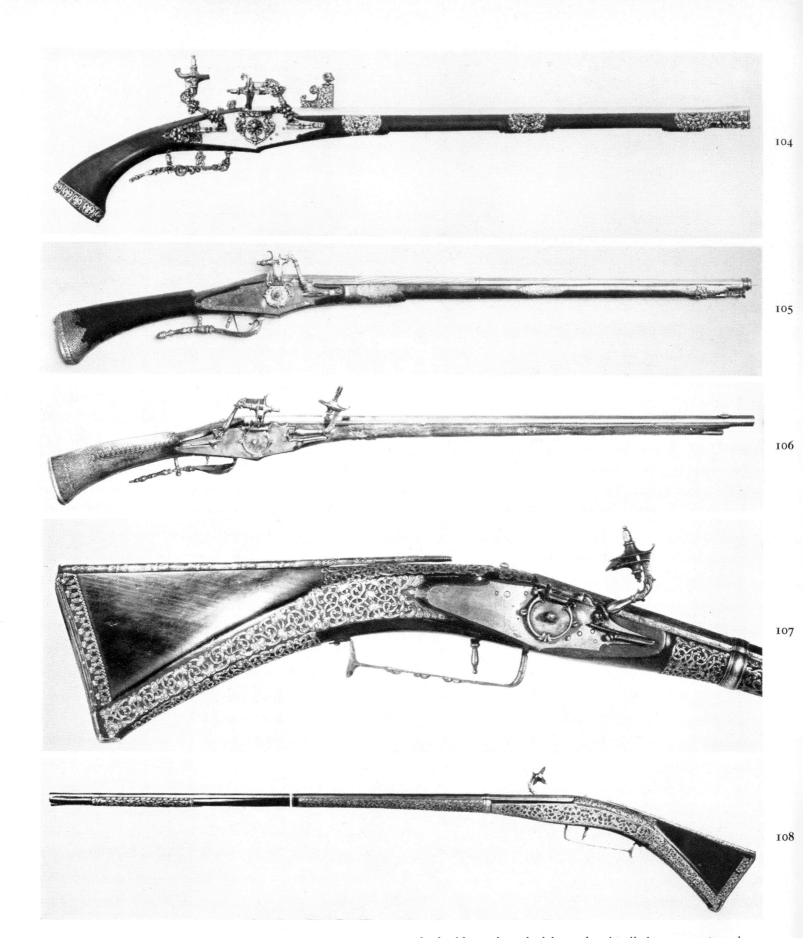

104

105

106

107

108

MEDITERRANEAN WHEELLOCK GUNS **104** Gun with double cock and elaborately chiselled mounts. Barrel signed by Lazarino Cominazzo. *Spanish (Neapolitan), c. 1660. Metropolitan Museum, New York (No. 04.3.162).* **105** Walnut stock with chiselled steel mounts bearing arms of Louis XIII of France (1610–43). Signed LAZZARINO COMINAZZO (barrel) and GIOVANNI ANTONIO GAVACCIOLO (inside lock). *N. Italian (Brescia), c. 1630. Livrustkammaren, Stockholm (No. 1782). B. 30·6 in. Cal. 0·63 in.* **106** Lock with two cocks, marked MM. Walnut stock decorated with steel tracery. *N. Italian, dated 1642. Historisches Museum, Bern (No. 2224). B. 35·3 in. Cal. 0·55 in.* **107–8** Italian lock. Ebony stock decorated with bands of steel repoussé ornament. Barrel marked A PATIS and initials AL. *Sardinian, mid 17th century. Cleveland Museum of Art, Ohio (No. F. 9). B. 36 in.*

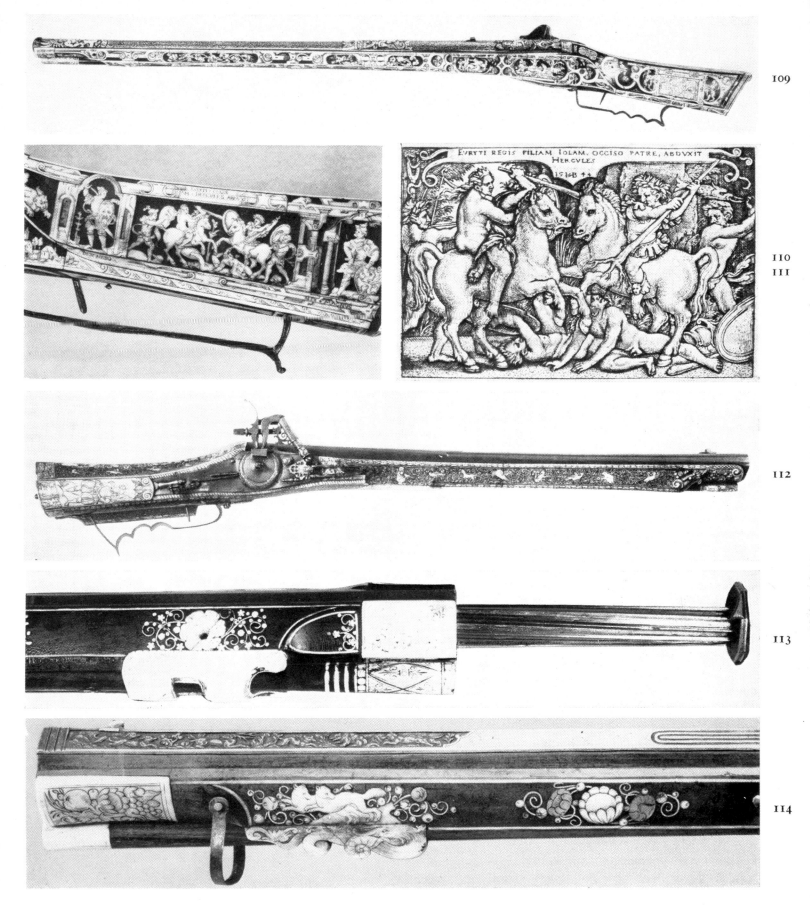

WHEELLOCK GUNS **109** Gun with combined match- and wheellock. Lock and barrel chiselled with satyrs and arabesque strap-work. Walnut stock inlaid with stag-horn strap-work and panels engraved with hunting and battle scenes. Cheek-piece inscribed HERCULES. *German, c. 1550. Wallace Collection* (No. A. 1073). *B. 34 in. Cal. 0·6 in.* **110** Cheek-piece of German wheellock gun *c. 1550* showing stag-horn inlay engraved with the 'Rape of Iole' from the 'Labours of Hercules'. *City Art Museum, St. Louis* (No. 74.39). **111** Original engraving by Hans Sebald Behan dated 1544 from which the decoration on **110** was copied. *City Art Museum, St. Louis* (No. 58.14). **112** Blunderbuss. Stock inlaid with stag-horn. *German, c. 1590. Wallace Collection* (No. A. 1078). *B. 26 in. Oval bore* $1\frac{7}{8} \times 1\frac{3}{16}$ *in.* **113** Muzzle of rifle inscribed CASPAR SOMMERFELD IN BRESLAW 1668, showing detachable small-bore rifled insert. *Kremlin, Moscow* (No. 6493). **114** Muzzle of wheellock rifle by Lorenz Helbe. *Strassburg, c. 1660. Historisches Museum, Bern* (No. 2306).

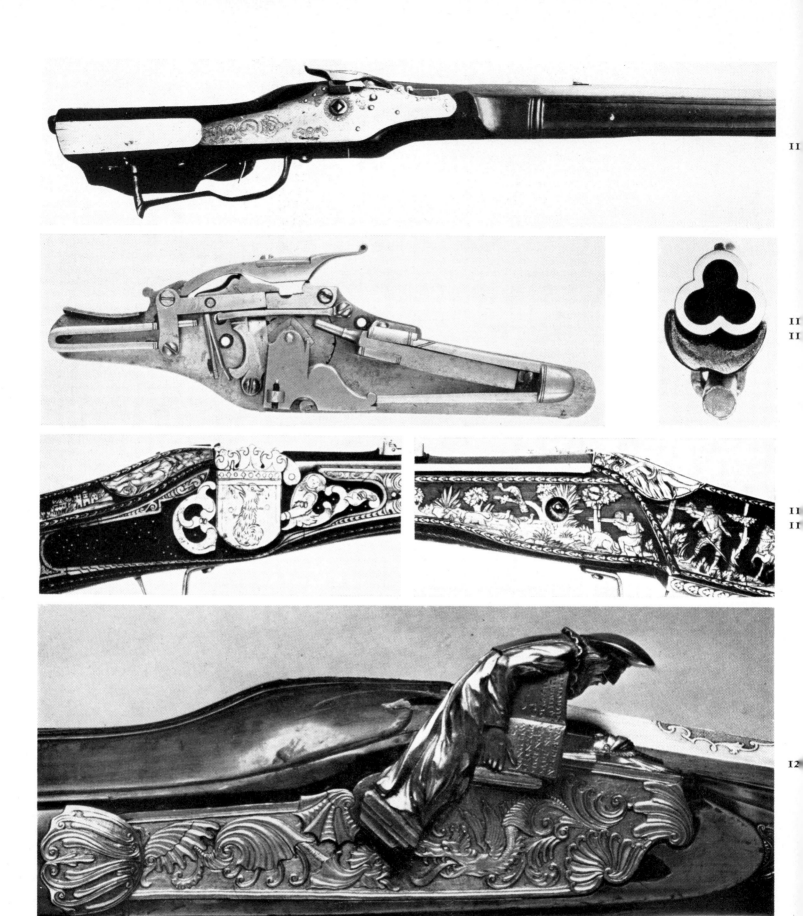

ENCLOSED WHEELLOCKS   **115** Wheellock gun by Andreas Neidhardt. *Danish*, dated 1643. *Tøjhusmuseet, Copenhagen* (No. B. 163).   **116** Interior of lock of **115**.   **117** Muzzle view of **115**.   **118** Rifle. Combined cock and pan cover. *German, c.* 1580. Wheel casing engraved with arms of the city of Stettin. *Tower of London* (No. XII–1547). *B.* 24·3 in. *Cal.* 0·415 in.   **119** Left-hand side of stock of **118** showing winding hole for lock.   **120** Waterproof wheellock, the cock in the form of a Doctor of Divinity holding a book engraved with Hebrew characters. *S. German*, dated 1726. *Bayerisches National-museum, Munich* (No. 13/551).

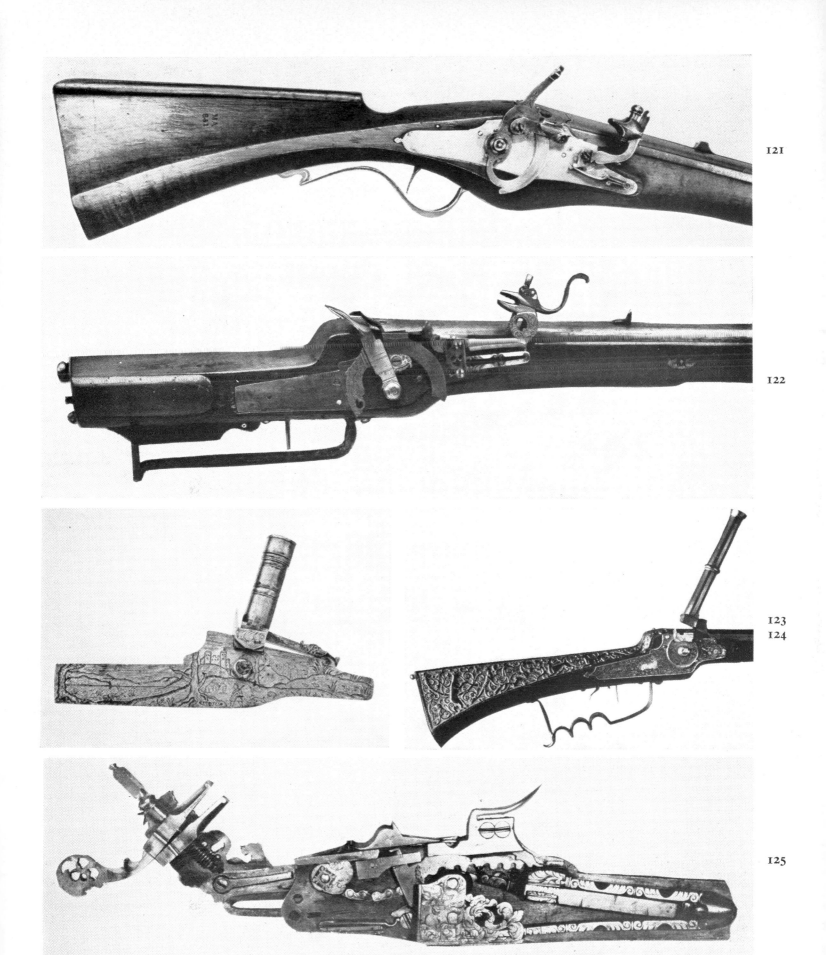

UNUSUAL WHEELLOCKS **121** Gun with segment lock inscribed RAF.VERD [Rafaelle Verdiani] F. 1619. *Italian (Florence).
Tower of London* (No. XII–1067). B. 38½ in. *Cal.* 0·65 in. **122** Gun with segment lock. Barrel bears the mark of Elias
Pedersen of Odense. *Danish, c.* 1665. *Tøjhusmuseet, Copenhagen* (No. B. 435). L. 46·2 in. *Cal.* 0·79 in. **123** Detached wheellock with smoke chimney (*Rauchfang Radschloss*). *Austrian, c.* 1660. *A. R. Dufty Collection.* **124** Rifle of the Emperor Ferdinand III (1637–57) by Hans Faschang, Vienna, *c.* 1640. *Kunsthistorisches Museum, Vienna* (No. D. 101). **125** Interior view of
a self-spanning wheellock. *German, c.* 1660. *C. O. von Kienbusch Collection.*

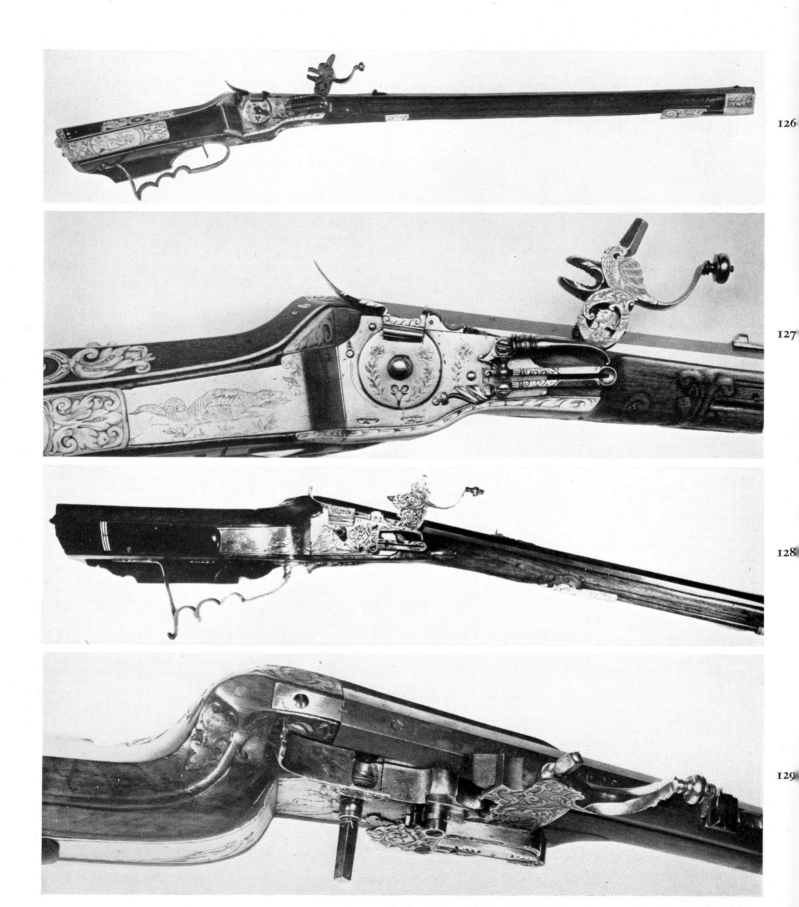

WHEELLOCK GUNS WITH BENT STOCKS   **126** Rifle made for right-handed man using left eye. *German*, dated
1669. *Porte de Hal, Brussels* (No. 83D/45). *B.* 30·5 in. *Cal.* 0·75 in.   **127** Close-up of the lock of **126.**   **128** Similarly bent gun.
Austrian, c. 1700. *C. O. von Kienbusch Collection.*   **129** Top view of the lock of **128.**

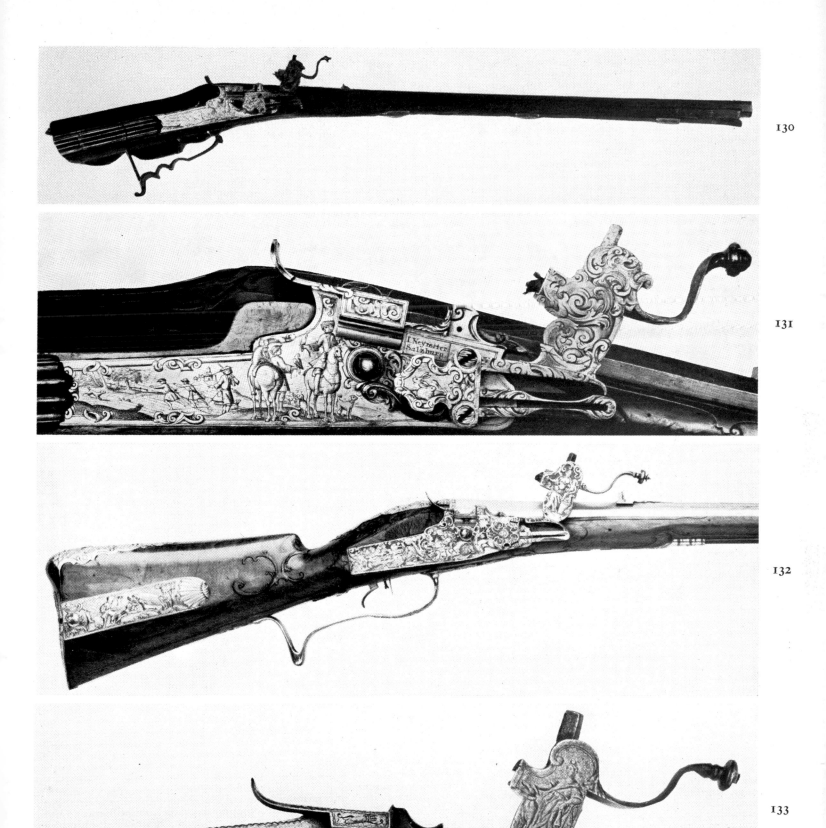

130

131

132

133

LATE WHEELLOCKS **130** Lock signed I. NEYREITER, SALZBURG. Barrel blued and signed in gold IO CASPAR RUDOLPH IN
CREMPS. *German, c. 1710. Porte de Hal, Brussels* (No. 85D/48). *B.* 33·5 in. *Cal.* 0·55 in. **131** Close-up of the lock of **130**. The
engraving signed I. C. STENGEL SCULPSIT. **132** Wheellock rifle signed GOTLIB STEEGER. *German, c. 1735. Tøjhusmuseet,
Copenhagen* (No. B. 1375). *B.* 27·8 in. *Cal.* 0·59 in. **133** Detached wheellock. *German, c. 1740. Author's Collection (ex
Metropolitan Museum, New York).*

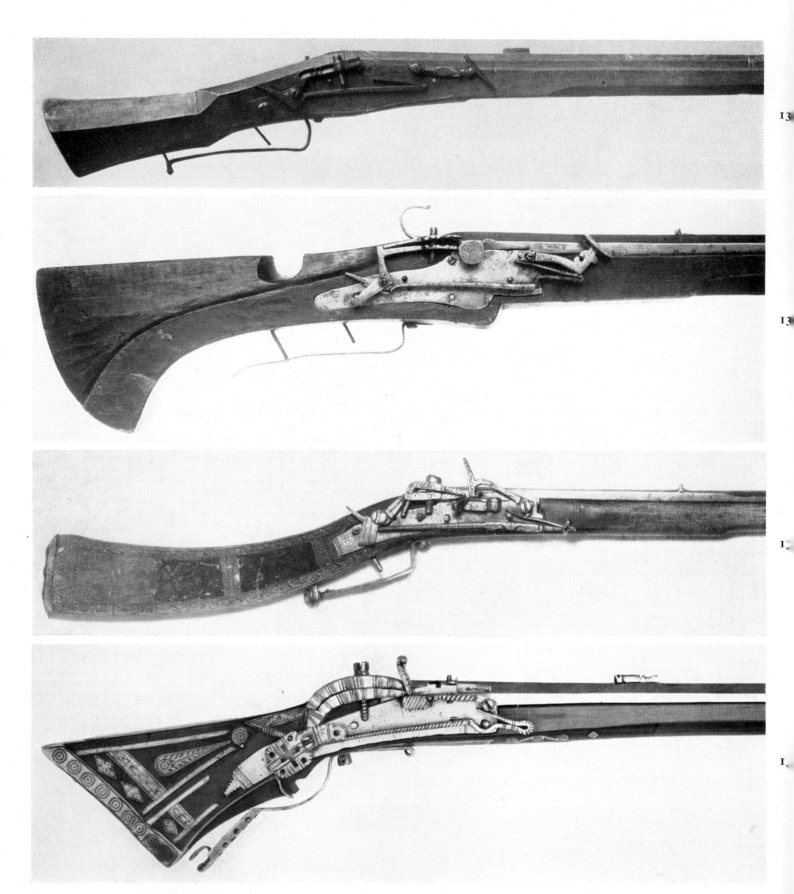

SCANDINAVIAN FLINTLOCKS **134** Snaphance arquebus. Barrel stamped with maker's mark CK and Nuremberg town mark. Possibly one of the Nuremberg arquebuses fitted with snap-locks in the Swedish royal workshop at Arboga in 1556. *Livrustkammaren, Stockholm* (No. 1341). **135** Snaphance musket. *Swedish*, late 16th century. *Livrustkammaren, Stockholm* (No. 4916). *B. 57 in. Cal. 0·87 in.* **136** Snaphance gun. *Norwegian*, late 17th century. *Norsk Folkemuseum, Oslo* (No. 34–29). **137** Flintlock gun with swivelling steel. Stock decorated with engraved horn (*Göinge-bössa*). *S. Swedish*, mid 17th century. *Livrustkammaren, Stockholm* (No. 1795). *B. 35·3 in. Cal. 0·39 in.*

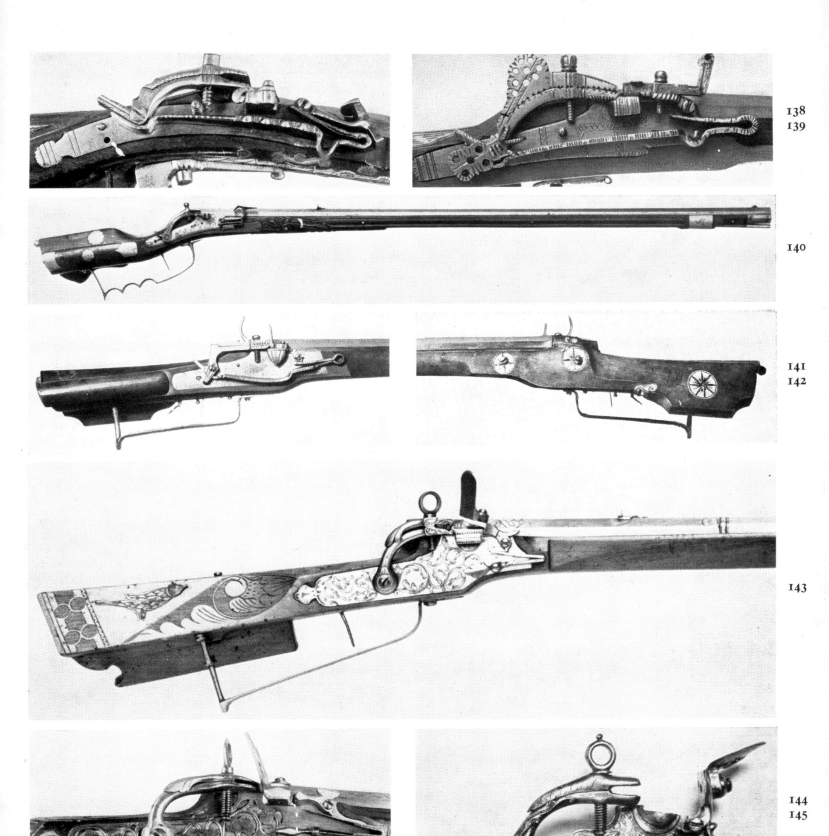

138
139
140
141
142
143
144
145

BALTIC FLINTLOCKS   **138** Lock of snaphance rifle. *Swedish, 17th century. Kremlin, Moscow (No. 6829).*   **139** Lock of gun with swivelling steel. *S. Swedish, 17th century. Skokloster, Sweden (No. 457).*   **140** One of a pair of snaphance guns made by Daniel Danatz for Karl XI (1675–97). *Pomeranian, c. 1685. Livrustkammaren, Stockholm (No. 1319). B. 37·9 in. Cal. 0·31 in.*   **141–2** Lock and side views of Swedish rifle with set trigger. *17th century. Skokloster, Sweden (No. BB. 143).*   **143** Rifle with brass barrel. *Swedish, c. 1650. Tøjhusmuseet, Copenhagen (No. B. 883). B. 23·6 in. Cal. 0·27 in.*   **144** Lock of Swedish rifle. *17th century. Kremlin, Moscow (No. 6822).*   **145** Detached lock with swivelling steel. *c. 1680. Victoria and Albert Museum (No. M. 548–1924).*

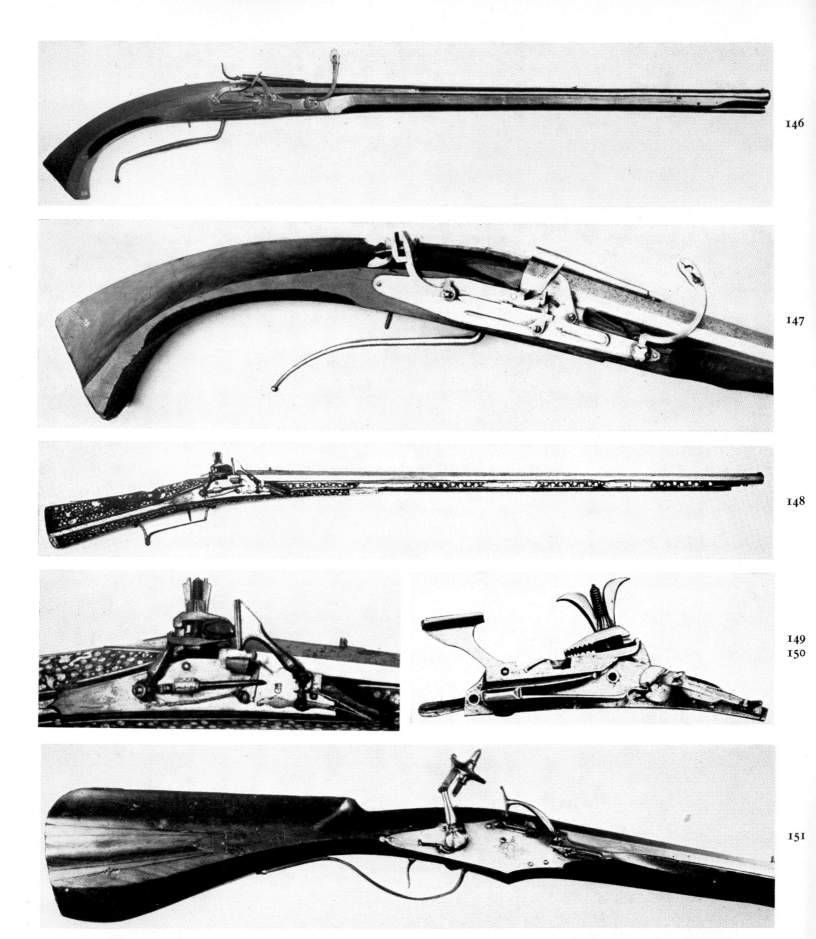

FRENCH AND GERMAN SNAPHANCE GUNS **146** Combined snaphance and matchlock musket. *German, c.*
1575. Tøjhusmuseet, Copenhagen (No. B. 154). *B.* 40·4 in. *Cal.* 0·71 in. **147** Similar gun to **146**. Makers' marks on barrel,
WW (underneath) and MF with date 1572. *Germanisches Museum, Nuremberg* (No. W. 411). **148** Stock inlaid with engraved
stag-horn. *German* (?), late 16th century. *Pitt Rivers Museum, Oxford* (No. PR.IV.69). *B.* 42½ in. *Cal.* 0·8 in. **149** Close-up
of lock of **148**. **150** Interior view of lock of pistol with Nuremberg Barrel, *c.* 1590. *Tower of London* (No. XII–736).
151 Lock with 'dog' catch under cock. From *Cabinet d'Armes of Louis XIII* (No. 138). *French, c.* 1630. *Victoria and Albert*
Museum (No. M. 4–1949). *L.* 78 in. *Cal.* 0·52 in.

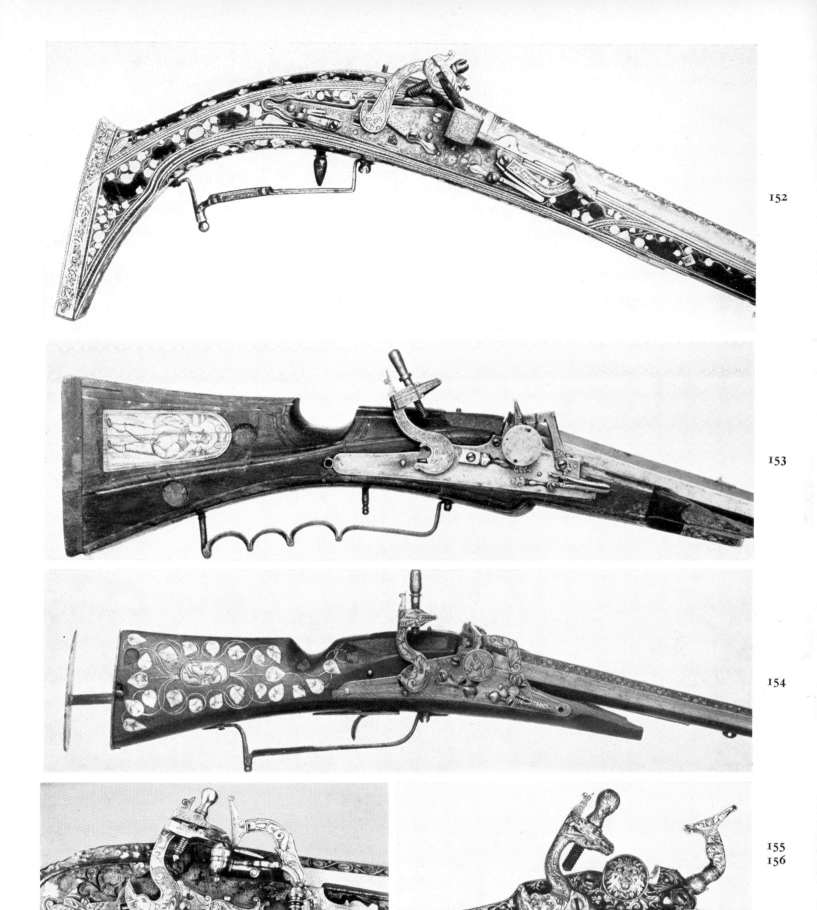

ENGLISH SNAPHANCE GUNS   **152** Petronel. Lock and barrel damascened in gold and silver. Both bear maker's mark RA under fleur-de-lis. Stock inlaid with engraved mother-of-pearl and stag-horn. Stockmaker's initials DI. *English*, dated 1584. *National Museum, Copenhagen* (No. 10428). L. 43·3 in.   **153** Gun with damaged stock from the armoury of Gustav II Adolf (1611–32). *English* (?), late 16th century. *Livrustkammaren, Stockholm* (No. 1251). B. 50·77 in. *Cal.* 0·5 in.   **154** Gun with extension butt-plate bearing the arms of the Scottish family of Spens. *English* (?), late 16th century. *Livrustkammaren, Stockholm* (No. 1349). B. 31·8 in. *Cal.* 0·47 in. (*See p.* 99.)   **155** Gun given to Tsar Michael Romanoff by Fabian Smith in 1625. Snaphance-type steel is fitted with pan-cover base. *Kremlin, Moscow* (No. 6783).   **156** Detached lock from fowling-piece presented by King James I to King Philip III of Spain, probably in 1614. *English. Royal Armoury, Madrid* (No. K. 128). L. 7·4 in.

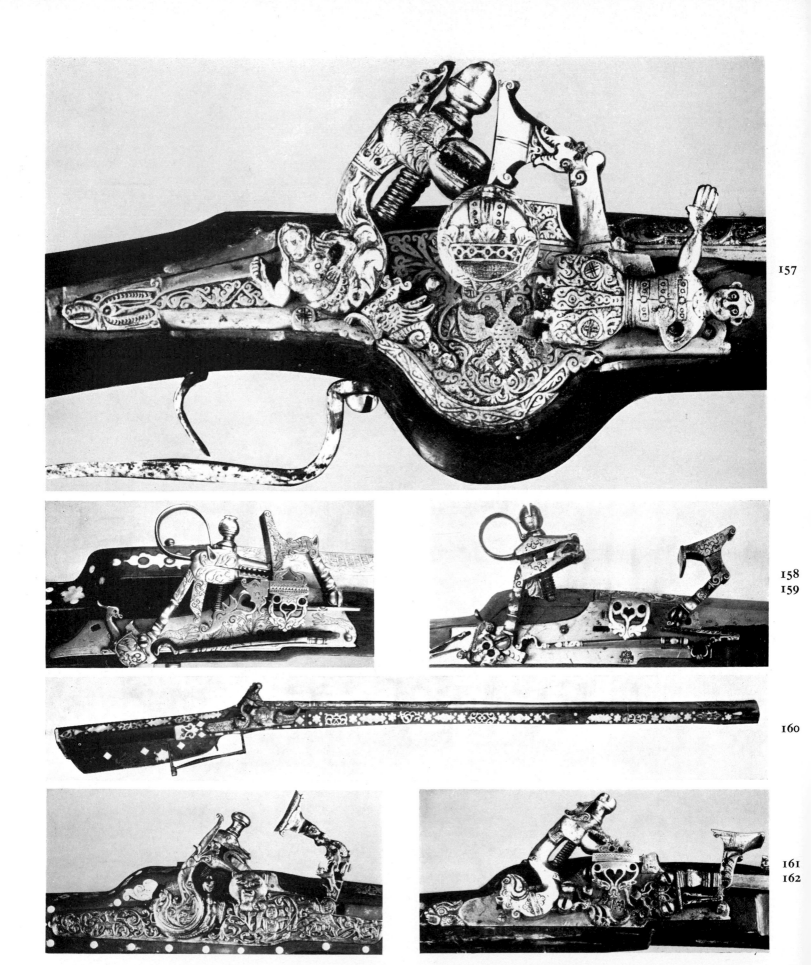

RUSSIAN SNAPHANCE GUNS **157** Lock of 17th-century carbine. *Kremlin, Moscow* (No. 7446). **158** Lock of arquebus by Gregory Vyatkin, dated 1654. *Kremlin* (No. 6763). **159** Lock of 17th-century arquebus by Kusma Martinov. Note pan cover on base of steel. *Kremlin* (No. 6626). **160** Barrel by Dronov Vasily, the lock marked ANDRON. Late 17th century. *Kremlin* (No. 6616). **161** Lock of an arquebus which belonged to Peter I, dated 1692. *Kremlin* (No. 7458). **162** Lock of a 17th-century arquebus by Artemy Andronov (barrel by Vasily Titov). *Kremlin* (No. 7464).

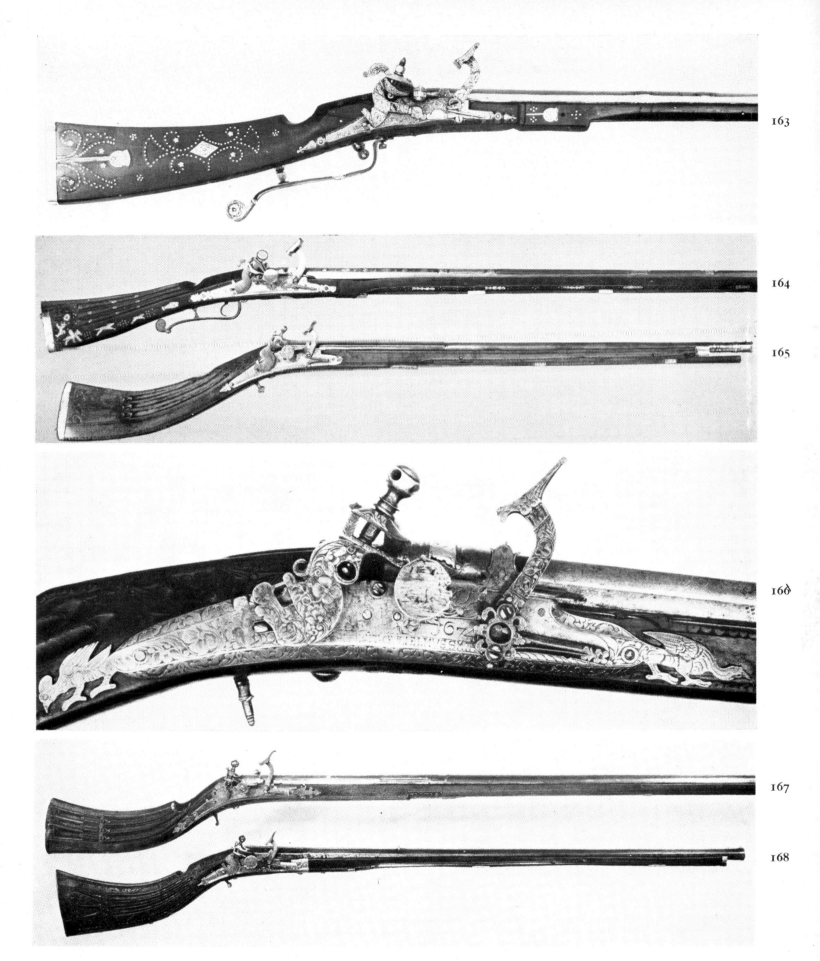

163

164

165

166

167

168

SCOTTISH SNAPHANCE GUNS **163** Lock engraved and gilded. Stock of red Brazil wood inlaid with silver decoration. Lock and barrel stamped RA and date 1614. *Tower of London* (No. XII–63). *B.* 38 in. *Cal.* 0·46 in. **164** Gun bearing the arms and initials of Sir John Grant (1596–1617). Brass lock stamped AP [Andrew Philp of Dundee]. *Countess of Seafield Collection.* (*See p. 99.*) **165** Sir John Grant's carbine, re-stocked and locked in 1673. *Countess of Seafield Collection.* **166** Lock signed ME FECIT GULIELMUS SMITH [the Grant family gunsmith] and dated 1674. *Countess of Seafield Collection.* **167** Gun signed BELLACHASTEL GULIELMUS SMITH. Bellachastel was the old name for the family seat of Castle Grant. *Countess of Seafield Collection.* **168** Breechloading gun dated 1686. Barrel and fore-end unscrew from breech. *Countess of Seafield Collection.*

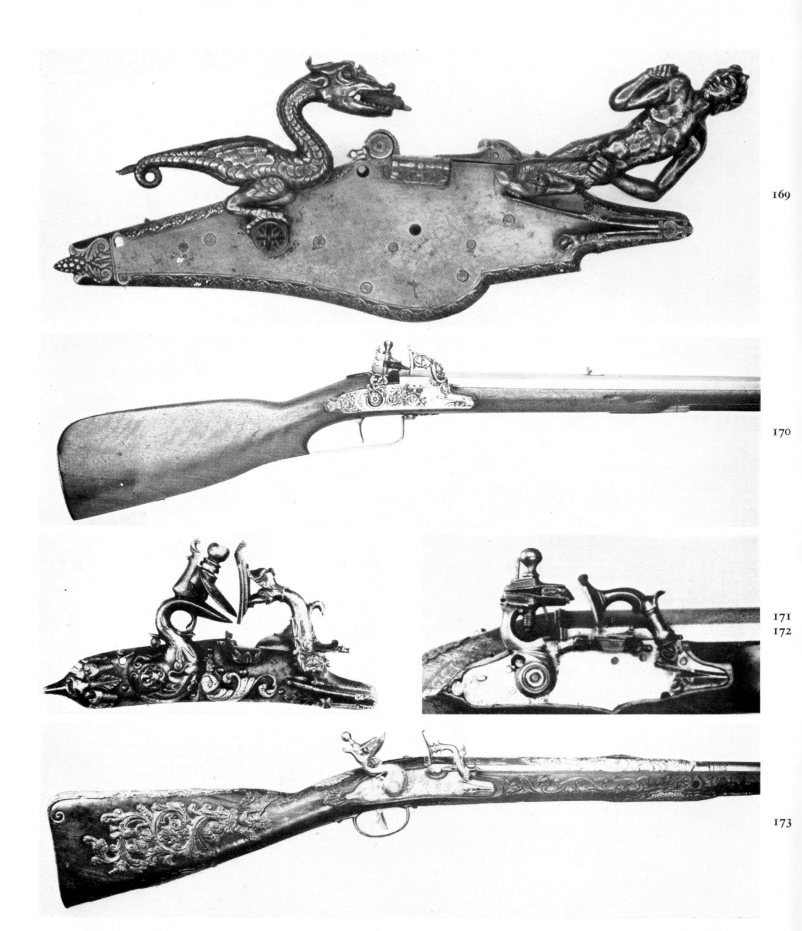

ITALIAN SNAPHANCES **169** Detached lock with sculptured cock and steel. *Italian (?)*, *c. 1625. Odescalchi Collection, Rome (No. 895).* **170** Rifle. *N. Italian, dated on barrel 1675. Tøjhusmuseet, Copenhagen (No. B. 1004). B. 34·4 in. Cal. 0·55 in.* **171** Detached lock signed on inside ROMANO. *N. Italian, late 16th century. Peel Park Museum, Salford.* **172** Detail of carbine. Barrel signed LAZARINO COMINAZZO. *N. Italian, c. 1680. Victoria and Albert Museum (No. M. 620–1927).* **173** Sporting gun. Chiselled steel mounts. Barrel encased with panels of embossed silver. *Tuscan, c. 1750. Birmingham Museum and Art Gallery. L. 52½ in. Cal. 0·62 in.*

174

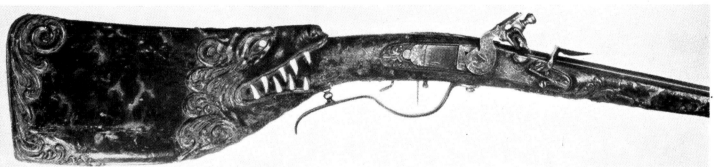

175

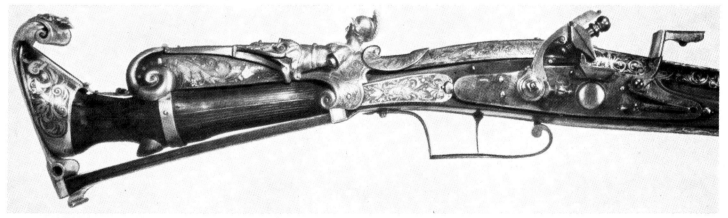

176

177

DECORATED FLINTLOCKS   **174** Detached lock of sculptured steel bearing the arms of an armillary sphere and the motto UNDIQUE MAGNAS. Signed inside PETRUS ANCINUS REGIENSUS F. MDCXXXXIII. *N. Italian,* dated 1643. *Odescalchi Collection, Rome* (No. 946). (*See p. 99.*)   **175** Small-bore rifle. The stock painted to resemble tortoiseshell. *French, c.* 1640. *A. R. Dufty Collection. B.* 49 in. *Cal.* 0·187 in.   **176** Gun by Marin le Bourgeoys of Lisieux. *French, c.* 1605–10. *State Hermitage, Leningrad* (No. F. 281).   **177** Stock inlaid with coloured and engraved stag-horn and brass wire by Jean Conrad Tornier of Massevaux, Alsace. Dated 1646. *Tower of London* (No. XII–1549). *B.* 44 in. *Cal.* 0·39 in.

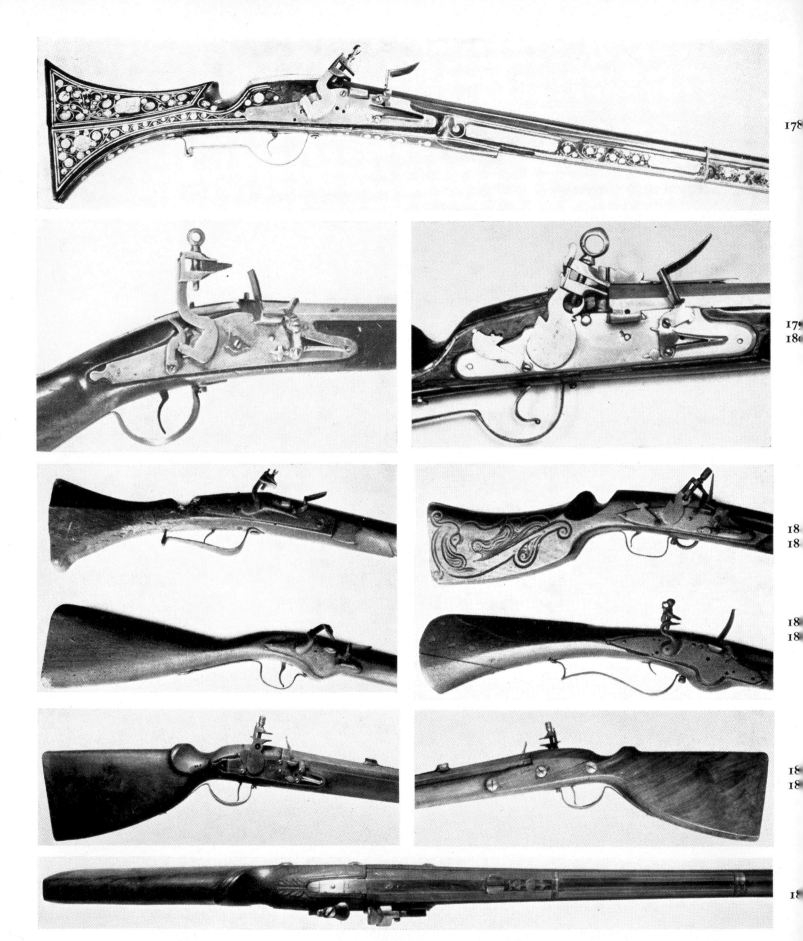

ENGLISH 17TH-CENTURY FLINTLOCK GUNS **178** Musket with 'English' lock (dog-catch and cock-stop missing). Stock bears arms of the Stationers' Company, the initials JR and the date 1619. *Windsor Castle* (No. 364). *B.* 44½ in. *Cal.* 1·0 in. **179** 'English' lock on musket, *c.* 1640. *Tower of London* (No. XII–1694). **180** Dog lock on musket, *c.* 1650. *Tower of London* (No. XII–48). **181–4** Unusual flintlocks on muskets bearing the proof marks of the London Gunmakers' Company, *c.* 1640–60. *Littlecote, Berkshire, England.* **185–7** Lock, side and top views of one of a pair of guns bearing the mark of George Fisher, and the proof marks of the Armourers' Company of London. *c.* 1650. *Skokloster, Sweden* (W. 265). *B.* 53·7 in. *Cal.* 0·8 in. (*See p.* 99.)

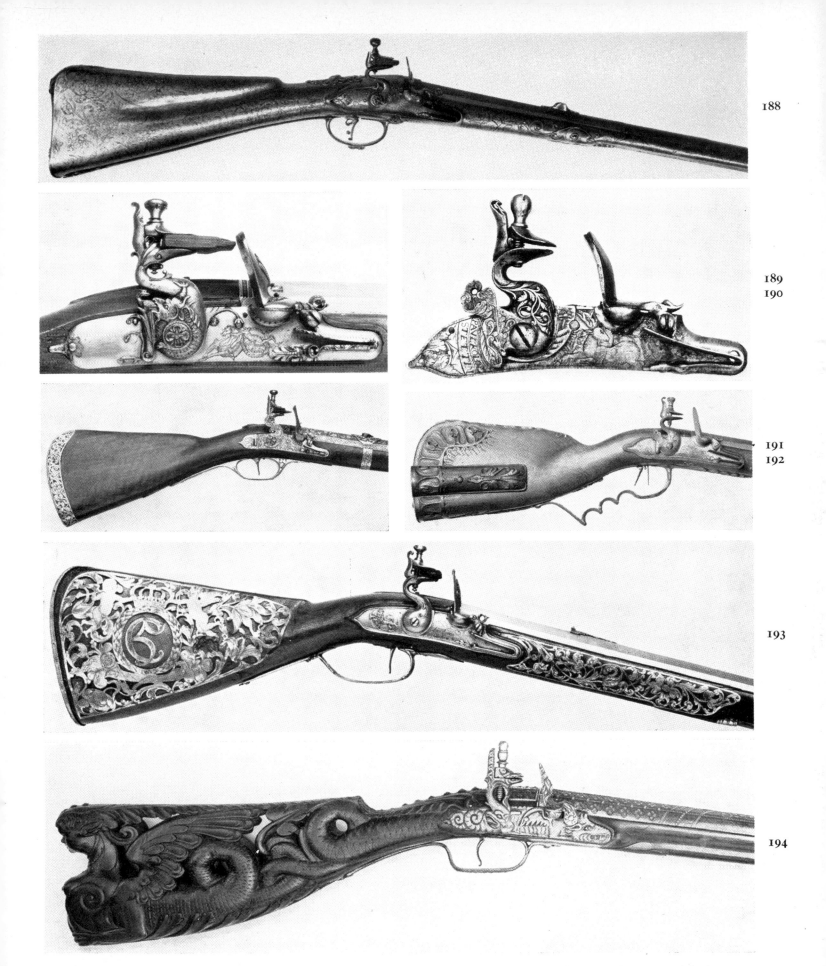

CONTINENTAL 17TH-CENTURY FLINTLOCKS **188** All-steel sporting gun, Hollow metal stock and lock engraved and chiselled by Stefano Scioli. Barrel by Gironimo Mutto. *Italian (Brescia), c.* 1680. *Tower of London* (No. XII–1752). B. 43¾ in. *Cal.* 0·595 in. **189** Lock on one of a pair of rifles, signed MUNIER A GENEVE. *Swiss, c.* 1680. *Skokloster, Sweden* (No. W. 492). B. 30·7 in. *Cal.* 0·63 in. **190** Detached dog-lock signed PAUL ROLOF, STETTIN. *German, c.* 1680. *Livrustkammaren, Stockholm.* **191** Sporting gun signed JEAN KNOOP, UTRECHT. *Dutch, c.* 1655. *Tøjhusmuseet, Copenhagen* (No. B. 602). B. 45·8 in. *Cal.* 0·71 in. **192** Sporting rifle by BERNT ORTHER, STETTIN. *German, c.* 1690. *Livrustkammaren, Stockholm.* **193** Christian V's rifle signed LARS BERRIG, TRUNHIEM. *Norwegian, c.* 1685. *Tøjhusmuseet, Copenhagen* (No. B. 836). B. 37·7 in. *Cal.* 0·6 in. **194** Charles XI's gun. *Swedish, c.* 1650. *Livrustkammaren, Stockholm* (No. 1333).

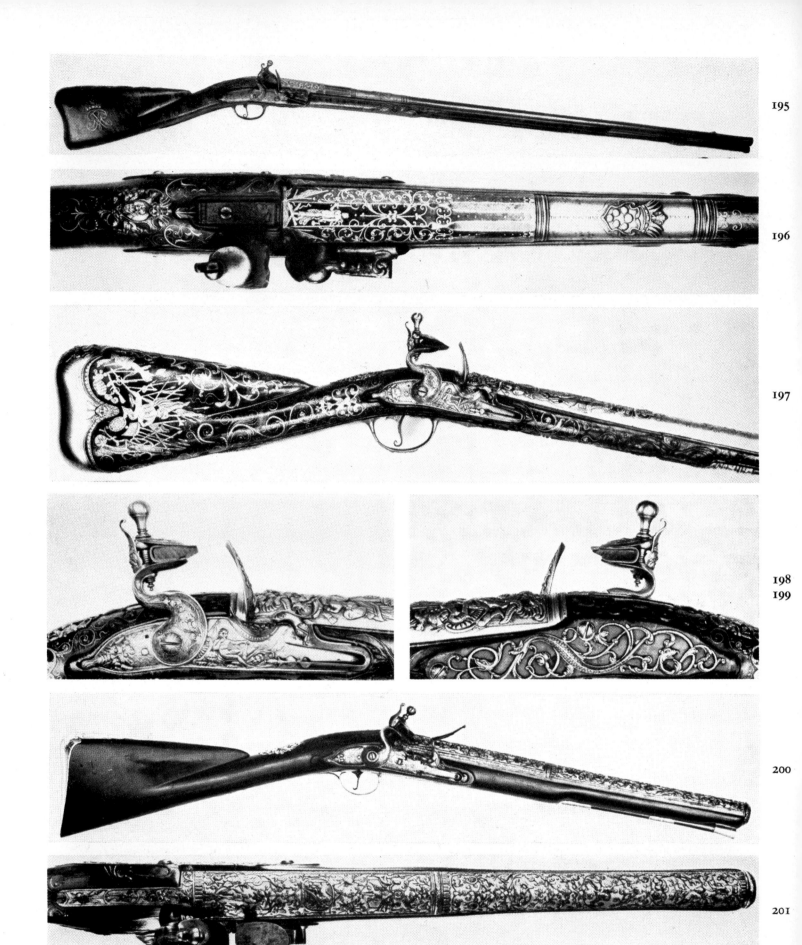

DECORATED ENGLISH FLINTLOCKS **195** Fowling-piece to fire two superimposed charges, bearing the arms of the Medici family, made by Andrew Dolep of London, c. 1685. *Royal Armoury, Turin (No. T. 105). B. 36·3 in. Cal.* 0·67 in. *(See p.* 99.) **196** Top view of **195**. Signature reads DOLEP LONDINI FECIT. **197** Silver-decorated fowling-piece signed F. MADDOCK, CASTEL YARDE, DUBLIN. *c.* 1685. *Tower of London (No.* XII-1554). *(See p.* 99.) **198-9** Lock and side-plate view of **197**. **200** Carbine by Peter Gandon of London, *c.* 1750. *A. R. Dufty Collection. B.* 15½ in. *Cal.* 0·7 in. **201** Barrel of **200**. Chiselled and gilt by Daniel Sadeler, *c.* 1620.

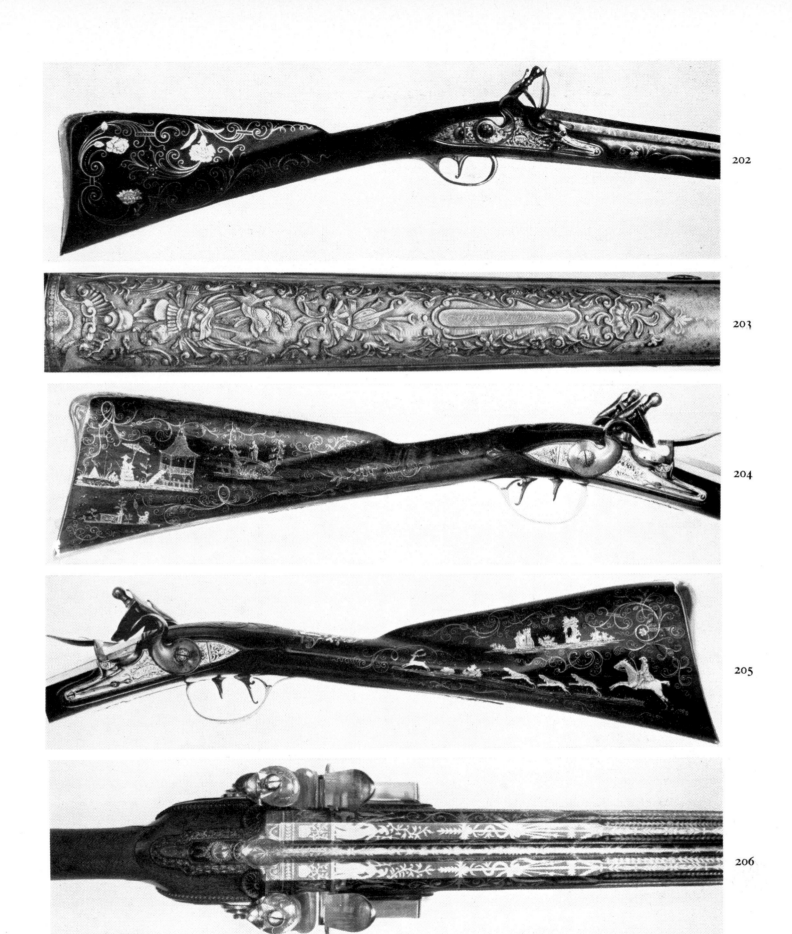

DECORATED ENGLISH FLINTLOCKS **202** Sporting gun with silver-decorated stock by Benjamin Griffin of London, *c*. 1740. *Capodimonte, Naples* (No. 2604). **203** Chiselled and gilt barrel of sporting gun by Richard Wilson, London. Silver mounts hall-marked 1749–50. *Victoria and Albert Museum* (No. 8–1883). **204–5** Both sides of the silver-decorated butt of a double-barrelled sporting gun by William Bailes, London. Hall-marked 1764. *A. R. Dufty Collection*. B. 38 in. *Cal*. 0·6 in. **206** Pair of gold-decorated barrels made by Ezekiel Baker, London, in 1828 for a Boutet gun belonging to George IV. *Windsor Castle* (No. 184). (*See pp*. 99 *and* 221.)

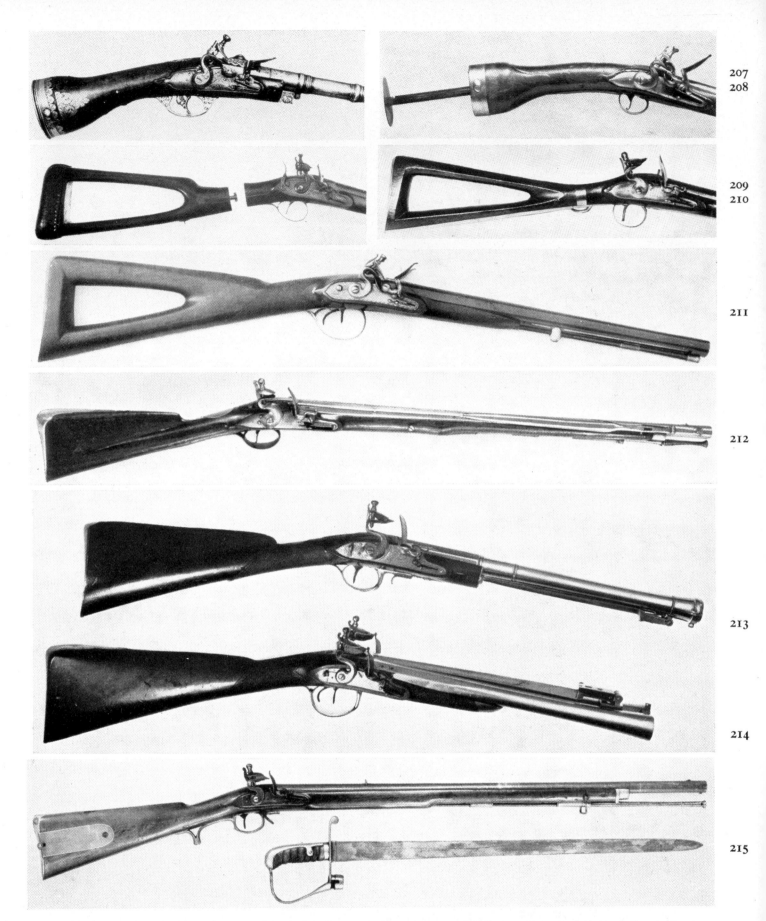

ENGLISH FLINTLOCK CARBINES AND BLUNDERBUSSES **207** Pistol carbine with extending butt-plate and turn-off barrel by Richard Hewse, Wootton Bassett. *English, c. 1660. Lord Howard de Walden Collection.* **208** Carbine with butt-plate extended. *English, c. 1690. Glasgow Museum (No. 39–65bai).* **209** Gun with detachable 'skeleton' butt, by Barton, London. *c. 1790. Tower of London (No. XII–1585).* **210** Military carbine by Fowler of Dublin. *1797. Edinburgh Castle (No. L, 1949–41). (See p. 99.)* **211** Double-barrelled carbine by Tatham & Egg, London. Sliding bayonet under barrel. *c. 1805. C. G. Vokes Collection. B. 16½ in. Cal. 0·59 in.* **212** Military Tower carbine with folding bayonet, *c. 1780. Tower of London (No. XII–692). B. 28 in. Cal. 0·67 in.* **213** Brass-barrelled blunderbuss with folding bayonet signed GRICE, LONDON. *c. 1780. Tower of London (No. XII–1742). B. 15·2 in. Cal. 1·0 in.* **214** Double brass-barrelled blunderbuss with folding bayonet, signed J & W RICHARDS, LONDON. *c. 1785. Tower of London (No. XII–1770). B. 13·7 in. Cal. 0·90 in.* **215** Rifled carbine with sword bayonet by Staudenmayer, London. *c. 1805. Tower of London (No. XII–1049). B. 30 in. Cal. 0·65 in.*

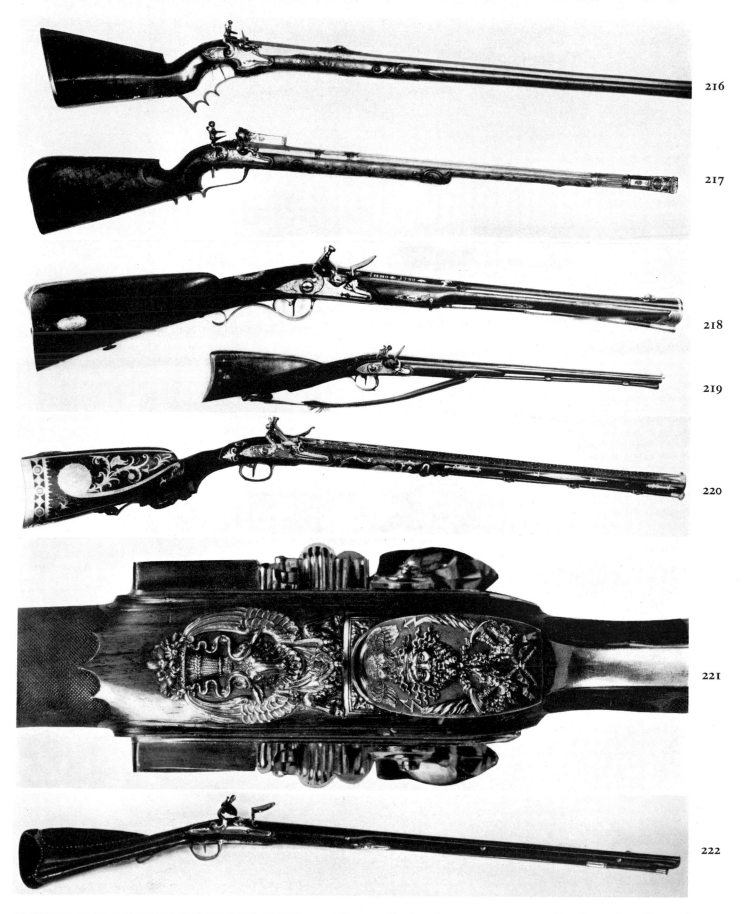

216

217

218

219

220

221

222

FRENCH AND RUSSIAN FLINTLOCK GUNS **216** Target rifle signed CUINOLET A DIJON. *French, c. 1675. Tower of London* (No. XII–1106). *B.* 36·8 in. *Cal.* 0·6 in. **217** Target rifle. Chiselled steel barrel and tubular rear-sight. Lock signed LES SOISSONS A GRENOBLE. *French, c. 1675. Tower of London* (No. XII–1570). *B.* 30·9 in. *Cal.* 0·635 in. **218** Blunderbuss signed JOHAN ADOLPH GRECKE A ST. PETERSBURG ANNO 1780. Stock bears cypher of Empress Catherine II. Swivelling safety steel on lock. *Wallace Collection* (No. A. 1124). *B.* 20 in. **219** Sporting gun made for a child. *Belgian or French, c. 1820. Wallace Collection* (No. A. 1133). *B.* 15½ in. **220** Rifle by Nicolas Boutet. Blued barrel decorated with gold ornament. Walnut stock inlaid with scroll work of red gold, with a grip of carved ebony. *French (Versailles), c. 1805. Wallace Collection* (No. A. 1131). *B.* 26 in. *Cal.* 0·4 in. **221** Silver trigger guard on a double-barrelled shotgun by Boutet. (see **206**). *Windsor Castle* (No. 184). **222** Boy's sporting gun by Dupont, Paris. Walnut stock padded with red velvet. *French, c. 1750. Windsor Castle* (No. 399). *B.* 30 in. *Cal.* 0·56 in.

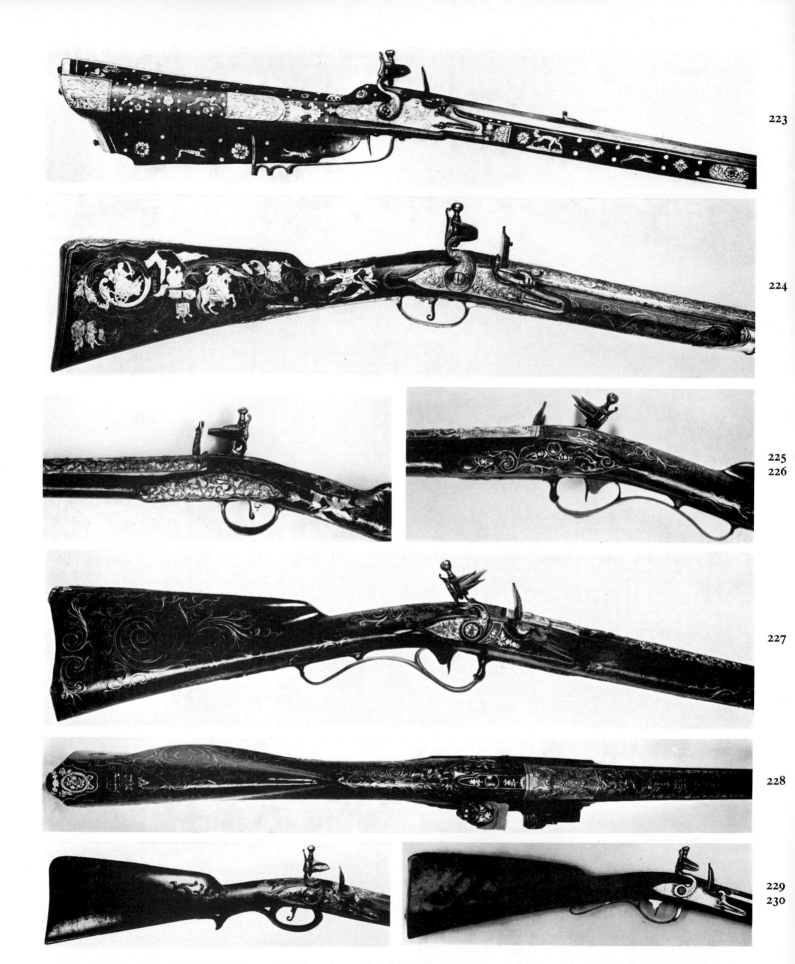

RUSSIAN FLINTLOCK GUNS **223** Rifle. The stock inlaid with stag-horn and brass wire. Late 17th century. *Victoria and Albert Museum* (No. M. 228–1919). *L.* 58 in. *Cal.* 0·37 in. **224** Sporting gun made at Tula for the Empress Elizabeth, dated 1749. *Tøjhusmuseet, Copenhagen* (No. B. 1533). *B.* 40·7 in. *Cal.* 0·65 in. **225** Side view of a gun made at Tula in 1752 Butt inlaid with silver after the design by Nicholas Guérard. *Tower of London* (No. XII–1504). *B.* 44 in. *Cal.* 0·60 in. **226–8** Side, lock and top views of a sporting gun signed A. LEONTIEW. Blued barrel and mounts encrusted with gold floral decoration. *Tula, c.* 1775. *Victoria and Albert Museum* (No. M. 3–1961). *L.* 38 in. *Cal.* 0·6 in. (*See p.* 100.) **229** Sporting gun made at Tula in 1752. Barrel bears cypher of Empress Elizabeth. *Kunsthistorisches Museum, Vienna* (No. HGK. 195). *B.* 43·9 in. *Cal.* 0·63 in. **230** Sporting gun made at Tula in 1790. *Capodimonte, Naples* (No. 2451).

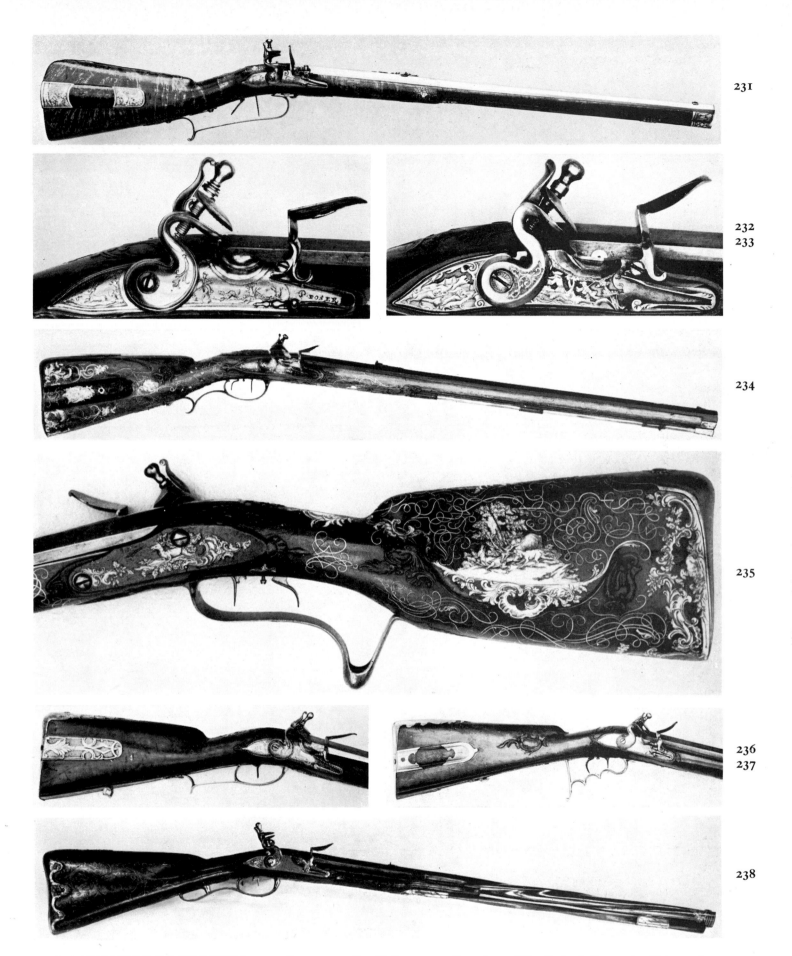

EUROPEAN FLINTLOCK RIFLES **231** *German, c.* 1685. *Tøjhusmuseet, Copenhagen (No. B. 875). B.* 30·4 in. *Cal.* 0·59 in.
232 Lock of a rifle by Paul Poser, Prague. *c.* 1720. *B. W. Muir Collection.* **233** Lock of a rifle by I. O. Voisskouski. *Polish (?).*
c. 1740. *B. W. Muir Collection.* **234** Lock signed I. G. HORNEFFER. Walnut stock inlaid with stag-horn. *East German, c.* 1740.
B. W. Muir Collection. **235** Unsigned rifle with stock by the same maker as **234**. *German, c.* 1740. *Author's Collection. B.* 31¼
in. *Cal.* 0·54 in. (*See p.* 100.) **236** Signed FRANZ GORBER. *German, c.* 1720. *B. W. Muir Collection.* **237** Signed I. KUCHEN-
REUTER. *German, c.* 1775. *B. W. Muir Collection.* **238** Twisted barrel with heart-shaped rifling. Signed WALSTER A SAARBRUCK.
German, c. 1770. *Windsor Castle (No. 401). B.* 27 in.

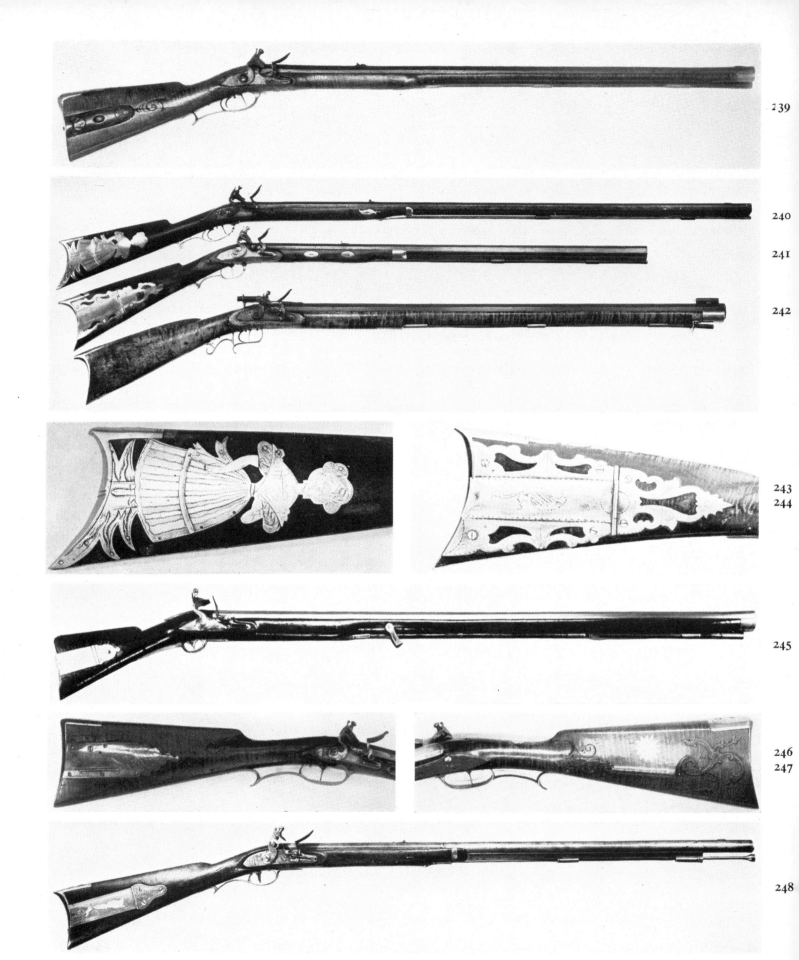

AMERICAN FLINTLOCK RIFLES **239** Rifle carried by Edward Marshall on his 'Indian Walk' of 1737. Barrel marked II. A. D. ROTHENBERG, *American (Pennsylvania), c.* 1730. *Bucks County Historical Society. B.* 38 in. *Cal.* 0·68 in. **240–2** Three unsigned examples of the so-called Kentucky rifle, *c.* 1825–35. *Winchester Gun Museum.* Barrel of longest rifle 41½ in. **243** Butt decoration of **240**. Inlay of silver, brass and copper. **244** Patch box decoration on a Pennsylvanian rifle signed N. KILE 1817. *Smithsonian Institution, Washington* (No. 215418). **245** Rifled wall gun. Patch-box lid engraved AMERICAN LIBERTY. *c.* 1775. *Tower of London* (No. XII–559). *B.* 54½ in. *Cal.* 0·96 in. **246–7** Lock and side views of rifle, *c.* 1775. Silver star on butt inscribed STATES UNITED WE ARE ONE. *Windsor Castle* (No. 270). *B.* 44 in. *Cal.* 0·48 in. (*See p.* 100.) **248** Military rifle, U.S. Model 1814. Lock marked HARPERS FERRY 1815. *Smithsonian Institution. B.* 33 in. *Cal.* 0·54 in.

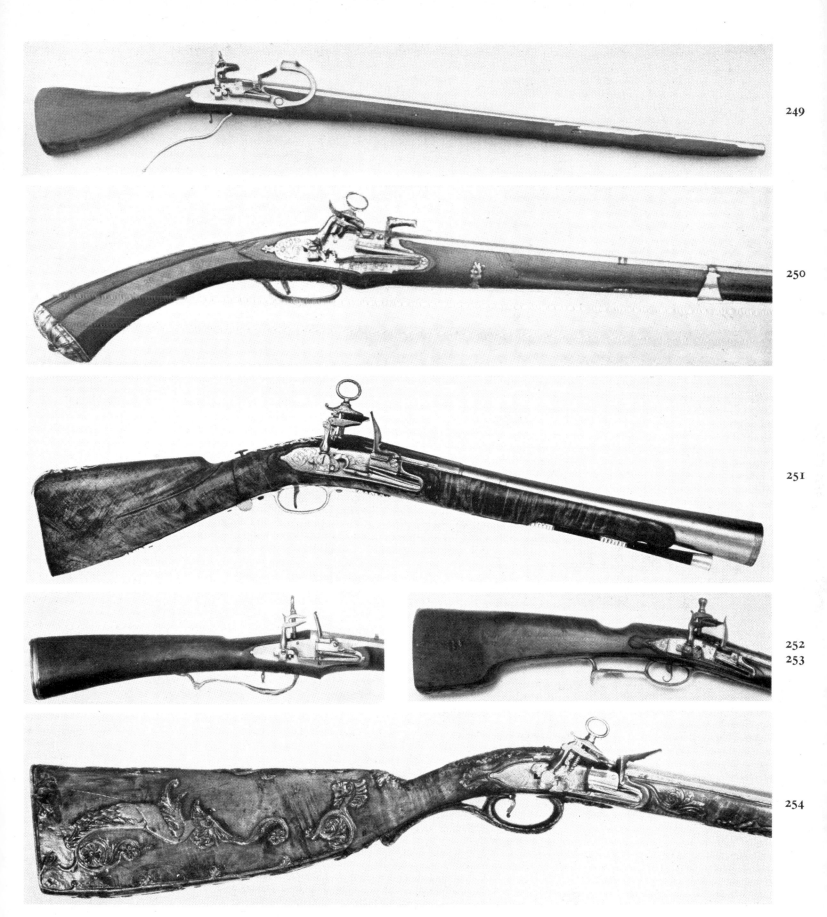

ITALIAN FLINTLOCK GUNS **249** Combined matchlock and 'toe-lock' musket. *c.* 1690. *Museum of Artillery, Turin* (No. M. 36). **250** Sporting gun. *Brescia, c.* 1660. *Museum of Artillery, Turin* (No. M. 30). **251** Silver-mounted blunderbuss with folding butt. Barrel by Lazarino Cominazzo. Late 17th century. *Winchester Gun Museum. B.* 16½ in. *Cal.* (at muzzle) 1¾ in. **252** Barrel signed ANGONE, the stock HGA. Early 17th century. *Schwarzburg, Germany* (No. 988). **253** Lock signed F. ROSSI. *S. Italian, c.* 1750. *Tower of London* (No. XII–1096). *B.* 34·5 in. *Cal.* 0·7 in. **254** Silver-mounted birding gun, *c.* 1700. *A. R. Dufty Collection. B.* 46½ in. *Cal.* 0·375 in.

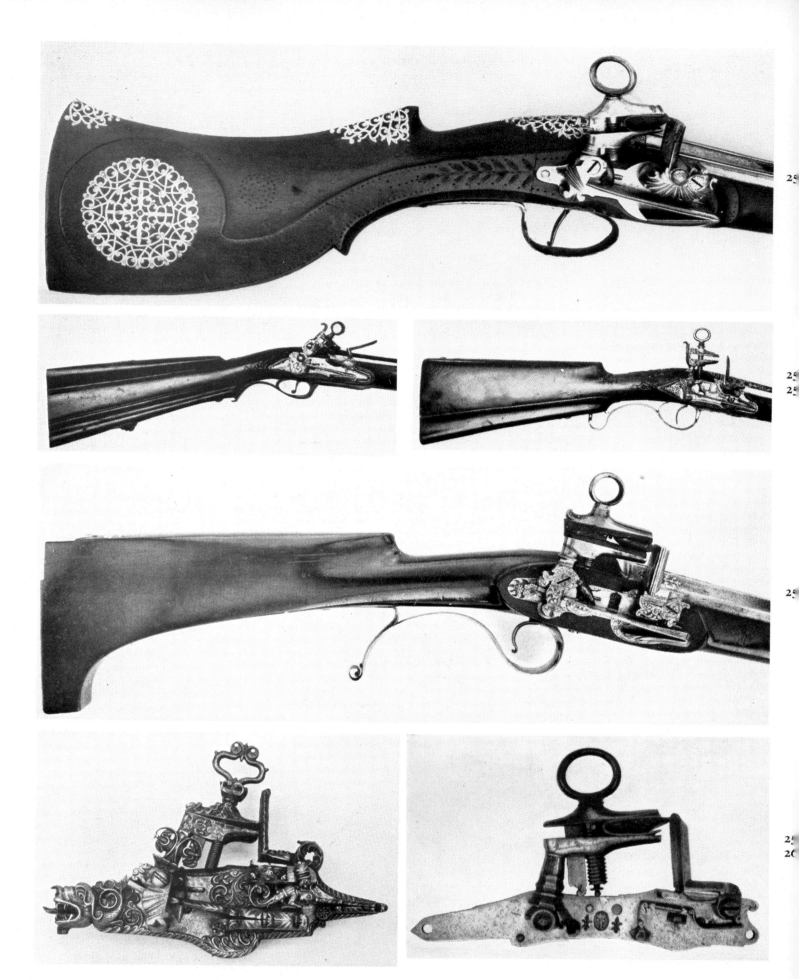

SPANISH FLINTLOCKS **255** Decorated Ripoll carbine signed ROVIRA 1694. *W. Keith Neal Collection.* **256** Miquelet-lock gun with 'Madrid' stock signed P. STEVAN. *c.* 1780. **257** Miquelet-lock gun with 'Madrid' stock by Juan Esteban Bustindui, dated 1792. *Tower of London* (No. XII–1634). *B.* 30·3 in. *Cal.* 0·6 in. **258** Miquelet-lock gun with 'Catalan' stock, dated 1806. *W. Keith Neal Collection.* **259** Chiselled miquelet lock signed PAABLO. 17th century. *Metropolitan Museum, New York* (No. 19.53.28). **260** Lock with interior mainspring and horizontally-acting sear. *c.* 1780. *W. Keith Neal Collection.*

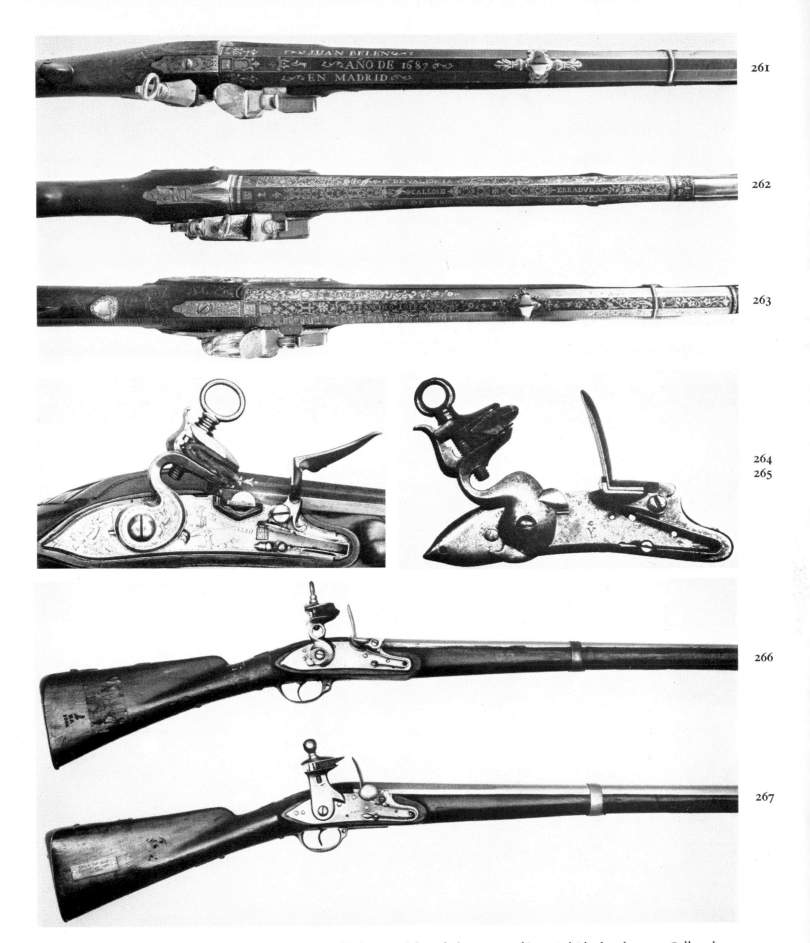

261

262

263

264
265

266

267

SPANISH FLINTLOCKS **261-3** Top views of gold-decorated barrels by Juan Belén, Madrid, dated 1687; Callos de Herraduras, Valencia, dated 1810; and Francisco Lopez, Madrid, dated 1756. *Royal Armoury, Madrid* (Nos. K. 131, 165, 158). **264** 'Madrid' lock by Joaquin de Zelaya, Court gunmaker to Ferdinand VI. *c*. 1750. *B. W. Muir Collection.* **265** Military version of the 'Madrid' lock in the fully-cocked position. *Private Collection.* **266** Musket with exterior sear under cock. Barrel dated 1808. *Tower of London* (No. XXIV–638). *B*. 43 in. *Cal.* 0·72 in. **267** Musket. Modified miquelet lock, signed F. MUNIZ. *c*. 1800. *Tower of London* (No. XII–215). *B*. 43½ in. *Cal.* 0·72 in.

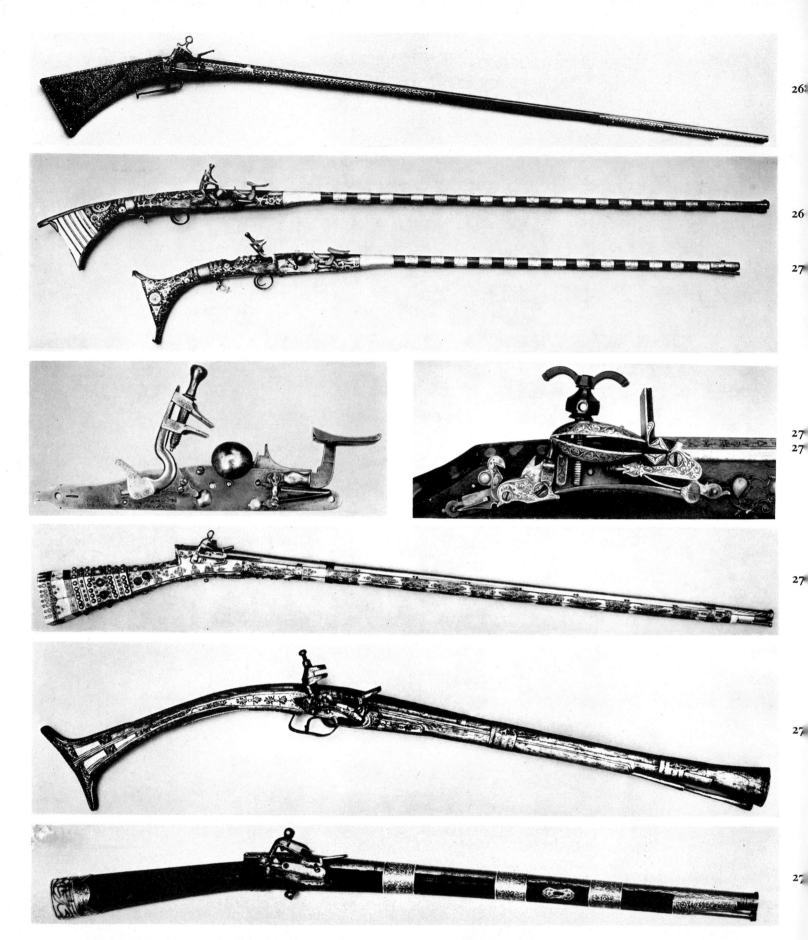

268

269

270

272
273

274

275

MEDITERRANEAN FLINTLOCK GUNS　268 Miquelet-lock gun signed TOM CAFFARO. *Sardinian, early 18th century.* *Metropolitan Museum, New York (No. 14.25.1382).* 269 Snaphance gun. *North African (Kabyle), 19th century. Metropolitan Museum, New York (No. 36.25.2230). B. 64 in.* 270 Snaphance gun. *North African (Kabyle), 19th century. Metropolitan Museum, New York (No. 36.25.2229). B. 61 in.* 271 Lock of 269. 272 Detail of Moroccan gun showing Arab toe-lock. *Mid 18th century. Metropolitan New Museum, York (No. 32.75.274).* 273 Miquelet-lock gun. *Turkish, 18th century. Metropolitan Museum, New York (No. 32.75.270).* 274 Miquelet-lock blunderbuss. *Albanian, 18th century. Metropolitan Museum New York (No. 36.25.2194).* 275 Child's miquelet-lock gun. *Circassian, late 18th century. Wallace Collection (No. 2100).*

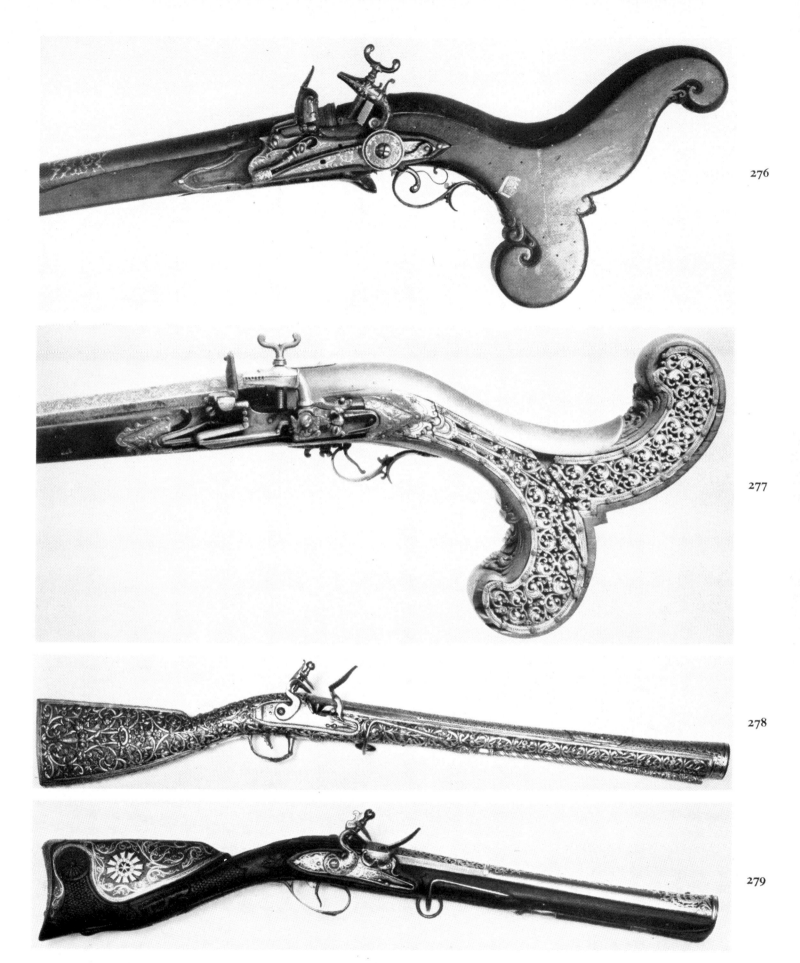

CINGALESE AND TURKISH FLINTLOCK GUNS **276** Toe-lock gun. *Cingalese*, lock early 18th century. Stock and barrel earlier. *W. Keith Neal Collection. (See p. 100.)* **277** Toe-lock gun with ivory-inlaid butt. *Cingalese*, early 18th century. *Metropolitan Museum, New York (No. 91.1.907).* **278** Blunderbuss. Wooden stock overlaid with copper-gilt. Lock marked IONDON WARANTED. *Turkish*, early 19th century. *Wallace Collection (No. 2086).* **279** Blunderbuss. Rosewood stock inlaid with silver. *Turkish*, early 19th century. *Wallace Collection (No. 2066).*

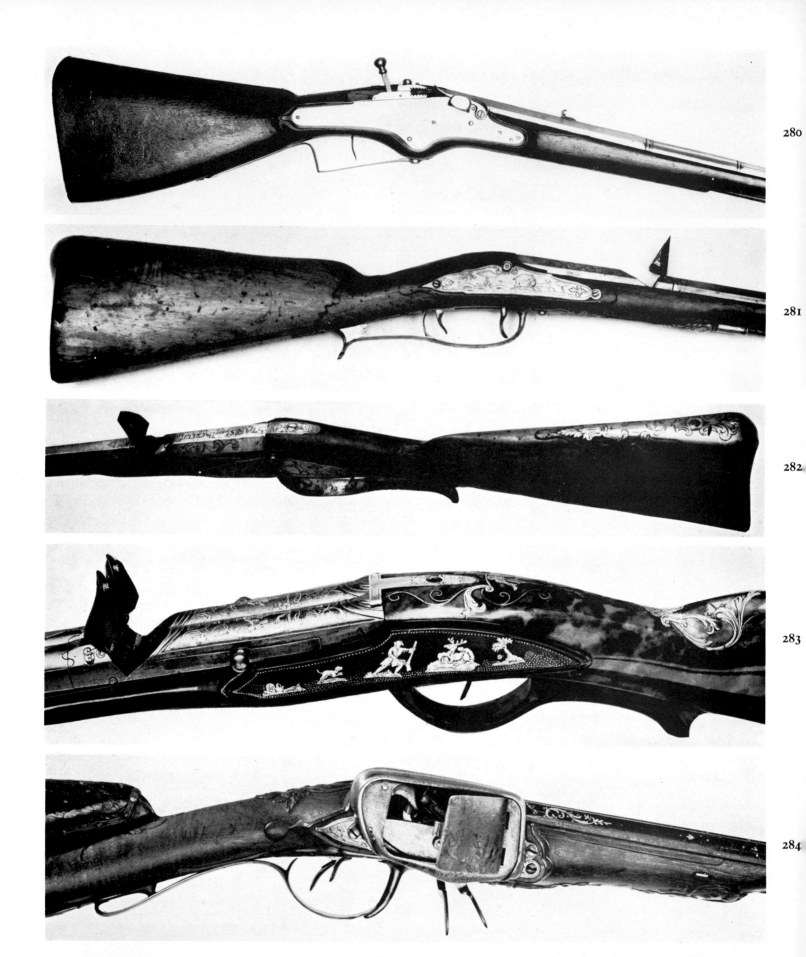

280

281

282

283

284

CONCEALED FLINTLOCK GUNS   **280** Gun with sliding exterior cock by M. Kalthoff. *Danish, c. 1660. Tøjhusmuseet, Copenhagen* (No. B. 478).   **281** Gun with sliding, interior cock. Steel raised for priming. Additional trigger for cocking. Signed STANISLAUS PACZELT. *Bohemian (Kuttenberg), dated 1738. Tower of London* (No. XII–627).   **282** Top view of **281**. **283** Double-barrelled gun with sliding, interior cocks. Stock veneered with tortoiseshell and inlaid with silver. Cocking knobs on side of breech. *German, 1740. Bayerisches Nationalmuseum, Munich* (No. 13/589).   **284** Double-barrelled gun with locks enclosed in metal boxes. Cocking levers in front of guard. Signed BOUILLET A PARIS. *c. 1780. Tower of London* (No. XII–1755).

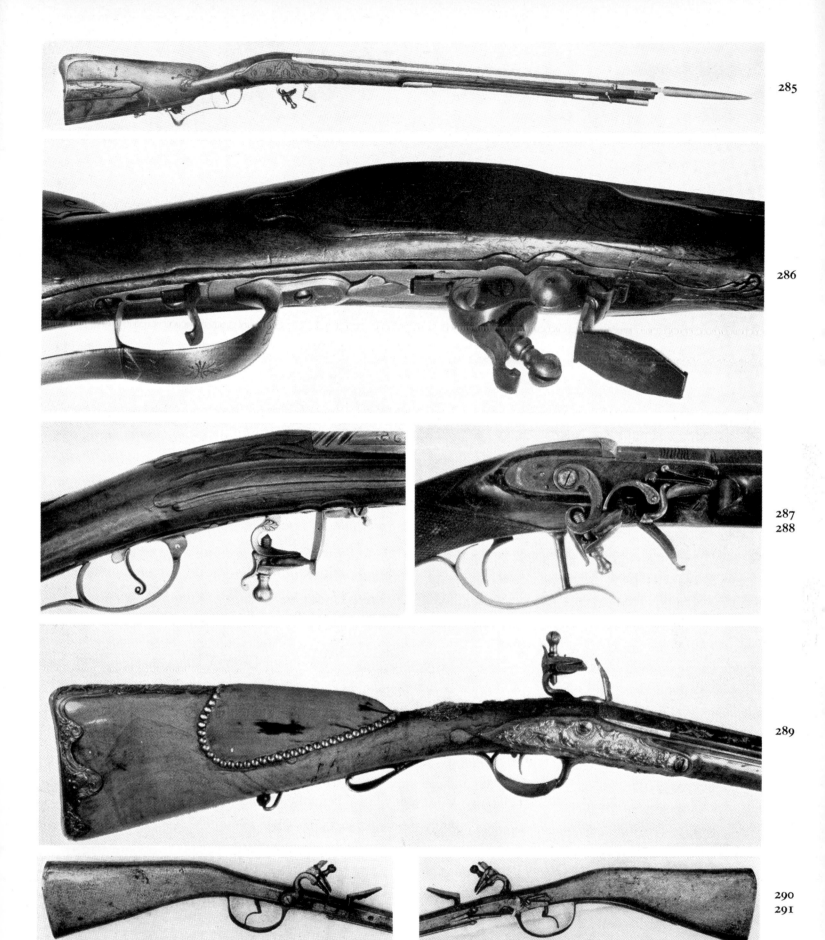

UNUSUAL FLINTLOCK GUNS **285** Rifle with lock underneath and folding bayonet. *German, c. 1740. Livrustkammaren, Stockholm (No. 2941).* **286** Close-up view of lock of **285.** **287** Under-lock rifle, probably by same maker as **285.** *German, c. 1740. W. Keith Neal Collection.* **288** Joseph Egg's patent lock. *English, c. 1815. State Hermitage, Leningrad.* **289** Sporting gun with left-hand lock signed DELETY A PARIS RUE COQUILLIERE. Silver mounts hall-marked 1777–8. *Victoria and Albert Museum (No. 2195–1855).* **290–1** Lock and side views of gun with all-steel stock and exterior mechanism, probably by Jan Cloeter. *German, c. 1650. Mark Dineley Collection.*

EXPERIMENTAL FLINTLOCKS **292** Henry Nock's enclosed, screwless lock, 1786. *Private Collection*. **293** Left-hand screwless lock. *French (?), c. 1790. Private Collection*. **294–5** Self-priming lock by Parkes. *English, c. 1800. Private Collection*. **296** George Bolton's screwless, enclosed lock with adjustable cock jaws. *English, c. 1795. Private Collection*. **297** Sir Howard Douglas's double-headed lock on a sporting gun by Theophilus Richards, Birmingham. *English, c. 1820. Glasgow Museum*. **298** Lock with external spiral springs and sear trigger. *French, c. 1790. Tower of London* (No. XXIV–525). (*See p.* 100) **299** Lock invented by Ezekiel Baker with enclosed spiral mainspring. *English, c. 1820. Tower of London* (Study Collection).

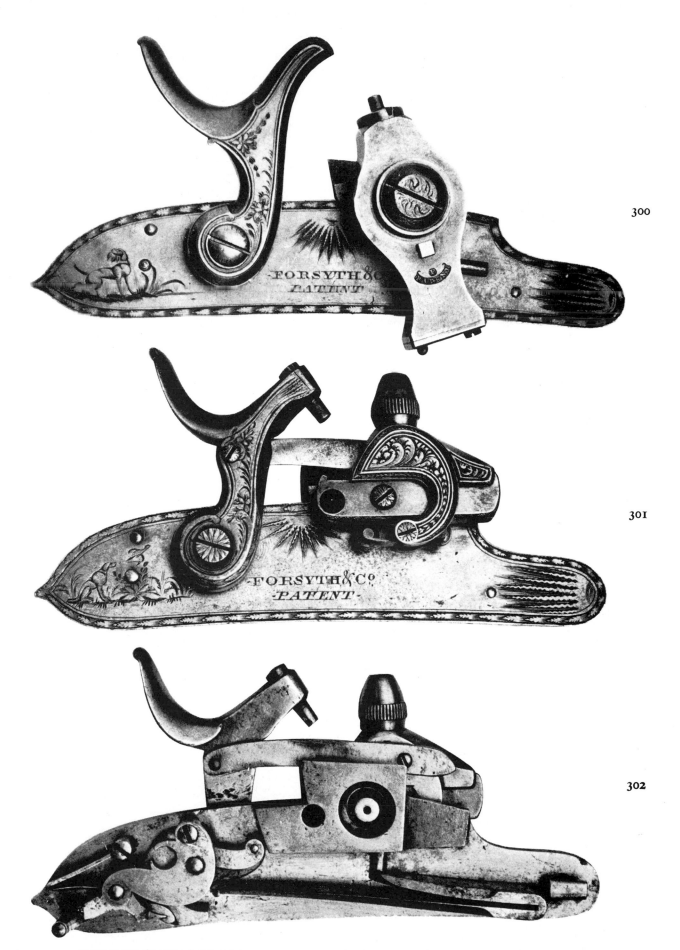

300

301

302

FORSYTH'S PERCUSSION LOCKS   **300** The 'scent-bottle' powder magazine lock.
c. 1810.   **301** Pellet lock with sliding magazine connected to hammer. *c.* 1815.   **302** Interior view of **301**. Both these locks were designed to interchange with flintlocks. *W. ·
Keith Neal Collection.*

303
304

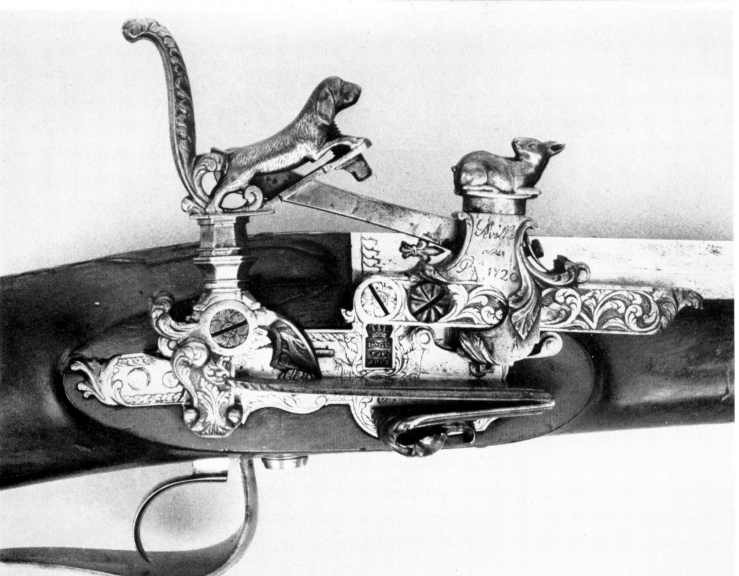

305

PERCUSSION POWDER AND PELLET LOCKS **303** Another version of the Forsyth 'scent-bottle' lock, *c.* 1815.
304 Powder magazine lock by John Jones & Co., London. *c.* 1825. (*See p.* 100.) **305** Miquelet lock by Joseph Gutierrez,
Seville. Dated 1820. *W. Keith Neal Collection.*

PERCUSSION LOCK GUNS (*OPPOSITE*) **306** Tower musket converted to pellet lock by T. H. Hayward for British
percussion trials of 1834. **307** Rifle with Westley Richards's patent cap magazine of 1838. **308** Baron Heurteloup's
koptipteur gun with under-hammer action made for a British Ordnance trial in 1837. **309** U.S. Springfield rifle of 1858 with
Maynard tape primer. **310** Maynard breechloader with tape primer. **311** Sharp's breechloading rifle with disc primer
and Richard Lawrence's patent cut-off of 1859, which allowed percussion caps to be used when necessary. **312** 1859 Enfield
rifle fitted with the Chester disc primer. **313** Breechloading rifle with Della Noce and Bianchi automatic capper.
From an old photograph of the former H. H. Harrod Collection.

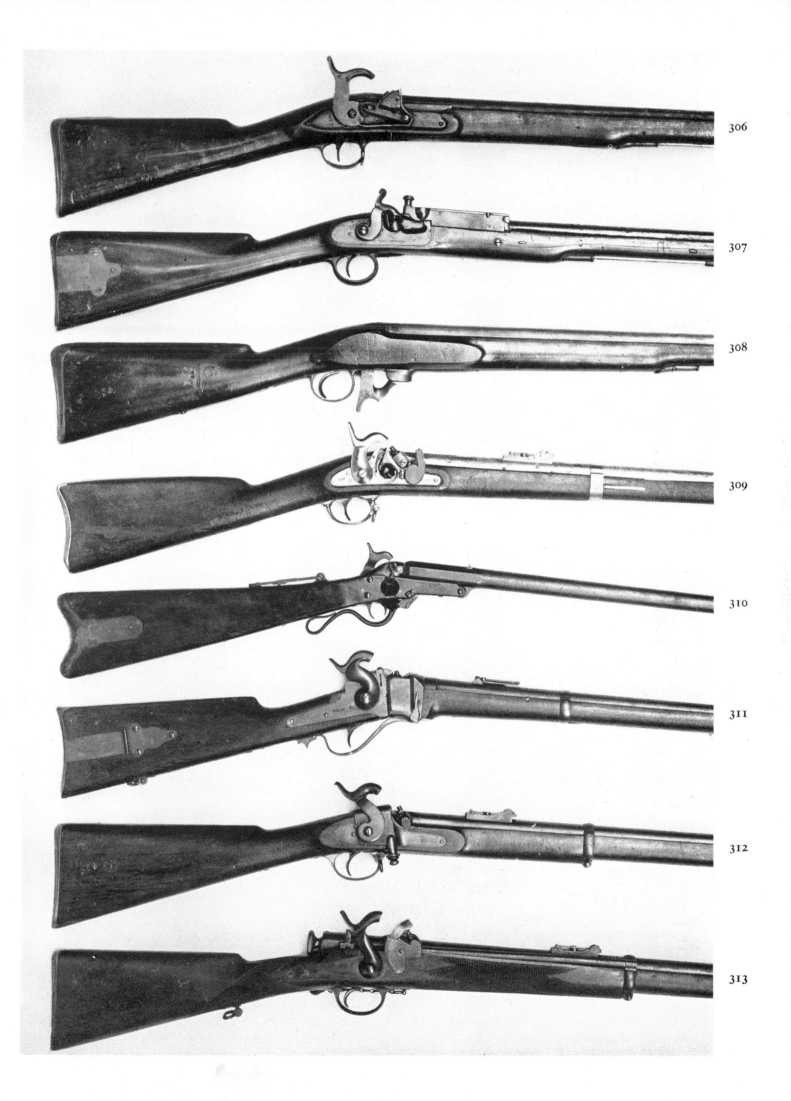

306

307

308

309

310

311

312

313

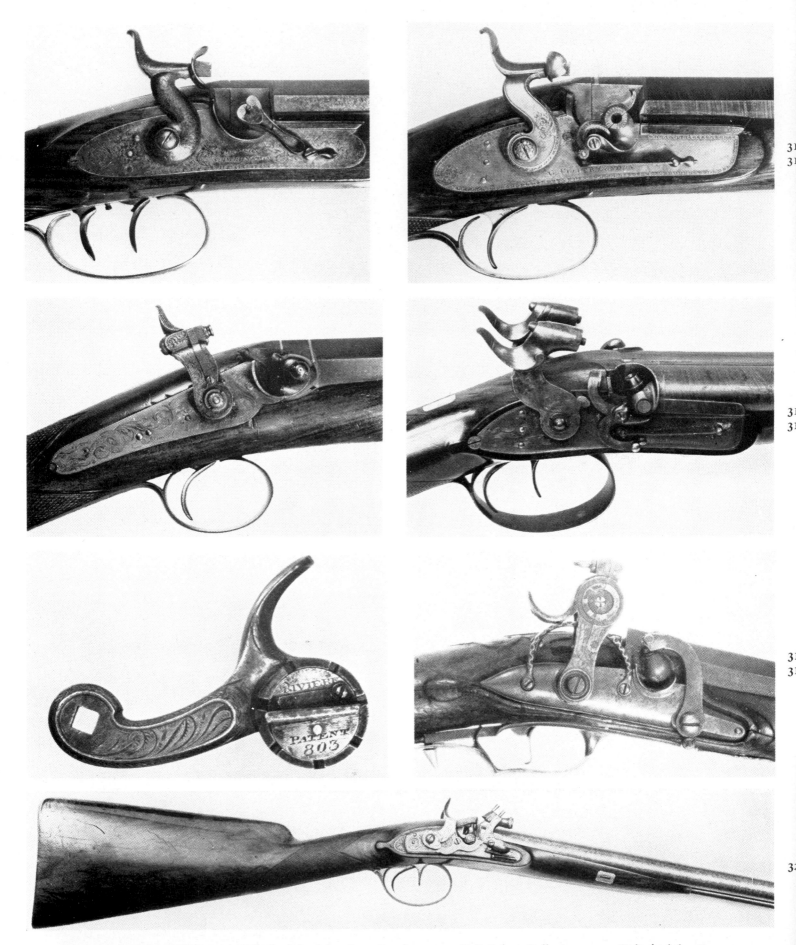

PERCUSSION LOCKS **314** Tube-lock by John Cox, Southampton. *F. J. Bubear Collection.* **315** Tube lock by George Fuller, London. *F. J. Bubear Collection.* **316** Pellet lock by Samuel Nock, London. *F. J. Bubear Collection.* **317** Pellet locks on a double-barrelled gun by Charles Moore, London. *Museum of Applied Arts and Sciences, Sydney.* **318** Hammer with circular pellet magazine marked RIVIERE PATENT 803. *Private Collection.* **319** Pellet lock with revolving magazine head. *German, c. 1825. Tower of London (Study Collection). (See p. 100.)* **320** Double-barrelled shotgun with Westley Richards's patent powder or pellet lock of 1821. *Tower of London (No. XII–1607).*

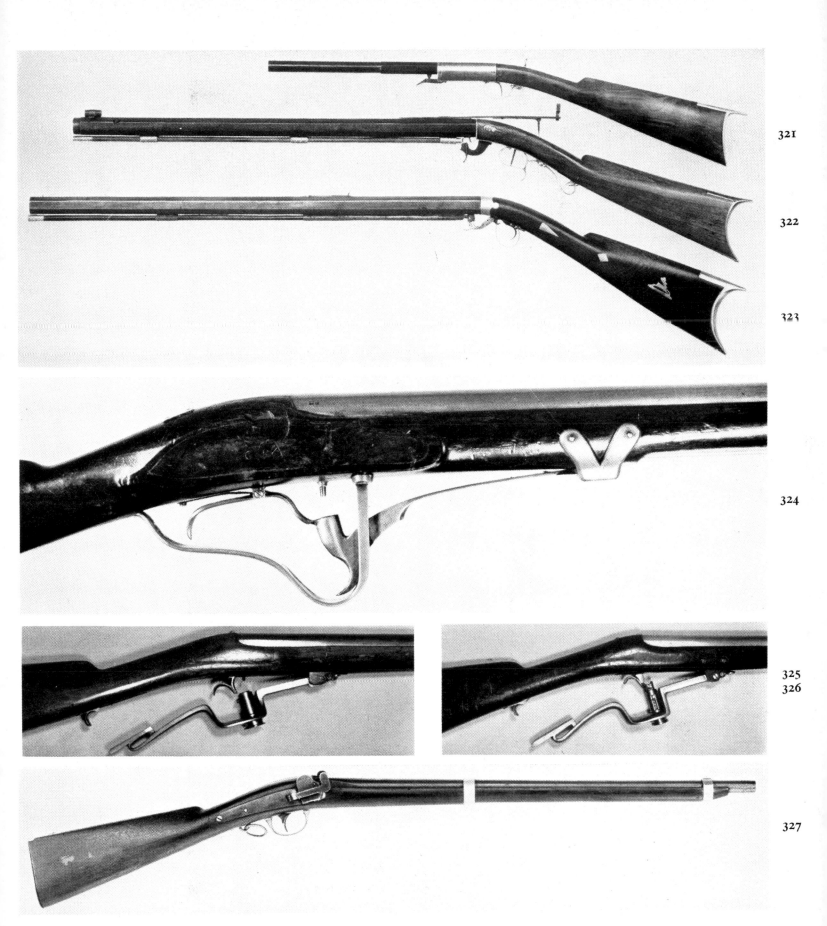

PERCUSSION UNDER- AND SIDE-HAMMER GUNS **321** Carbine. *American, c. 1850. Winchester Gun Museum. B. 10¼ in. Cal. 0·32 in.* **322** Rifle with extension rear-sight, marked D. H. HILLIARD, CORNISH, NEW HAMPSHIRE. *American, c. 1860. Winchester Gun Museum. B. 24 in. Cal. 0·38 in.* **323** Rifle marked W. F. ROBBINS, MANESBURY, PA. *American, c. 1870. Winchester Gun Museum. B. 27 in. Cal. 0·55 in.* **324** Tower musket converted to Henry Wilkinson's lock of 1839. *Tower of London (No. XII–703).* **325–6** Two models of the *koptipteur* lock of Gustaf Fleetwood. *Swedish, 1837. Tøjhusmuseet, Copenhagen (Nos. B. 2163–4).* **327** Jenks breechloading Navy carbine with side-hammer and Maynard's tape primer. *American, 1847. Winchester Gun Museum. B. 25 in. Cal. 0·52 in.*

PERCUSSION PISTOL-CARBINES   **328** U.S. Springfield model 1855 carbine with Maynard primer. *Winchester Gun Museum. L.* (with stock) 28¼ in.   **329** Under-hammer pistol with clip-on metal skeleton stock. *American,* dated 1870. *Herschel C. Logan Collection. L.* (pistol only) 19 in. *Cal.* 0·34 in.   **330** Pistol-carbine with telescopic sight, from a cased set by W. Billinghurst, Rochester, N.Y., together with its loading accessories. *Herschel C. Logan Collection. L.* (pistol only) 19 in. *Cal.* 0·38 in.

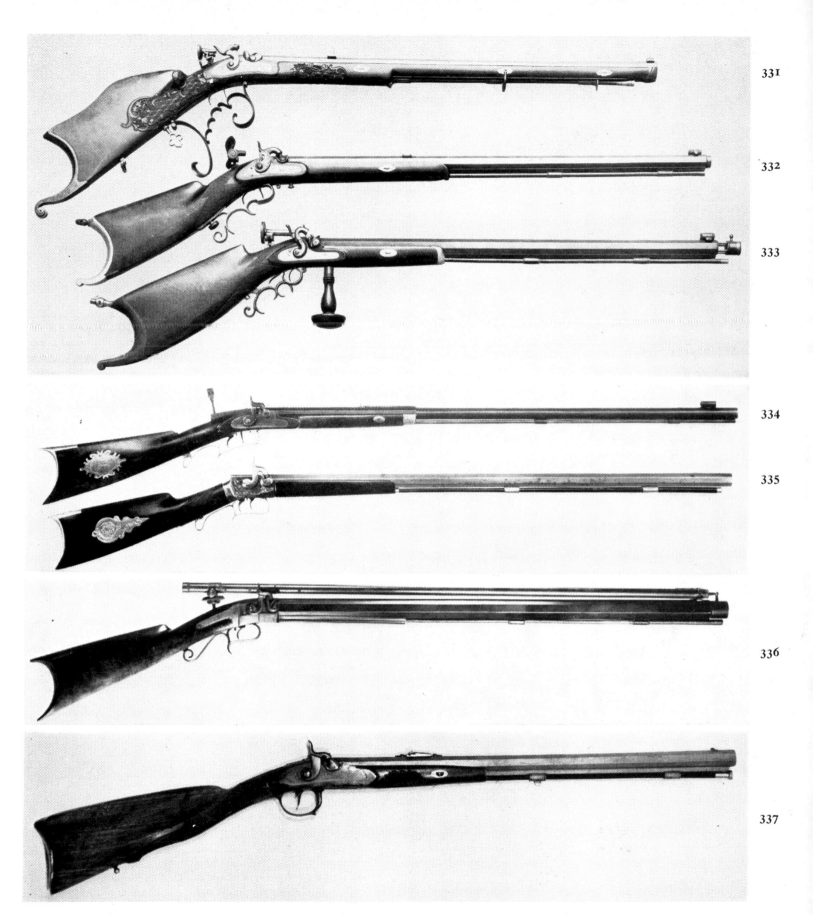

331

332

333

334

335

336

337

PERCUSSION RIFLES   **331** Schuetzen butt. Signed A. ZENKE A COLOGNE. *German, c.* 1850. *Milwaukee Museum (No. N.* 562). *B.* 31½ in. *Cal.* 0·372 in.   **332** Schuetzen butt. Signed PH. KLEIN, N.Y. *American, c.* 1860. *Milwaukee Museum (No. N.* 3614). *B.* 33 in. *Cal.* 0·41 in.   **333** Schuetzen butt, palm rest and false muzzle. Signed J. MEUNIER, MILWAUKEE, WIS. *American, c.* 1860. *Milwaukee Museum (No. N.* 2168). *B.* 30½ in. *Cal.* 0·4 in.   **334** Target rifle by John Smith, Ohio. *American,* dated 1869. *Winchester Gun Museum. B.* 34 in. *Cal.* 0·36 in.   **335** Rifle with engraved action marked G.P.F. BRISTOL, RHODE ISLAND. *American, c.* 1870. *Winchester Gun Museum. B.* 23½ in. *Cal.* 0·48 in.   **336** Rifle with telescopic sight by Edwin Wessen, Hartford, Conn. Used as a sniper's rifle by Edwin Stanclift, 8th Battn of Sharpshooters, Army of the Potomac, during the American Civil War. *Smithsonian Institution, Washington. B.* 29½ in. *Cal.* 0·45 in.   **337** Sporting rifle from a cased set. Barrel marked E. COLLETTE: Lock marked ARSENAL WARSZAWSKI 1827. *Muzeum Wojska Polskiego, Warsaw (No.* 24984 MWP).

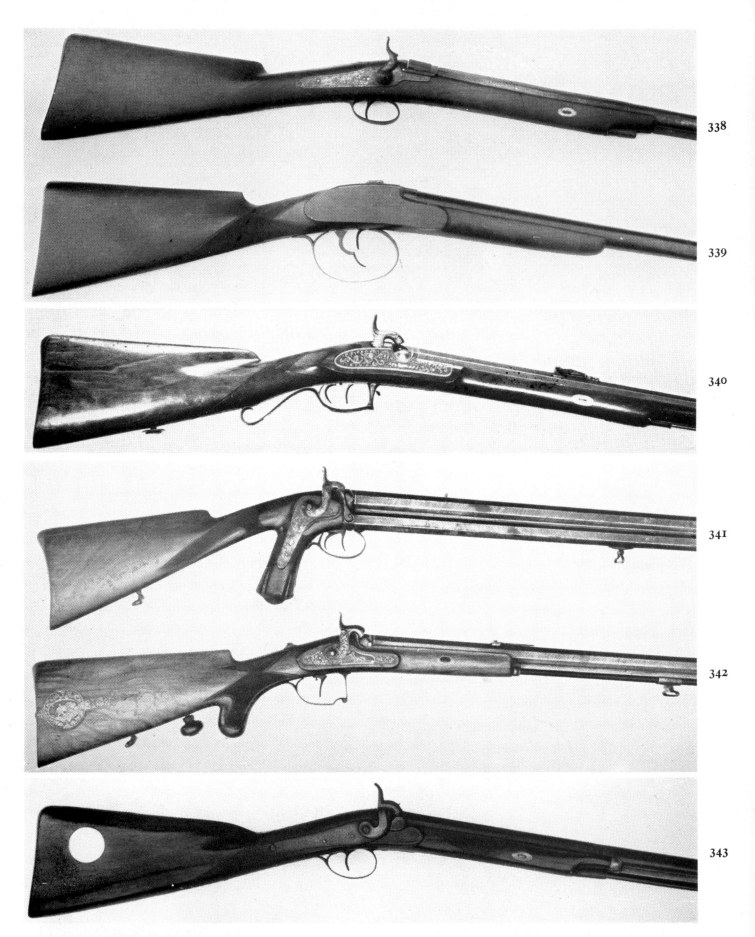

338

339

340

341

342

343

PERCUSSION SPORTING GUNS **338** Gun with Bentley's patent enclosed lock of 1839. *English. C. G. Vokes Collection. B.* 32 in. **339** Gun with enclosed action and large cocking lever behind trigger. Marked BARON DE BERENGER PATENT NO. 52. *English, c.* 1835. *C. G. Vokes Collection. B.* 30 in. *Cal.* 12 bore. **340** Rifle signed N. S. JESSEN. *Danish,* dated 1852. *Tøjhusmuseet, Copenhagen* (No. B. 2598). *B.* 32·7 in. *Cal.* 0·58 in. **341** Rifle with over-and-under barrels. *French, c.* 1850. *Tower of London* (Study Collection). *B.* 24 in. *Cal.* 0·69 in. **342** Rifle signed SCHENK IN MARIENBAD. *German, c.* 1850. *Tower of London* (Study Collection). *B.* 27¼ in. *Cal.* 0·67 in. **343** Gun signed BRIDLE. *English, c.* 1850. *Author's Collection. B.* 32 in. *Cal.* 0·69 in. (*See p.* 100.)

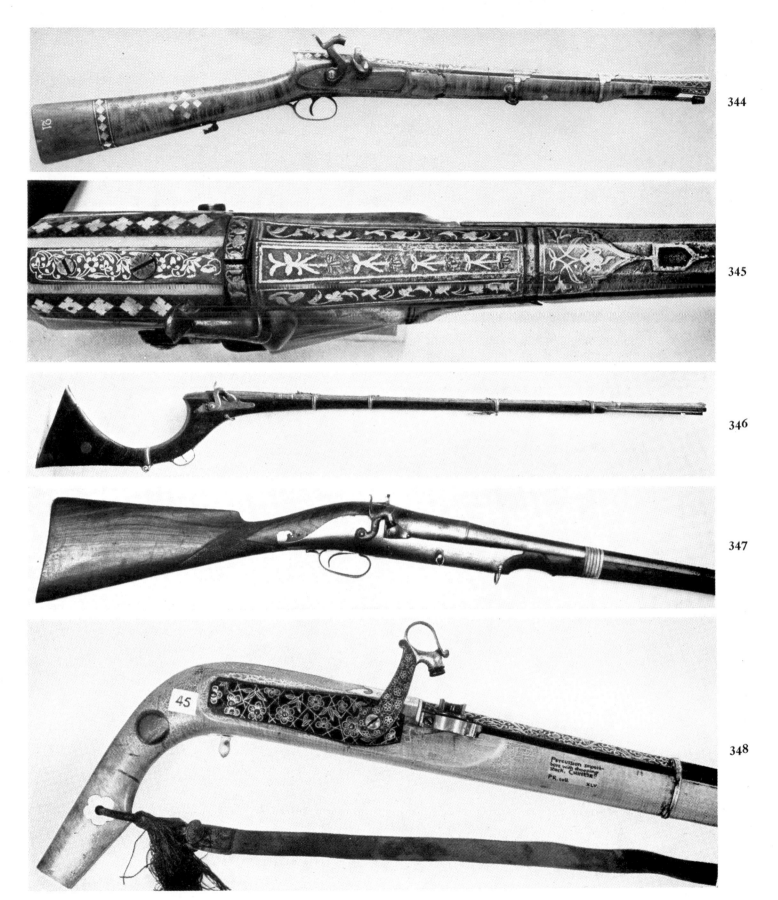

ORIENTAL PERCUSSION GUNS **344** Persian carbine (*Tufangcha*). Lock of European form inscribed 'the work of Rustam.' *Historisches Museum, Bern* (No. 751). B. 17·4 in. *Cal.* 0·59 in. **345** Top view of the breech of **344**. **346** Afghan gun with European lock. *Historisches Museum, Bern.* B. 46·7 in. *Cal.* 0·67 in. **347** Indian sporting gun with European-type butt. *Tower of London* (No. XXVI–110F). B. 45¼ in. **348** Chinese gun. Lock and barrel damascened in gold. *Pitt Rivers Collection, Oxford* (No. PR. 45). B. 47¼ in. *Cal.* 0·45 in.

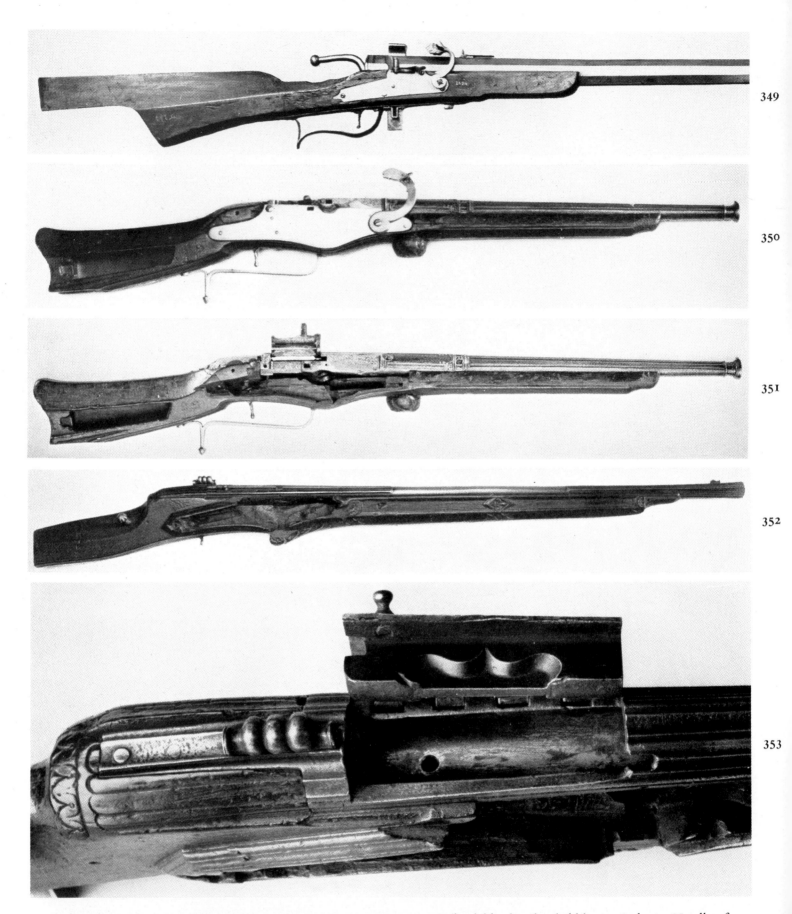

349

350

351

352

353

MATCHLOCK AND WHEELLOCK BREECHLOADERS **349** Reloadable chamber held by vertical peg. Handle of chamber protrudes at rear of breech. *German*, early 17th century. *Historisches Museum, Bern* (No. 2216). *B.* 41 in. *Cal.* 0·98 in. **350** Henry VIII's carbine, fitted with a later matchlock. *English* (?), dated 1537. *Tower of London* (No. XII–1). *B.* 26 in. *Cal.* 0·54 in. **351** The same gun without its matchlock and with its breech block raised. **352** Henry VIII's long gun. *English* (?), *c.* 1535. *Tower of London* (No. XII–2). *B.* 43½ in. *Cal.* 0·71 in. **353** Close-up of the open breech of **352**.

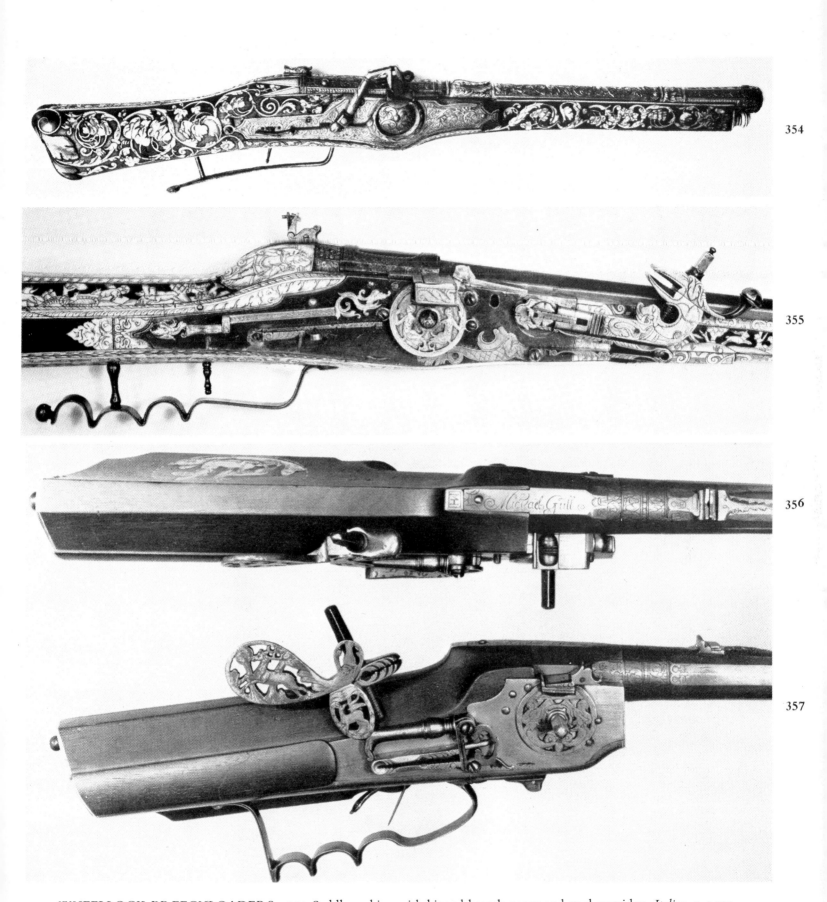

354

355

356

357

WHEELLOCK BREECHLOADERS **354** Saddle carbine with hinged breech-cover and steel cartridge. *Italian, c.* 1550. *Royal Armoury, Turin* (No. N. 10). *B.* 17·6 in. *Cal.* 0·51 in. **355** Close-up of gun with hinged breech-cover and steel cartridge. Self-spanning lock. *German (Augsburg), c.* 1600. *Wallace Collection* (No. A. 1081). **356–7** Lock and top views of a gun with turn-off barrel by Michael Gull, Vienna. *c.* 1650. *Kunsthistorisches Museum, Vienna* (No. HGK. 673).

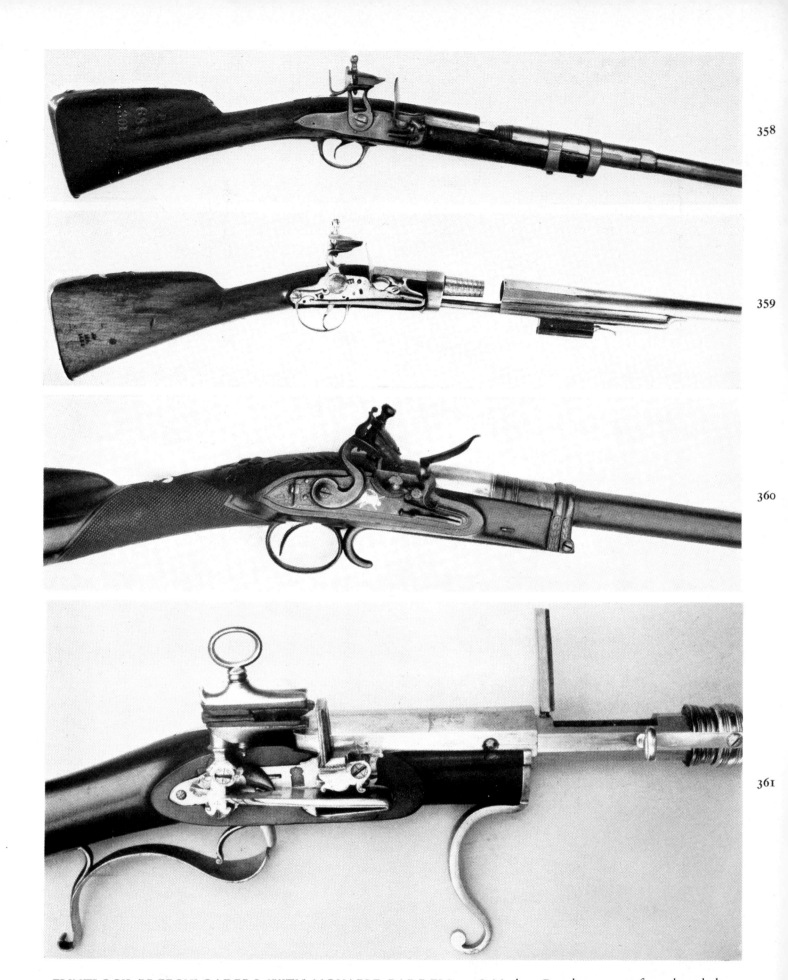

FLINTLOCK BREECHLOADERS WITH MOVABLE BARRELS **358** Musket. Barrel unscrews from breech by tapered quick thread. Lock signed F. BERNIER. *French, c. 1760. Tower of London (No. XII–259). B. 49·5 in. Cal. 0·69 in.* **359** Musket. Barrel slides forward to admit charge. *French, c. 1770. Tower of London (No. XII–1126). B. 46·8 in. Cal. 0·71 in.* (*See p.* 100.) **360** Rifle by Durs Egg, London. Barrel unscrews to disclose loading aperture on top of chamber. *English, c. 1790. Mark Dineley Collection.* **361** Sporting gun by F. Castano. Barrel pulled out and hinged lid of chamber open for loading. *Spanish, c. 1800. W. Keith Neal Collection.*

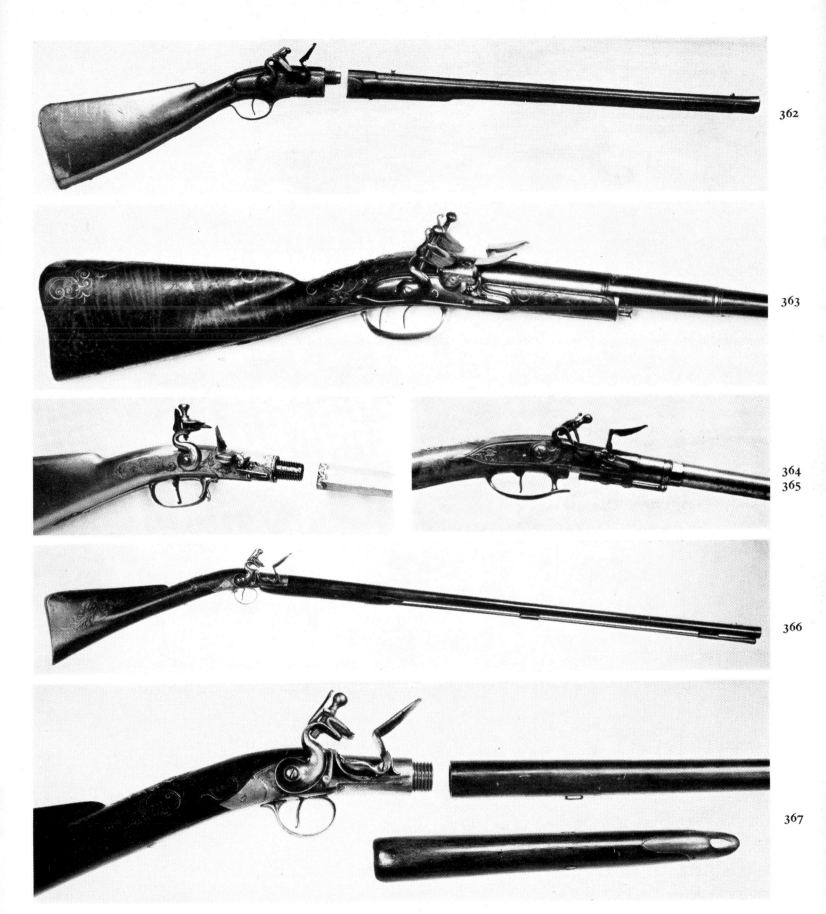

FLINTLOCK BREECHLOADERS WITH TURN-OFF BARRELS   **362** Rifle by Trulocke, London. *English, c.* 1670. *Glasgow Museum* (No. 39–65vx). *B.* 25 in. *Cal.* 0·70 in.   **363** Sporting gun with two chambers and locks. Signed GORGO LONDINI FECIT. *English, c.* 1690. *Lord Braybrooke Collection (On loan to Tower of London).*   **364** All-steel rifle signed J. CLOETER A GREVENBROCH. *W. German, c.* 1680. *Tøjhusmuseet, Copenhagen* (No. B. 903).   **365** Rifled carbine by Pochard, Paris. *French, c.* 1730. *Glasgow Museum* (No. 39–65vo).   **366** Butt and action, *c.* 1740. Barrel by Ezekiel Baker & Son, London, *c.* 1830. *Winchester Gun Museum. B.* 24¾ in. *Cal.* 0·54 in.   **367** Close-up of **366** with barrel unscrewed and fore-end detached.

368

369

370

371

FLINTLOCK BREECHLOADERS WITH PIVOTED CHAMBERS **368** Combined matchlock and flintlock gun. Barrel joined to chamber by interrupted screw-thread. Lock signed PETER DURINGER, MAINTZ. *German, c. 1660. Rotunda, Woolwich (No. IX–9). B. 44·75 in. Cal. 0·56 in.* **369** Close-up of **368** showing barrel mechanism and chamber in loading position. **370** Gun signed JOHN BICKNELL, LONDINI. *English, c. 1660. Tower of London (No. XII–1617). B. 49 in. Cal. 0·64 in.* **371** The same gun with its trigger guard depressed and chamber open.

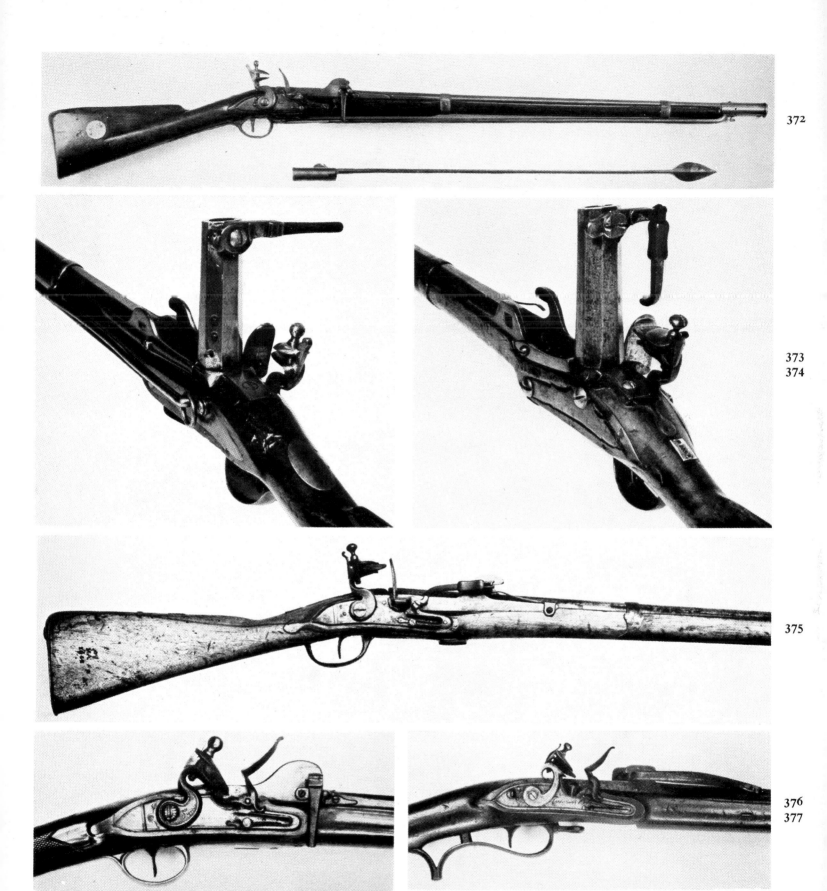

FLINTLOCK BREECHLOADERS (CRESPI SYSTEM) **372** Experimental cavalry rifle with spear bayonet (one on the rifle and one shown separately) by Durs Egg, London. *English, c.* 1785. *Tower of London* (No. XII–1034). *B.* 35 in. *Cal.* 0·65 in. **373** Breech of **372**. Chamber raised for loading. **374** Breech of **375** in loading position. **375** Austrian military rifle, *c.* 1775. *Tower of London* (No. XXIV–416). *B.* 33¼ in. *Cal.* 0·72 in. **376** Close-up of rifle made by Durs Egg for English Volunteer Company, *c.* 1790. Fitted with Hennem's screwless lock. **377** Breech of rifle by Tatham & Egg, London. *c.* 1810.

FLINTLOCK BREECHLOADERS WITH PIVOTED CHAMBERS 378 Rifle with folding bayonet by Durs Egg, London. Chamber raised for loading. *English, c. 1800. Glasgow Museum* (No. 39–65vr). 379 U.S. rifle Model 1819 with J. H. Hall breech action. Made at Harper's Ferry Armoury in 1838. Chamber raised. *West Point Museum* (No. 5552). *B.* 32·75 in. *Cal.* 0·52 in. 380 Breech of 379 closed. 381 Breech of 382 open. 382 Rifle of doubtful authenticity. Barrel and lock by Ezekiel Baker & Son, *c.* 1830. Rolling collar breech similar to Edward Lindner patent of 1859. Stock from Austrian Jaeger rifle (?), *c.* 1845. *Winchester Gun Museum.* 383 Double-barrelled gun. Folding levers unlock barrels which move forward to open breech. *English, c. 1820. Royal Armoury, Turin* (No. M. 61). *B.* 21·5 in. *Cal.* 0·63 in.

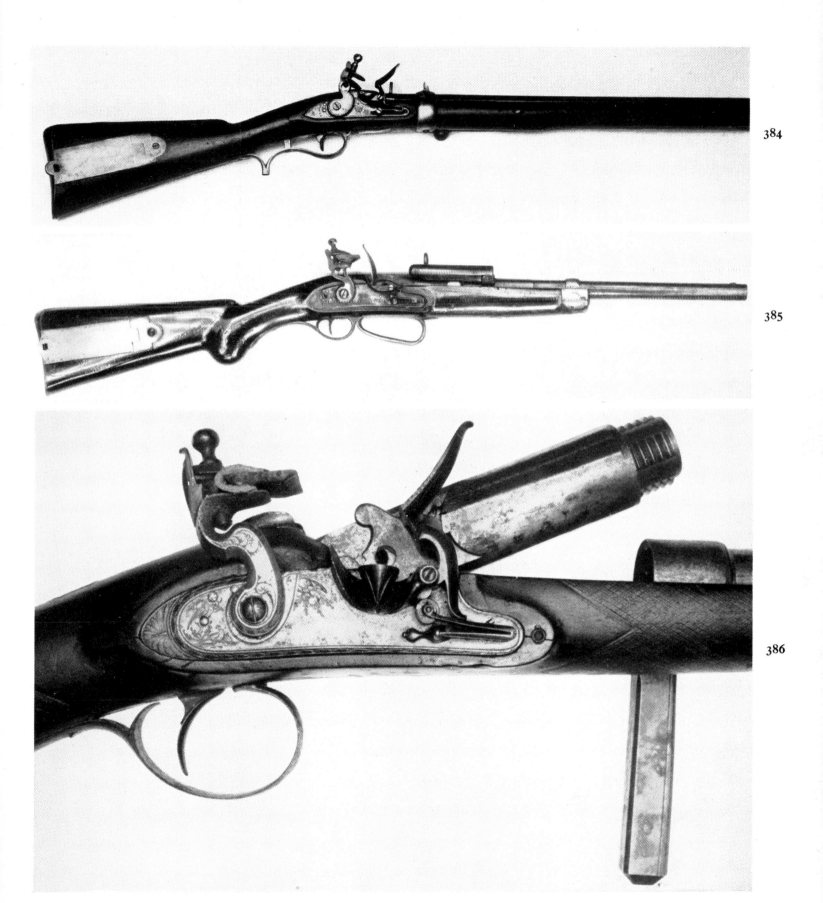

SARTORIS FLINTLOCK BREECHLOADERS **384** Sartoris action fitted to a Baker rifle. *English, c.* 1820. **385** Cavalry carbine made for a Volunteer Company (?). *English, c.* 1820. **386** Close-up of sporting gun with Sartoris action open. Fitted with self-priming device. *English, c.* 1820. *Noel Corry Collection.*

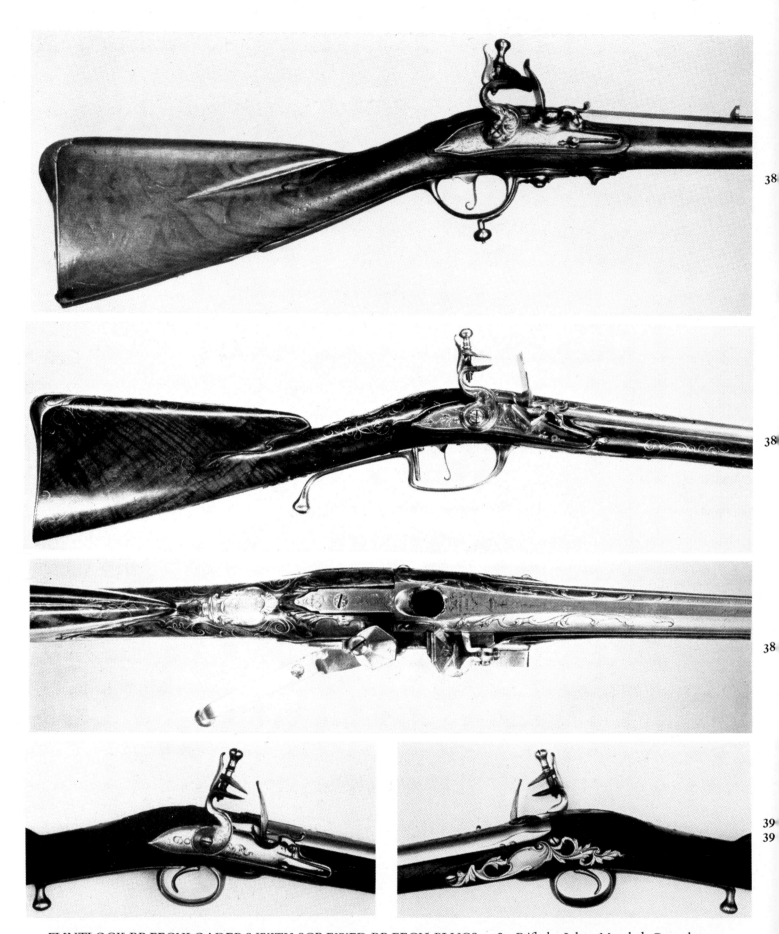

FLINTLOCK BREECHLOADERS WITH SCREWED BREECH-PLUGS **387** Rifle by Johan Merckel, Copenhagen. *Danish, c.* 1710. *Tøjhusmuseet, Copenhagen* (No. B. 1140). **388** La Chaumette gun signed BIDET, LONDINI. Made for George I. *English, c.* 1725. *Duke of Brunswick Collection.* **389** Top view of breech of **388**, with loading aperture open. **390–1** Lock and side views of La Chaumette gun by Bidet. *English, c.* 1730. *Wapenmuseum Generaal Hoefer, Leiden.*

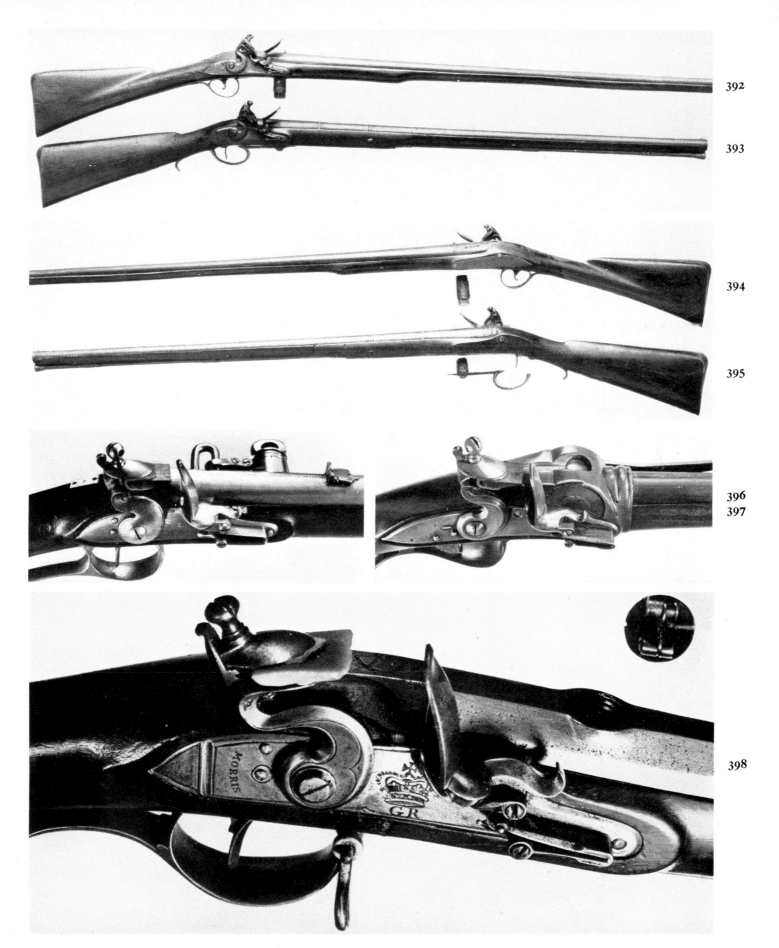

FLINTLOCK BREECHLOADERS WITH MOVABLE BREECH-PLUGS   **392** Rifle. Screwed plug with nut head under barrel. *English, c. 1760. Milwaukee Museum* (No. N. 7151).   **393** Gun signed FOSTER. Screwed plug under barrel connected to trigger guard. *English, c. 1790. Milwaukee Museum* (No. N. 6196).   **394** No. **392** with plug removed.   **395** No. **393** with plug removed.   **396** Experimental cavalry rifle by James Wilkes, London, 1801. Screwed plug on side of breech linked to barrel. *Tower of London* (No. XII–258).   **397** Breech of Hulme's rifle made for British Army trial in 1807. Rolling-block breech with loading aperture on top. *Tower of London* (No. XII–256).   **398** Light Infantry rifle by Morris, Birmingham. Screw plug removed. *c. 1810. F. J. Bubear Collection.*

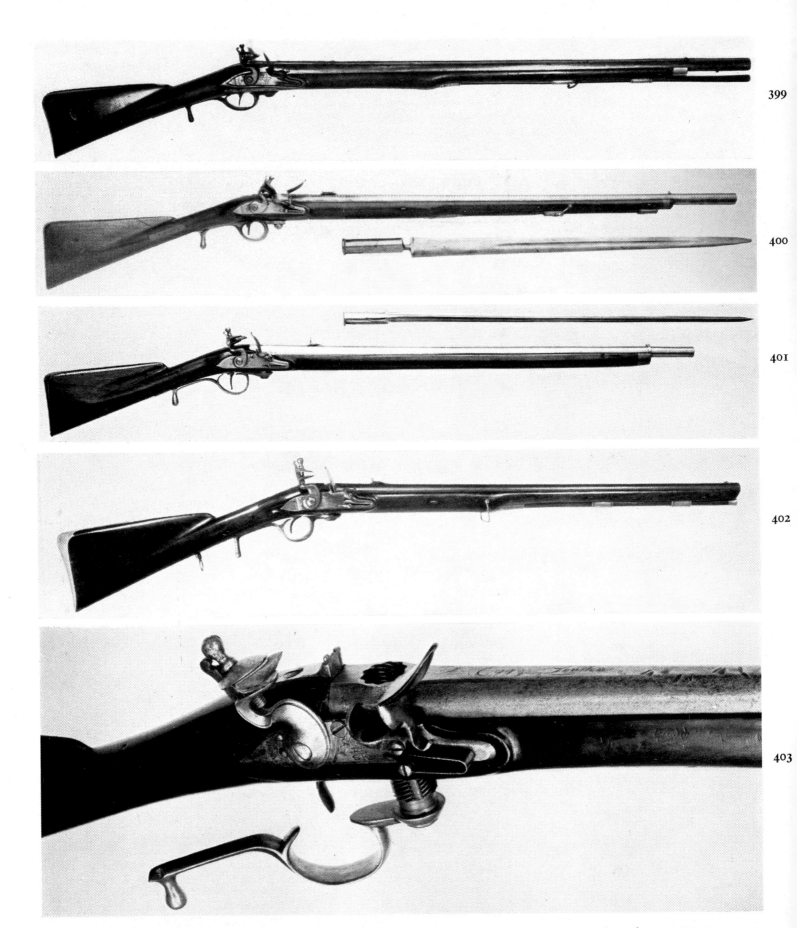

FERGUSON MILITARY BREECHLOADERS **399** One of the original-issue Ferguson rifles of 1776. *Morristown National Historical Park.* B. 34 in. *Cal.* 0·68 in. 8-groove rifling. **400** Rifle by Durs Egg. *c.* 1795. *Smithsonian Institution, Washington* (No. 42402-A). B. 34 in. *Cal.* 0·69 in. 8 grooves. Bayonet L. 25 in. **401** Rifle and bayonet with special fastening. No marks. *English (?), c.* 1795. *Tøjhusmuseet, Copenhagen* (No. B. 1863). B. 31·6 in. *Cal.* 0·63 in. 8 grooves. Bayonet L. 26·6 in. **402** Cavalry rifle made for the East India Company by Henry Nock. Dated 1776. *Author's Collection.* B. 29 in. *Cal.* 0·61 in. **403** Breech of Volunteer rifle by Durs Egg. Plug withdrawn showing anti-fouling grooves. *Jac Weller Collection.*

FERGUSON SPORTING BREECHLOADERS **404** Rifle by Durs Egg. Made for George IV when Prince of Wales. Blued barrel and lock inlaid with gold. Silver mounts hall-marked 1782. *Windsor Castle* (No. 420). *B.* 34 in. 12 grooves. **405** Rifle with sliding bayonet by Durs Egg, *c.* 1780. *West Point Museum* (No. 5530). *B.* 24 in. *Cal.* 0·58 in. 8 grooves. **406** Top view of breech of **405**. **407** Breech (in open position) of rifle by Durs Egg. Silver mounts hall-marked 1777. *W. Keith Neal Collection.*

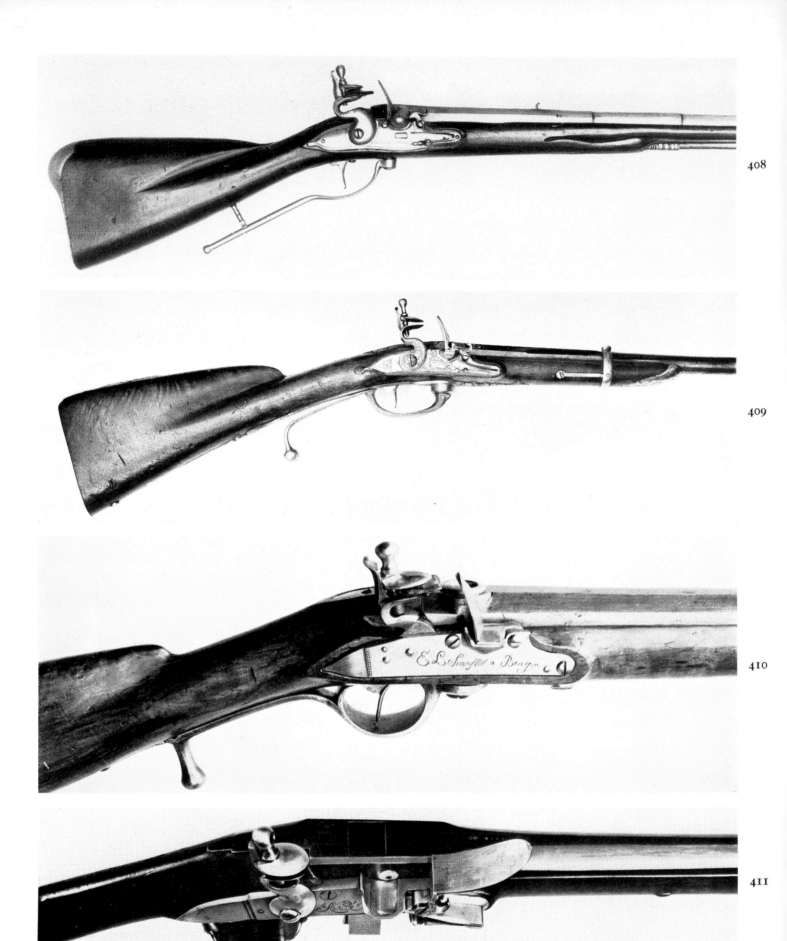

FLINTLOCK BREECHLOADERS WITH MOVABLE PLUGS · 408 Rifle with horizontal breech block worked by trigger guard. Signed HEINRICH KAPPEL. *Danish (Copenhagen), c.* 1690. *Tøjhusmuseet, Copenhagen* (No. B. 1034). *B.* 38·4 in. *Cal.* 0·79 in. (*See p.* 100.) 409 Gun with screwed breech-plug by Brion, Paris, *c.* 1740. Formerly *Ettersburg Castle Collection.* 410 Rifle with screwed breech-plug signed E. L. SVORSDØL A BERGEN. *Norwegian, c.* 1810. *Tøjhusmuseet, Copenhagen* (No. 1950). *B.* 32·6 in. *Cal.* 0·6 in. (*See p.* 100.) 411 Gun with vertically-falling breech block signed RIVES A PARIS. *French, c.* 1780. *Tower of London* (No. XII–1125). *B.* 39½ in. *Cal.* 0·65 in.

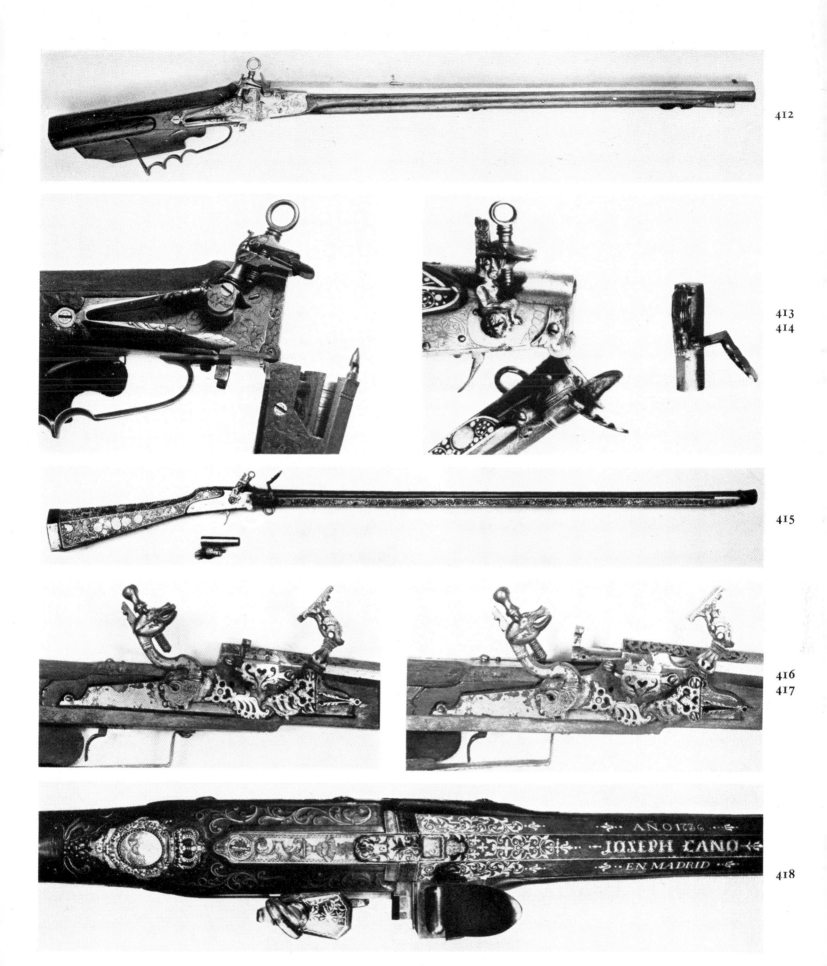

412

413
414

415

416
417

418

FLINTLOCK BREECHLOADERS WITH SEPARATE CHAMBERS **412** Rifle with miquelet-type lock and break-action by Franz Jeiadtel. *Austrian (Vienna), c. 1650. Tøjhusmuseet, Copenhagen* (No. B. 570). *B. 28·3 in. Cal. 0·51 in.* **413** Close-up of open breech of **412**. **414** Close-up of open breech of **415** with spare chamber. **415** Break-action gun with spare chamber. *N. German, early 17th century. Royal Armoury, Turin* (No. M. 55). *B. 36·6 in. Cal. 0·59 in.* **416** Breech of a snaphance gun with pull-out chamber. *Russian, 17th century. Kremlin, Moscow* (No. 7424). **417** Same gun with chamber half-way out. **418** Top view of break-action gun by Joseph Cano. *Madrid. Dated 1736. Royal Armoury, Madrid* (No. K. 156).

FLINTLOCK BREECHLOADERS WITH SEPARATE CHAMBERS **419** Break-action gun with spare chamber. Lock marked LONDON. *Flemish (?), c. 1740. Tower of London (No. XII–252).* **420** Close-up of open breech and steel chamber of gun by Johann Georg Polz, Carlsbad, *c.* 1790. *Noel Corry Collection.* **421** Close-up of open breech and brass chamber of gun by Henry Delany, London, *c.* 1730. *Noel Corry Collection.* **422** Musket with pull-out chamber by Henry Nock, London, 1786. *Tower of London (No. XII–250). B.* 42½ in. *Cal.* 0·75 in. **423** Close-up of breech of **422** opened for loading. **424** Gun by Michael Gull, Vienna, with hinged breech block open and chamber partly extracted. *Austrian, c.* 1670. *Kunsthistorisches Museum, Vienna (No. D. 378).*

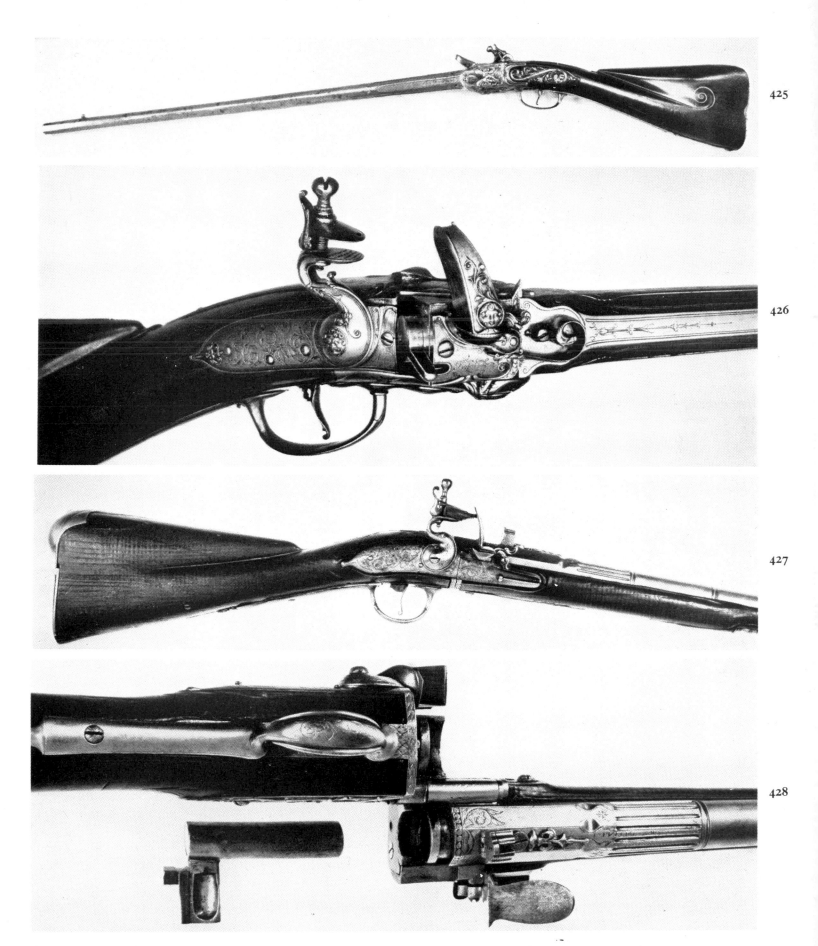

FLINTLOCK BREECHLOADERS WITH SEPARATE CHAMBERS **425** Break-action gun signed ACQUA FRESCA.
Barrel breaks sideways. *N. Italian (Bargi)*, dated 1694. *City Museum, Birmingham.* **426** Close-up of breech of **425**. Chamber
partly extracted. **427** Rifle signed I. FULLICK, SARUM. Barrel swivels sideways for loading. *English, c. 1680. Countess of
Seafield Collection.* **428** Close-up of breech of **427** (from underneath trigger guard) with chamber extracted.

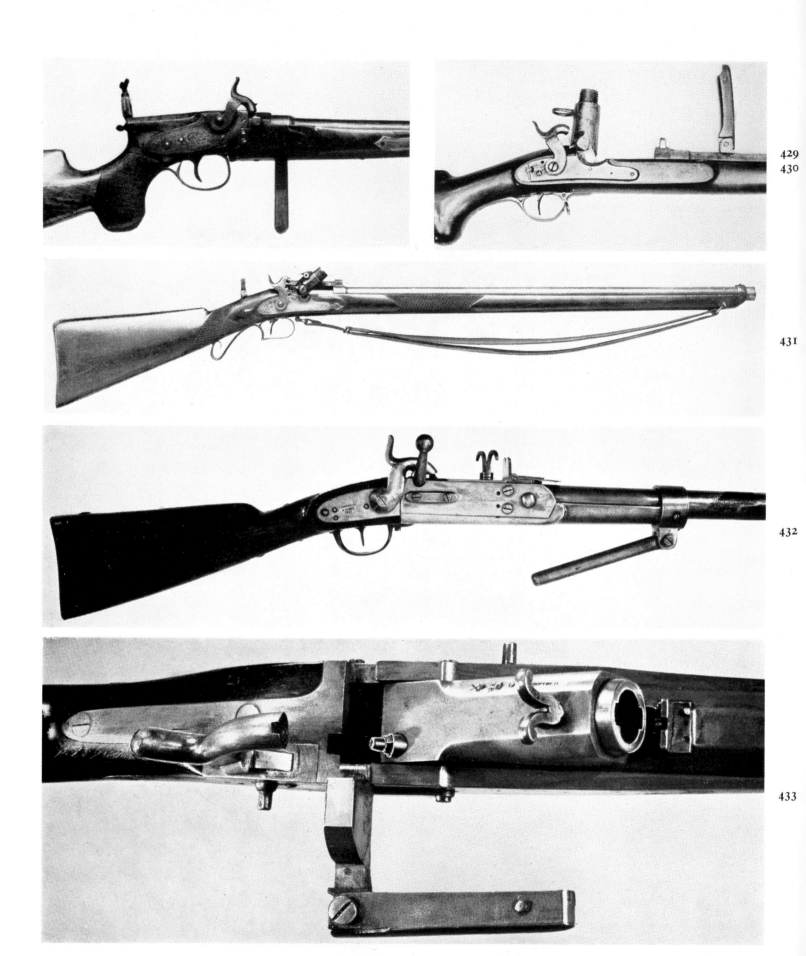

429
430

431

432

433

PERCUSSION BREECHLOADERS   **429** Rifle with separate chamber. Movable barrel joined to breech by interrupted screw-thread. Signed DURS EGG, LONDON. *c.* 1830. *Glasgow Museum.*   **430** Sartoris flintlock rifle converted to percussion, breech open. *c.* 1825. *Small Arms Factory, Enfield.*   **431** Sartoris rifle signed A. F. BIVEN, REGENT ST. WATERLOO PLACE. *English, c.* 1825. *Milwaukee Museum* (No. N. 565). *B.* $27\frac{1}{2}$ in. *Cal.* 0·58 in.   **432** Military wall rifle with tip-up chamber by P. J. Malherbe, Liège. Dated 1837. *Tower of London* (No. XII–575).   **433** Top view of open breech of similar gun made at Enfield Small Arms Factory, for use with a belted ball. *English,* dated 1839. *Tower of London* (No. XII–564).

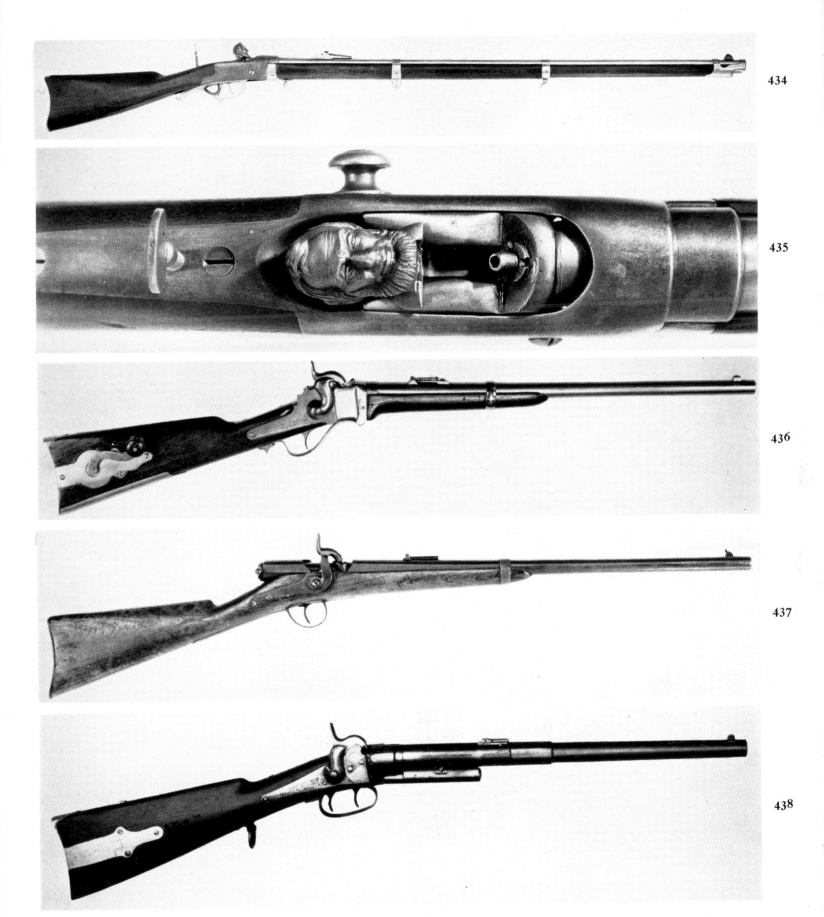

PERCUSSION BREECHLOADERS   **434** Rifle with lever-action breech and ramrod bayonet. Hammer cast in likeness of Abraham Lincoln. *American (?), c. 1860. Winchester Gun Museum.*   **435** Top view of breech of **434**.   **436** Model 1863 Sharps's carbine with disc primer and coffee mill in butt. *American. Winchester Gun Museum. B. 22 in. Cal. 0·52 in.*   **437** Confederate carbine. Burton's first-model bolt-action. *American, c. 1860. Winchester Gun Museum. B. 22 in. Cal. 0·52 in.*   **438** Greene cavalry carbine with side-swivelling barrel and Maynard's tape primer. Made in America for British Army, 1856. *Tower of London (Study Collection). B. 18 in. Cal. 0·52 in.*

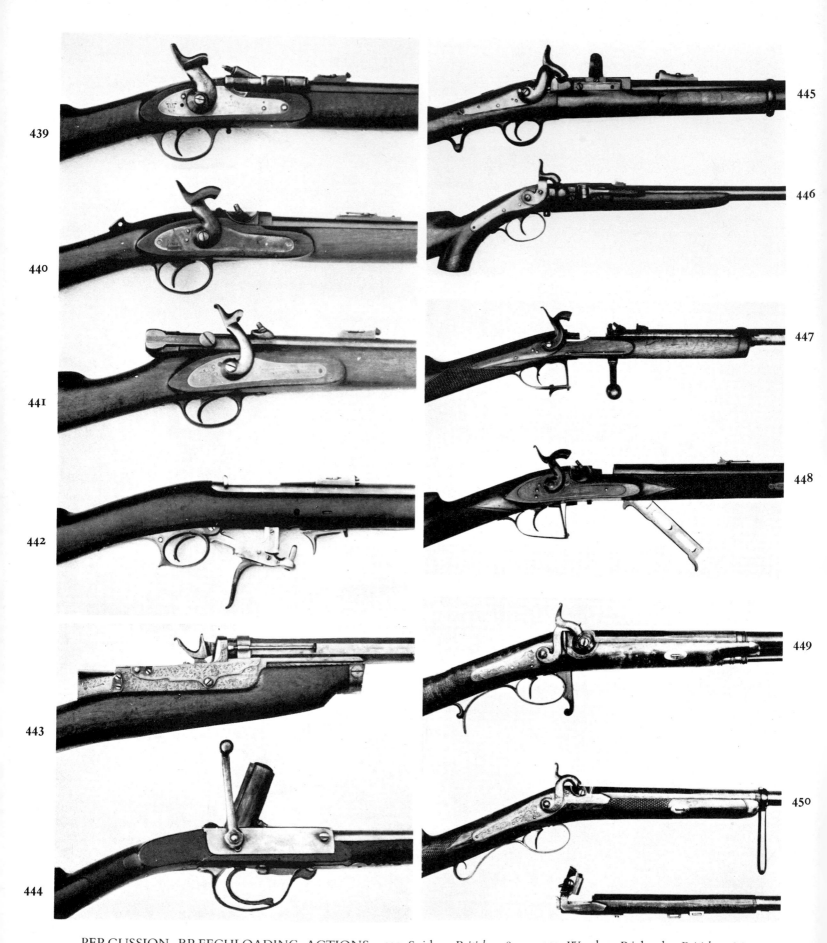

PERCUSSION BREECHLOADING ACTIONS 439 Snider. *British*, 1872. 440 Westley Richards. *British*, 1867.
441 Calisher & Terry. *British*, 1869. 442 F. Prince. *British*, 1859. (*See p.* 100). 443 Renson. *Belgian*, 1863. (*See p.* 101.)
444 I. Grindreng. *Danish, c.* 1860. *C. G. Vokes Collection* (439–444).
445 J. Leetch. *British*, 1854. 446 J. Leetch. *British*, 1855. 447 F. Prince. *British*, 1855. 448 T. Murcott. *British, c.* 1860.
449 Golden. *British, c.* 1845. 450 Williams & Powell. *British, c.* 1845. (*See p.* 101.) *Tower of London* (*Study Collection*)
(445–50).

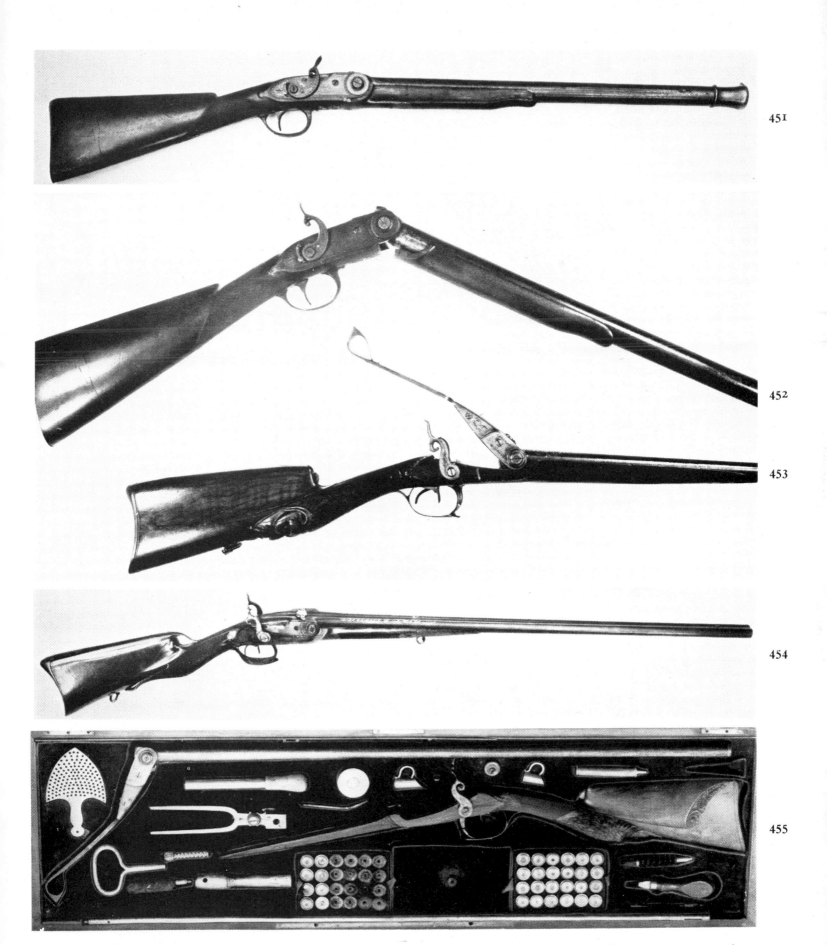

PAULY BREECHLOADERS **451–2** Seven-barrelled volley gun of the design patented in London in 1814. *Tower of London* (No. XII–1761). *B.* 22·3 in. *Cal.* 0·3 in. **453** Double-barrelled gun with breech raised. Made by A. Renette after design patented in Paris in 1812. *Tower of London* (No. XII–1565). *B.* 29·75 in. *Cal.* 0·615 in. **454** Double-barrelled gun signed in gold on breech INVENTION PAULY BREVETÉE À PARIS. **455** Double-barrelled gun in case with loading tools and brass cartridge bases. Barrels bear mark of A. Renette, Paris. Serial No. 241. *C. R. Clare Collection. B.* 31·75 in. *Cal.* 0·63 in.

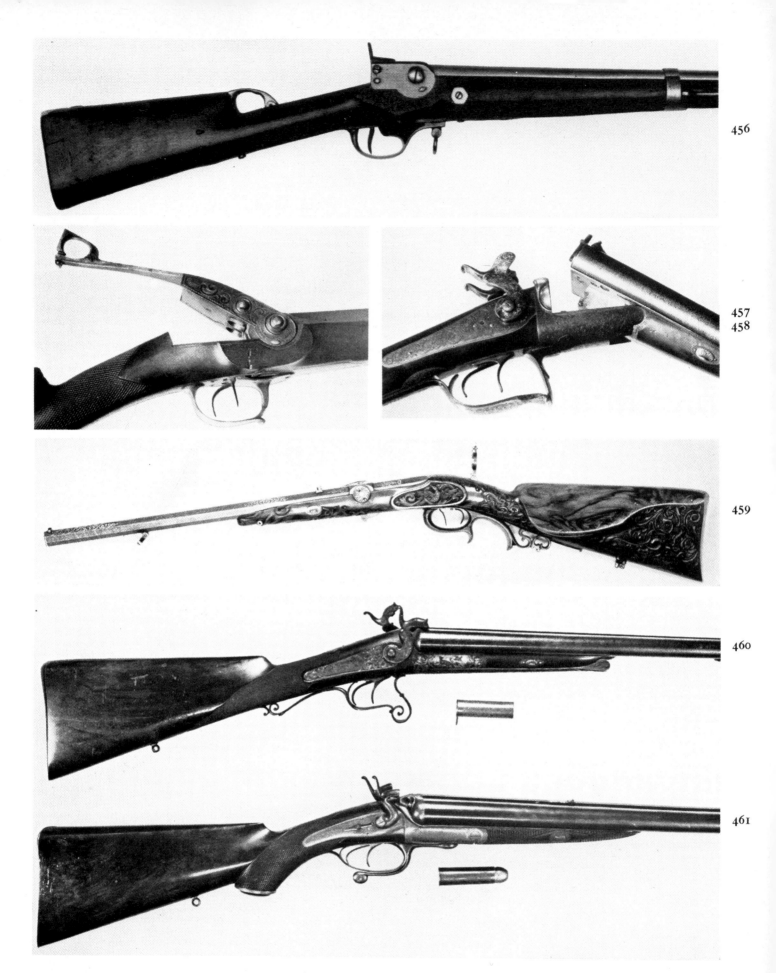

CARTRIDGE BREECHLOADERS **456** Belgian military musket, Robert system. *c.* 1835. *Tower of London* (No. XII–1052). *B.* 41·5 in. *Cal.* 0·63 in. **457** Open breech of double-barrelled sporting gun by J. Robert. Patented 1831. French, *c.* 1835. *Arms Museum, Liège* (No. Aj 2/2444). **458** Open breech of double-barrelled sporting gun by Béringer. Patented 1834. *French, c.* 1840. *Arms Museum, Liège* (No. Aj 6/5355). **459** Gallery gun by Carl Stiegele, Munich. Revolving breech using fulminated, hollow bullet. *John T. Amber Collection.* **460** Double-barrelled pin-fire shotgun (with cartridge) by Ronge Bros. *French, c.* 1865. **461** Double-barrelled centre-fire big-game rifle (with cartridge) by Joseph Lang, London, *c.* 1880.

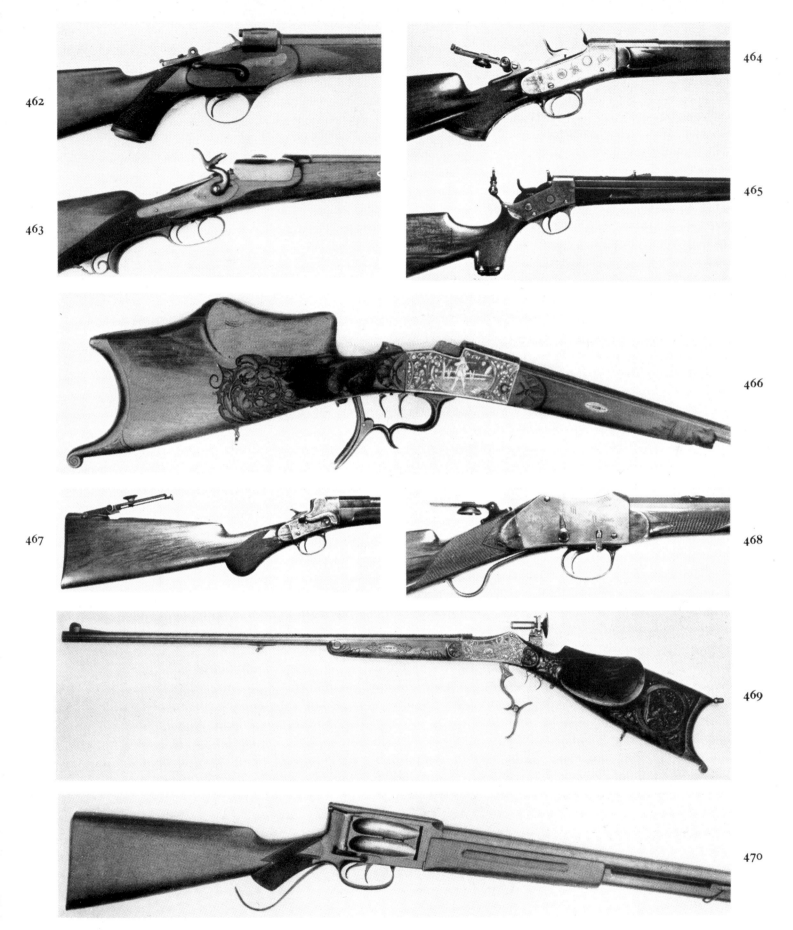

CARTRIDGE BREECHLOADERS **462** Soper breech action. *British, c. 1870.* **463** Werndl breech action. *Austrian, c. 1865. C. G. Vokes Collection.* **464** Remington rolling-block target rifle. *American, c. 1880.* **465** Remington rolling-block sporting rifle. *American, c. 1880.* **466** Vertically-falling block Schuetzen rifle (*System Kolbe*) signed AUGUST STUKENBROK EINBECK. *German, c. 1890. C. G. Vokes Collection.* **467** Remington-Hepburn long-range Creedmoor rifle. *American, c. 1880.* **468** Peabody-Martini rifle. *American, c. 1870.* **469** Martini-action Schuetzen rifle by Carl Stiegele, Munich. *German, 1890. John T. Amber Collection.* **470** Over-and-under shotgun with side-swivelling breech block. *Russian, c. 1900. C. G. Vokes Collection.*

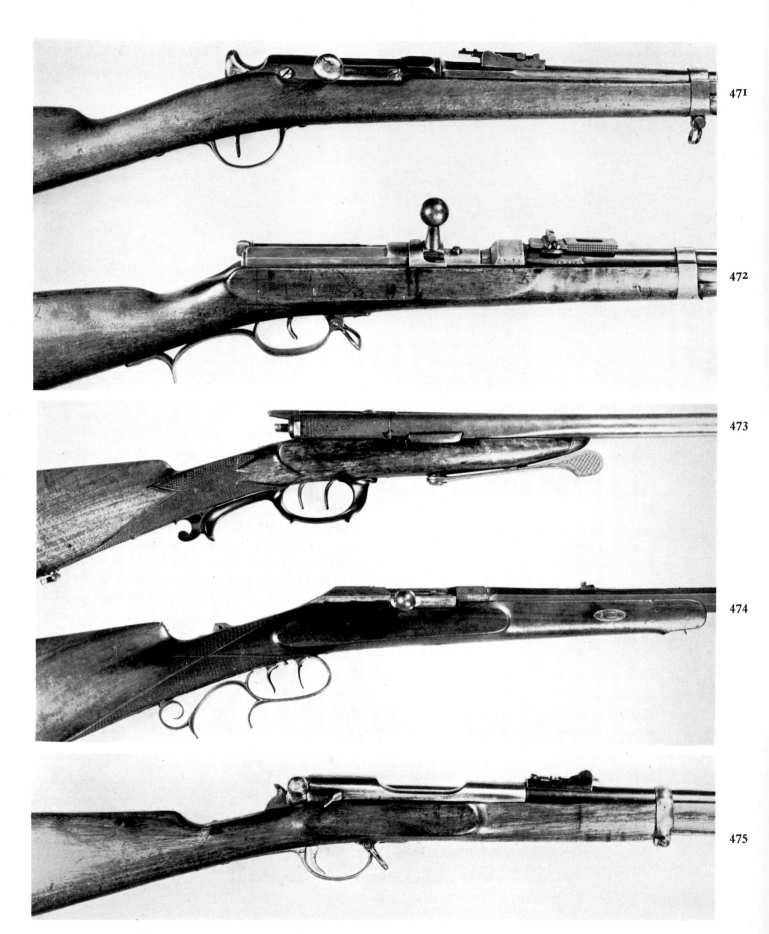

BOLT-ACTION BREECHLOADERS **471** Chassepot military centre-fire rifle. *French*. Model 1866. **472** Von Dreyse military needle-fire rifle. *German*, Model 1841. **473** Double-barrelled needle-fire sporting rifle signed F. V. DREYSE SOMMERDA. Barrels move forward and then swing sideways for loading. *German*, 1860. **474** Centre-fire sporting rifle signed LALLERSTEDT IN BERLIN. *German*, c. 1880. **475** Centre-fire military rifle by Brown Mfg. Co., Newburyport, Mass. *American*, patented 1871.

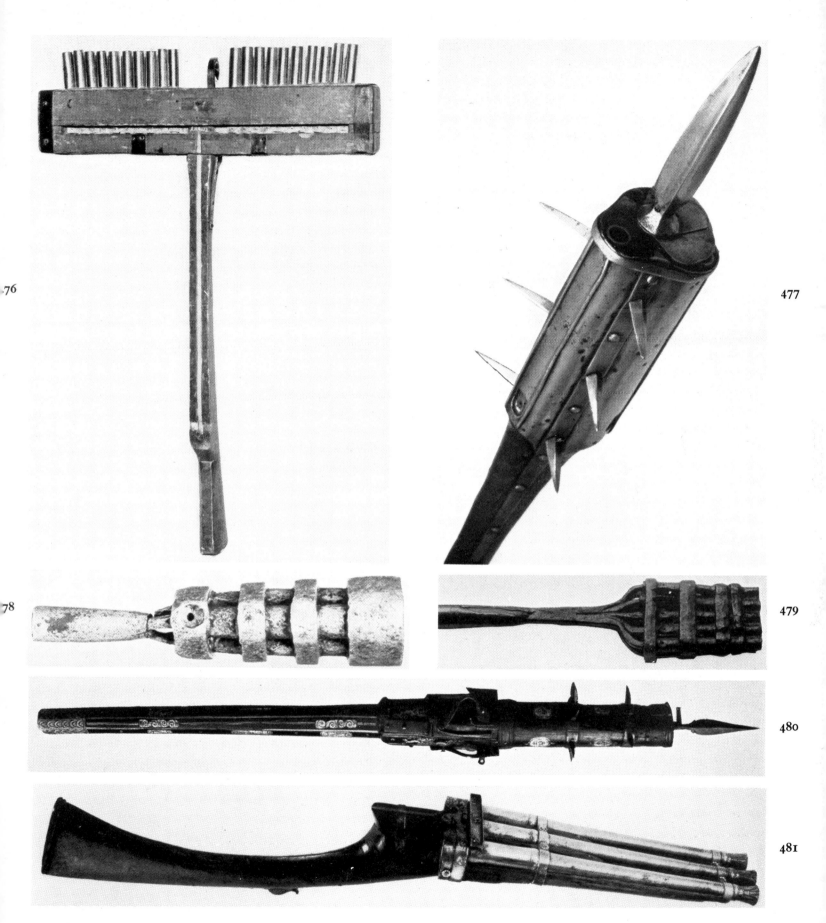

MULTI-BARRELLED GUNS 476 Wall gun with 20 sawn-off musket barrels fired by powder train in grooves. *Swedish* (?), *c.* 1660. *Royal Army Museum, Stockholm* (No. AM. 4053). *B.* 7·3 *in. Cal.* 0·79 *in.* 477 Head of 'holy-water sprinkler' with three barrels. *English* (?), early 16th century. *Tower of London* (No. XIV–1). 478 Three-barrelled signal gun. *Korean* (?), 18th century. *Author's Collection. L.* 7¼ *in.* 479 Ten-barrelled gun on pole. *Formosan*, 18th century. *Rotunda, Woolwich* (No. XI–21). 480 Three-barrelled 'holy-water sprinkler' with snap-matchlocks. *S. German*, late 17th century. *Metropolitan Museum, New York* (No. 19.53.70). 481 Three-barrelled matchlock gun. *Indian*, 18th century. *Tower of London* (No. XXVI–64F). *B.* 11¼ *in.*

482

483

484

485

486

DOUBLE-BARRELLED OVER-AND-UNDER GUNS **482** Wheellock rifle. *S. German, dated 1588. Windsor Castle* (No. 327). *B.* 32½ in. *Cal.* 0·47 in. **483** Flintlock gun signed ABRAHAM MUNIER A GENEVE. *Swiss, c. 1650. Tøjhusmuseet, Copenhagen* (No. B. 680). *B.* 46·7 in. *Cal.* 0·52 in. **484** Flintlock gun signed PONSIN. *French, c. 1740. C. G. Vokes Collection. B.* 36 in. **485** Flintlock rifle with single lock and tap-action priming-pan. Fine Damascus barrels with Persian inscription mounted in England. *c.* 1820. *C. G. Vokes Collection. B.* 24½ in. **486** Percussion rifle with 'mule's ear' side hammers by W. E. Robbins, Mansbury, Roaring Springs & Elk Run, Pennsylvania. *American, c.* 1860. *Winchester Gun Museum. B.* 33 in. *Cal.* 0·41 in.

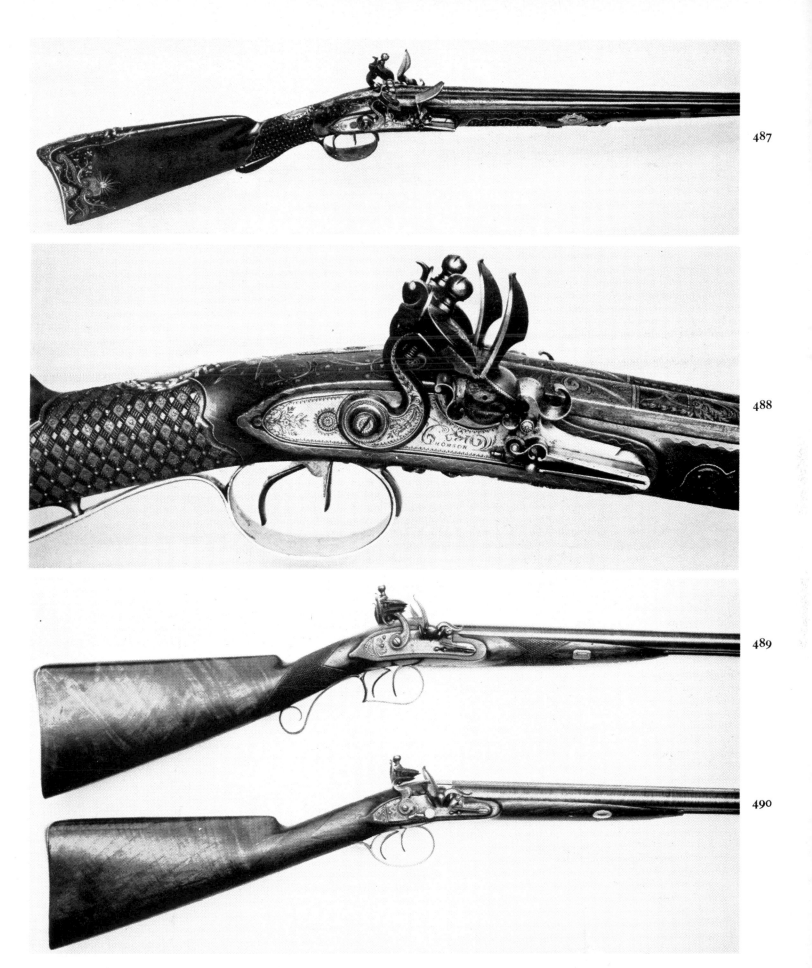

DOUBLE-BARRELLED SIDE-BY-SIDE GUNS **487** Flintlock shotgun signed THOMSON A STRASSBOURG on locks. Barrels marked cⁿ. TORDU FLP ETOFFE. *French, c. 1810. Bayerisches Nationalmuseum, Munich* (No. 13/587). **488** Close-up of locks of **487**. **489** Flintlock shotgun signed ALEXR. WILSON PATENT LONDON with circular priming pans. *c. 1820. Tower of London* (No. XII–1604). *B. 30 in. Cal.* 0·6 in. **490** Flintlock shotgun signed JOSEPH MANTON LONDON. Fitted with his patent 'gravitating stops' of 1812. Serial No. 6197. *Tower of London* (No. XII–1597). (*See p.* 101.)

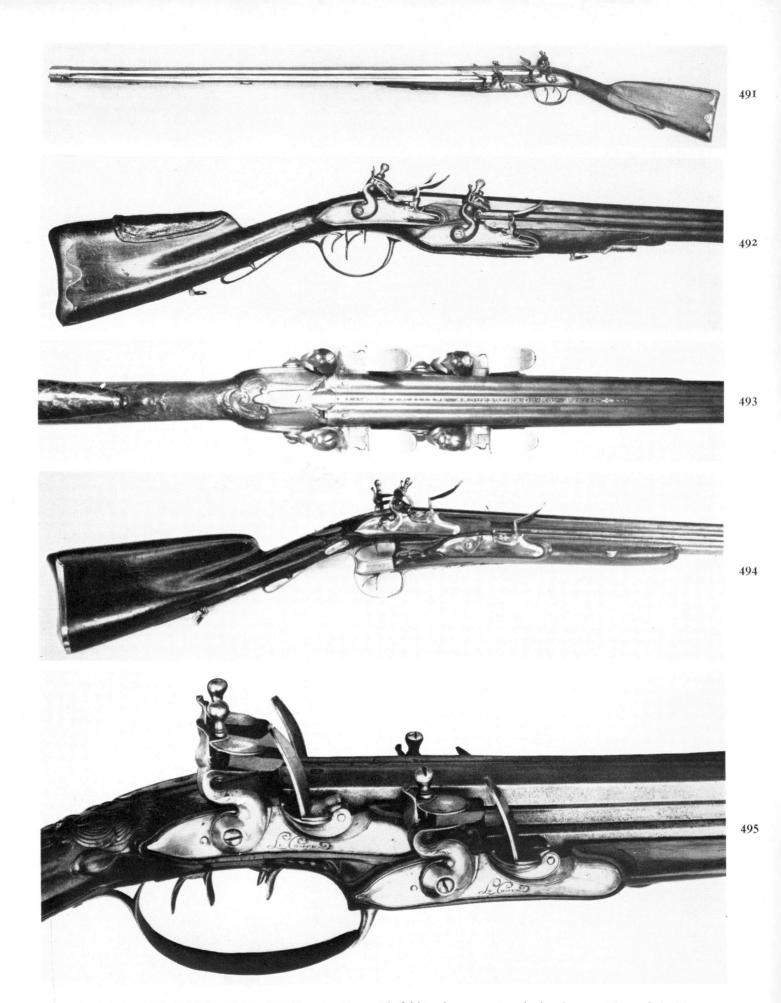

491

492

493

494

495

FLINTLOCK FOUR-BARRELLED GUNS **491** Gun with folding bayonet. *French, dated 1797. Metropolitan Museum, New York (No. 32.75.109). L. 54½ in.* **492** Gun signed ESCALLERE ARQUEBUSIER DU ROY A PARIS. *French, c. 1780. Glasgow Museum (No. 39–65wk).* **493** Top view of **492**. **494** Gun signed VE PEYRE DUBOIS ET FILS A ST. ETIENNE. *French, c. 1785. Windsor Castle (No. 192). B. 36½ in. Cal. 0·52 in.* **495** Close-up of lock of gun signed LE COMTE. *French, c. 1780. W. Keith Neal Collection.*

496

497

498

499

500

SEVEN-BARRELLED GUNS   **496** Flintlock naval carbine by H. Nock. *English, c.* 1780. *Tower of London* (No. XII–480). *B.* 20 in.   **497** Flintlock naval carbine by Henry Nock. Second model 1787. *Tower of London* (No. XII–1030). *B.* 20 in. **498** Flintlock sporting rifle by Staudenmayer, London. *c.* 1810. *B.* 21 in. *Cal.* 0·4 in.   **499** Colonel Thomas Thornton's gun with two sets of seven barrels. *English, c.* 1790. *Arms Museum, Liège* (No. AeI/5866). *B.* 20·2 in. (*See p.* 101.)   **500** Percussion sporting rifle from a cased set. Signed FORSYTH & CO. PATENT GUNMAKERS LONDON. Serial No. 3732. *c.* 1825. *Tower of London* (No. XII–1467). *B.* 20·5 in. *Cal.* 0·38 in.

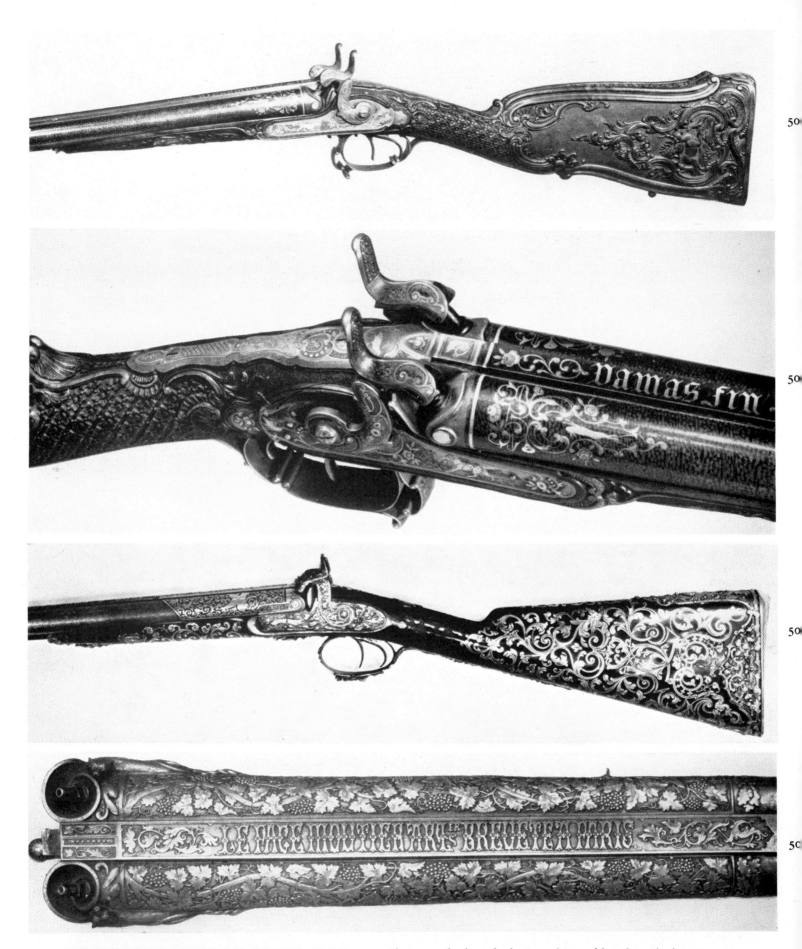

PERCUSSION DOUBLE-BARRELLED GUNS   **501** Shotgun, the barrels decorated in gold and marked DAMAS FIN.
Stock carved in deep relief by J. M. Tinlot. *Belgian (Liège), c. 1860. Arms Museum, Liège* (No. Mc 10/4717).   **502** Close-up
of the locks of **501**.   **503** Shotgun. Ebony stock inlaid with silver decoration. Silver butt-plate engraved EXPOSITION 1844.
Locks signed DEVISME À PARIS. *Windsor Castle.* B. 29 in. Cal. 0·67 in. (*See p.* 101.)   **504** Chiselled barrels of shotgun signed
LE PAGE MOUTIER ARQ[er] BREVETE A PARIS. *c. 1860. Harold's Club, Reno, U.S.A.* (*See p.* 101.)

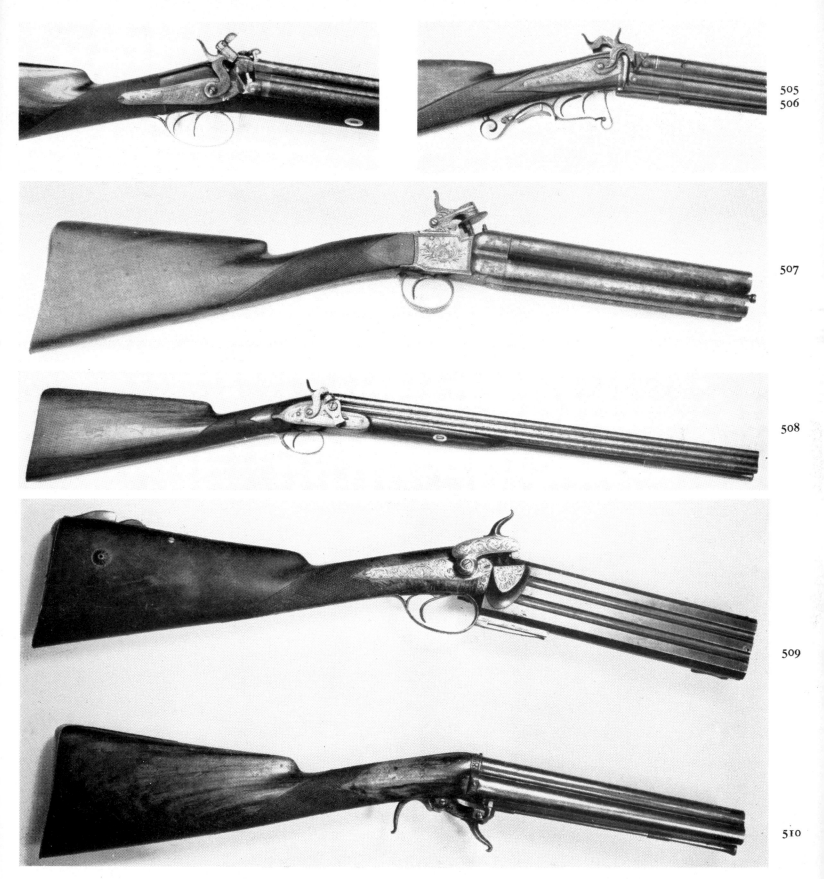

505
506

507

508

509

510

MULTI-BARRELLED PERCUSSION GUNS 505 Four-barrelled gun with two locks. Hammers with swivelling extensions for top barrels. Signed REILLY, LONDON. *c.* 1850. 506 Four-barrelled gun with two locks. Hammers have adjustable heads. Barrels marked in gold C. V. HEINLEIN IN BAMBERG. Trigger guard with 'squeeze' safety device. *German, c. 1860. C. G. Vokes Collection.*   507 Four-barrelled carbine with hand-revolved 'turret' hammer by William & John Rigby, Dublin. *c. 1860. C. G. Vokes Collection.* B. 9½ in. 508 Five-barrelled gun by Forsyth & Co. with patent 'scent-bottle' lock. Serial No. 3235. *c. 1820. Tower of London* (No. XII–1589). B. 24·2 in. Cal. 0·4 in. 509 Carbine with three rifled barrels in vertical line. Hammer with automatically-moving striker. Wheel-shaped cap holder in butt. By John Gurd, London, Ontario. *Canadian, c. 1850. Royal Ontario Museum, Toronto.* B. 10¼ in. Cal. 0·5 in. 510 Five-barrelled smooth-bore carbine. Under-hammer with moving striker by John Gurd, London, Ontario. *Canadian, c. 1845. Royal Ontario Museum, Toronto.* B. 10½ in. Cal. 0·516 in.

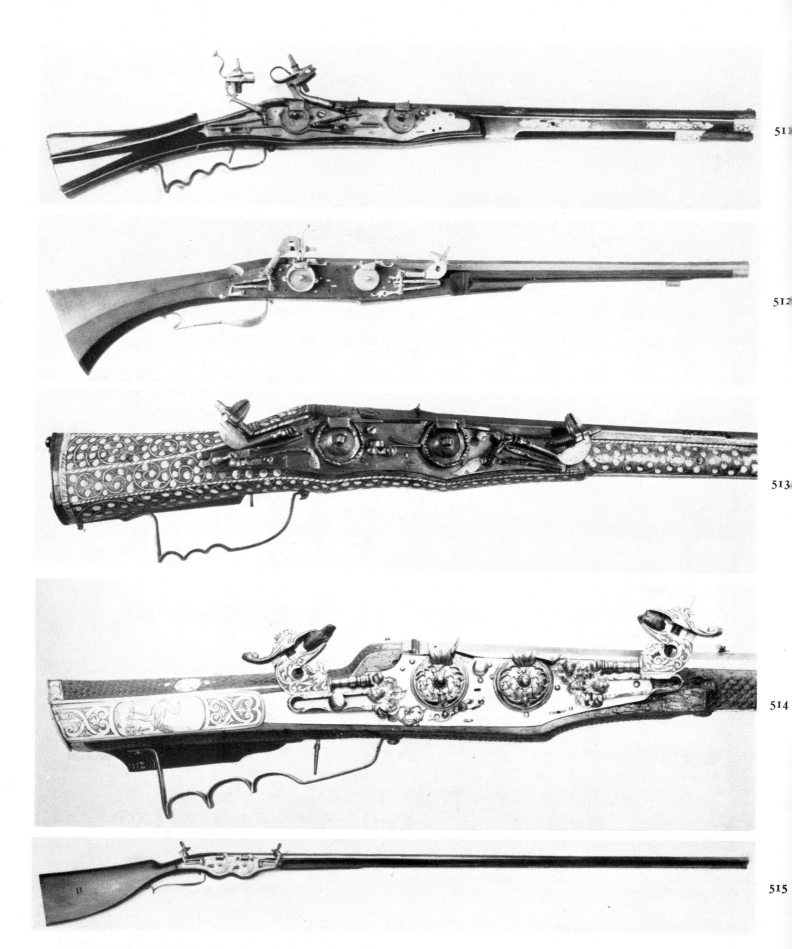

TWO-SHOT SUPERIMPOSED-CHARGE GUNS **511** Wheellock arquebus. *German (Augsburg), c. 1585. Museum of Art, Geneva (No. K. 184). B. 27·7 in.* **512** Wheellock carbine. *French (?), c. 1600. Livrustkammaren, Stockholm (No. 1213). B. 27·7 in. Cal. 0·69 in.* **513** Wheellock gun. *German, dated 1581. Victoria and Albert Museum (No. M. 615–1927). L. 45 in. Cal. 0·68 in.* **514** Wheellock rifle. *German (Saxony), dated 1634. Tøjhusmuseet, Copenhagen (No. B. 211). B. 44·7 in. Cal. 0·47 in.* **515** Long wheellock gun. *French, c. 1620. Tower of London (No. XII–1066). B. 49·7 in. Cal. 0·52 in.*

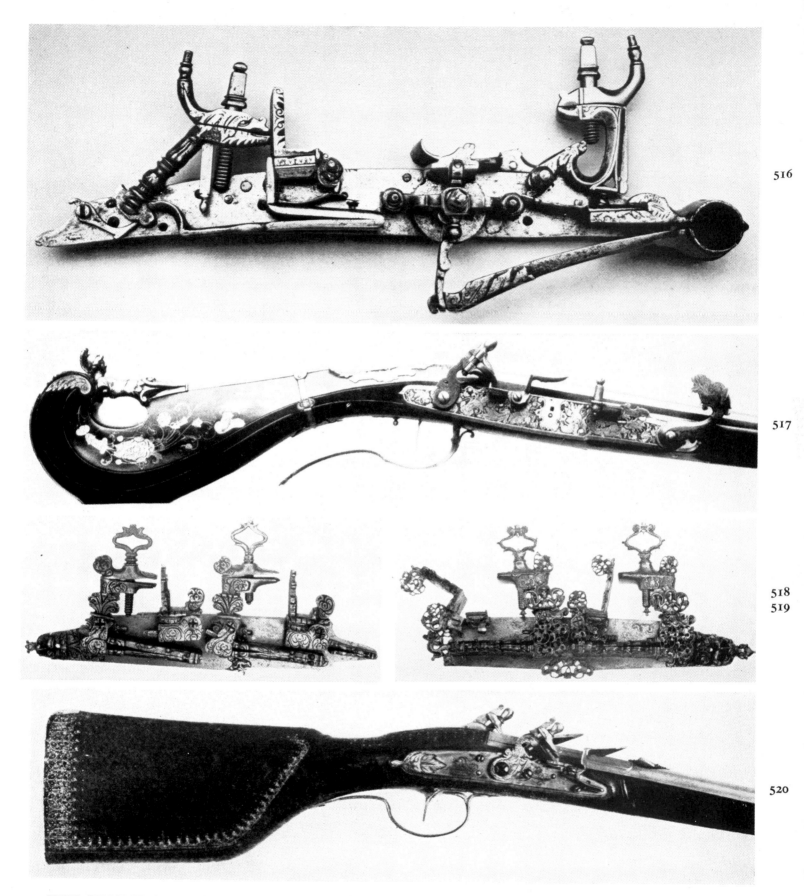

516

517

518
519

520

TWO-SHOT SUPERIMPOSED-CHARGE GUNS AND LOCKS **516** Combined wheellock and flintlock. *Italian*, late 16th century. *Museum of Artillery, Turin*. **517** Flintlock and matchlock musket. Ebony stock decorated with silver. Caryatids in gilt bronze. From *Cabinet d'Armes* of Louis XIII. *French, dated 1636. Army Museum, Paris* (No. M. 410). *B.* 44·6 in. *Cal.* 0·67 in. **518** Right-hand miquelet lock. *Neapolitan*, 17th century. *Odescalchi Collection, Rome* (No. U.887). **519** Left-hand miquelet lock. *Neapolitan*, 17th century. *Odescalchi Collection, Rome* (No. U. 901). **520** Double flintlock gun. Butt decorated with silver. *S. German, c.* 1650. *Kunsthistorisches Museum, Vienna* (No. HGK. 505). *B.* 24·8 in. *Cal.* 0·59 in.

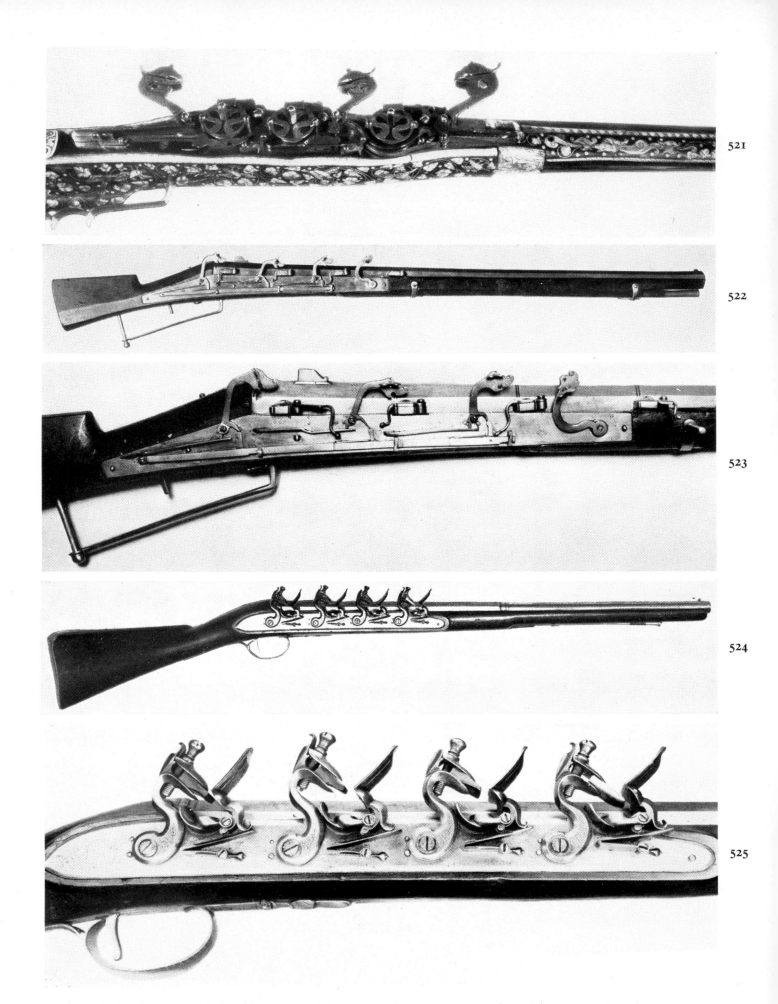

SUPERIMPOSED-CHARGE GUNS **521** Three-shot wheellock. *German, late 16th century. State Hermitage, Leningrad (No. 3.0.5835). B.* 38·9 in. *Cal.* 0·59 in. **522** Four-shot matchlock. *German, early 17th century. Royal Museum of Arms, Brussels (No. 56 D/5). B.* 45·9 in. *Cal.* 0·87 in. **523** Close-up of locks of **522**. **524** Four-shot flintlock with sliding trigger. Signed JACAUD, LONDON. *c.* 1820. *C. G. Vokes Collection. B.* 32 in. *Cal.* 0·75 in. **525** Close-up of locks of **524**.

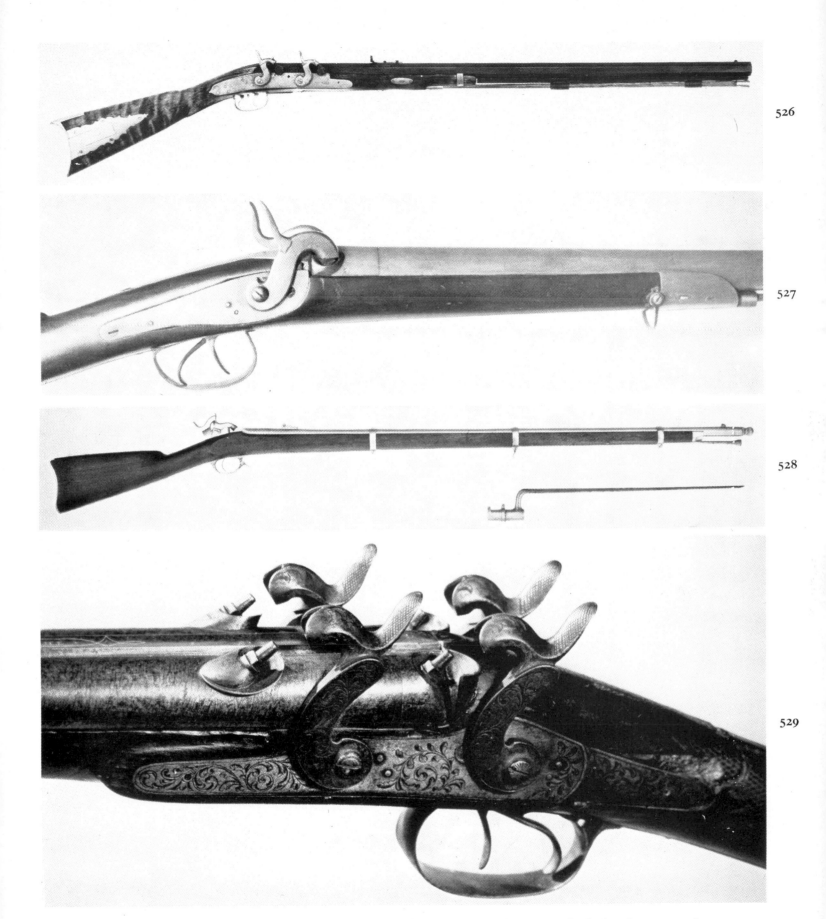

526

527

528

529

PERCUSSION SUPERIMPOSED-CHARGE GUNS   **526** Two-shot Kentucky-type flintlock rifle converted to percussion. *American, c. 1825. Winchester Gun Museum. B.* 33 in. *Cal.* 0·50 in.   **527** Two-shot side-by-side locks. *French, c.1850. Arms Museum, Liège* (No. Ah. 11/659). *B.* 37·5 in.   **528** U.S. musket Model 1863 with two side-by-side locks. *Winchester Gun Museum. B.* 41 in. *Cal.* 0·58 in.   **529** Double-barrelled shotgun with four locks, signed THORY ARQ A AMIENS. Presented by Governor of New Zealand, Sir George Grey, to a Maori chief in 1853. *French, c. 1850. Dominion Museum, Wellington.*

530

531
532

533
534

535

536

MULTIPLE SUPERIMPOSED-CHARGE GUNS **530** Sixteen-shot wheellock gun. *German, c.* 1580. *(See p.* 101.)
531 Four-barrel 29-shot flintlock carbine signed FRANCISCO MAMBACH. *German, c.* 1660. *Tower of London* (No. XII–1122).
B. 17 in. *Cal.* 0·46 in. **532** Muzzle of **531**. **533** Four-barrelled flintlock carbine. *German, c.* 1640 (lock later). *Army Museum, Warsaw* (No. 611/11). **534** Five-barrelled flintlock carbine. *German, c.* 1650. *Army Museum, Warsaw* (No. 610/11).
535 India Pattern musket converted to Chambers system (12 shots). *English,* 1815. *Tower of London.* **536** Seven-barrelled
Chambers swivel gun. (224 shots) *American, c.* 1815. *Arms Museum, Liège* (No. Hj 7/1834). *B.* 48·7 in. *Cal.* 0·75 in.

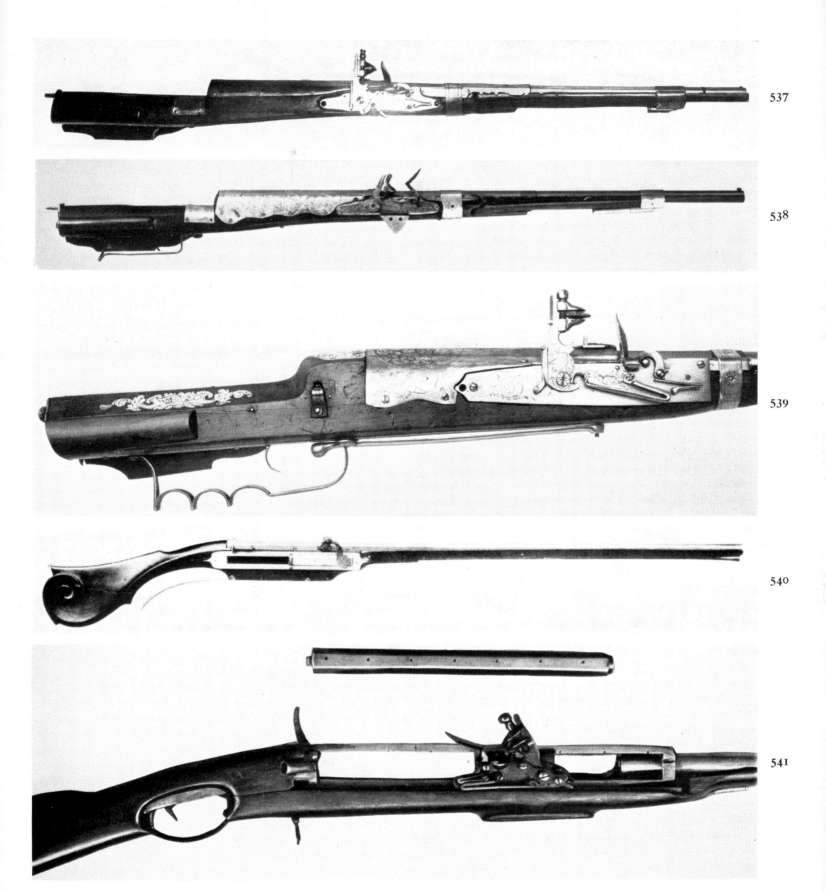

MULTIPLE SUPERIMPOSED-CHARGE GUNS **537** Ten-shot flintlock gun with moving barrel. Probably by Heinrich Habrecht, Schleswig, *c.* 1650. *Kremlin, Moscow* (No. 7542). **538** Flintlock gun with moving barrel owned by Charles X Gustavus (1654–60). By same maker. *Livrustkammaren, Stockholm* (No. 3868). *B.* 25·8 in. *Cal.* 0·63 in. **539** Flintlock gun with moving barrel, by same maker. *Tøjhusmuseet, Copenhagen* (No. B. 500). *B.* 40 in. *Cal.* 0·7 in. **540** Matchlock musket with sliding lock for two shots. From *Cabinet d'Armes* of Louis XIII. *French, c.* 1630. *Army Museum, Paris* (No. M. 401). *B.* 40 in. *Cal.* 0·63 in. **541** Musket with sliding flintlock made for the East India Company. Detachable chamber for seven charges. Lock signed JOVER & BELTON. *English, dated 1786. Tower of London (Study Collection). B.* 29 in. *Chamber* 10¾ in. *Cal.* 0·65 in.

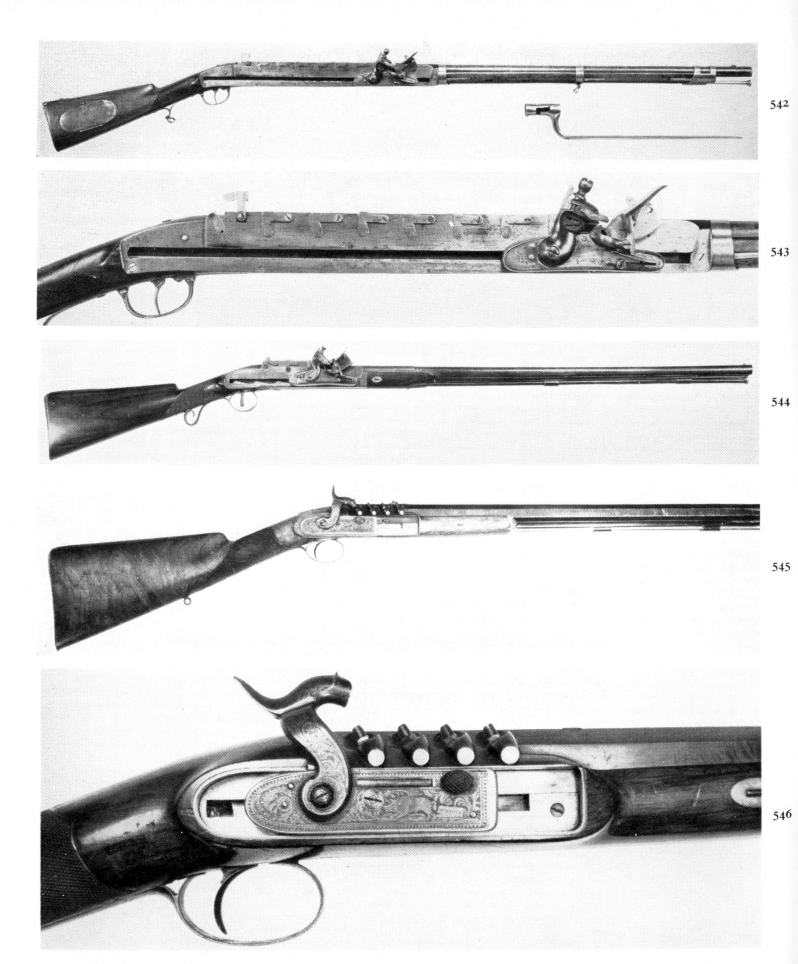

SUPERIMPOSED-CHARGE GUNS WITH SLIDING LOCKS **542** Ten-shot flintlock rifle by S. North, Middleton, Conn. *American, dated 1825. Winchester Gun Museum. B. 41½ in. Cal. 0·54 in.* **543** Action of **542**. **544** Four-shot flintlock gun by H. W. Mortimer, London. Serial No. 44. *English, c. 1805. Winchester Gun Museum. B. 35½ in. Cal. 0·643 in.* **545** Four-shot percussion gun. Barrel inscribed CAPTⁿ RITSO PATENTEE, W. MILLS MAKER 120 HIGH HOLBORN LONDON. Serial No. 1610. *c. 1830. Tower of London (No. XII–1408). B. 24·3 in. Cal. 0·6 in.* **546** Close-up of sliding percussion lock on four-shot rifle by W. Mills, London. *c. 1840. Noel Corry Collection.*

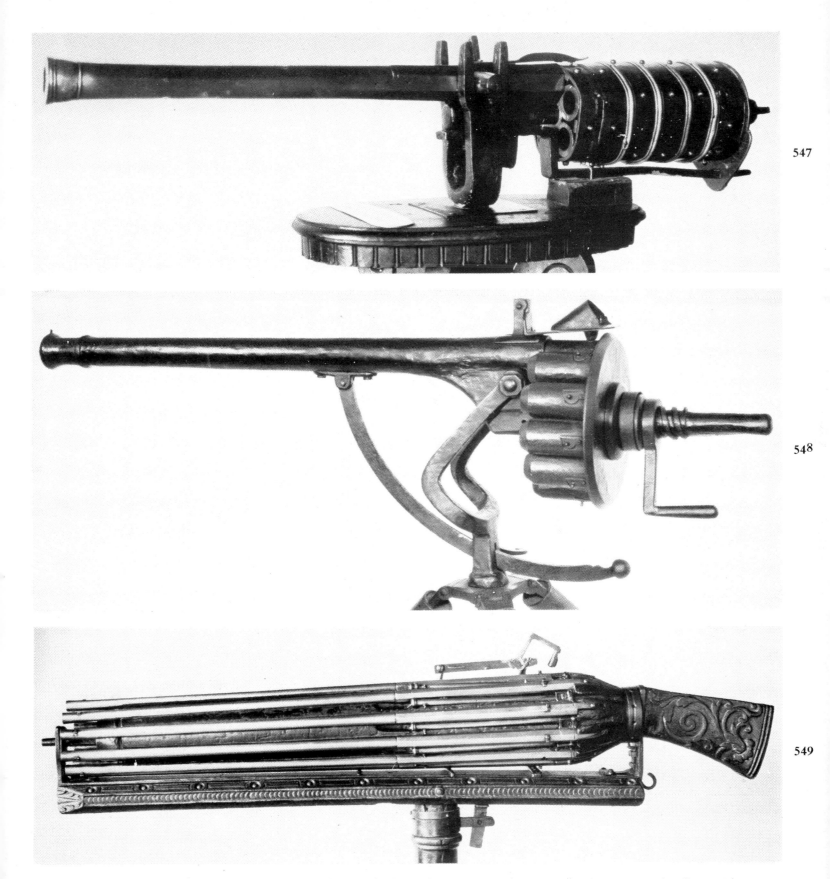

547

548

549

REVOLVERS   **547** Wall gun with five-chambered cylinder. *Italian, c. 1600. Palazzo Ducale, Venice. B. 33·4 in. Cal. 1·58 in.*
548 James Puckle's 'Defence' or wall gun. Iron model with square-bored 11-chambered cylinder, fired by match. Handle at rear controls backward and forward movement of cylinder which is hand-revolved. *English, c. 1720. Tower of London* (No. XII–125). *B. 35 in. Cal. 1·6 in.*   **549** Matchlock wall gun with revolving barrels. *Italian, 17th century. Palazzo Ducale, Venice.*

MATCHLOCK REVOLVERS   **550** Four-barrelled carbine. *Indian, 18th century. Royal Scottish Museum, Edinburgh* (No. 1956.612). *L.* 32 in. *Cal.* 0·63 in.   **551** Five-barrelled Indian gun. 18th century. *Tower of London* (No. XXVI–70F). *B.* 27½ in. *Cal.* 0·46 in.   **552** Three-barrelled carbine. *Japanese, early 17th century. Smithsonian Institution, Washington. B.* 11½ in. *Cal.* 0·4 in. (*See p.* 101.)   **553** Top view of **552**.   **554** Gun with four-chambered cylinder. *Indian, 18th century. Wadsworth Atheneum, Hartford* (No. 1905.1024).   **555** Gun with six-chambered cylinder, signed DEVANAGRI. *Indian,* dated 1689. *C. G. Vokes Collection. B.* 31 in. *Cal.* 0·55 in.

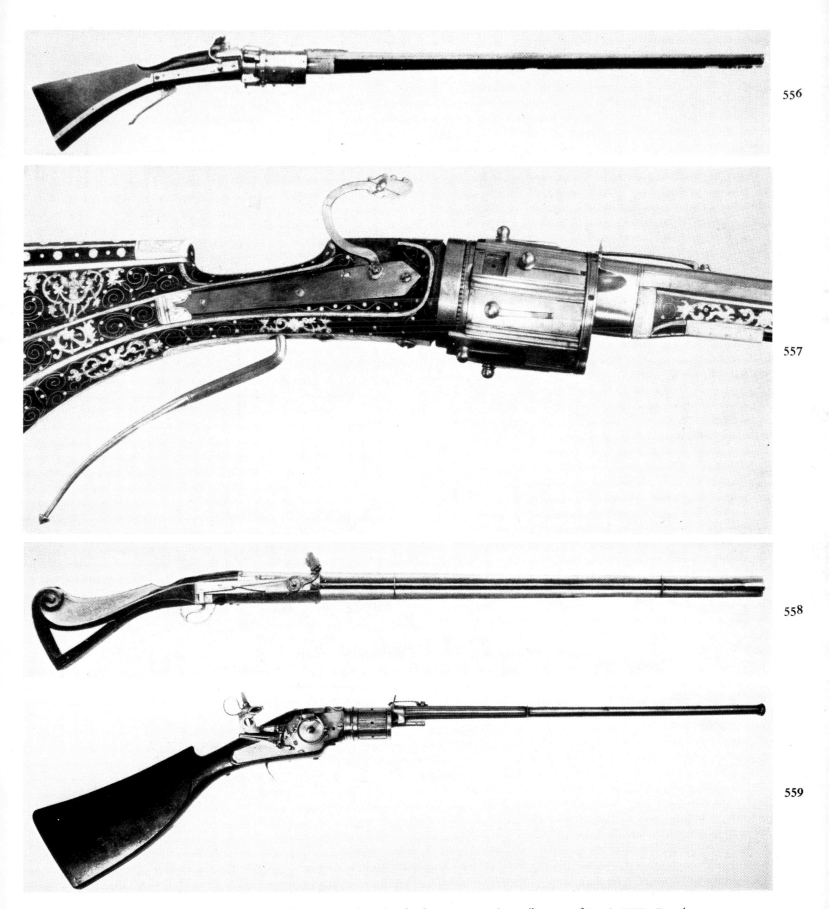

556

557

558

559

REVOLVERS **556** Matchlock gun with five-chambered cylinder. From *Cabinet d'Armes* of Louis XIII. *French, c.* 1620. *Army Museum, Paris* (No. M. 1067). *B.* 32·6 in. *Cal.* 0·55 in. **557** Matchlock gun with eight-chambered cylinder. *French, c.* 1620. *State Hermitage, Leningrad. B.* 37·2 in. *Cal.* 0·71 in. **558** Matchlock gun with double turn-over barrels. From *Cabinet d'Armes* of Louis XIII. *French, c.* 1620. *Army Museum, Paris* (No. M. 369). *B.* 38·2 in. *Cal.* 0·75 in. **559** Wheellock carbine with six-chambered cylinder. Lock stamped with maker's mark of HK and pair of spectacles. *German, c.* 1600. *Tower of London* (No. XII–471). *B.* 18¼ in. *Cal.* 0·35 in.

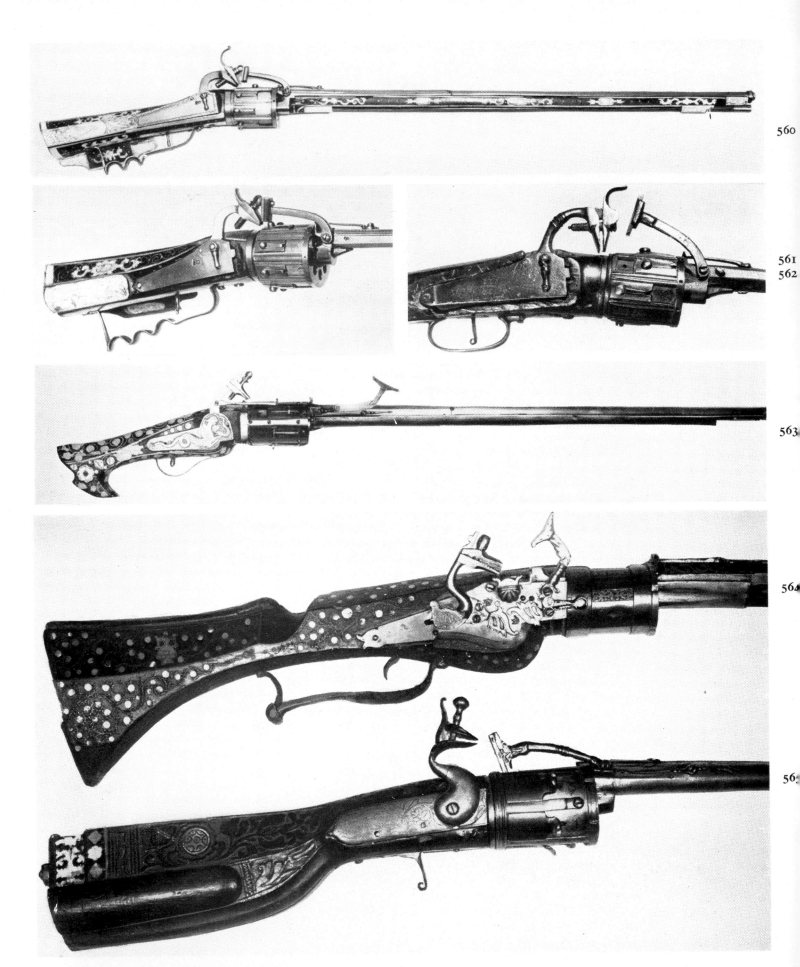

560

**561
562**

563

564

565

SNAPHANCE REVOLVERS **560** Rifle with eight-chambered cylinder. *German (Nuremberg), dated 1597. Tøjhusmuseet, Copenhagen (No. B. 294). B. 27·7 in. Cal. 0·42 in.* **561** Rifle with eight-chambered cylinder. *German (Nuremberg), c. 1600. Tøjhusmuseet, Copenhagen (No. B. 295). B. 27·8 in. Cal. 0·4 in.* **562** Rifle with eight-chambered cylinder. *German, c. 1600. Royal Scottish Museum, Edinburgh (No. 1876.29.22). L. 48 in. Cal. 0·4 in.* **563** Pistol-carbine with six-chambered cylinder. *German, c. 1600. Kremlin, Moscow (No. 8352).* **564** Gun with six-chambered cylinder by lsay Pervuskin. *Russian, c. 1620. Kremlin, Moscow (No. 7595).* **565** Rifle with six-chambered cylinder. *Russian, c. 1680. Kremlin, Moscow (No. 7544).*

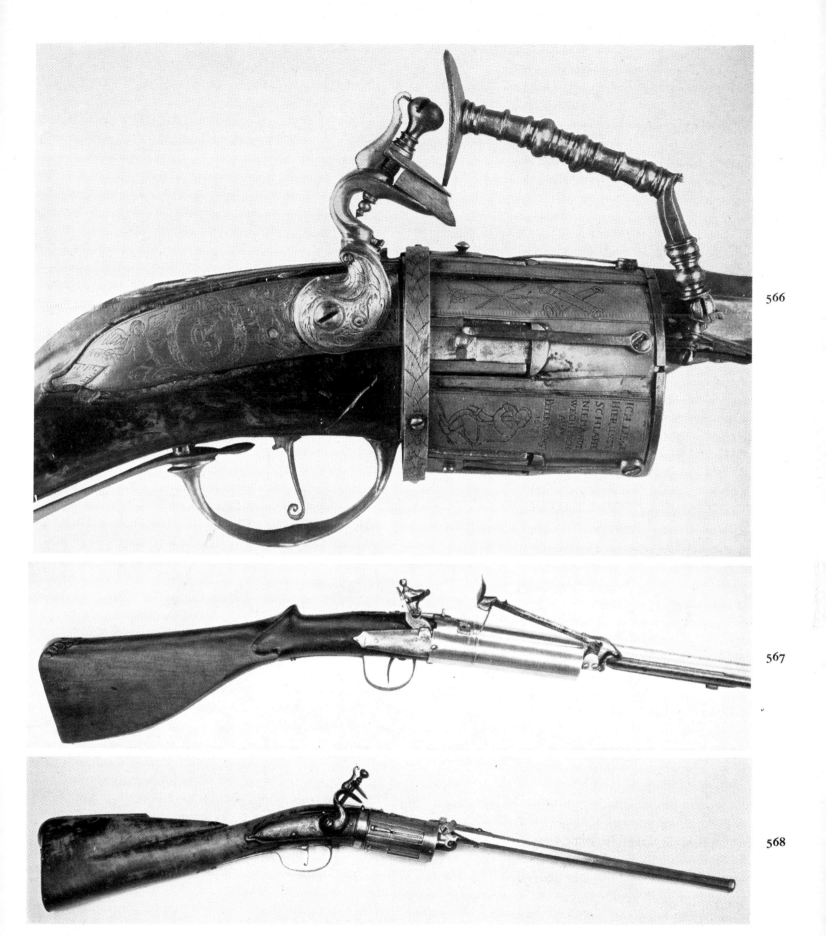

566

567

568

SNAPHANCE REVOLVERS **566** Rifle with five-chambered cylinder inscribed ICH LIEGE HIER UNDT SCHLAFFE NIEMANDT WECHT MICH AUFF [I lie here and sleep. Nobody wakes me up.] PETER DACHY 1695. *Kremlin, Moscow* (No. 7556). **567** Gun with six-chambered cylinder. *French, c. 1660. Wadsworth Atheneum, Hartford* (No. 1905.1031). *B.* 44 in. **568** Carbine (steel missing from lock) with six-chambered cylinder. Signed JOHN DAFTE, LONDINI. *English, c. 1680. Wadsworth Atheneum, Hartford* (No. 1905.1022). *L.* 33 in. *Cal.* 0·4 in.

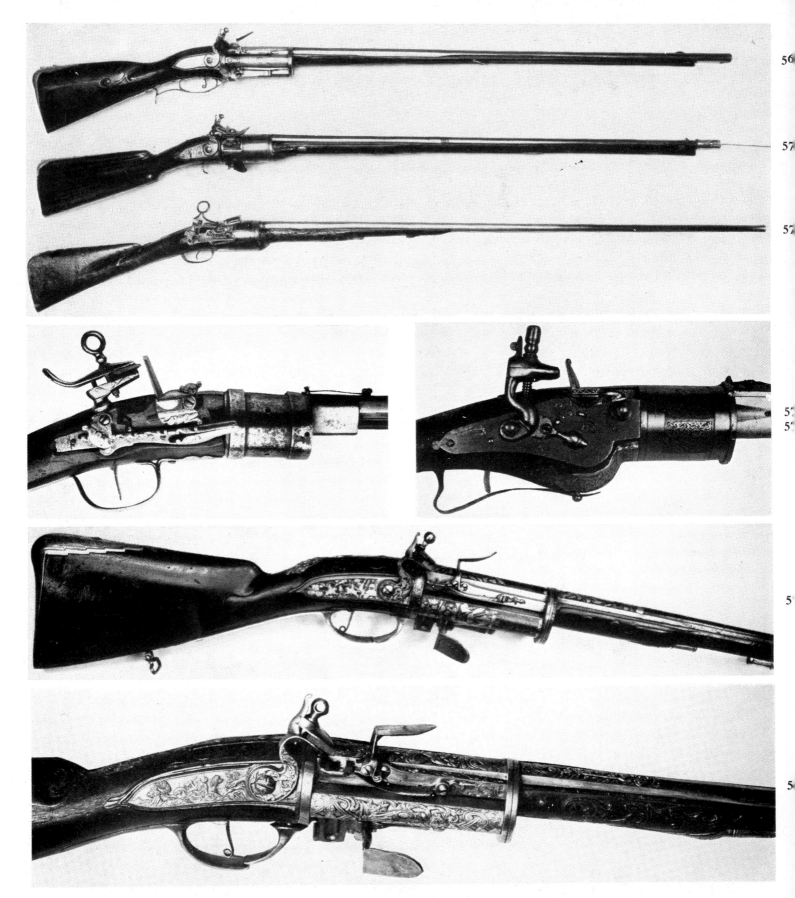

FLINTLOCK REVOLVERS **569** Gun with four chambers. Brass lock-plate and mounts. *German*, dated 1732. *Tower of London* (No. XII–477). *B.* 36 in. *Cal.* 0·6 in. **570** Gun with four-chambered brass cylinder. Socket bayonet on muzzle. Brass lock signed DULACHS. Side-plate inscribed IASINTO IAVMANDREV M. F. MANRESA 1739. *Spanish. Tower of London* (No. XII–476). *B.* 27½ in. *Cal.* 0·64 in. **571** Hand-revolved four-chambered cylinder. Lock with priming magazine signed ROVIRA. Breech tang inscribed PERA CARBUNELL EN BARCELONA. *Spanish*, dated 1702. *Tower of London* (No. XII–1123). *B.* 42·4 in. *Cal.* 0·6 in. **572** Miquelet-lock gun with four-chambered cylinder. *Spanish, c.* 1740. *W. Keith Neal Collection.* **573** Six-chambered gun by Isay Pervuskin. *Russian, c.* 1630. *Kremlin, Moscow* (No. 8351). **574** Gun with three chambers damascened with gold. *German*, early 18th century. **575** Gun with three chambers. *German*, early 18th century. *Royal Arms Museum, Brussels* (No. 788/72).

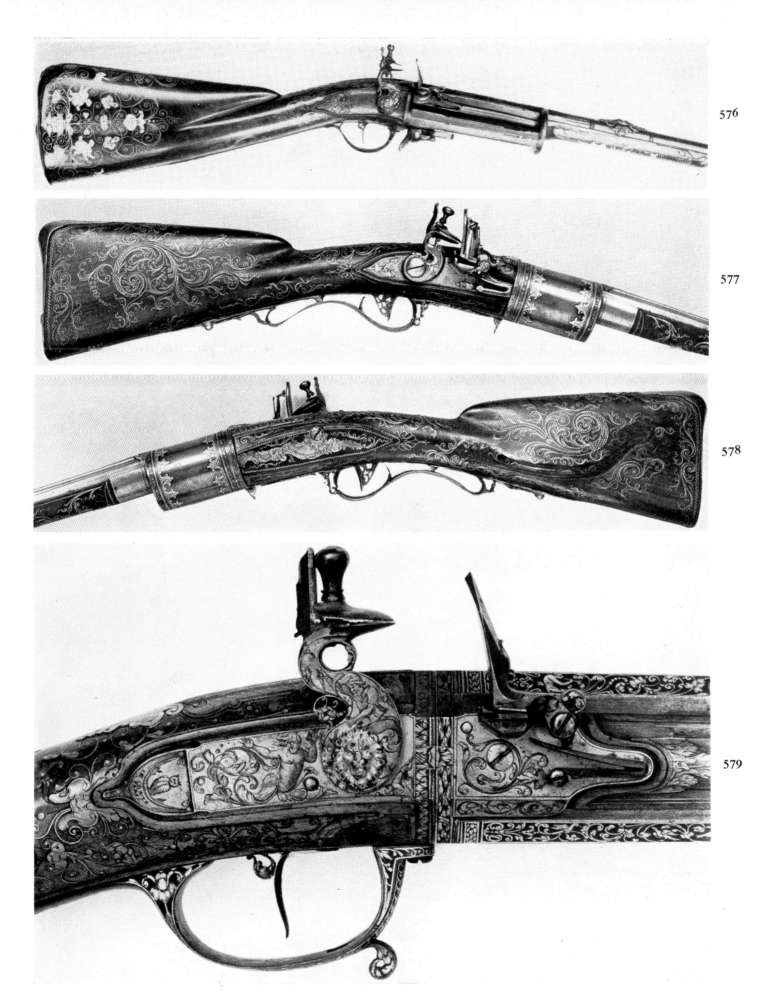

576

577

578

579

FLINTLOCK REVOLVERS **576** Gun with three chambers. Stock inlaid with silver. *French, c.* 1670. *Tower of London* (No. XII–1553). *B.* 31¼ in. *Cal.* 0·59 in. **577** Gun with six-chambered cylinder and magazine primer. Signed (in Cyrillic) B. KALESNIKOW. *Russian, c.* 1780. *Bayerisches Nationalmuseum, Munich* (No. W. 2843). **578** Reverse side of **577**. **579** Lock of double-barrelled turn-over gun signed LE CONTE A PARIS. Stock inlaid with silver and signed BERAIN FECIT. Presented by Louis XIV of France to Charles XI of Sweden in 1673. *Livrustkammaren, Stockholm* (No. 3888).

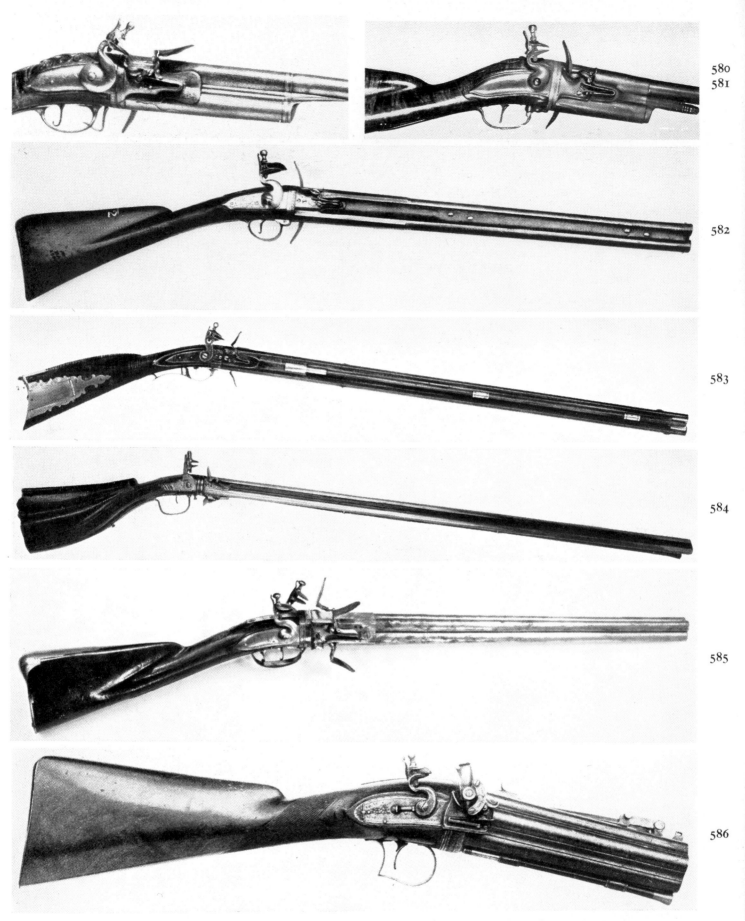

FLINTLOCK REVOLVERS **580** Gun with two 'turn-over' chambers, signed LANDREVILLE. *English, c. 1690. Glasgow Museum (No. 39.65vv).* **581** Gun with two 'turn-over' chambers signed GORGO A LONDRES. *English, c. 1695. Joe Kindig Collection.* **582** Double-barrelled turn-over carbine, signed BRAZIER LONDON. *English, c. 1770. Tower of London (No. XII–1458). B. 22·25 in. Cal. 0·6 in.* **583** Double-barrelled turn-over Kentucky rifle. *American, c. 1820. Winchester Gun Museum. B. 37½ in. Cal. 0·45 in.* **584** Three-barrelled turn-over gun signed TILMAN KEVCKS. *German, c. 1660. George F. Harding Museum, Chicago (No. 187). B. 39¾ in. Cal. 0·43 in.* **585** Four-barrelled turn-over carbine with side-by-side locks. Signed BARBAR. *English, c. 1730. Windsor Castle (No. 400). B. 22 in. Cal. 0·51 in.* **586** Seven-barrelled pepper-box carbine with magazine primer and spring bayonet, signed RIGBY DUBLIN. *Irish, c. 1820. National Museum of Ireland, Dublin. L. 24¾ in. Cal. 0·58 in. (See p. 101.)*

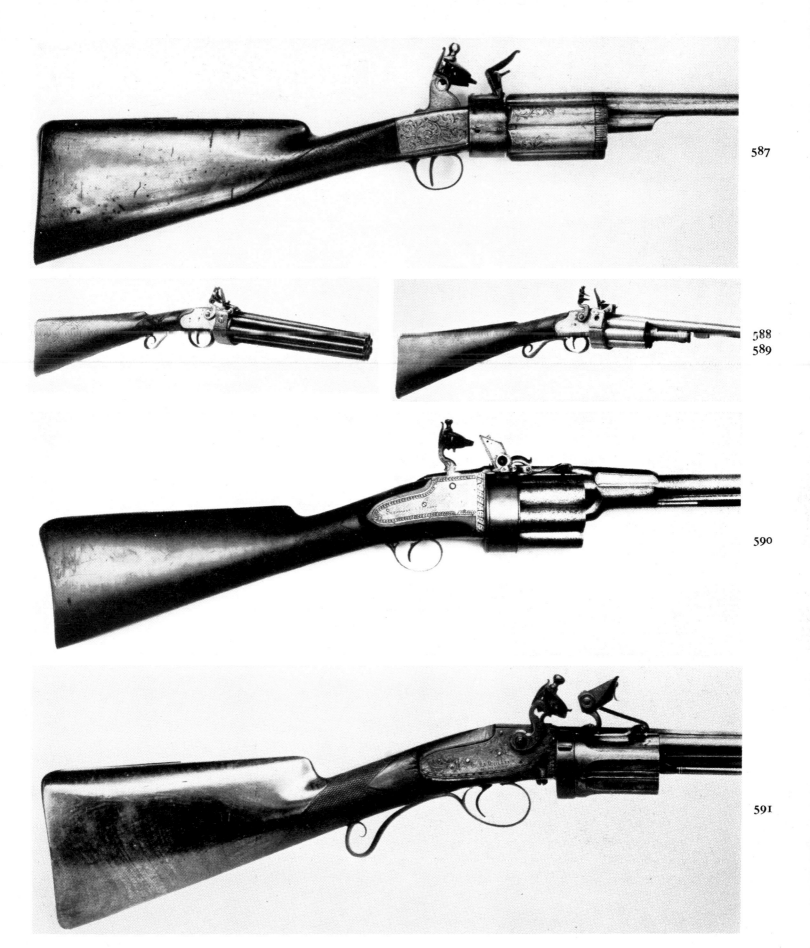

587

588
589

590

591

FLINTLOCK REVOLVERS   **587** Collier-type gun with hand-revolved six-chambered cylinder, signed ROBERT WOOD. *English, c.* 1825.   **588** Wheeler seven-barrelled carbine, hand revolved. *American, c.* 1820. *Smithsonian Institution, Washington.* B. 11 in. Cal. 0·5 in.   **589** Wheeler musket, hand-revolved seven-chambered cylinder. *American, c.* 1820. *Smithsonian Institution, Washington.* B. 32 in. Cal. 0·5 in.   **590** Gun with six chambers and magazine primer signed E. H. COLLIER No. 4. *English, c.* 1825. *Tower of London* (No. XII–1503). *B.* 25·7 in. *Cal.* 0·69 in.   **591** Gun with four chambers and magazine primer signed E. H. COLLIER 117 PATENT. Hand revolved. *English, c.* 1825.

PERCUSSION REVOLVERS 592 Rifle with six-chambered cylinder and 'push-in' ramrod. *English, c.* 1845. *C. G. Vokes Collection. B.* 28 in. *Cal.* 0·45 in. 593 Rifle with six-chambered cylinder by Witton, Daw & Co., London. *c.* 1850. *B.* 25 in. *Cal.* 0·5 in. 594 Rifle with hinged loading lever marked JOHN BLISSETT'S PATENT IMPROVEMENT [English Patent No. 2069 of 1855]. *Tower of London* (Study Collection). 595 Action of four-chambered gun with separate ramrod signed LE LYON A PARIS, patented in France in 1826. *William M. Locke Collection.*

596

597

598

599

600

601

PERCUSSION REVOLVERS **596** Double-barrelled (one rifled, one smooth) 'turn-over' rifle signed F. BAADER (on lock), HORRMANN IN MÜNCHEN (on barrel). *German, c. 1840. Tower of London (No. XII–1412). B. 26 in. Cal. 0·52 in.* **597** Three-barrelled 'turn-over' rifle. Barrels stamped E. S. SWEET, CAST STEEL WARRANTED. *American (Kalamazoo), c. 1855. Milwaukee Museum (No. N. 3620). B. 29¾ in. Cal. 0·36 in.* **598** Four-barrelled rifle by Walter Adams. *English, c. 1860. B, 27 in.* **599** Six-barrelled rifle by W. Briggs. *American, c. 1850. Winchester Gun Museum. B. 22 in. Cal. 0·34 in.* **600** Four-barrelled self-cocking and revolving carbine, signed BECKWITH, LONDON. *c. 1845. C. G. Vokes Collection. B. 11½ in. Cal. 0·67 in.* **601** Six-barrelled wall gun. Barrels revolved by curled trigger. Inscribed J. R. COOPER 7th DECEMBER 1843 [Date of Registered Design]. *English. Royal Armoury, Turin (No. M. 69). B. 30·6 in. Cal. 0·52 in.*

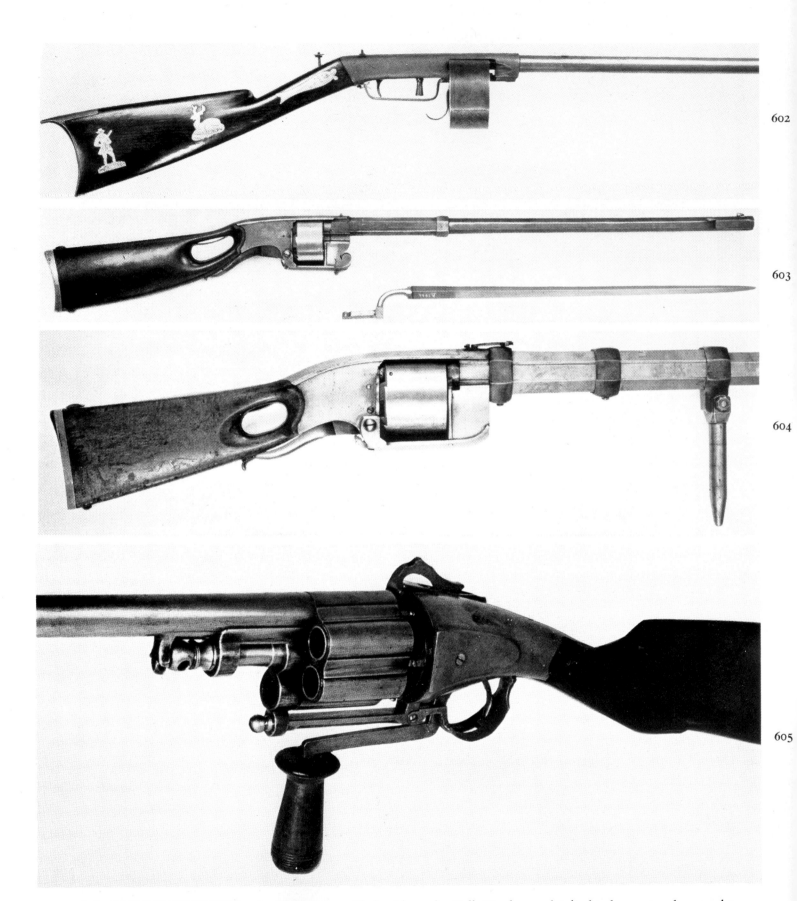

PERCUSSION REVOLVERS **602** Fifteen-shot rifle by Alexander Hall. Hand-turned cylinder does not make complete revolution. *American, c. 1860. Winchester Gun Museum. B. 25 in. Cal. 0·38 in.* **603** Eight-shot military rifle and bayonet designed by Peder Rasmussen. *Danish, c. 1845. Tøjhusmuseet, Copenhagen (No. B. 2444). B. 27 in. Cal. 0·62 in.* **604** Rasmussen's rifled wall gun. *Danish, c. 1845. Tøjhusmuseet, Copenhagen (No. B. 2446). B. 43 in. Cal. 0·77 in.* **605** Six-shot gun. Probably by Cesare Rosaglio. Cylinder turned by handle. *Austrian (Vienna), c. 1830. Schloss Ambras, Innsbruck.*

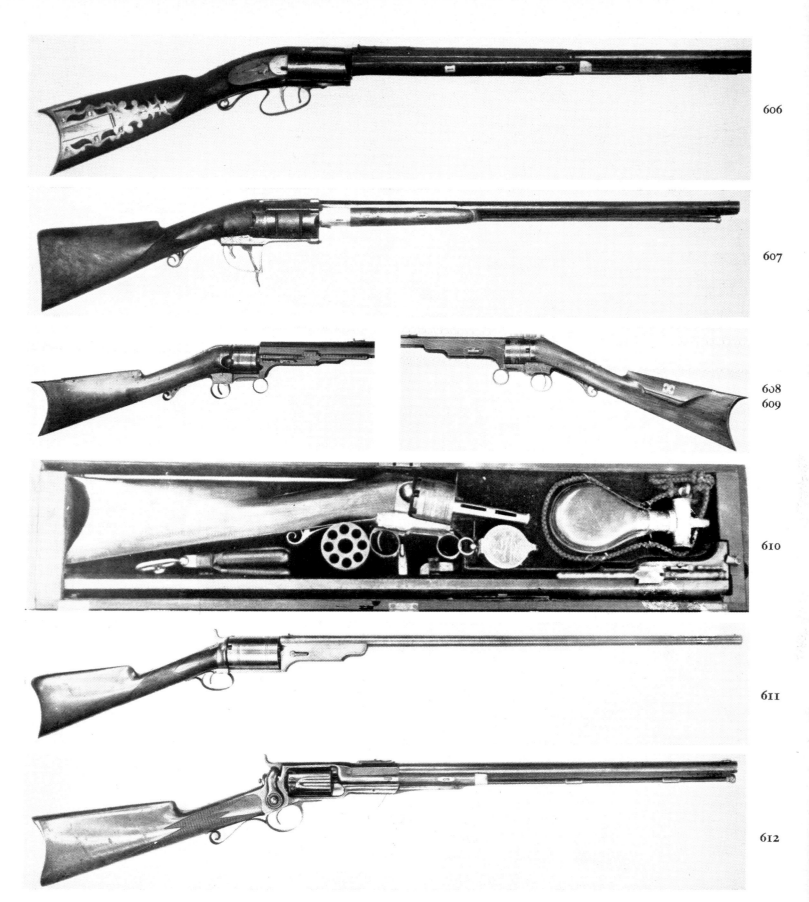

COLT REVOLVERS **606** Experimental nine-shot rifle by Anson Chase & W. H. Rowe, Hartford, 1832. *Wadsworth Atheneum, Hartford* (No. 1905.1032). *B.* 35½ in. *Cal.* 0·37 in. **607** Experimental six-shot shotgun by John Pearson, Baltimore, *c.* 1834–5. *Wadsworth Atheneum, Hartford* (No. 1905.1025). *B.* 30½ in. *Cal.* 0·66 in. **608** Paterson eight-shot ring-lever rifle with rounded-back cylinder showing folding rammer. *c.* 1840. *William M. Locke Collection.* **609** Reverse side of Paterson ring-lever with square-back cylinder. *c.* 1840. *Wadsworth Atheneum, Hartford* (No. 1905.969). **610** Cased Paterson ring-lever rifle with accessories. Serial No. 144. *B. R. Lewis Collection.* **611** Paterson eight-shot shotgun. Cylinder turned by hammer. Serial No. 135. *c.* 1840. *William M. Locke Collection.* *B.* 32 in. *Cal.* 0·648 in. **612** Six-shot rifle made at Hartford with Thuer conversion for use with metallic cartridges. Serial No. 2926. *William M. Locke Collection. B.* 24 in. *Cal.* 0·44 in. (*See* p. 101.)

AMERICAN PERCUSSION REVOLVERS **613** Six-shot rifle by James Warner, Springfield, Mass. *c.* 1855. *Winchester Gun Museum. B.* 22½ in. *Cal.* 0·38 in. **614** Seven-shot rifle (pill-lock) by T. P. Cherington. *c.* 1850. *B.* 30 in. *Cal.* 0·4 in. **615** Seven-shot rifle by H. Volpius with extension rear-sight, *c.* 1860. *B.* 22¾ in. *Cal.* 0·36 in. **616** Six-shot rifle by William Billinghurst, Rochester, N.Y., converted to ·45 Colt metallic cartridges, *c.* 1875. *Winchester Gun Museum. B.* 28 in. **617** North & Orange six-shot shotgun, *c.* 1855. *Winchester Gun Museum. B.* 22½ in. *Cal.* 0·83 in.

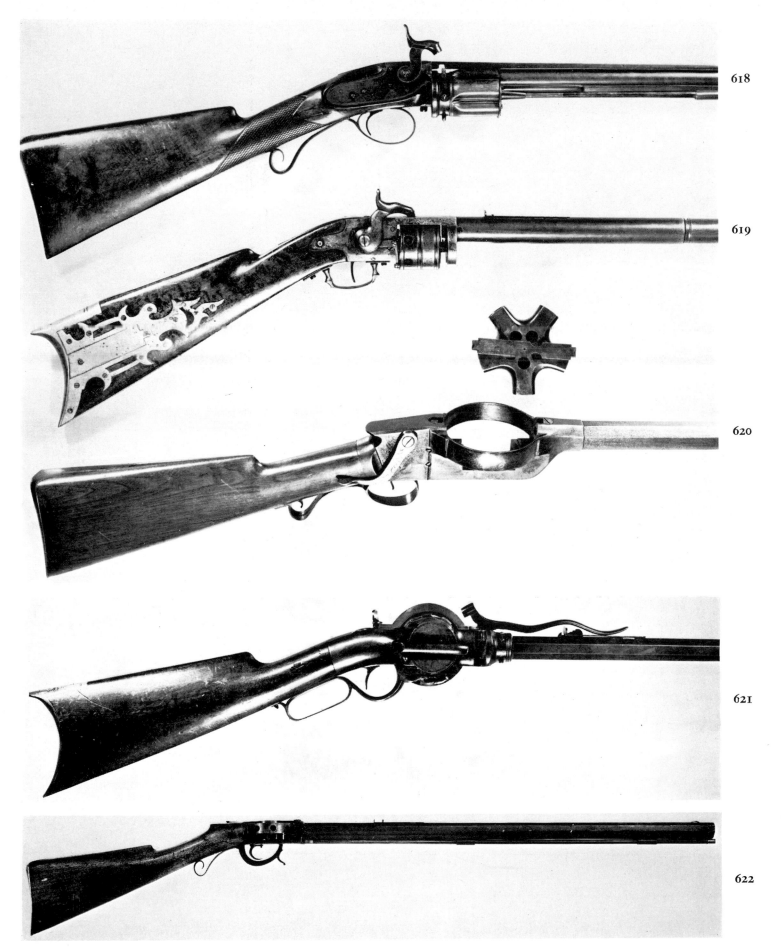

PERCUSSION REVOLVERS **618** Five-shot shotgun marked EDWARDS MAKER–COLLIER'S PATENT. *English, c. 1845.*
B. 28 in. *Cal.* 0·57 in. **619** Six-shot rifle marked NICHOLS & CHILDS PATENT CONWAY MASS 1838. *American. B.* 29 in. *Cal.*
0·44 in. **620** Five-shot 'turret' rifle marked E. H. GRAHAM'S PATENT. *American, c. 1840. B.* 25 in. *Cal.* 0·6 in. **621** Nine-shot
pill-lock 'turret' rifle marked E. W. PORTER NEW YORK–PORTER'S PATENT 1851. *B.* 27½ in. *Cal.* 0·49 in. **622** Nine-shot 'turret'
rifle by Cochran. *American, c. 1837-8. Winchester Gun Museum. B.* 28¾ in. *Cal.* 0·38 in.

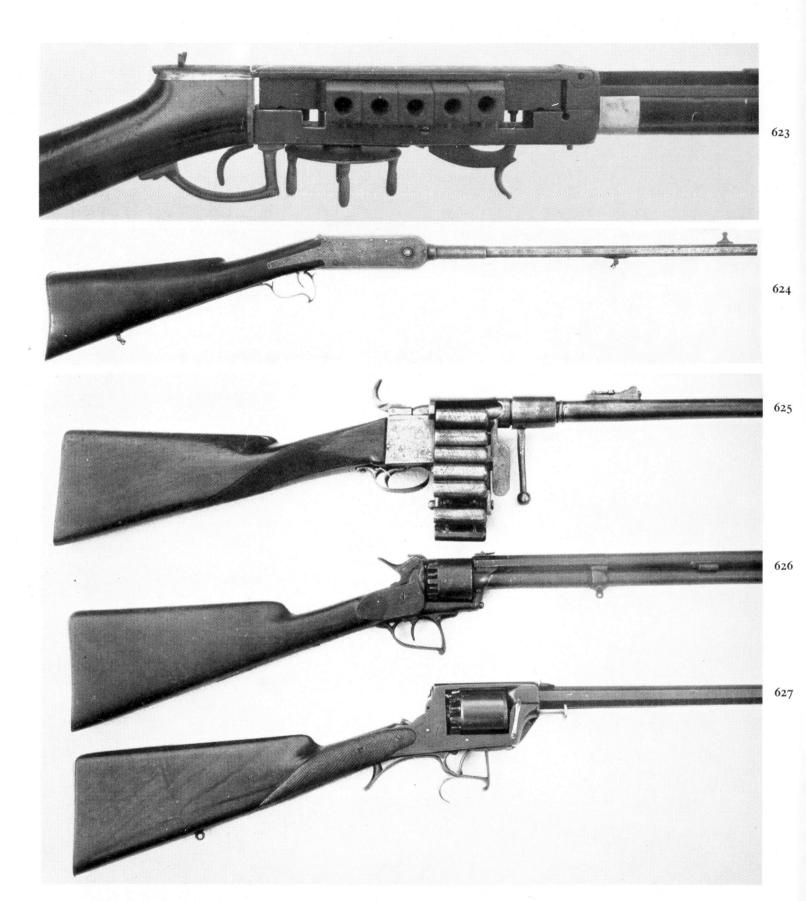

PERCUSSION REVOLVERS **623** Action of 12-shot 'chain' rifle by Bennett & Haviland, patented 1838. *B. R. Lewis Collection.* **624** One hundred-shot 'chain' rifle. *French (?), c. 1875. Winchester Gun Museum. B. 19 in. Cal. 0·45 in.* **625** Fourteen-shot 'chain' gun by T. W. G. Treeby, London, *c. 1855. C. G. Vokes Collection. B. 20½ in. Cal. 0·51 in.* **626** Nine-shot Le Mat shotgun/rifle. *c. 1860. C. G. Vokes Collection. B. (Shot) 18 in. B. (Rifle) 20 in.* **627** Five-shot Tranter rifle by Charles Nephew & Co., Calcutta. Serial No. 5518T. *C. G. Vokes Collection. B. 21½ in. Cal. 0·52 in.*

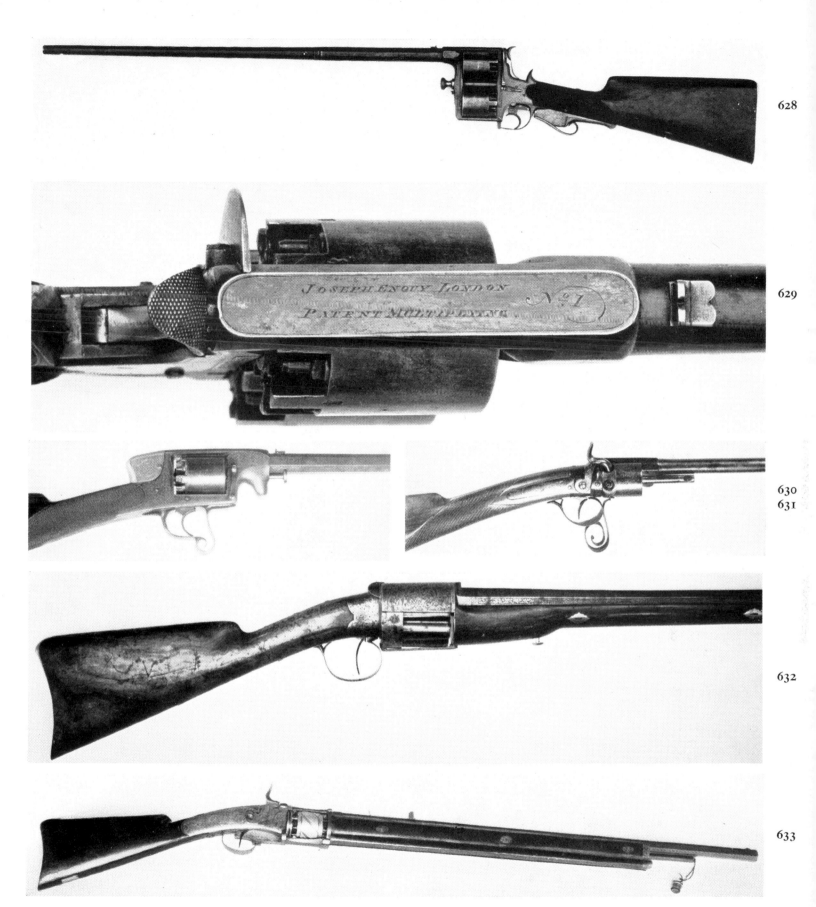

628

629

630
631

632

633

PERCUSSION REVOLVERS   628 Rifle with two cylinders, marked JOSEPH ENOUY LONDON PATENT MULTIPLYING N°. 1.
c. 1855. *Museum of Artillery, Turin* (No. 301).   629 Top view of action of 628.   630 Action of five-shot rifle by Robert
Adams, London, with shield over hammer. *Arms Museum, Liège* (No. Ch 17/2251).   631 Action of unnamed six-shot rifle.
Barrel swings up on hinge for loading.   632 Six-shot double-action gun signed DEVISME BTE A PARIS. Barrel inlaid in gold
with name ABDULLAH IBN BELGASIM (in Turkish characters). *French, c.* 1850. *Tower of London* (No. XII-1522). *B.* 51 in. *Cal.*
0·65 in.   633 Rifle with revolving cylinder fed by tubular magazine under barrel. Patented by Edward Lindner, New York,
in 1854. *Arms Museum, Liège* (No. Ch 14/900). *B.* 32·3 in.

CARTRIDGE REVOLVERS **634** Six-shot centre-fire rifle signed F. CLAUDIN BLD DES ITALIENS 38 PARIS. *c.* 1870. *C. G. Vokes Collection. B. 26½ in. Cal. 0·41 in.* **635** Ten-shot pin-fire rifle unmarked. *French (?), c.* 1860. *C. G. Vokes Collection. B. 21 in. Cal. 0·41 in.* **636** Seven-shot rim-fire rifle unmarked. *English (?), c.* 1870. *C. G. Vokes Collection. B. 21 in.* **637** Presentation set of pin-fire rifle, bayonet and pistol by Lefaucheux in glass-top case lined with blue velvet. Stocks of carved ebony, actions etched and damascened. *French, c.* 1860. **638** Action of rim-fire rifle signed PIEPER-GHAYE. *Belgian, c.* 1870. *Arms Museum, Liège* (No. Ch 28/5696). **639** Action of pin-fire sporting rifle by E. Lefaucheux. *French,* dated 1854. *Arms Museum, Liège* (No. Ch 18/2253). **640** Smith & Wesson centre-fire rifle, *c.* 1885. *Winchester Gun Museum. B. 18 in. Cal. 0·32 in.*

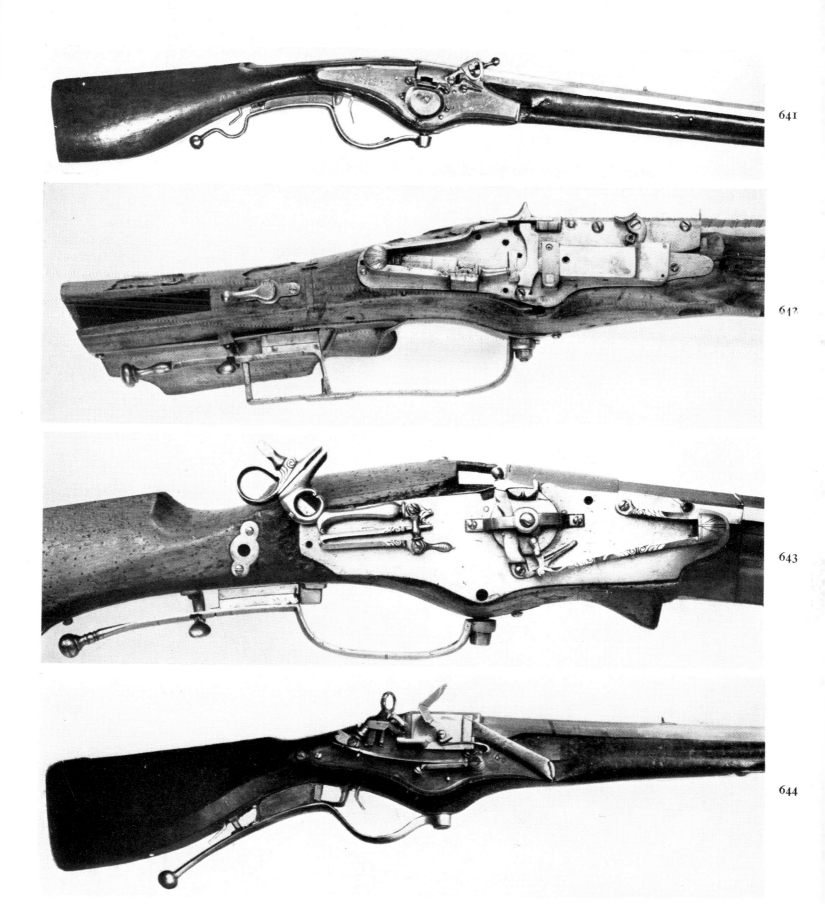

KALTHOFF MAGAZINE GUNS **641** Wheellock rifle by Peter Kalthoff. Inscribed ANNO 1645 DAS ERSTE. *Tøjhusmuseet, Copenhagen* (No. B. 180). *B.* 37·3 in. *Cal.* 0·38 in. **642** Wheellock gun by Heinrich Habrecht, Schleswig, the 'Master from Gottorp'. *German, c.* 1645. *Tøjhusmuseet, Copenhagen* (No. B. 188). *B.* 35·5 in. *Cal.* 0·64 in. **643** Wheellock gun, by same maker. *c.* 1650. *Tøjhusmuseet, Copenhagen* (No. B. 497). *B.* 43·8 in. *Cal.* 0·67 in. **644** Flintlock rifle by H. Bartmans. *Dutch (The Hague), c.* 1645. *Tøjhusmuseet, Copenhagen* (No. B. 182). *B.* 33·7 in. *Cal.* 0·67 in.

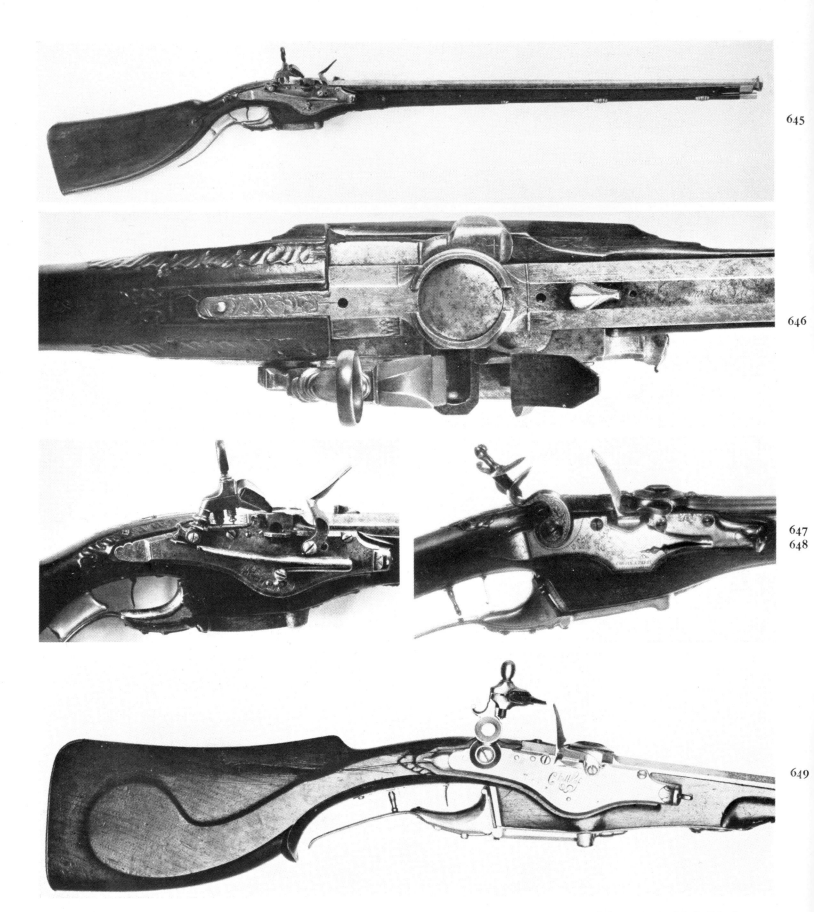

645

646

647
648

649

KALTHOFF MAGAZINE GUNS   **645** Flintlock gun signed HARMAN BARNE, LONDINI. *English, c.* 1650. *Mark Dineley Collection.*   **646** Top view of action of **645**.   **647** Close-up of lock of **645**.   **648** Close-up of lock of flintlock gun signed COUSIN A PARIS. *c.* 1680. *State Hermitage, Leningrad* (No. 3.0.638).   **649** Flintlock gun signed C. KALTHOF. *English, c.* 1660. *Tøjhusmuseet, Copenhagen* (No. B. 762). *B.* 43·5 in. *Cal.* 0·63 in.

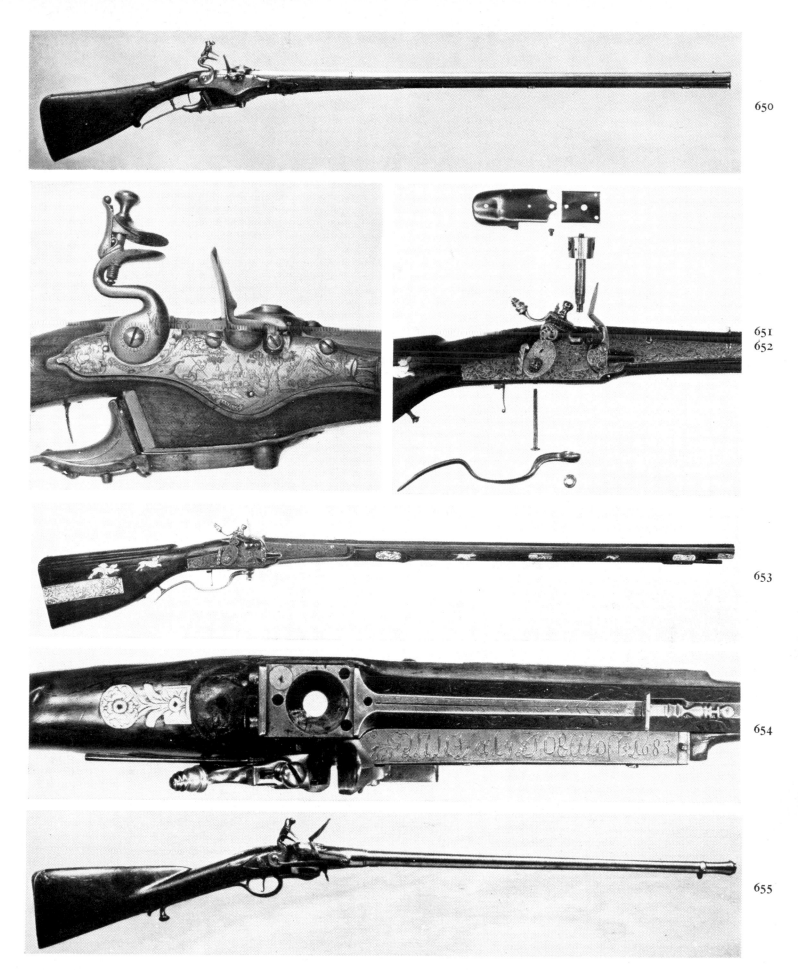

FLINTLOCK MAGAZINE GUNS   **650** Gun on Kalthoff system signed IAN FLOCK, UTRECHT. *Dutch, c.* 1680. *Livrustkam-maren, Stockholm* (No. 1334). *B.* 44·3 in. *Cal.* 0·51 in.   **651** Close up of lock of **650**.   **652** Action of **653** with breech block removed.   **653** Repeating rifle signed MICHAEL DORTTLOFF 1683. *Winchester Gun Museum. B.* 36 in. *Cal.* 0·35 in.   **654** Top view of action of **653** with breech block removed.   **655** Rifle with vertically-revolving breech block and external lock mechanism by Clarkson. *English, c.* 1740. *Glasgow Museum* (No. 39–65we). *B.* 22¼ in. *Cal.* 0·56 in.

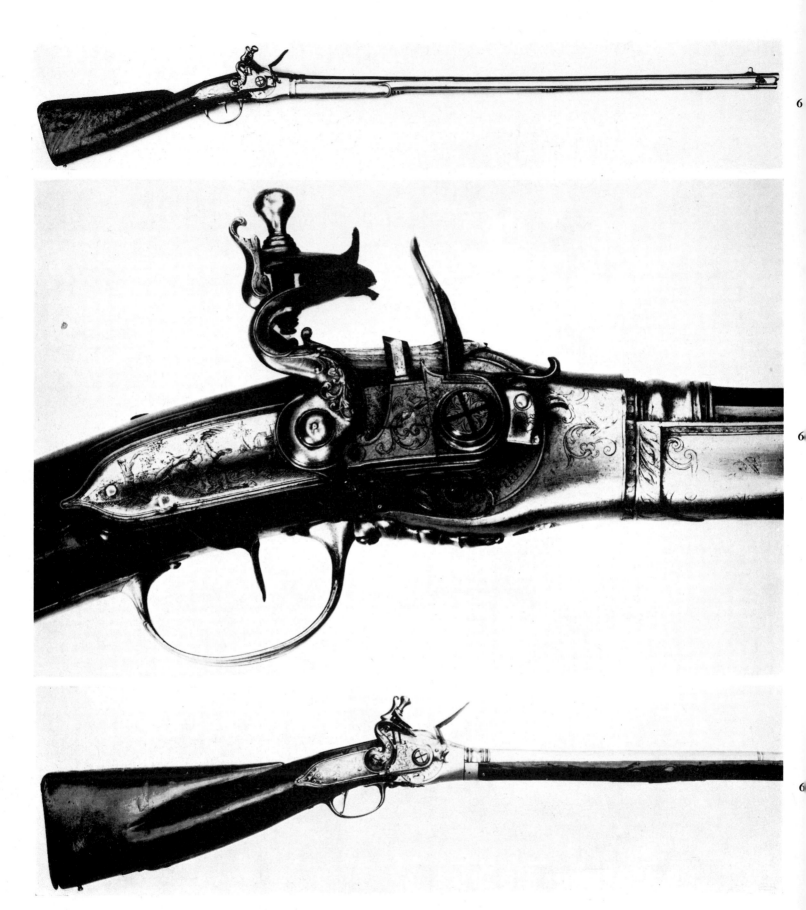

FLINTLOCK MAGAZINE GUNS   **656** Gun with horizontally-revolving breech block signed MICHELE LORENZONI DI FIRENZE. *Italian*, c. 1685. *Royal Armoury, Turin* (No. M. 64). *B.* 34·3 in. *Cal.* 0·52 in.   **657** Close-up of action of **656**.   **658** Gun with similar action by same maker, c. 1690. *Tøjhusmuseet, Copenhagen* (No. B. 1006). *B.* 35·5 in. *Cal.* 0·52 in.

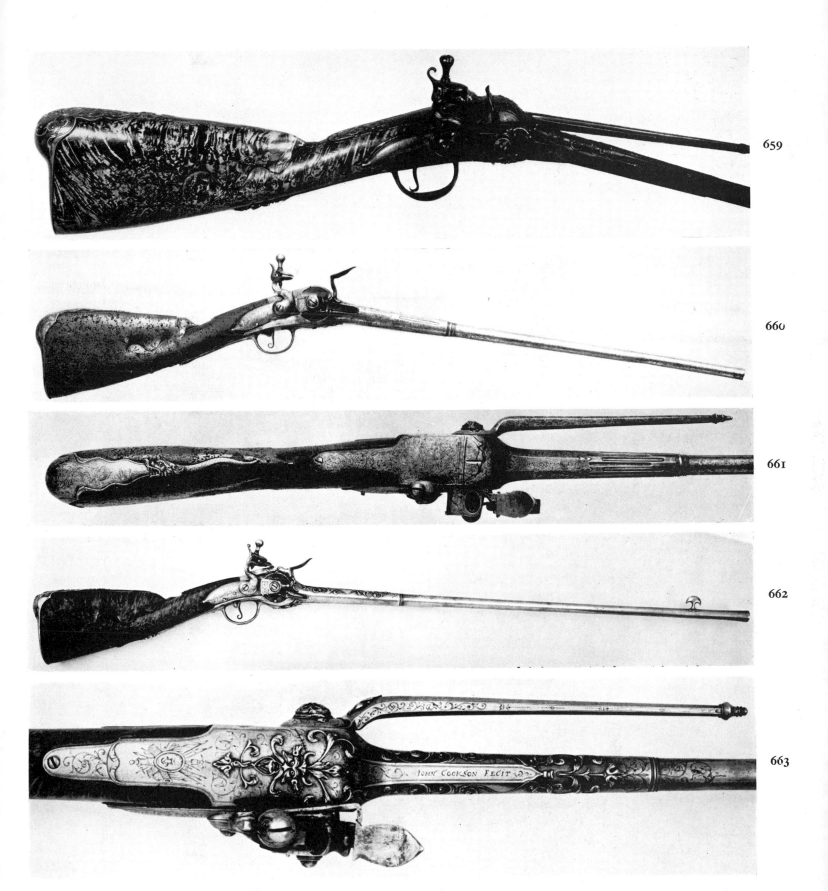

MAGAZINE GUNS BY JOHN COOKSON, *c.* 1690.   **659** Gun with burr-walnut stock and deep-chiselled steel mounts, signed JOHN COOKSON. *Victoria and Albert Museum* (No. 77-1893).   **660** Gun with plain walnut stock and engraved mounts signed JOHN COOKSON FECIT. *Milwaukee Museum* (No. N. 6316). *B.* 25 in. *Cal.* 0·55 in.   **661** Top view of **660**.   **662** Gun with burr-walnut stock and deep-chiselled steel mounts and curious fore-sight signed JOHN COOKSON FECIT and dated 1686 (?). *William M. Locke Collection. B.* 31½ in. *Cal.* 0·55 in.   **663** Top view of action of **662**.

664

665

666

667

FLINTLOCK MAGAZINE GUNS **664** Action of gun with horizontally-revolving breech block signed GIACOMO BERSELLI. *Italian, c. 1700. Royal Armoury, Turin, (No. M. 65).* **665** Gun with similar action signed C. NUTERISCH A WIEN. *Austrian, c. 1730. Tower of London (No. XII–472). B. 23·5 in. Cal. 0·47 in.* **666** Similar gun with brass action cast as a monster's head. *Austrian, c. 1730. Tower of London (No. XII–1273). B. 20·25 in. Cal. 0·57 in.* **667** Close-up of action of **666**.

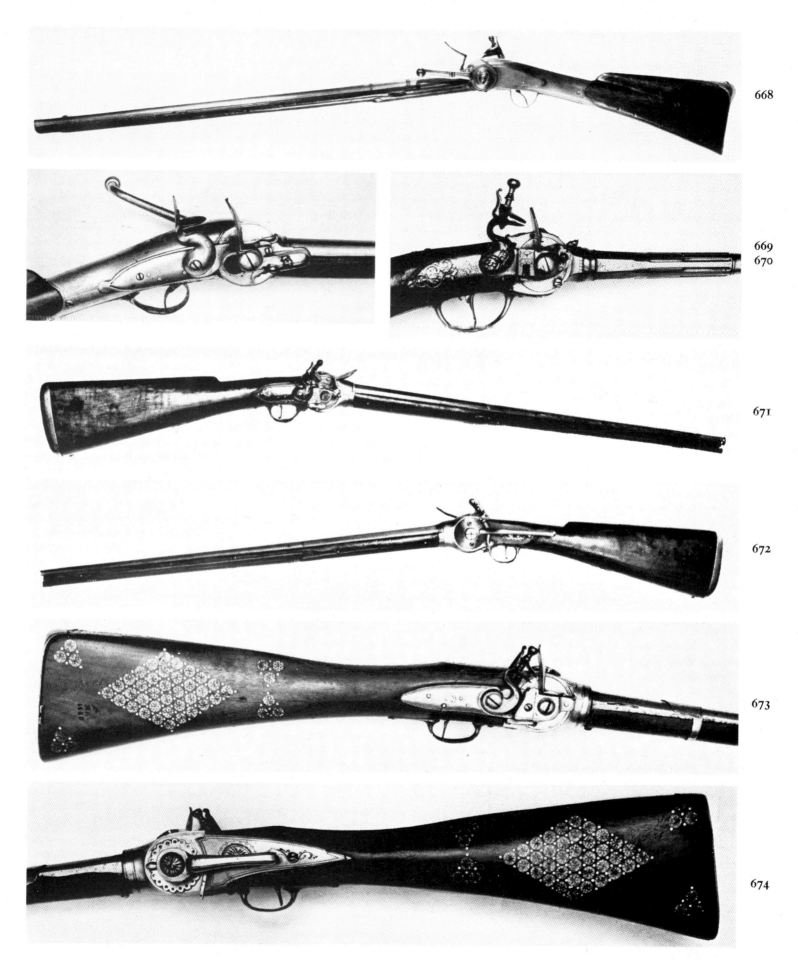

668

669
670

671

672

673

674

FLINTLOCK MAGAZINE GUNS **668** Reverse side of Lorenzoni-type gun. *English* (?), *c.* 1740. *Smithsonian Institution, Washington. B.* 28½ in. *Cal.* 0·70 in. **669** Close-up of similar gun. *Tower of London* (No. XII–474). **670** Close-up of action of gun signed BARTOLOMEO COTEL. *Italian, c.* 1690. *Tower of London* (No. XII–473). **671–2** Lock and reverse-side views of gun by Antonio Constantini, Bologna. *Italian, c.* 1700. *Birmingham Museum.* **673–4** Lock and reverse-side views of Turkish copy of a Lorenzoni-type gun. 18th century. *Tower of London* (No. XXVI–3F).

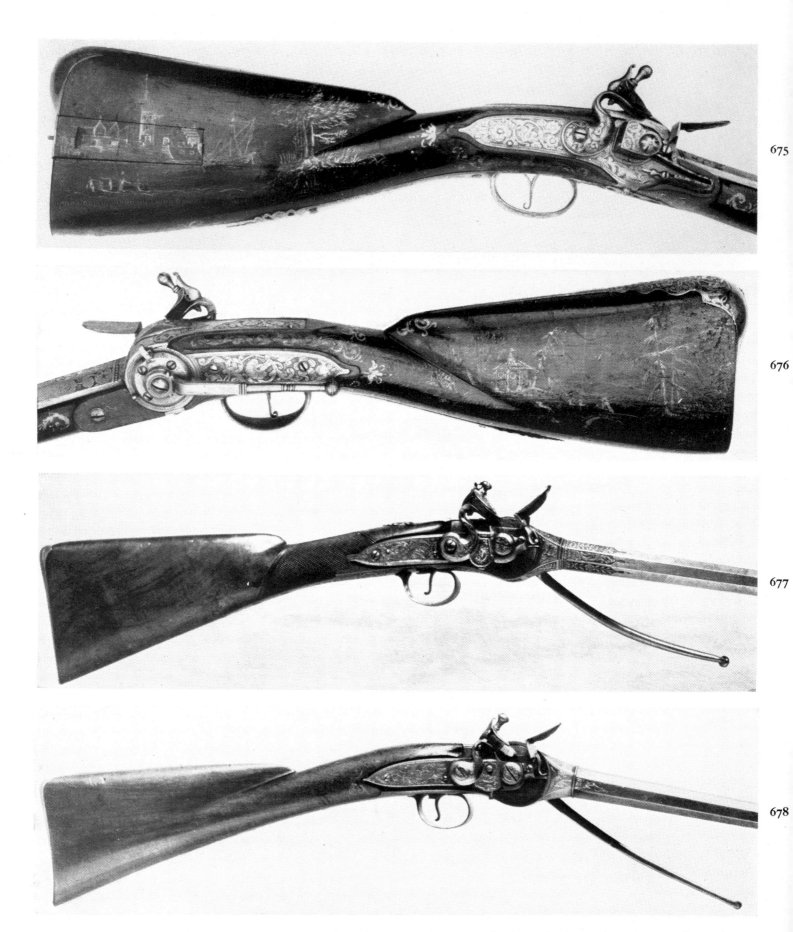

675

676

677

678

FLINTLOCK MAGAZINE GUNS **675–6** Lock and reverse-side views of rifle with ebonised stock painted in gilt. *Dutch, c. 1690. C. G. Vokes Collection.* **677** Gun with etched lock and breech signed PARIS, DERBY. *English, c. 1780. Glasgow Muse. n* (No. 39–65wd). **678** Gun with engraved lock and breech signed JOHN PRATT. *English, c. 1770. Glasgow Museum* (No. 39–65wf).

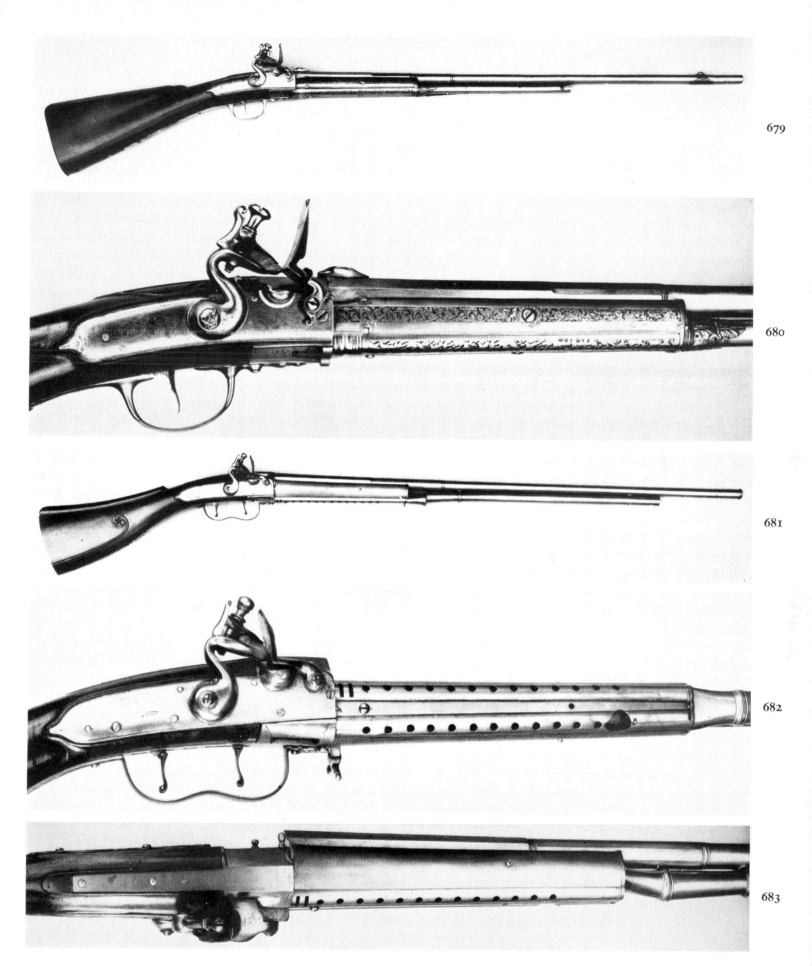

679

680

681

682

683

FLINTLOCK MAGAZINE GUNS   679 Gun with turn-over barrel assembly with tubular magazines underneath, signed
MICHAEL LORENZONUS. *Italian, c.* 1685. *Royal Armoury, Turin* (No. M. 63). *B.* 31·8 in. *Cal.* 0·51 in.   680 Close-up of engraved and chiselled action of 679.   681 Gun with similar action signed GIO PIETRO CALLIN A GENOVA 1685. *Royal Armoury,
Turin* (No. M. 62).   682 Close-up of 681 with barrel twisted to one side showing perforated bullet magazines.   683 Top
view of 681 in same state.

FLINTLOCK MAGAZINE GUNS **684** Silver-mounted gun signed CHELEMBRON A PONDICHERY. From Collection of George III. *French, c.* 1780. *Windsor Castle* (No. 413). B. 35¼ in. *Cal.* 0·61 in. **685** Indian copy of **684** dated 1217 A.H. (A.D. 1802/3). *Windsor Castle* (No. 430). B. 38¼ in. *Cal.* 0·56 in. **686** Unnamed fowling-piece on Chelembron system. *French, c.* 1780. **687** Close-up of gun inscribed on barrel in silver FAIT PAR CHELEBROM 1781. *Mark Dineley Collection.* **688** Reverse side of **687**.

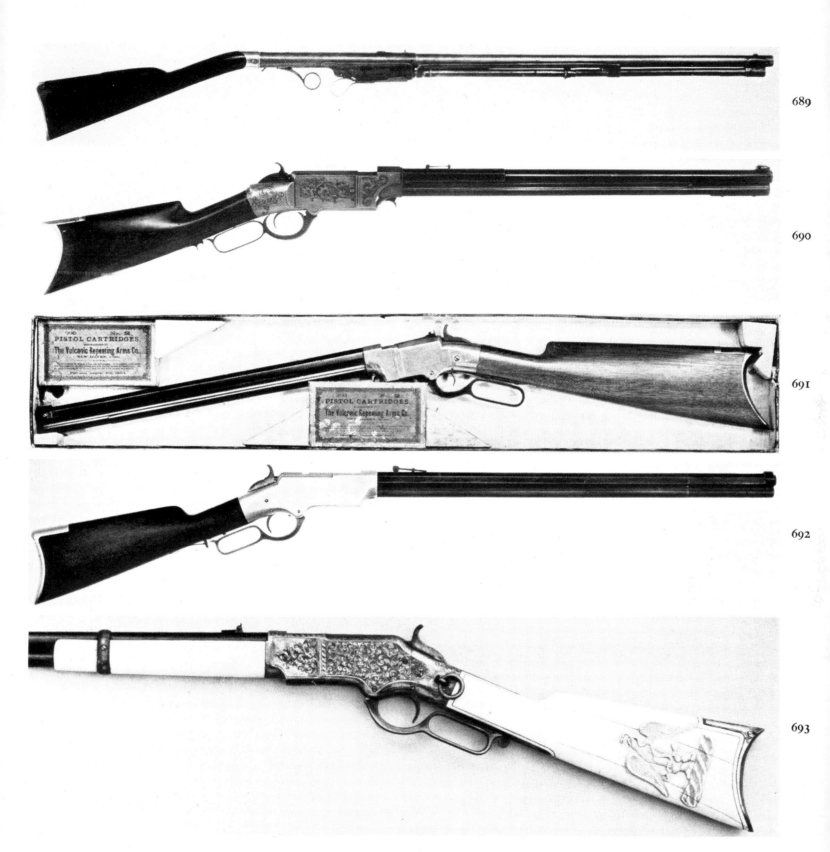

689

690

691

692

693

DEVELOPMENT OF WINCHESTER MAGAZINE RIFLE **689** Walter Hunt's rifle, patented 1847–9. *Winchester Gun Museum. B.* 25½ in. *Cal.* 0·54 in. **690** Smith & Wesson experimental rim-fire rifle, 1854–5. *Winchester Gun Museum. B.* 23 in. *Cal.* 0·50 in. **691** 'Volcanic' rifle made by New Haven Arms Co., in original box, *c.* 1858–60. *Winchester Gun Museum. B.* 16½ in. *Cal.* 0·3 in. **692** Henry rifle with brass frame. Serial No. 2928. *c.* 1864. *Winchester Gun Museum. B.* 24 in. *Cal.* 0·44 in. **693** Silver-plated Winchester Model 1866 rifle with carved ivory stock probably made for the Mexican Market. Serial No. 21,921. *William M. Locke Collection. B.* 20 in. *Cal.* 0·44 in.

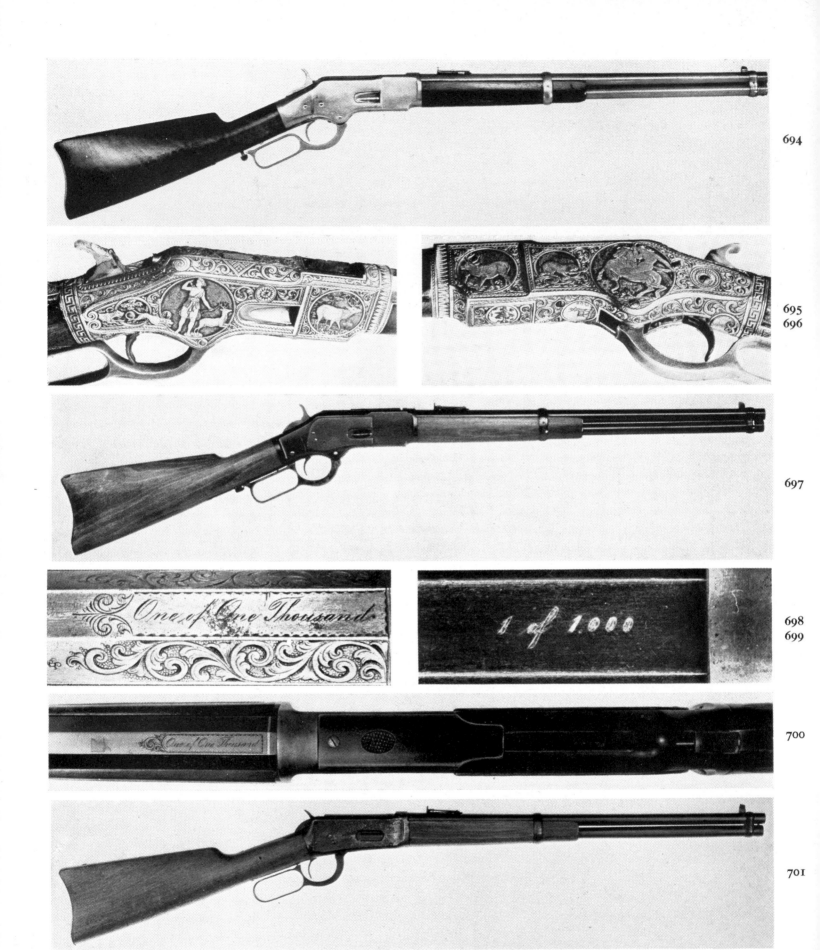

WINCHESTER MAGAZINE RIFLES **694** Model 1866 carbine, Serial No. 164,554. *Winchester Gun Museum. B.* 20 in.
Cal. 0·44 in.   **695–6** Close-up of both sides of the chiselled gilt–brass action of a presentation Model 1866 rifle. *C. G. Vokes
Collection.*   **697** Model 1873 carbine. *Winchester Gun Museum. B.* 20 in. *Cal.* 0·44 in.   **698–9** Two examples of the inscription on 'One of One Thousand' rifles.   **700** Top view of 'One of One Thousand' Model 1876 rifle, showing slim lines of
the Winchester action. *Winchester Gun Museum.*   **701** Model 1894 carbine. *Winchester Gun Museum. B.* 20 in. *Cal.* 0·30–30 in.

MISCELLANEOUS MAGAZINE RIFLES **702** Evans carbine made in Mechanic Falls, Maine, U.S.A., *c.* 1870. *Winchester Gun Museum.* **703** Spencer carbine Model 1865 with Stabler cut-off. *Winchester Gun Museum. B.* 20 in. *Cal.* 0·50 in. **704** Roper shotgun with detachable muzzle choke, *c.* 1866–8. *Winchester Gun Museum. B.* 28 in. *Cal.* 16ga. **705** Pin-fire 'mouth-organ' rifle with four horizontal chambers, signed INV^on JARRE A PARIS. Serial No. 79. *C. G. Vokes Collection. B.* 26 in. *Cal.* 0·62 in. **706** Underneath view of 'mouth-organ' rifle with five-shot magazine, signed N. KENDALL, WINDSOR, VT, PATENT. *American, c.* 1870. *Milwaukee Museum* (No. N. 589). *Cal.* 0·43 in.

707

708

709

710

711

712

PUMP-ACTION MAGAZINE GUNS   **707** Gun patented in England by W. Krutzsch, 1866.   **708** Margot gun patented in France, 1880.   **709** Spencer 12-bore shotgun of 1885.   **710** Winchester 12-bore shotgun, Model 1893.   **711** Colt Lightning rifle, *c.* 1890. *Cal.* 0·40 in.   **712** Winchester Trench gun and bayonet, Model 1897. All from *Winchester Gun Museum*.

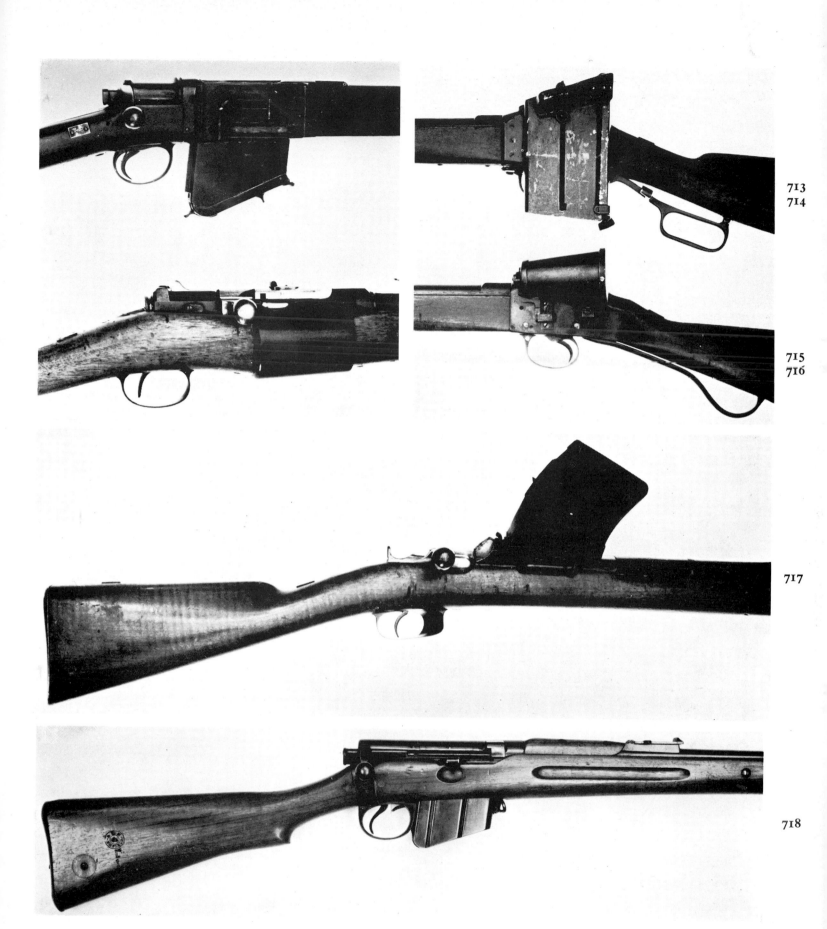

MILITARY MAGAZINE RIFLES 713 Lee experimental rifle and magazine made at Enfield, 1886. 714 Martini-Henry rifle with C. G. Harston's patent spring-loaded magazine, 1887. 715 Spitalsky (Steyr) rifle of 1883 with rotary magazine. 716 Martini-Henry rifle with experimental rotary magazine with gravity feed, c. 1886. 717 Dutch rifle with spring-loaded magazine, patented in England in 1882 by J. S. Jarmann. 718 Lee-Metford rifle with box-magazine, 1889. All from *Tower of London* (Study Collection).

719

720

721

722

723

BOLT-ACTION MAGAZINE RIFLES **719** German Mannlicher rifle, Model 1888. *Cal.* 7·9 mm. **720** Russian Mosin-Nagant rifle, Model 1891. *Cal.* 7·62 mm. **721** Swiss Vetterli rifle, Model 1867–71 No. 2. *Cal.* 10·4 mm. **722** Danish Krag-Jorgensen rifle. *Cal.* 6·5 mm. **723** Dutch Beaumont-Vitale Model 1871–88. *Cal.* 11 mm.

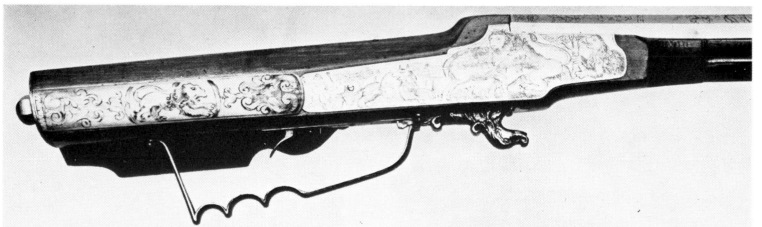

AIR-GUNS **724** Pump-up gun of Queen Christina (1644-54). Copper barrel inscribed MACHT MICHS HANS KOĽER VON KITZING ANNO 1644. *Livrustkammaren, Stockholm* (No. 1252). *B.* 40·6 in. *Cal.* 0·48 in. **725** Close-up of **724**. **726** Pump-up gun signed and dated GEORGE FEHR DRESDEN 1653. *Tøjhusmuseet, Copenhagen* (No. B. 527). *B.* 34·6 in. *Cal.* 0·43 in. **727** Pump-up gun signed and dated GEORGE FEHR DRESDEN 1655. *Tøjhusmuseet, Copenhagen* (No. B. 526). *L.* 45·7 in. *Cal.* 0·42 in.

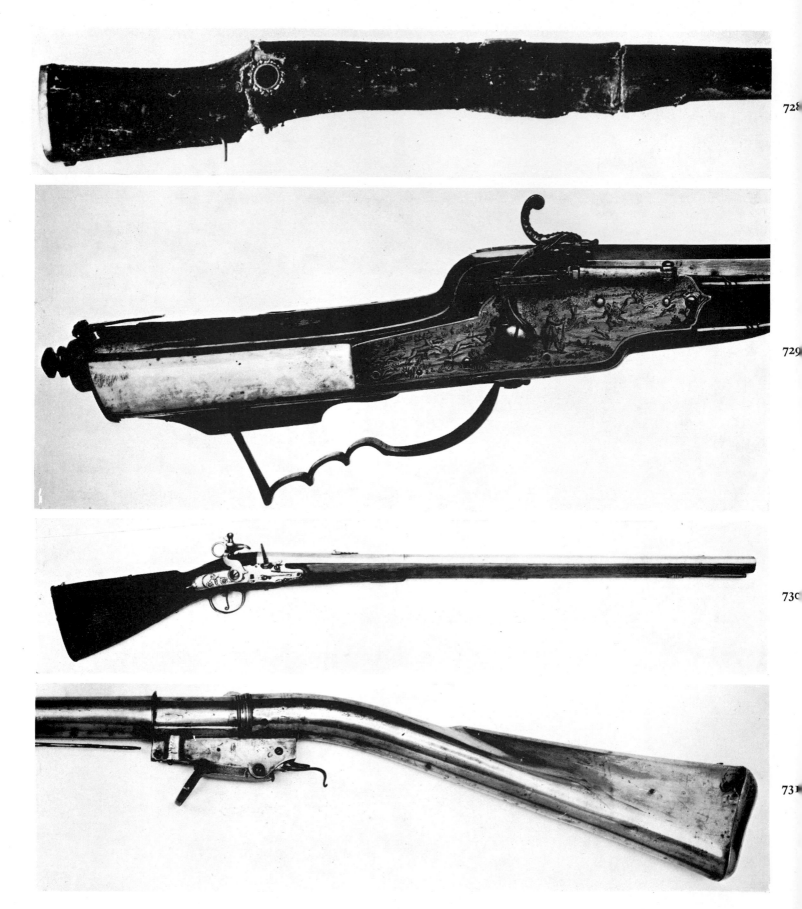

728

729

730

731

AIR-GUNS **728** Spring-gun, stock and barrel covered with velvet. *German*, late 16th century. *Livrustkammaren, Stock-holm* (No. 1196). **729** Action of pump-up gun signed JOHANN KOCK IN CÖLLEN 1654. *Skokloster, Sweden* (No. BB. 52). B. 31·5 in. *Cal.* 0·43 in. **730** Pump-up gun with barrel reservoir. *German, c.* 1690. *Tøjhusmuseet, Copenhagen* (No. B. 1025). **731** All-brass pump-up gun with butt reservoir. *German* (?), early 18th century. *Pitt Rivers Museum, Oxford* (No. PR. 74). B. 28½ in. *Cal.* 0·35 in.

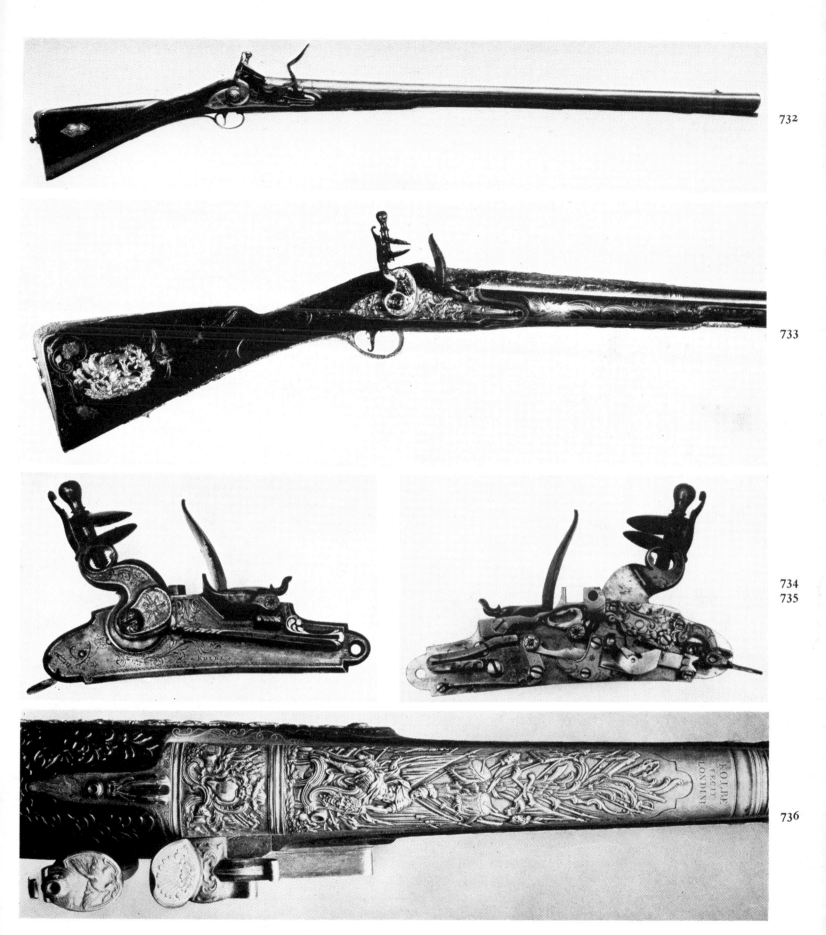

732

733

734
735

736

AIR-GUNS BY JOHANN KOLBE   **732** Gun with butt pump and barrel reservoir, *c.* 1730. *Glasgow Museum* (No. 39–65wm). *B.* 37½ in. *Cal.* 0·5 in.   **733** Silver-mounted gun with same action. Gilt-brass barrel encased with silver at breech. Believed to have belonged to George II (1727–60). *c.* 1740. *Victoria and Albert Museum* (No. 494–1894). *L.* 53½ in. *Cal.* 0·4 in. **734–5** Front and rear views of detached air-gun lock. *Tower of London* (No. XII–941).   **736** View of silver decoration on breech of **733**, signed KOLBE FECIT LONDINI.

AIR-GUNS **737** Military magazine rifle with butt reservoir. Serial No. G1223 (action), G1239 (butt). *Austrian, c.* 1780. *C. G. Vokes Collection. B.* 32½ in. *Cal.* 13 mm. **738** Gun with similar action signed CONTRINER IN WIEN. *Austrian, c.* 1790. *C. G. Vokes Collection. B.* 34 in. **739** Top view of **738** showing decorated gilt-brass breech and tubular magazine. **740** Breechloading bellows gun. *German, c.* 1780. *Tower of London* (No. XII–714). *B.* 31 in. *Cal.* 0·42 in. **741** Rifle with butt reservoir signed BOSLER A DARMSTADT. *German, c.* 1750. *Tower of London* (No. XII–715). *B.* 38 in. *Cal.* 0·48 in. **742** Rifle with brass barrel-reservoir signed JOVER LONDON. *c.* 1780. *Tower of London* (No. XII–1763). *B.* 37 in. *Cal.* 0·4 in.

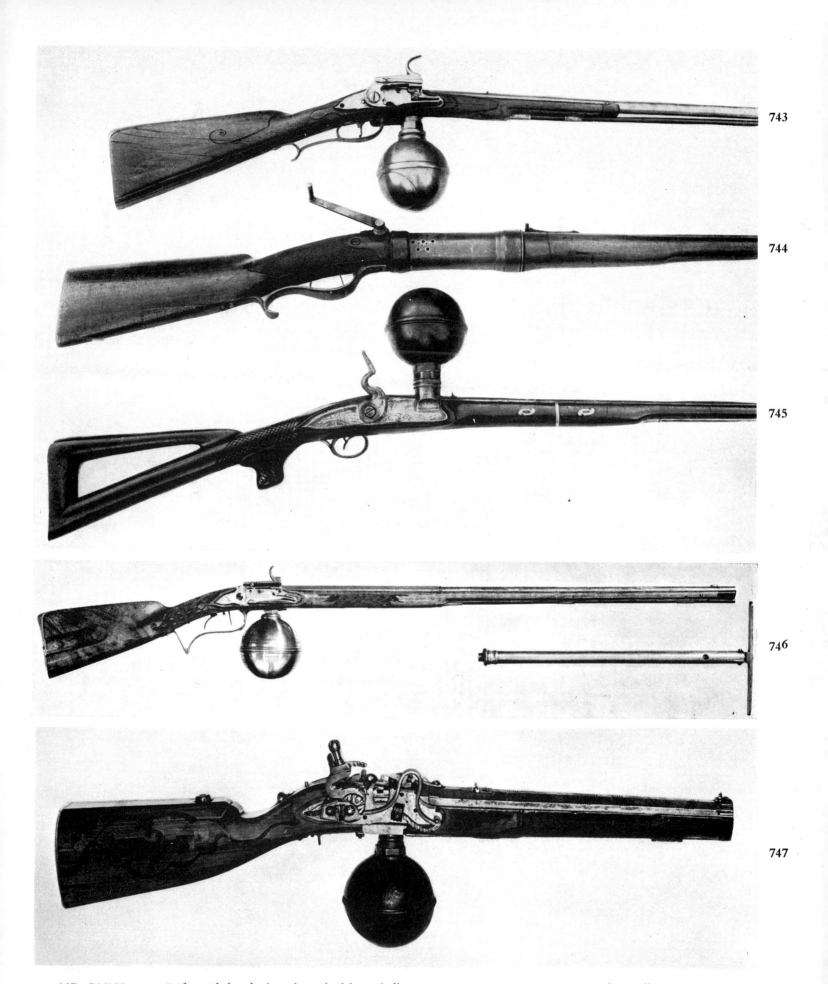

AIR-GUNS **743** Rifle with bar-lock and patched brass-ball reservoir. *German, c. 1800. C. G. Vokes Collection. B.* 33 in.
744 Spring-gun with brass compression cylinder (winder in position). *German, c. 1850. C. G. Vokes Collection. B.* 20½ in.
745 Silver-mounted gun with ball reservoir signed BATE LONDON. Hall-marked 1778. *C. G. Vokes Collection. B.* 30 in. *Cal.*
0·25 in. **746** Toy air-gun with butt reservoir and pump signed H. F. JACOBI IN DRESDEN. *German, c. 1800. A. R. Dufty*
Collection. L. 23¼ in. *B.* 16 in. *Cal.* 0·175 in. **747** Heavy carbine with ball reservoir. Stock of inlaid wood and lock probably of modern construction.

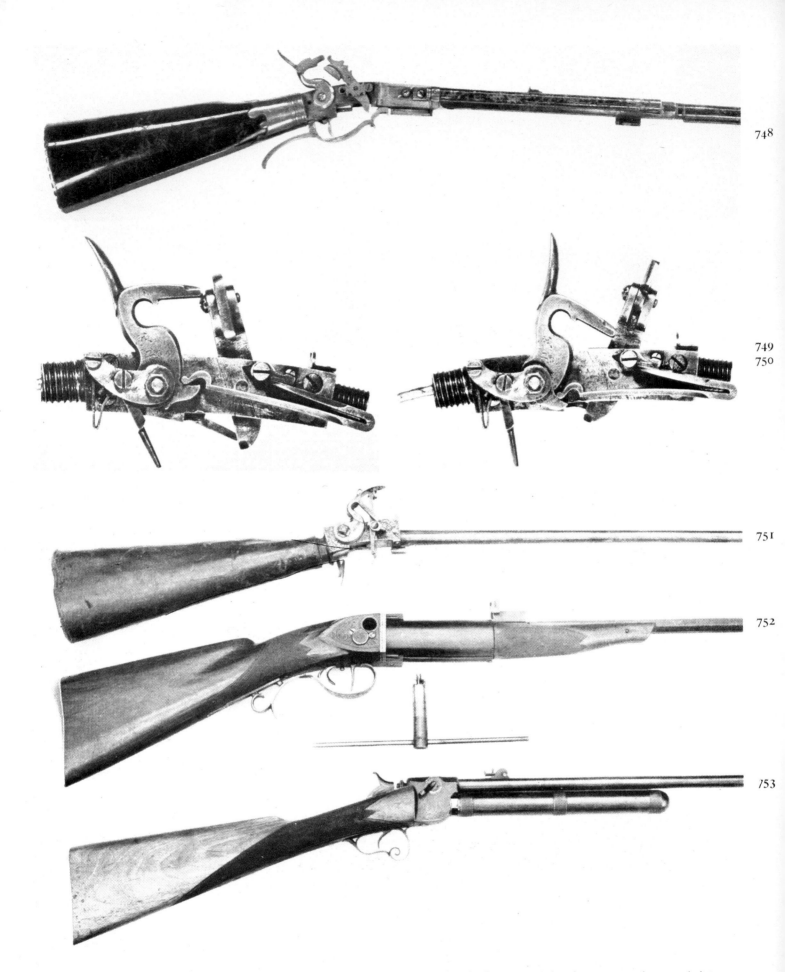

AIR-GUNS **748** Military magazine rifle with butt reservoir and external lock. *German*, dated 1804. *Windsor Castle* (No. 432). *B.* 37½ in. *Cal.* 0·51 in. (*See p.* 101.) **749–50** Detached external lock from a similar gun shown in cocked, and fired (note plunger extended) position. **751** Gun with leather-covered butt signed KUHNLENTZ. *German, c.* 1820. *C. G. Vokes Collection. B.* 35 in. **752** Spring-gun with white metal mounts. Winding key detached. *German, c.* 1870. *C. G. Vokes Collection. B.* 24 in. **753** Giffard gas gun signed RIVOLIER ET FILS, ST ETIENNE. Serial No. 94. *French, c.* 1885. *C. G. Vokes Collection. B.* 25 in.

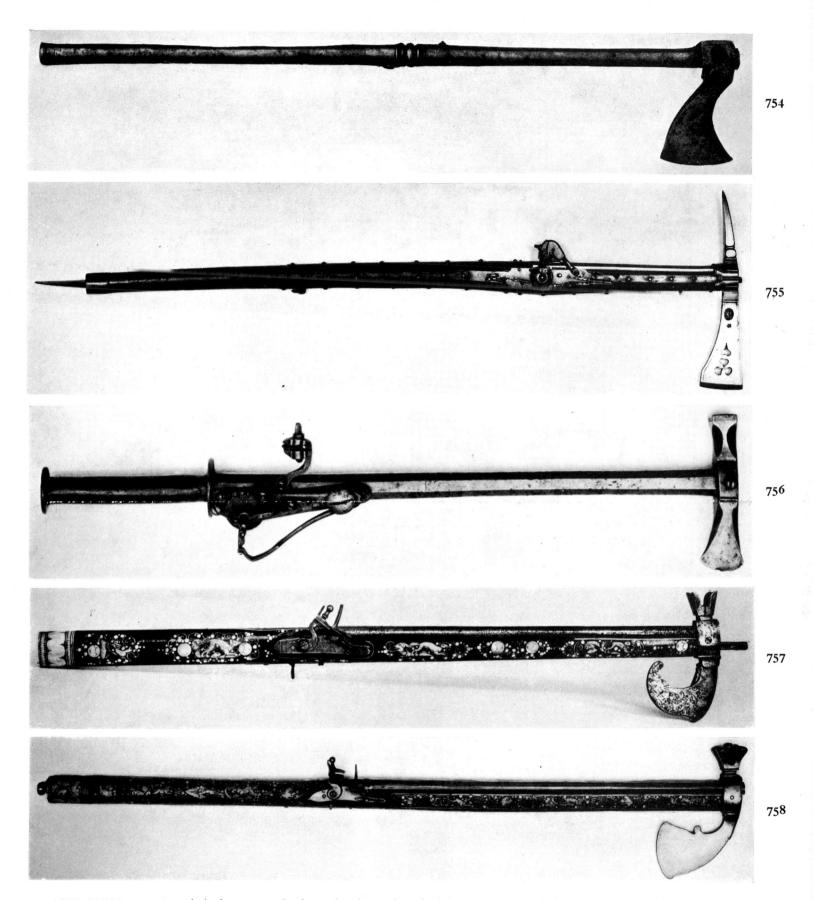

754

755

756

757

758

AXE GUNS   **754** Metal shaft composed of two hand-gun barrels firing in opposite directions. Touch-holes in centre. *Indian*, 17th century.   **755** Wooden stock with spike. Wheellock fired by button trigger near spike. *German*, c. 1570. *Wallace Collection* (No. A. 1239). *L.* 40 in.   **756** Battle hammer with wheellock gun barrel as shaft. *Italian*, late 16th century. **757** Flintlock gun and ceremonial axe. Stock inlaid with mother-of-pearl and stag-horn (probably same maker as **88**). *Silesian*, c. 1660.   **758** Stock inlaid stag-horn. *Silesian*, c. 1700.

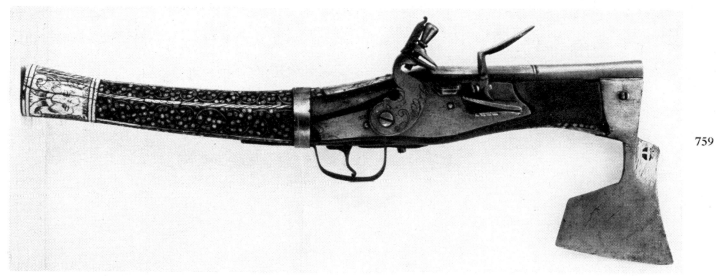

759

760

761

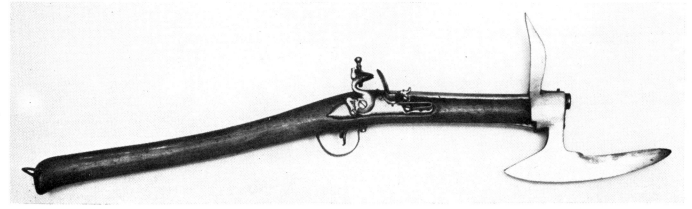

762

FLINTLOCK AXE GUNS **759** Stock inlaid stag-horn. *German, 17th century. George F. Harding Museum, Chicago* (No. 1299). *L.* 19¼ in. *B.* 6½ in. *Cal.* 0·48 in. **760** Blade with armourer's mark of PB. *Italian (?), 17th century.* **761** Carbine with war hammer signed BIANCO. *Italian, c. 1690. Tøjhusmuseet, Copenhagen* (No. B. 878). *L.* 32·4 in. *B.* 16·4 in. *Cal.* 0·5 in. **762** Carbine with dog-lock. *German, c. 1720. Tower of London* (No. XIV–7). *L.* 33 in. *B.* 9¾ in. *Cal.* 0·56 in.

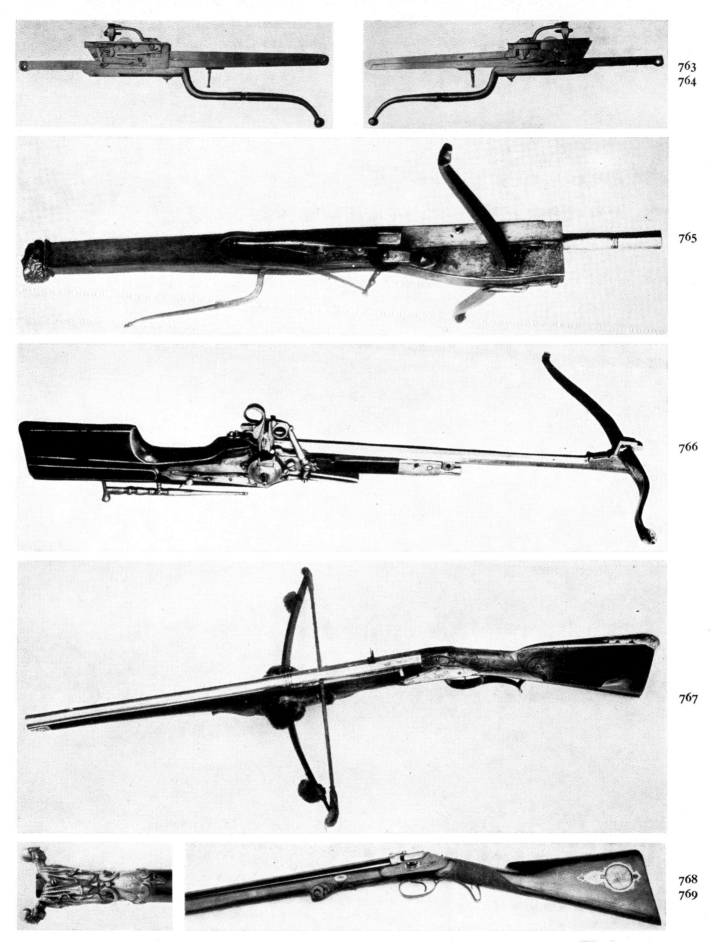

763
764

765

766

767

768
769

CROSSBOW AND CATAPULT GUNS 763–4 Both sides of the action of a combined crossbow and self-spanning wheellock gun. *German, c. 1520 (?). Kunsthistorisches Museum, Vienna (No. D. 200).* 765 All-steel wheellock (cock missing) gun and crossbow. Bronze lion mask on butt. *N. Italian, c. 1520 (?). Palazzo Ducale, Venice (No. Q. 1).* 766 Wheellock gun and stone bow (lever missing). *German, c. 1610. Victoria and Albert Museum (No. M. 618–1927).* 767 Bullet crossbow with brass barrel. *German, dated 1742. A. R. Dufty Collection. L. 38 in.* 768 Muzzle of 769. 769 Catapult gun. *English, c. 1850. C. G. Vokes Collection. L. 46 in. B. 30 in.*

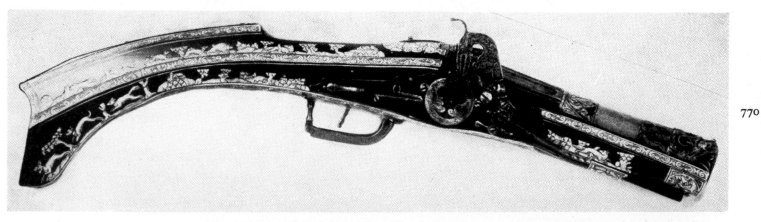

770

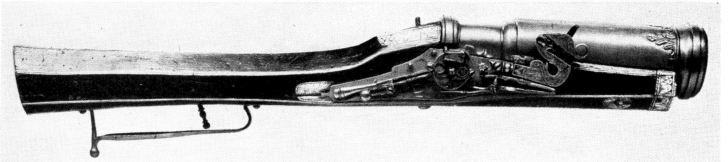

771

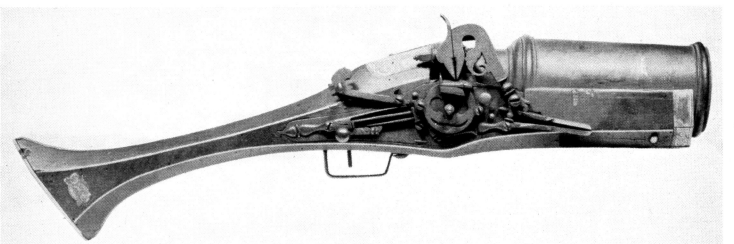

772

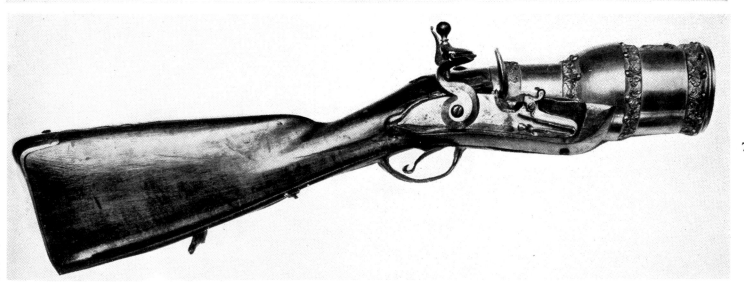

773

HAND-MORTAR GUNS **770** Wheellock, with chiselled steel barrel. *German (probably Augsburg), c. 1590. Wallace Collection* (No. A. 1077). L. 25½ in. B. 10½ in. Cal. 1·45 in. **771** Wheellock, with bronze barrel. *German, c. 1580. Glasgow Museum* (No. 39–65ye). L. 28 in. B. 10¾ in. Cal. 2·06 in. **772** Combined wheellock and matchlock. Lock with maker's mark GH over pierced heart. Bronze barrel. *German (Nuremberg), c. 1590. British Museum* (No. 81.8–2.135). L. 24¾ in. Cal. 2·8 in. **773** Flintlock. Bronze barrel cast with arms of Wurtemberg. *German, c. 1740. Historisches Museum, Bern* (No. 2322). L. 25·6 in. B. 8 in. Cal. 3 in.

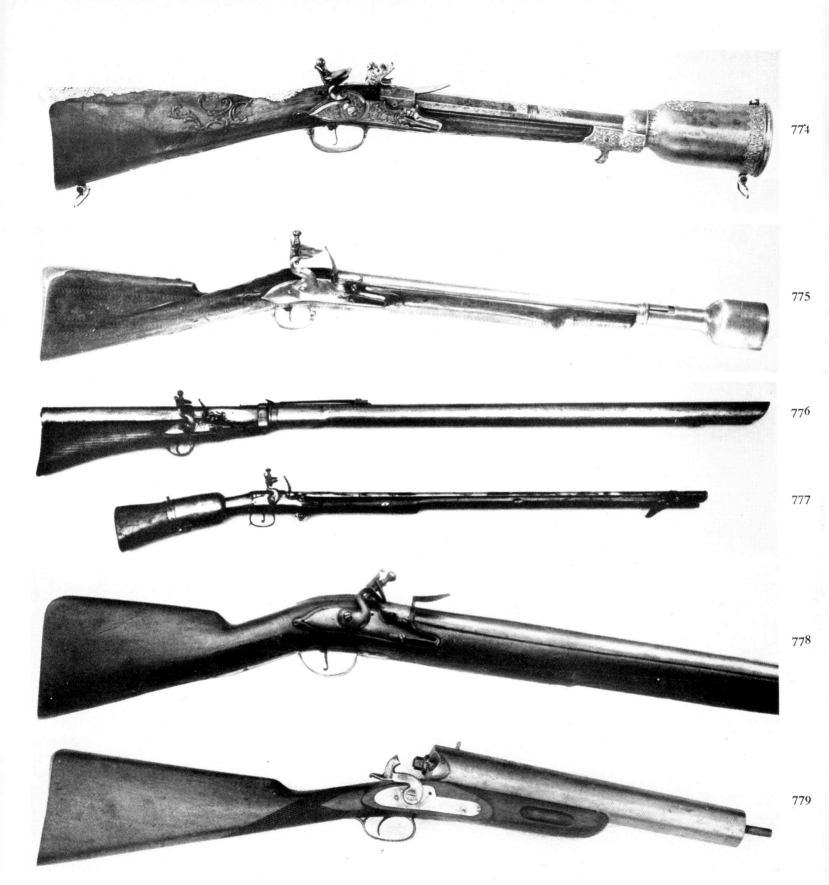

774

775

776

777

778

779

GRENADE, ROCKET AND LINE GUNS **774** Flintlock grenade gun with chiselled steel barrel and discharge cup. Gilt brass mounts. Signed GRAFENSTEIN A GOTHA. *German, dated* 1731. *Bayerisches Nationalmuseum, Munich* (No. 13/725). L. 32·2 in. *Cal.* 2·8 in. **775** Short flintlock musket with detachable grenade cup. *English, dated* 1728. *Tower of London* (No. XII–266). B. 21¼ in. *Cal.* 0·75 in. **776** Flintlock rocket launcher with steel tube. *English, c.* 1810. *Tower of London* (No. XII–589). L. 66 in. *Cal.* 2 × 1·6 in. **777** Flintlock carbine with grenade cup in butt (wooden end folds back in use). Folding stand under barrel. Signed I. HARTWELL. *English, c.* 1685. *Tower of London* (No. XII–261). B. 38½ in. *Cal.* 0·65 in. **778** Flintlock rocket launcher with copper barrel. *English* (?), *c.* 1720. B. 35½ in. *Cal.* 1·75 in. **779** Percussion line thrower with brass barrel and tubular spigot. *English, c.* 1860. *C. G. Vokes Collection.* B. 14 in.

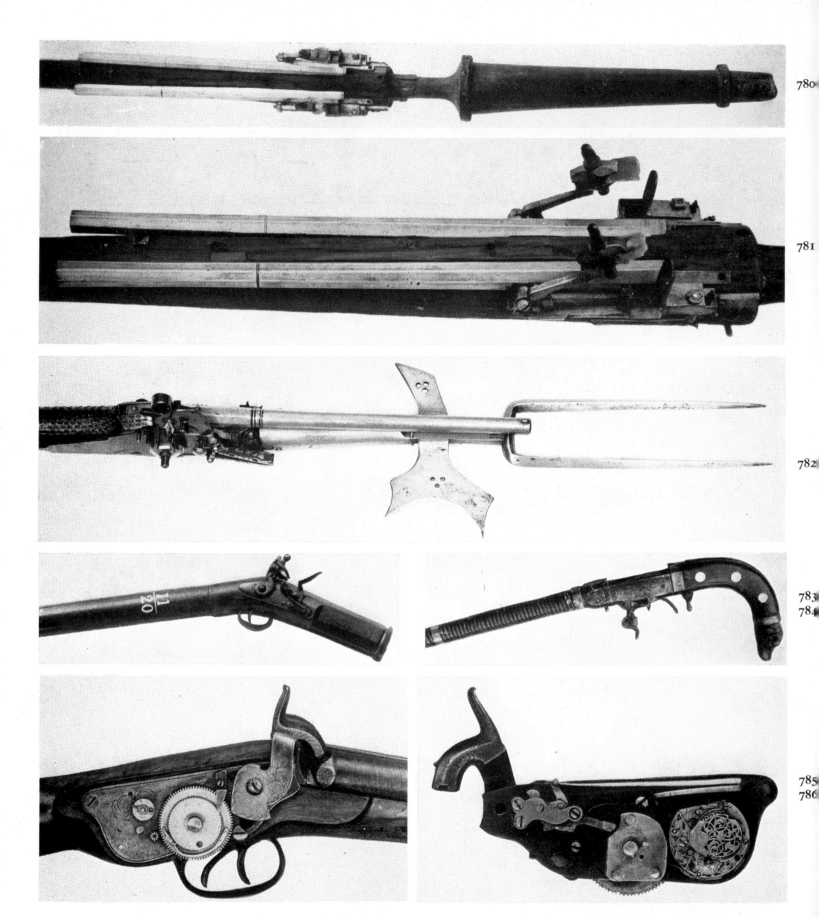

COMBINATION WEAPONS **780** Wooden lance with two miquelet-lock pistols. *Spanish, c. 1580. Royal Armoury, Madrid* (No. I. 20). **781** Close-up of locks of **780**, with sliding steels and pan-cover. **782** Head of combined halberd, fork and wheellock pistol. *German, c. 1580. Wallace Collection* (No. A. 1238). *L. 85 in. B. 12½ in. Cal. 0·4 in.* **783** Staff gun. Heavy brass barrel of 1 in. bore set at angle of 135° on wooden pole 5½ ft. long. *English, c. 1810. Rotunda, Woolwich* (No. XI-20). **784** Walking-stick gun with carved horn handle. Under-hammer percussion lock. *C. G. Vokes Collection.* **785** Double-barrelled percussion shotgun with time-lock. *English, c. 1850. (See p. 101.)* **786** Interior of lock of **785** showing verge watch-movement of earlier date.

CARTRIDGE HOLDERS   **787** Wooden box with metal surround and spring lid. *German, c. 1590. H. L. Peterson Collection.*   **788** Cartridge box with engraved stag-horn panels. *Dutch, c. 1570. Metropolitan Museum, New York (No. 14.25.1502).*
789 Cartridge box with engraved mounts. *Saxon, c. 1580. Metropolitan Museum, New York (No. 29.158.701).*   **790** Bandoleer. *Swedish, mid 17th century. Royal Army Museum, Stockholm (No. AM. 3024).*   **791** Iron cartridge box damascened in gold and silver. *Indian, c. 1850. Author's Collection.*   **792** Cartridge case. Ebony tubes decorated with silver niello work. Worn on the breast of the coat. *Russian, early 19th century. Wallace Collection (No. 2095).*

EUROPEAN POWDER FLASKS **793** All steel. Engraved with arms of the Roman family of Chigi. *Italian, c. 1600. Tower of London (No. XIII-156).* **794** Steel casing with embossing of Samson and Delilah and arms of Medici. *Italian, c. 1620. Tower of London (No. XIII-10).* **795** Ebony inlaid with stag-horn and mother-of-pearl. *German, dated 1616. Tower of London (No. XIII-17).* **796** Wood inlaid with stag-horn and bands of gilt brass. *German, c. 1590. Tower of London (No. XIII-41).* **797** Turned ivory. Nozzle has three wheellock spanner sockets. *German (?), c. 1600. Tower of London (No. XIII-43).* **798** Antler, engraved with figure of Lucretia. *German, c. 1600. Tower of London (No. XIII-5).* **799** Blue enamel, gilt brass mounts. *German, c. 1640. Victoria and Albert Museum (No. 2198-1855).* **800** Carved box-wood, silver mounts with Augsburg mark. *German, c. 1600. Private Collection.* **801** Copper gilt. *German, c. 1570. Wallace Collection (No. A. 1297).*

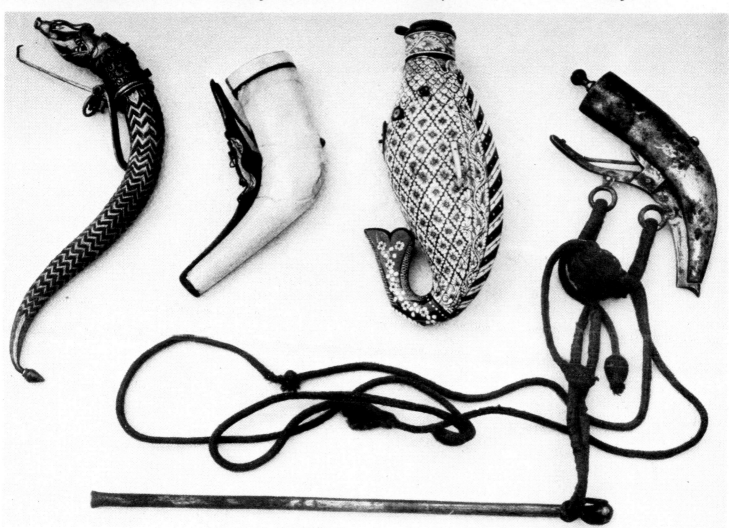

INDIAN AND TURKISH POWDER FLASKS (*C. G. Vokes Collection*) **802** Brass gilt, *Indian*, 18th century. **803** Ivory. *Turkish*, 18th century. **804** Wood inlaid with ivory. *Indian*, 18th century. **805** All-steel, with ramrod. *Turkish*, 18th century.

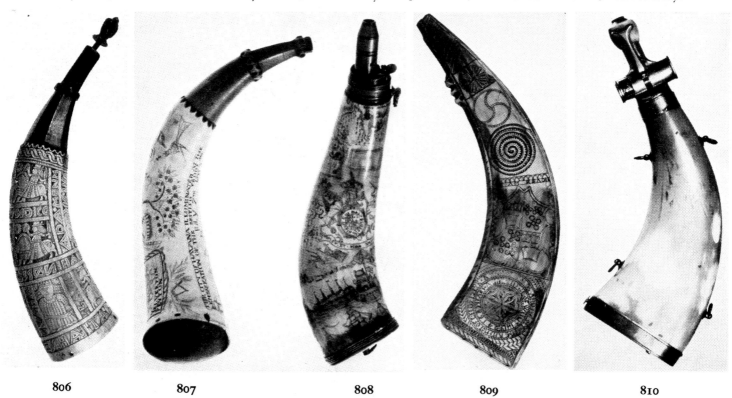

| 806 | 807 | 808 | 809 | 810 |

HORN POWDER FLASKS (*See also pp.* 101–2). **806** Carved with personages from Old Testament. *Norwegian*, 17th century. *Tower of London* (No. XIII–28). **807** Engraved with scenes commemorating withdrawal of British troops from Havana, 7 July 1763. *Tower of London* (No. XIII–161). **808** Engraved with Royal arms and map showing forts on rivers Hudson and Mohawk. *Colonial American*, c. 1750. *Tower of London* (No. XIII–126). **809** Engraved with arms of Fraser family. *Scottish*, dated 24 July 1683. *Glasgow Museum* (No. 94–179e). **810** Push-in automatic filler nozzle marked BOCHE B^te A PARIS. *French*, c. 1850.

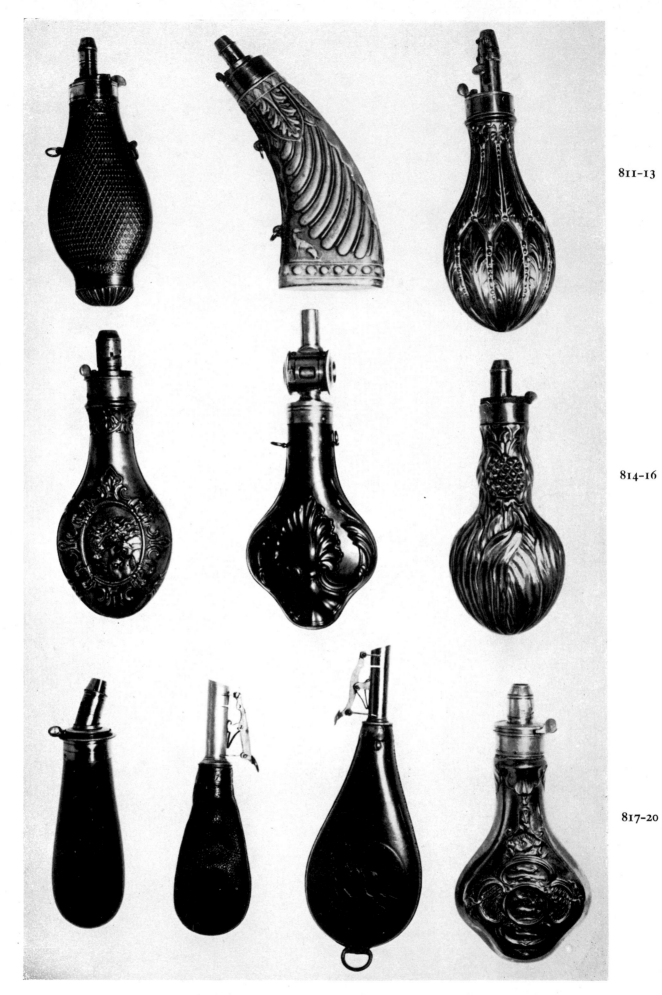

811–13

814–16

817–20

NINETEENTH-CENTURY EUROPEAN POWDER AND SHOT FLASKS
811–20 *Late F. J. Bubear Collection, (See p.* 102)

821   822   823   824

825   826   827   828

GUN TOOLS   **821–8** *Private Collection.* (*See pp.* 102–3.)

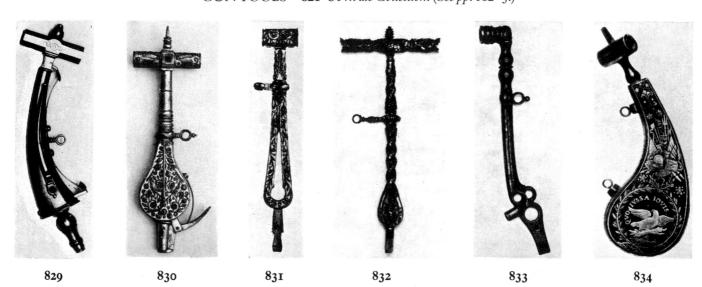

829   830   831   832   833   834

WHEELLOCK KEYS   **829–34** (*See p.* 103.)

835   836

837   838

839   840   841   842   843

GUN TOOLS AND ACCESSORIES **835** Pocket set of tools by Dolep, London. *En suite* with gun **195**. *The Trustees of late R. Holland-Martin (on loan to Tower of London).* **836** Lock spring vices. *English*, 19th century. *Author's Collection.* (*See* p. 103.) **837** Percussion nipple primers. *British*, 19th century. *J. B. Bell, W. S. Curtis and R. Bedford Collections.* (*See* p. 103.) **838** Various types of nipple keys. *English*, 19th century. *Author's Collection.* **839–43** Percussion tube and cap dispensers. *English*, 19th century. *W. Keïth Neal Collection.*

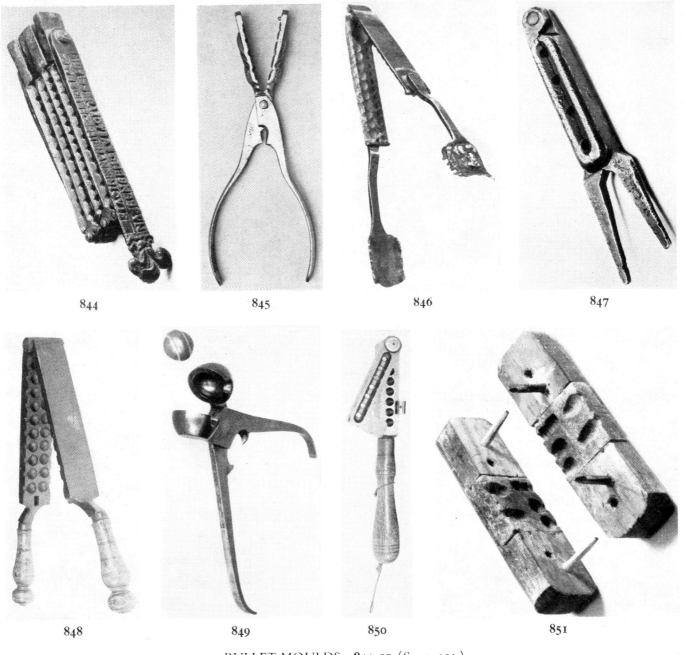

844   845   846   847

848   849   850   851

BULLET MOULDS   **844–51** (*See p.* 103.)

852   853   854   855   856   857   858

GAUGES   **852–8** (*See p.* 103.)

859   860   861   862   863   864

PLUG BAYONETS   **859** Oak handle. *English*, 17th century. *Tower of London* (no number).   **860** Ivory handle with silver piqué. *English, c.* 1680. *Tower of London* (No. X–193).   **861** Horn grip. *Spanish*, 18th century. *Tower of London* (No. X–73). **862** Reversible ebony handle. *French, c.* 1760. *J. R. Winsbury Collection.*   **863** *Spanish*, 19th century. *J. R. Winsbury Collection.*   **864** Chiselled gilt steel signed IACOBUS LAVAU INVENIT ET SCULPTIT MADRID. *c.* 1770. *Victoria and Albert Museum* (No. 2238–1855).

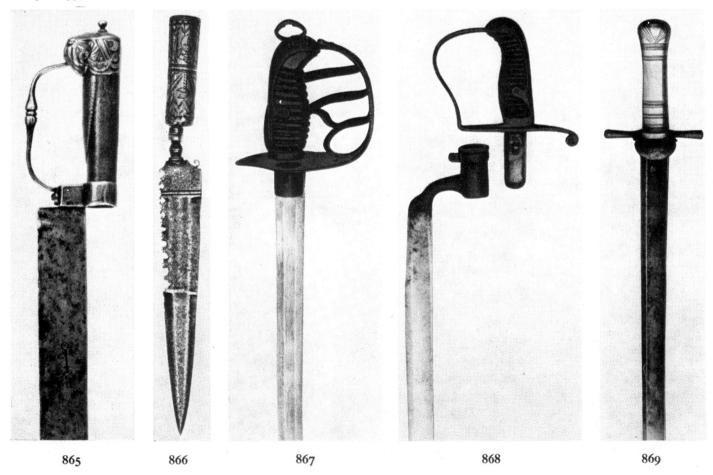

865   866   867   868   869

SOCKET BAYONETS   **865** Chiselled steel hilt. *English, c.* 1680. *Tower of London* (No. X–248).   **866** Brass hilt. *Spanish*, 18th century. *Tower of London* (No. X–209).   **867** Sword with bayonet socket. *English, c.* 1795.   **868** Sword with detachable blade bayonet. *English, c.* 1795.   **869** Brass hilt. Rifle sword bayonet. *German, c.* 1800. *J. R. Winsbury Collection.*

NOTES ON THE PLATES

67 The inscription on the lock reads POR BENITO FRESNEDO SOI DEL AÑO DE 1844. NI ME PRESTO NI ME BENNDO SOLO DE MI DUEÑO SOI. [By Benito Fresnedo I am from the year 1844. I neither lend myself nor sell myself. I belong only to my master].

69 The inscription on the top of the barrel reads TENWA GO-NEN ECHIZEN NO KAMI KORE WO KAZARU [The Lord of Echizen caused this to be decorated in the year Tenwa 5 (A.D. 1685)]. The barrel has been remounted in a nineteenth-century stock and another inscription underneath describes this work. It reads in part 'Enami Kanzaemon living on the border between Settsu and Izumi Provinces made the back [i.e. the stock].' Twelve other assistant workmen from the Isshi District, Ise Province are also listed. The date is given as Spring of Kaei 5 (A.D. 1852), and there is also a description of the type of metal used CHI TETSU TAN SA-U SANJŪ MAKIBARI [crude iron tempered each side in threefold layers]. See D. B. Waterhouse, 'Fire-arms in Japanese History; With notes on a Japanese Wall Gun', *The British Museum Quarterly*, Vol. XXVII, No. 3/4, Winter 1963/4, pp. 94–7.

154 From the initials IS on the barrel it is probable that this gun belonged to the Scottish nobleman Jakob Spens, who raised soldiers for Sweden in Scotland and was made a Swedish colonel in 1608. He died in 1632 and is buried in the Riddarholms Kyrkan in Stockholm.

164 A narrow silver strip along the barrel is inscribed with the spurious legend DOMINUS JOHANNES GRANT MILES WICECOMES DE INNERNES ME FECIT IN GERMANIA ANNO 1434. The red Brazil wood stock is inlaid on the reverse side with a design representing the arms of Dundee. The gunsmith Andrew Philp was admitted to the Hammermen of Dundee in 1596. The round pan of the lock is a replacement dated 1635.

174 Piétro Ancino (1616–1702) of Reggio Emilia (an ancient province in North Italy) was a pupil of the medallist Ruspagiari, and became a painter and sculptor of some renown. The trigger guard which was made for the same gun is in the Metropolitan Museum, New York (No. 56.23) and bears a similar inscription.

185–7 The proof marks of the Armourers' Company—A and P crowned—are rarely found on firearms. George Fisher was made a freeman of the Company in 1631. These guns are believed to have been made for the Englishman George Fleetwood (1605–67) who, in 1629, raised a squadron of cavalry for the Swedish Army in Germany. He became a colonel in 1630 and remained in Sweden until his death.

195 This fowling-piece is part of a suite of arms probably made for Francesco Maria de' Medici (1660–1710), a younger brother of the Grand Duke of Tuscany. His initials FM in the form of a mirror cypher are inlaid in silver on the butt. A pair of pistols from the suite is in the Museo di Capodimonte, Naples, and the set of tools is in the Tower of London (**835**).

197 The only other known example of this gunmaker's work is a pistol in the W. Keith Neal Collection. In a list of gunsmith's estimates for new military arms for the Duke of Ormond in 1705 (*Trinity College Library*, *Dublin, MS. 1180, No. 46*) is a note that he was 'one of her majesty's armourers in pay'.

206 This double-barrelled gun was originally made by Nicolas Boutet for Napoleon I, who presented it to André Garnerin, the balloonist. It was acquired by Durs Egg who sold it to the Prince Regent in 1824 for £100. The barrels were then damaged during a proof by Ezekiel Baker who supplied a new pair of barrels for £65. See H. L. Blackmore, 'The Prince Regent as a Gun Collector', *The Connoisseur*, December, 1960, pp. 230–6.

210 Carbine designed by Lord Ancram for the Midlothian Fencible Cavalry in 1797. It is illustrated and described in the *Transactions of the Royal Society of Edinburgh*, Vol. IV (1798).

226–8 The maker of the gun, Archip Leontiev, is recorded working at the Tula factory from 1762 to 1778, mainly as a steel-chiseller and decorator. The gun probably belonged to Lord George Augustus Herbert (1759–1827) who was travelling in Russia in 1778–9. See C. Blair, 'Archip Leontiev's Gun', *The Connoisseur*, February, 1962, pp. 116–17.

235 This rifle came from a small collection of arms reputed to have formed part of the loot acquired by Napoleon Bonaparte during the invasion of Russia. They were brought to England by the Chevalier Bruslart who was employed by the Bourbons to follow the French Army. A suite of arms made at Tula from the same collection is in the Tower of London (**225**). No signatures or marks are on this rifle, but another example of the same stock-maker's work is found on the rifle in the Royal Scottish Museum, Edinburgh (No. 1872.25.20) which is signed, on the lock, SCHLEGELMILCH A SUHL.

246–7 This rifle belonged to Colonel Thomas of the American Riflemen, who was killed in action in South Carolina by the British Legion. It was presented to the Royal Collection by Colonel George Hanger. It was repaired by Durs Egg whose bill dated 26 Jan. 1803 reads—

> To Cleaning a longe American Rifle Gun, the Barrel Straightened repaired and leaded a Strong Ramrod with cleaning implements a new Bullet Mould, and barrel Brown'd a new cock nail altering lock & case hardening..£2.5.6

> *(Royal Archives, Windsor Castle*
> *Accounts of George IV 29107)*

276 The steel of the lock has side shields. A similar device formed part of Henry Shrapnel's English patent of 1834 'to guide sparks downwards to the pan'.

298 This military musket formerly bore a label inscribed 'Projet du Gen Delcassin de Charleville en l'an 2 pour que tous serrurier puit faire alors une Platine'.

304 This lock was an improved version of Westley Richards's patent of 1821. When the hammer fell the magazine was knocked out of the way, the hole at the base of the magazine being opened and shut by a spring shutter.

319 The lock is apparently a conversion of a flintlock sporting gun, *c.* 1780. When the hammer is cocked a new primer is brought into position, an indicator on the side showing the number remaining. Before firing a lever cover over the nipple is withdrawn by pulling back the knob behind the trigger guard.

343 This gun belonged to the author's great-grandfather. Inscription on silver butt plate reads 'This was the gun of Richard Blackmore of Dean Rew Farm, Barnstaple. It was last used by his son Richard who with a heavy charge killed fourteen birds and broke the stock in two.'

359 The barrel is inscribed UN DES PROJETS DE FUSIL COMPOSÉ ET PROPOSÉ PAR LE Sr BERTHIER INGre DES CAMPS AT ARMÉES DU ROY ATACHÉ A LA SUITE DU MINISTRE DE LA GUERRE. EXECUTÉ PAR DESAINTE. Butt tang engraved with Royal arms of France.

408 Rotation of the trigger guard moves the horizontal breech block to one side, leaving the breech end of the barrel open. Part of the stock by the breech is then removed for insertion of the charge.

410 Erik Larsen Svorsdøl (1762–1825) was a Norwegian gunmaker. In 1810, as master gunmaker of the Bergen-hus infantry regiment, he presented this gun as his invention to the Danish-Norwegian King Frederick VI.

442 This action was patented in 1859. A vertically-sliding breech block was pulled down in cocking the under-hammer, and a self-consuming cartridge was pushed into the breech. When the hammer was released a percussion cap was fed on to the nipple in the manner of Heurteloup's *koptipteur*. Two claws on the side of the hammer head withdrew the spent cap.

443 The action is based on British patent No. 2998 of 1863 taken out by the American, Regulus Pilon. Recoil of barrel and sliding breech block is used to re-cock the gun. Single shot only. The trigger is hidden under the cover on top of the butt at rear of the action.

450 This breechloading rifle has two interchangeable barrels. Each barrel rotates inside a breech sleeve withdrawing it sufficiently from the coned end of the hinged breech block which springs up for loading (as in the detached barrel).

490 The silver escutcheon plate bears the crest of the Ashburnham family, probably of George, 3rd Earl of Ashburnham (1760–1830).

499 Locks signed DUPE & CO. The two sets of seven barrels could be removed from the stock and one set used in a separate single stock. Inscription on one set of barrels is PERDITION TO CONSPIRATORS and on the other GLENMORE FOREST 1793. The latter was Thornton's favourite hunting ground in Scotland. On the intersecting strip between the barrels is inscribed WITH THIS ALONE I'LL DEFEND ROBRO CAMP 1795. Roborough Camp, near Plymouth, was commanded by Thornton and was the scene of a mutiny in that year.

503 This gun is illustrated and described in the *Illustrated London News* of 11 January 1845. It was presented to Prince Albert by Louis Philippe of France. A smaller gun not so well decorated was presented at the same time to the Prince of Wales.

504 This shotgun, which has a deeply carved ebony stock and elaborately chiselled steel mounts, was presented in 1879 by M. Paul Jules Grevy, President of France, to Don Manuel Gonzales, President of Mexico.

530 The rear lock is connected by a tube to the front charge of a series of seven perforated bullets. In front of these are nine more bullets which are ignited by the second lock. Both locks are set off by an ingenious single trigger, a safety-catch preventing the rear wheel from moving when the first lock is fired. The gun could also be used as a single-shot.

552 Barrels bear the crest of the Tokugawa family. The inscription indicates that the gun was owned by an officer named Slichezalman and was made by Umetada Muneshige of Machi.

586 The police registration number W-X 5592 has been stamped on the barrel. Under an Act of 1843 (6 & 7 Victoria c.74) all owners of firearms in Ireland were compelled to take out licences and deliver the arms to the police for marking. The prefixing letters indicate the place of registration, which in this case was Wexford.

612 Under the terms of an American patent taken out by Rollin White in 1855, no gunmaker could use a bored-through cylinder except under licence. This in effect prevented the use of metallic cartridges in revolvers which were normally inserted in the rear of the cylinder. To get round this F. Alexander Thuer, a Colt employee, developed a system, patented in America and England in 1868, by which a rimless centre-fire cartridge could be loaded through the front of the Colt cylinder. The percussion nipples were removed, and an ingenious ring or plate at the rear of the cylinder enabled the spent cartridge to be ejected by the blow of the hammer.

748 The magazine could hold 20 bullets. The silver plate attached to the lock bears the inscription—MILITARY AIR-GUN, INVENTED BY BARON LUTGENDORF, AULIC COUNCILLOR OF HIS HIGHNESS THE REIGNING PRINCE OF THURN AND TAXIS AT RATISBON IN GERMANY, 1804. Bought from the Baron by George IV in 1806.

785 The gun could be set to fire at a certain time, could be used as a trap gun by means of a pull-out peg, or could be fired like a normal gun.

806 The Society of Antiquaries of Scotland has a number of these Scandinavian horns in its collection at Edinburgh. The figures and inscriptions carved on them all relate to Biblical subjects or to heroes of the Charlemagne cycle of romances. See *Proceedings of the Society of Antiquaries of Scotland*, Vol. XXII (1888), pp. 157–63, 320–31.

807 Inscriptions read YELVERTON PEYTON CAPT. 9th REGT FOOT ST. AUGUSTINE EAST FLORIDA JENY 30th 1767 and THE CITY OF HAVANA ILLUMINATED AT THE EMBARKATION OF THE BRITISH TROOPS JULY 7th 1763. By the Peace of Paris in 1763 Spain ceded Florida to the British in exchange for Cuba.

808 Most of the American map horns date to the period of the French and Indian Wars (1757–63) when few printed maps of the regions concerned were available. On the majority, the map starts at the base of the horn with a view of New York and the compass pointing to the north. From here to the tip of the horn the map shows the main villages, forts, supply stations, rivers and lakes along the routes connecting New York and Canada. The Hudson-Champlain route to Eastern Canada and the Hudson-Mohawk route to Lake Ontario and the West were both paths of trade and warfare. The engraving, particularly on presentation pieces to officers, is often the work of the professional horn-maker and is of fine quality. Some of the horns, however, are of cruder design, being engraved by the soldiers and settlers. These usually bear the owner's name with some doggerel verse: 'Steal not this horn for fear of shame', etc., 'The rose is red, the grass is green', etc., 'Powder and Ball conquers all', etc. Two horns are recorded dated 1756 which bear the verse adopted by James Puckle for his revolving gun (**548**) of 1718—

> 'Defending King George
> Your country and laws
> Is defending yourselves
> and ye Protestant cause.'

The verse on the Scottish powder horn of 1683 (**809**) is also found on an American horn dated 1748. See Stephen V. Grancsay, *American Engraved Powder Horns*, New York, 1945.

809 The horn is also engraved with the motto I AM READIE and the inscription A MAN OF WORDS AND NOT OF DEEDS AND NOT OF DEEDS [sic] IS LYK A GARDENFUL OF WEEDS.

810 This type of charger was patented in the United States in 1875 by T. Hick and G. W. Weatherwax, but this patent is an obvious copy of Boche's earlier French design.

811 Copper, with brass charger. Diaper pattern, marked B. A PARIS.

812 Pewter, with brass charger, marked 50 55 60 65. Leaf pattern with greyhound.

813 Copper, with brass charger, marked GRAINS 70 75 80 85 90.

814 Copper, with panel embossed with three horses' heads. Brass charger marked DRAMS $2\frac{1}{4}$ $2\frac{1}{2}$ $2\frac{3}{4}$ 3 and G. & J. W. HAWKESLEY SHEFFIELD.

815 Copper, shell pattern. Brass charger with transparent window, as patented by Michel Boche of Paris in England in 1845 (No. 10,683).

816 Copper. Foliage design with pineapple. Brass charger.

817 Copper, lacquered grey. Brass charger marked SYKES PATENT.

818 Soft black leather shot flask. German silver charger marked DIXON & SONS. OZ I $1\frac{1}{4}$.

819 Stiff brown leather shot flask embossed with medallion of huntsman and animals. Brass charger marked OZ I $1\frac{1}{4}$.

820 Copper embossed with game motif. Brass charger marked DRAMS 2 $2\frac{1}{4}$ $2\frac{1}{2}$ $2\frac{3}{4}$ 3 and HEATH PATENT.

821 Set of tools (screwdriver, drifts, hammer, pincer, jags, etc.) screwing into central vice. Inscribed J. DELPIRE ARMURIER DU 7em REGT SUISSE DE LA GARDE ROYALE PARIS. *French, c.* 1820.

822–3 Similar set of tools and a bullet mould *cum* breech wrench from a cased gun. *French, c.* 1820.

824 Patch or wad cutter. *English,* 19th century.

825 Hammer and pricker screwing into triple screwdriver. *German*, 17th century.

826 Huntsman's set of tools (pliers, hammer, flint-knapper, bullet-drawer and whistle). *German*, early 18th century.

827 Similar set. The hammer portion unscrews to release pliers. *French*, late 17th century.

828 Wheellock key. *German*, early 17th century.

829 Combined all-steel priming flask and wheellock key. *German*, early 17th century. *Wallace Collection* (No. A.1308).

830 Combined primer, screwdriver and spanner by Daniel Sadeler, Munich. *c.* 1610. *Metropolitan Museum, New York* (No. 14.25.1528).

831 Chiselled steel spanner and screwdriver. *German, c.* 1640. *Odescalchi Collection, Rome.*

832 Chiselled steel spanner and screwdriver. *Italian, c.* 1630. *Wallace Collection* (No. A.1325).

833 Wheellock key and screwdriver. *German, c.* 1620. *Wallace Collection* (No. A.1320).

834 Combined priming flask, spanner and screwdriver. Iron inlaid with silver. Belonged to the Duc de Sully (1560–1641). *French, c.* 1600. *State Hermitage, Leningrad* (No. 3.0.6306).

836 The lock was cocked and the vice fitted over the compressed spring. When the cock was released the spring could be unclipped from the lock-plate. Top right-hand vice is marked T. BRAZIER REGISTERED MARCH 11th 1859 [a Registered Design].

837 These primers were designed to clear a clogged nipple. The two right-hand specimens, patented by Paton and Walsh of Perth, Scotland, in 1856, consist of a pricker, a powder primer and a cap magazine. See R. Bedford 'Percussion Nipple Primers', *Journal of Arms and Armour Society*, London, Vol. IV, No. 3 (September, 1962), pp. 51–67.

844 Bronze. Multi-chamber for spherical, tear-drop and barrel-shaped shot. *French*, late 16th century. *H. L. Peterson Collection.*

845 Steel. Four chambers. *French*, 17th century. *Metropolitan Museum, New York* (No. 14.25.1439).

846 Bronze. Multi-shot. *French*, 17th century. *H. L. Peterson Collection.*

847 Bronze. Engraved SETH POMEROY'S MOLD 1760. *American. H. L. Peterson Collection.*

848 Iron, turned wood handles. *English, c.* 1800. *Winchester Gun Museum.*

849 Iron, for Brunswick belted ball. *English, c.* 1845. *Jac Weller Collection.*

850 Iron, for conical bullets. *American, c.* 1860. *Winchester Gun Museum.*

851 Soapstone with wood frame. 19th century. *H. L. Peterson Collection.*

852 W. W. Greener's shot counter. *English*, 19th century. *F. J. Bubear Collection.*

853 W. & C. Eley percussion-cap gauge. *English*, 19th century. *R. Bedford Collection.*

854 Brass powder measure. *English*, 18th century. *Author's Collection.*

855 Iron powder measure. *German*, 17th century. *Author's Collection.*

856 Barrel gauge. *English*, 19th century. *Author's Collection.*

857–8 Powder measures (*Wazna-I-Barut*). Iron inlaid with silver and engraved brass. *Persian*, 18th century. *J. R. Winsbury Collection.*

BAYONETS

The bayonet is first mentioned in Cotgrave's *Dictionary* of 1611 as 'a kind of small flat pocket-dagger, furnished with knives; or a great knife to hang at the girdle, like a dagger'. De Puysegur in his *Mémoires* for 1647 describes soldiers carrying bayonets with blades a foot long, whose handles could be jammed in the muzzle of their muskets. The word itself is apparently derived from Bayonne, a French town noted for its cutlery (*see* Ménage's *Dictionnaire*, 1694). Although the first type of bayonet, now known as a plug bayonet, was superseded towards the end of the seventeenth century by ring and socket bayonets for military purposes, it continued in use as a sporting accessory, particularly in Spain, until the nineteenth century. The portrait of Charles IV of Spain by Francisco Goya in the Capodimonte Museum, Naples, shows him holding a sporting gun and wearing a plug bayonet on his waist belt.

The following are representative of the various types of blades and fastenings found on bayonets.

870 English plug bayonet of the type brought back by the British Army from Dunkirk in 1663 and first made by London cutlers in 1672.

871 Swedish plug bayonet, *c.* 1685. Handle fits into rings on side of muzzle. *Haermuseet, Akershus, Oslo* (No. 822).

872 English sword bayonet with plug handle, *c.* 1690. Formerly *Royal United Service Institution, London*.

873 Folding bayonet on Swedish flintlock musket, *c.* 1685. *Haermuseet, Akershus, Oslo* (No. 818). The breechloading gun **368** has a similar bayonet.

874 English plug bayonet, *c.* 1680, with brass socket on side of blade. *J. F. R. Winsbury Collection.*

875 German plug bayonet, *c.* 1690, with iron split socket attached to cross-piece. From Thierbach, *Handfeurwaffen*, fig. 187.

876 Early-type socket bayonet with flat blade, *c.* 1700.

877 Standard type of socket bayonet with reinforced rim and triangular section blade, 18th century.

878 Socket bayonet with locking ring on base with straight slot. Adopted by French Army in 1763. Used on Nock's musket *c.* 1790 and Baker rifle 1815.

879 Locking ring on reinforced middle section with zigzag slot. Used on most European and American rifles of 1855–70 period.

880 Folding knife with rings to act as bayonet. Designed by Isaac de la Chaumette, 1706; (see *Machines Approuvées par l'Académie Royale des Sciences*, Paris, Vol. II).

881 Sword bayonet with socketed handle. De la Chaumette, 1707 (*loc. cit.*). Actual example formerly in Royal Arms Museum, Dresden, is illustrated in *Zeitschrift für Historische Waffenkunde*, Dresden, Vol. III (1902–5), p. 46.

882 Socketed bayonet with detachable knife handle. Designed by M. Deschamps, 1718 (*Machines Approuvées*, etc., Vol. III, No. 205).

883 Folding bayonet attached to barrel. M. Deschamps, 1718 (*loc. cit.*).

884 Socketed spear bayonet made by Durs Egg for his breechloading carbine, 1785 (see **372**). Also used on some British muzzleloading carbines of the same period.

885 Indian socket bayonet with locking ring, late 18th century. Socket carved with tiger's head, blade shaped as tiger's tail.

886 First-model Baker rifle bayonet, *c.* 1800. Copied from type used on German Jaeger rifles of late 18th century.

887 Third-model Baker bayonet, *c.* 1825.

888 Brass-handled bayonet designed by Henry Wilkinson for double-barrelled Irish constabulary carbine, 1836.

889 British Brunswick rifle sword bayonet. Improved pattern, 1847.

890 British Sapper's saw bayonet. 1st model, 1841.

891 Belgian Comblain engineer's saw bayonet.

892 French Chassepot bayonet of 'yataghan' type. Type used on British Enfield Artillery rifle and U.S. rifle model, 1855.

893 Norwegian rifle sabre bayonet, 1851. Similar to Russian model.

894 Clip-on bayonet for double-barrelled rifle by A. Francotte, Liège.

895 Full-sized sword (30 in. blade) with hilt to fit double barrels of Jacob's rifle, *c.* 1860.

896 U.S. model 1873 trowel or spade bayonet (side and top views). Similar to 1868 British patent of E. Rice, which combined a muzzle stopper.

897 French Lebel Model 1886 bayonet with 'poignard' blade of +-shaped section and white metal handle.

898 Two types of U.S. model 1896 'bolo' knife bayonet.

899 Austrian knife bayonet, 1886—a type in almost universal use during World War I.

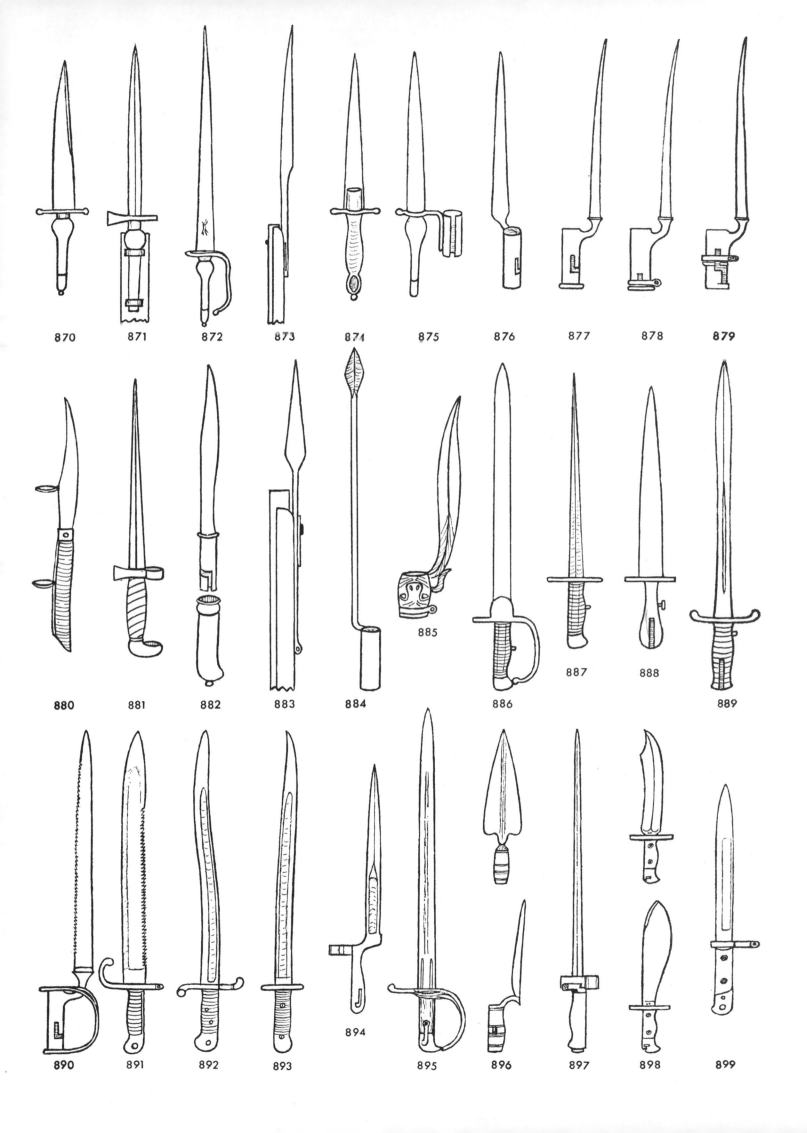

870   871   872   873   874   875   876   877   878   879

880   881   882   883   884   885   886   887   888   889

890   891   892   893   894   895   896   897   898   899

GUN BUTTS

The outline shape of a gun butt is by no means diagnostic. The triangular musket butt of the first half of the seventeenth century, for instance, was in use throughout Europe. Other shapes, e.g. the Cingalese butt, while firmly indicative of the country of origin, cannot be used as an accurate measure of the date of manufacture. Nevertheless the following outlines form a quick guide to identification and also illustrate the amazing way in which soldiers and sportsmen through the years have found it necessary to shape the stocks of their firearms.

Numbers in brackets refer to comparable examples illustrated in the plates.

Cheek Butts
900 Hand-gun, straight pole. *European, 14th century.*
901 Straight butt with shoulder niche. *European, 15th century.*
902 Elementarily-shaped butt. *German, c. 1500* (**43**).
903 The 'German' butt. Found mainly on wheellock rifles from *c. 1530 onwards* (**109, 112**).
904 Late type of German butt with more pronounced drop and deeper check-piece (**128, 130**).
905 Butt of snap-matchlock rifle. *North European, c. 1500.*
906 Later snap-matchlock, *c. 1600* (**59, 60**).
907 Wheellock 'tschinke' rifle. *Silesian, c. 1620–60* (**87–8**).
908 Wheellock rifle. *German, c. 1620* (**92, 100**).

Shoulder and Chest Butts
909 German-type butt lengthened to reach shoulder. *Russian, 17th century* (**160, 223**).
910 Transitional butt. *European, c. 1600* (**52–3**).
911 Triangular musket butt. *European, 17th century* (**54–6, 83**).
912 Petronel. *French, c. 1600* (**95**).
913 Petronel. *Swiss, c. 1590.*
914 Petronel. *English, dated 1584* (**152**).
915 Semi-rounded butt. *German, c. 1540.*
916 Rounded butt. *German, c. 1600* (**93**).
917 Paddle-shaped carbine butt. *North European, c. 1620–60* (**534**).

Development of the Pistol Grip Butt
918 *French, c. 1640* (**177**).
919 *English, c. 1650* (**183, 186**).
920 *Swiss, c. 1650* (**483**).
921 *French, c. 1675* (**217**).
922 *French, c. 1800* (**220**).
923 *German, c. 1850* (**342**)
924 *American, c. 1880* (**709**).
925 *American, c. 1880* (**465**).
926 *French, c. 1850* (**341**).

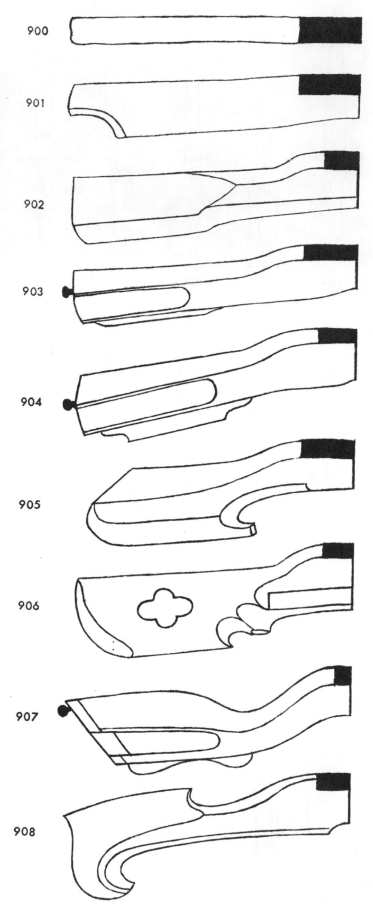

900

901

902

903

904

905

906

907

908

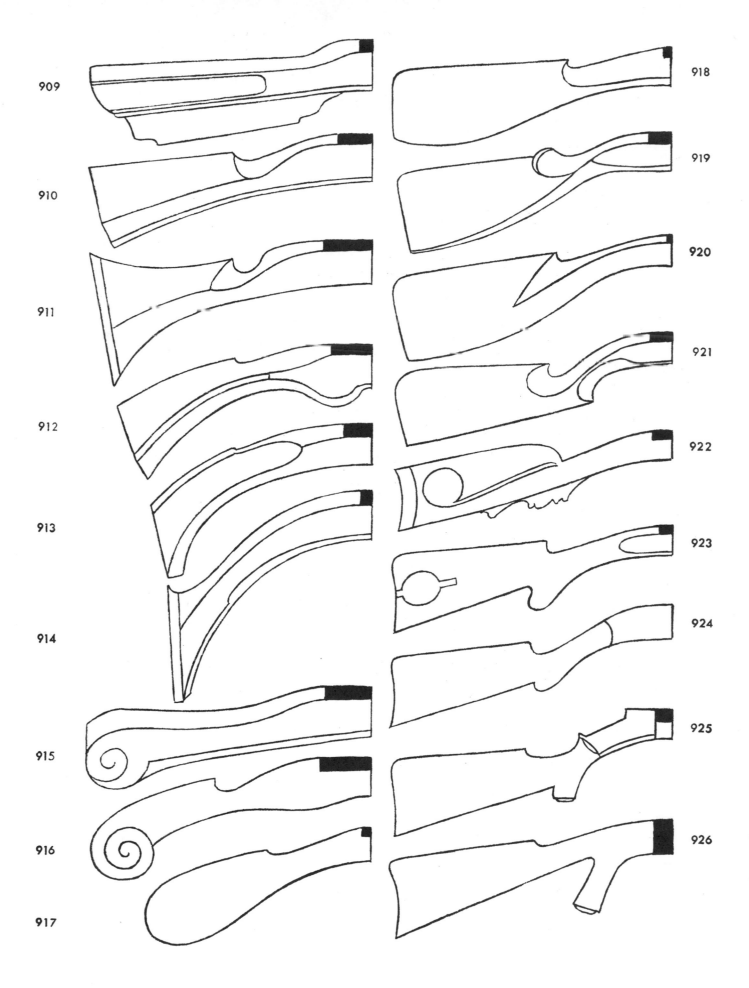

909

910

911

912

913

914

915

916

917

918

919

920

921

922

923

924

925

926

GUN BUTTS

Numbers in brackets refer to comparable examples illustrated in the plates.

Development of Straight European Butt

927 Rounded wrist extending down lower edge of butt. Flat butt-plate. *c.* 1680 (**188**).

928 Pronounced wrist, rounded butt-plate. *c.* 1700 (**197**).

929 Large bulbous 'heel' on butt-plate. *c.* 1690 (**408, 427**).

930 Less pronounced heel, toe of butt is pointed. Still with extended tubular wrist. *c.* 1740–90 (**300, 496–7**).

931 Tubular wrist extending to butt-plate. High comb. Found mainly on French and German muskets, *c.* 1740–80 (**494, 685–6**).

932 Straight line from pointed toe of butt-plate to lock, *c.* 1780 onwards (**498, 500**).

American and Schuetzen Butts

933 Heavy, curved butt-plate. Straight narrow butt, flat sides. *American, c.* 1780 onwards (**243–4**).

934 Schuetzen butt. Semi-circular butt-plate. Increased drop from line of barrel to allow for standing firing position. *American, c.* 1850 onwards (**332–3**).

935 Schuetzen butt of advanced design, with raised cheek rest. *German, c.* 1870 (**331, 466**).

Mediterranean Butts

936 *Spanish (Catalan),* 18–19th century (**258**).

937 *Spanish (Madrid),* 18–19th century (**256–7**).

938 *Sardinian,* 17–18th century (**107, 268**).

939 *Italian,* 17th century (**103, 250**).

940 *Albanian,* 18–19th century (**274**).

941 *Albanian,* 18–19th century.

942 *Turkish,* 18–19th century (**273**).

Oriental Butts

943 *Circassian,* 18–19th century (**275**).

944 *Afghan,* 18–19th century (**346**).

945 *Indian,* 18–19th century (**64**).

946 *Indian (Deccan),* 18–19th century (**65, 555**).

947 *South Indian (Coorg),* 18–19th century.

948 *South Indian (Coorg),* 18–19th century.

949 *Cingalese,* 17–18th century (**276–7**).

950 *Indonesian,* 18th century.

951 *Japanese,* 18–19th century (**68, 552**).

952 *Chinese,* 18–19th century (**348**).

953 *Formosan,* 18–19th century.

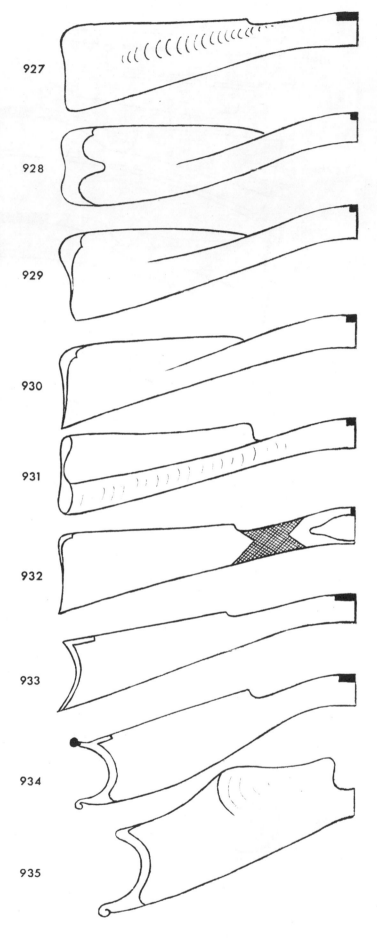

927

928

929

930

931

932

933

934

935

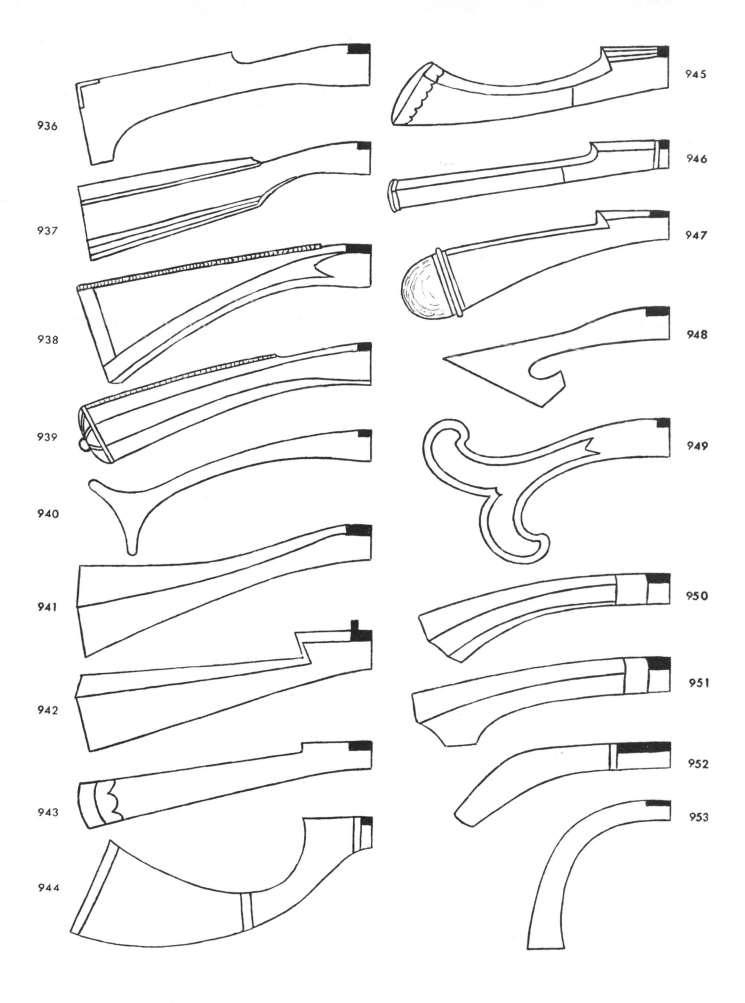

936

937

938

939

940

941

942

943

944

945

946

947

948

949

950

951

952

953

GUN LOCKS

954 *Left*—**European Matchlock**
The match-holder has a slotted tumbler into which is fitted the end of the sear-lever. This is operated either by a long extension or by a separate trigger. The whole mechanism fastened to a lock-plate.
Right—**Indian Matchlock**
The match-holder is connected to the sear-lever by a separate link. Both work in a vertical slot cut in the stock, and are pivoted in transverse pins.

955 European Snap-Matchlock
Interior mainspring *A* works on a tumbler. A spring *B* lying inside the lock has a stud *C* in the middle which protrudes through the lock-plate and acts as a sear by holding down the tail of the match-holder in the cocked position. This is released by pressure on the button trigger *D* which is fastened through the lock-plate to the end of the sear spring. *From an early 16th-century German lock in the Historisches Museum, Bern (No. 2211).*

956 European Snap-Matchlock
The mainspring *A* acts on the tail of the match-holder on the outside of the lock-plate. The sear *C* consists of a horizontally-acting lever pivoted in the middle. On one end is the stud which passes through the lock-plate and acts in the same way as that of the previous lock. The other end is bent at right angles so that the sear can be withdrawn (by a separate trigger) against the pressure of its spring *B*. *From a German wall-gun, dated 1562 on the barrel, in the Tower of London Armouries (No. XII–5).*

957 European Snap-Matchlock
This type of lock which has a set trigger is found only on a special group of European matchlocks (see **59–60**). The cock is controlled by a mainspring *A* which works on the tumbler. These two parts and the trigger *D* are attached to the inside of the lock-plate. Along the bottom of the lock-plate and at right angles to it is a base-plate to which are fitted the remaining parts. These are the sear-lever *C*, an intermediate lever *E*, and a spring *B* which controls both. One end of the sear catches in the tumbler and the other is pressed towards the lock-plate by the intermediate lever. In order to cock the lock, the intermediate lever is pulled away from the sear by a piece of string *F*, which is threaded through the lock-plate, until its pointed end is held by the rotating trigger stem. The match-holder can then be pulled back until the sear catches in the tumbler. When the trigger is pulled the intermediate lever is released. This gives the sear a smart blow causing it to release the tumbler and the match-holder falls into the pan. *From a late 16th-century German rifle in the Tower of London Armouries (No. XII–10).*

958 Japanese Snap-Matchlock
Made entirely of brass and constructed without any screws. Both the cock and the sear are motivated by coiled springs. The mainspring *A* is coiled round the tumbler which has a notch into which the sear *C* is pulled by another coiled spring *B* in the cocked position. To allow for any slackening in this brass spring additional fastening holes are provided on the sear in order to stretch the spring and increase its tension. *From an early 18th-century Japanese carbine in the Tower of London Armouries (No. XII–56).*

959 Javanese Snap-Matchlock
The brass mainspring *A* is fastened to the outside of the lock-plate where it presses upwards on the tail of the cock. The sear *C* is a simple piece of iron, one end bent to protrude through the lock-plate and catch on an indentation in the tail of the cock, and the other bent round so that the separate trigger can act on it. A flat leaf spring *B* bears on the end of the sear with a forked hook.

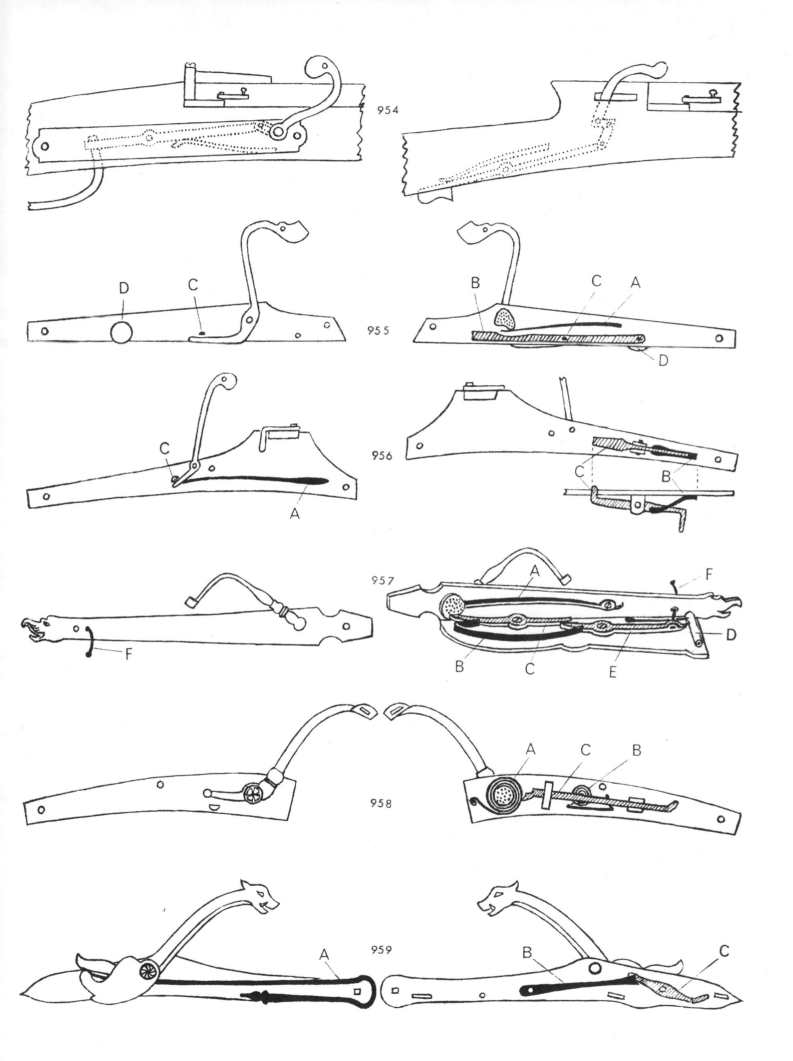

954

955

956

957

958

959

GUN LOCKS

960 Tschinke Wheellock
The wheel and its spring *A* are on the outside of the lock together with the cock and its spring. The sear *C* is pivoted to work horizontally and its stud protrudes through the lock-plate to catch in a hole on the inside of the wheel. To achieve this the button *B* has to be pressed when the wheel is wound up (in the majority of wheellocks a spring does this automatically). The sear is held by the sear catch *D* which juts out at right angles to the lock-plate so that it can be moved by the trigger. The pan-cover is kept shut by a small V-spring *E*, but it can be kept open for priming by a spring catch *F*. *From an early 17th-century Tschinke rifle in the Tower of London Armouries* (No. XII-1213).

961 Norwegian Flintlock
The exterior mainspring *A* controls both the cock (whose tail is pressed upwards by it) and the pan-cover. The latter has a swivelling steel positioned by a side-acting V-spring *D*. The right-angled sear *C* has a stud protruding through the lock-plate to catch the tail of the cock. Drawing shows the pan covered but with the steel swivelled to the front. *From a late 17th-century detached lock (maker's mark WL) in a private collection.*

962 Scottish Snaphance
The interior mainspring *A* acts on the toe of the tumbler, which has a long arm attached to push the sliding pan-cover out of the way when the cock falls. The pan-cover is held in both open and shut positions by a flat spring catch *D*. The cock is held in the cocked position by the stud of the sear *C* protruding through the lock-plate.

963 English Lock
The mainspring *A* bears on the toe of the tumbler. For full cock a stud on the horizontally-acting sear *C* protrudes through the lock-plate to engage the tail of the cock. There is also a half-cock position in which the hook nose of the sear catches a projection on the tumbler. *From an English musket, c. 1640, in the Tower of London Armouries.*

964 Dog Lock
The mainspring *A* acts as in the preceding lock, but the horizontally-acting sear *C* has a nose with two projections which catch on two lugs on the tumbler to hold the cock in the full- and half-cock positions. *From an English musket, c. 1650, in the Tower of London Armouries.*

965 French-type Flintlock
In this lock the sear *C* for the first time works in a vertical plane and engaged in two notches cut in the tumbler for half- and full-cock positions. This is an early form of the lock without a bridle, or supporting bridge, to the tumbler. *From a detached English military lock, c. 1690, in a private collection.*

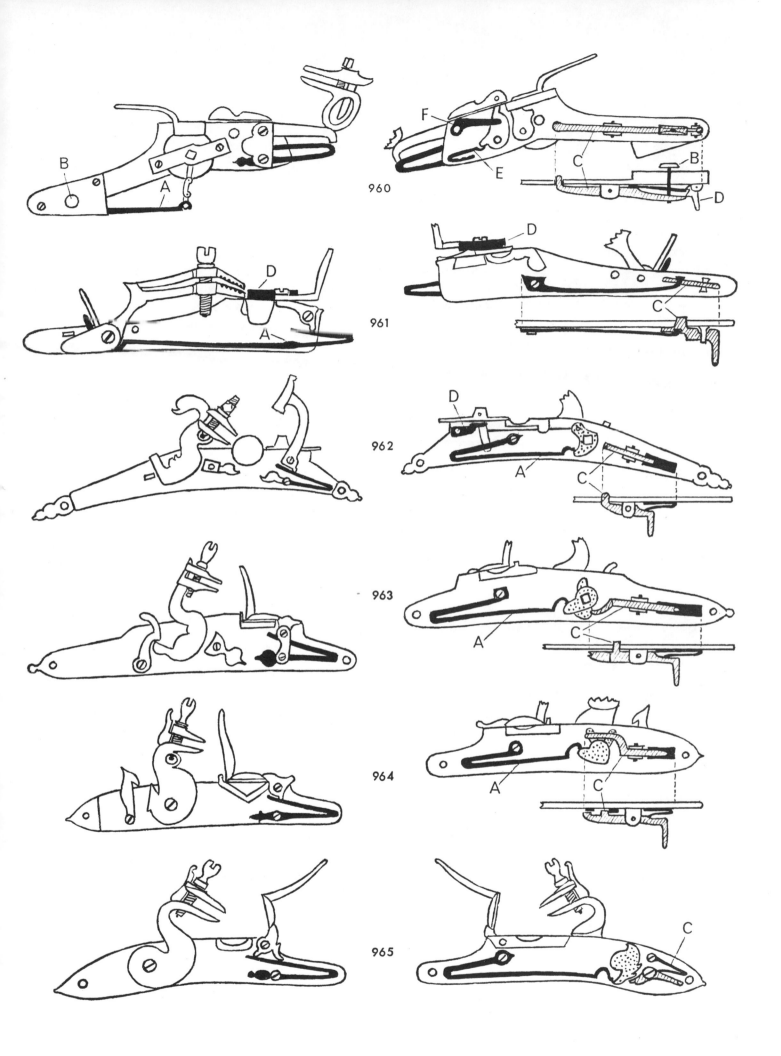

960

961

962

963

964

965

GUN LOCKS

966 Italian Lock

The exterior mainspring *A* bears down on the toe of the cock. Inside, the sear *C* engages through the lock-plate on top of the heel of the cock for the full-cock position. The sear catch *D* has an extension arm with a stud on its end which protrudes through the lock-plate to hold the toe of the cock in the half-cock position. A strong V-spring *B* acts on both levers. *From a South Italian sporting gun by P. Rossi, c. 1750, in the Tower of London Armouries* (No. XII–1096).

967 North African Lock

Large exterior mainspring *A* bears downwards on the toe of the cock as in the Italian lock. The full-cock position, however, is obtained by the stud of the sear *C* thrusting through the lock-plate to engage in an indentation in the rear or heel of the cock's base. The V-spring *B* also moves the sear-catch forward to hold the sear in position. A hook which catches behind the cock provides a safety or half-cock position. This hook has a small spring *E* which normally keeps it clear of the cock. *From a detached lock in a private collection.*

968 Spanish Miquelet Lock

The exterior mainspring *A* bears upwards on the heel of the cock. The horizontally-acting sear *C* has a large round stud with a slot in it which catches under the toe of the cock for the half-cock position only. Full cock is obtained by the toe of the cock being held by a smaller stud on the sear spring *B*. The spring of the combined pan-cover and steel is protected by an ornamental shield. *From a detached lock by Domingo Gabiola of Eibar, c. 1790, in a private collection.*

969 Madrid Lock

Although the mainspring *A* is placed inside the lock and bears on the toe of the tumbler, a similar sear to the miquelet lock is provided. In this case, however, the sear stud *C*, making the half-cock position, acts on a hook at the rear of the cock, while the sear-spring stud *B* engages a projection or toe on the front of the cock for full-cock. *From a detached lock (marked with a Y crowned) in a private collection.*

970 Side-action Percussion Lock

Perfection in lock work by Joseph Manton. The tumbler *B* is supported by a strong bridle and is worked by the mainspring *A* through a link to give a smoother action. The vertically-acting sear *C* is strengthened where it meets the notches of the tumbler. A sliding safety-catch *D* engages in both the hammer and the tumbler. *From a double-barrelled sporting gun, c. 1830, in the Tower of London Armouries (Study Collection).*

971 Back-action Percussion Lock

A clumsy-looking but simple and effective lock. The mainspring *A* acts on both the tumbler *B* (via a link) and the sear *C*. *From a French military musket marked M^re IMP^ale de MUTZIG and dated 1854 in the Tower of London Armouries (Study Collection).*

966

967

968

969

970

971

972 Colt Lightning Rifle, 1896

Cal. 0·22 rim-fire. Long and short cartridges can be used promiscuously in the magazine. The original Colt Lightning rifles were based on Dr. William H. Elliott's patents of 1883, which covered the 'trombone' pump or slide action mechanism. Other Colt associates patented improvements which led to the introduction of the 0·22 cal. model in 1888. The act of moving the handle A to the rear lifts the brace B, unlocks and moves to the rear the breech block G, cocks the hammer H, ejects the empty shell, raises the carrier lever L and the carrier I, presenting a loaded cartridge in the rear of and in line with the chamber. At the same time the magazine block e is pushed slightly to one side, closing the magazine. The forward motion of the handle A pushes the bolt G forward, moves the cartridge into the chamber, locks the breech-bolt by the brace B and opens the magazine for the passage of another cartridge into the chamber. The rifle is then ready for firing.

973 Evans Rifle, 1877

Cal. 0·44 rim-fire. The mechanism was invented by Warren R. Evans of Thomaston, Maine, and patented in 1868 and 1871. Outstanding feature is tubular magazine about 1½ inches in diameter extending from the butt-plate to the receiver and forming the butt framework and the small of the stock. In the magazine tube is a revolving four-fluted shaft, around which is coiled a spiral wire which keeps the cartridges apart. The feed system resembles the principle of the Archimedean screw. When the trigger guard is pressed downward and forward, the magazine revolves a quarter-turn and delivers a cartridge into position in front of the breech block. The action of returning the trigger guard to its normal position thrusts the cartridge into the breech. The lever's motion also cocks a hammer under the breech and operates the extractor and ejector. The original magazine held 34 cartridges but the later model of 1877 using longer cartridges only has a capacity of 26. The rifle can also be used as a single-shot by limiting the lever movement and feeding rounds individually through a side opening by hand.

974 Spencer Rifle

Cal. 0·52 and 0·50 rim-fire. Patented by Christopher M. Spencer of South Manchester, Conn., U.S.A., in 1860 and 1862. Tubular magazine with compressed spring passing through the butt holds seven copper cartridges.

Downward pressure on the trigger guard rolls down the breech block, extracts the fired cartridge and moves a fresh one from the magazine into the breech. On closing the trigger guard the cartridge is pushed into the chamber and both the barrel and magazine are closed by the breech assembly which holds the firing-pin. The rifle is fired by a separate side-hammer and back-action lock. In 1865 the Quaker inventor Edward M. Stabler designed a magazine cut-off which enabled the Spencer to be used as a single-shot.

975 Winchester Rifle Model 1873

Made in several calibres and barrel lengths, this was the most famous of the rugged Winchester repeaters which used the toggle-link breech-action derived from the Volcanic and Henry rifles. The tubular magazine under the barrel is loaded by pushing the bullet point first into the loading gate on the side of the receiver. A coiled spring then forces them back towards the breech and into the carrier. When the trigger-guard lever is depressed the breech-bolt slides back in line with the barrel, its rear end cocking the hammer while an extractor in the front withdraws the spent cartridge case. At the same time the carrier with a new cartridge is raised to the level of the chamber. On raising the trigger guard the breech block pushes the cartridge into the chamber and is locked into position, while the carrier descends to pick up another round. The makers claimed that the rifle could be fired at the rate of two shots per second.

976 Spencer Repeating Shotgun, 1882

Patented by C. M. Spencer and S. H. Roper in 1882. Cocking and re-charging is effected by a handle which slides along the magazine under the barrel and is connected to the breech mechanism by a forked lever and roller. This causes the breech block to swivel downwards while the fired case is extracted. During the last part of the backward motion of the roller the breech block is thrown upwards ejecting the empty case and bringing the carrier with an unused cartridge into line with the barrel. When the handle is moved forward this cartridge is pushed into the chamber and the breech block is lowered to the firing position. The carrier is then ready to receive another cartridge from the magazine. The gun can be cocked independently by a small lever in front of the trigger. As this is connected to the hammer it also indicates when the gun is cocked.

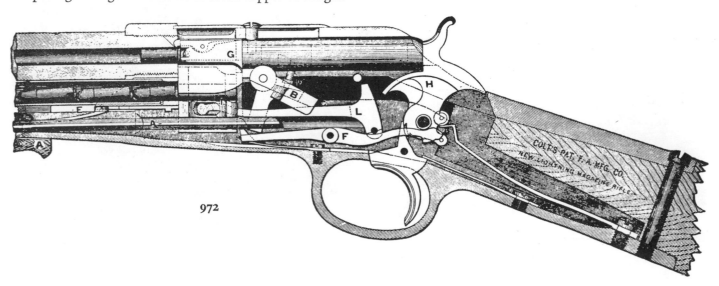

972

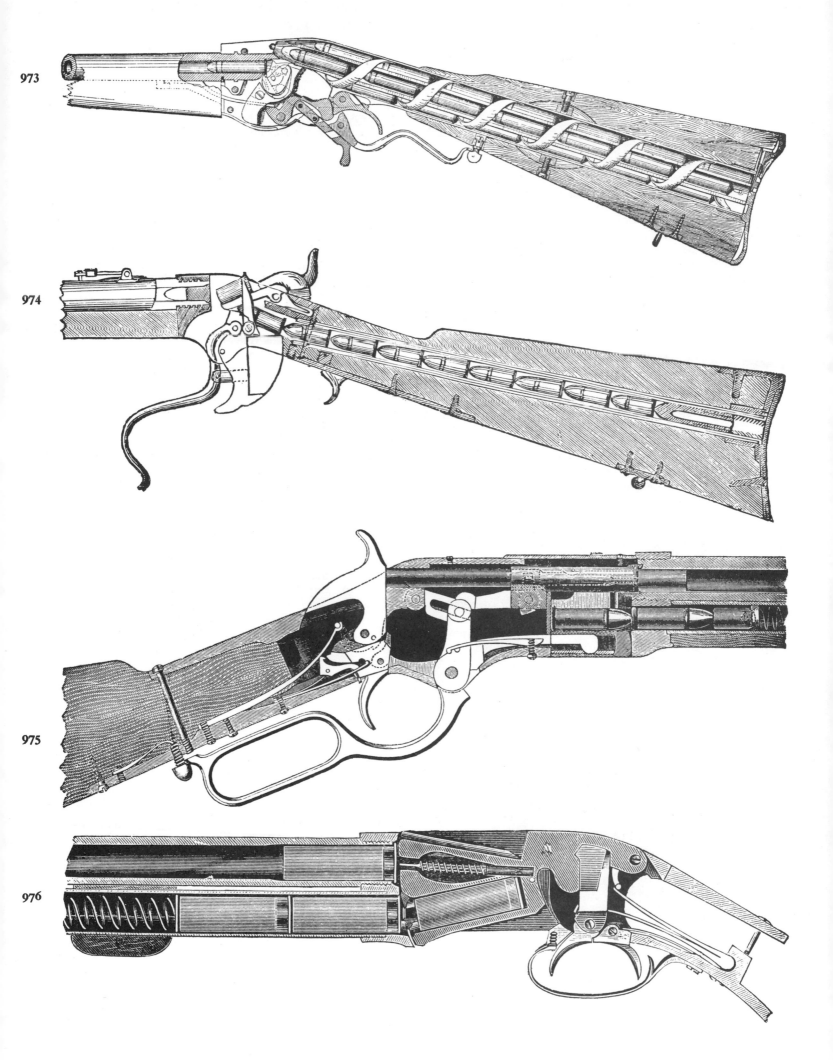

973

974

975

976

BOLT-ACTION MAGAZINE RIFLES

977 Krag-Jorgensen Rifle, 1889
Invented by Ole Herman Krag and Erik Jorgensen of Norway in 1888. Later adopted by Denmark, Norway and the United States. The horizontal box-type magazine passes underneath the bolt from right to left and turns up on the left side opposite the opening in the body. It accommodates five cartridges which are loaded separately through a gate on the right-hand side of the receiver. A strong following spring then moves them across to the other side and up in front of the bolt. A magazine cut-off enables single shots to be fired with the full magazine left in reserve.

978 Mannlicher Rifle Model 1880
This action is copied from that patented by J. Werndl in England in 1879. First produced by Ferdinand Ritter von Mannlicher in 1880 (patented in England in 1881) it uses the standard Austrian Army Werndl cartridge. These cartridges are housed in a group of three tubes located in the butt, which are fastened together in the form of a sheaf with a conical drum at its head. The outer surface of the drum is cut with zigzag grooves and by means of a studded repeating slide the magazine tube is revolved when the bolt is withdrawn. Each backward and forward movement of the bolt revolves the magazine assembly 60 degrees, so that whenever the breech is open one magazine tube is on top and a new cartridge is forced into the loading position by a strong coiled spring.

979 Mannlicher Rifle Model 1882
Set on top of the action in the manner of the magazine patented in England by J. Werndl in 1878 and 1882, the magazine developed by Mannlicher consists of a vertical box-type clip built on the slant with cut-away sides. There is a wide fluting to the rear of the clip which guides the rims of the cartridges and prevents them from being

displaced or shaken out when the magazine is partly empty. The guide is so efficient that no feeder spring is necessary, the cartridges being fed downwards by their own weight. The magazine is secured to the receiver by a spring-locked stud and is mounted on the right of the bolt so as not to interfere with the line of sight. When the bolt is withdrawn a lug on its side operates a right-angled lever at the bottom of the magazine which moves the cartridge sideways into the breech where the bolt can thrust it into the chamber.

980 Lebel Model 1886
One of the first small-bore rifles, this was the French Kropatchek rifle of 1885 modified to take a new 8 mm. cartridge of greater power using smokeless powder. The tubular magazine under the barrel holds eight cartridges which are pressed to the rear and on to a scoop-shaped carrier by a strong spiral spring. When the bolt is opened the carrier is raised and its cartridge pushed into the chamber by the returning bolt. The carrier can be immobilised and the rifle used as a single-shot.

981 Lee-Metford Rifle Mark II, 1892
This rifle embodies the bolt-action and vertical box magazine first patented by James P. Lee in 1879. The latter consists of a sheet-steel box inserted in an opening underneath the frame directly in front of the trigger guard, where it is held by a spring catch. A cut-off is fitted to the right side of the body which, when pressed inwards, stops the cartridge from rising out of the magazine and itself acts as a loading shelf. The rifle can then be fired and loaded singly. The Mark II magazine differs from its predecessor by holding ten cartridges in two columns instead of eight in one column. The magazine spring is C-shaped and is attached to the platform by a roller and slot connection.

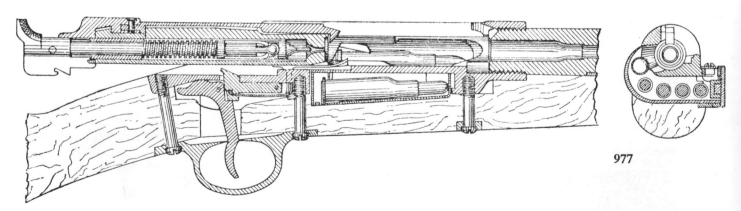

977

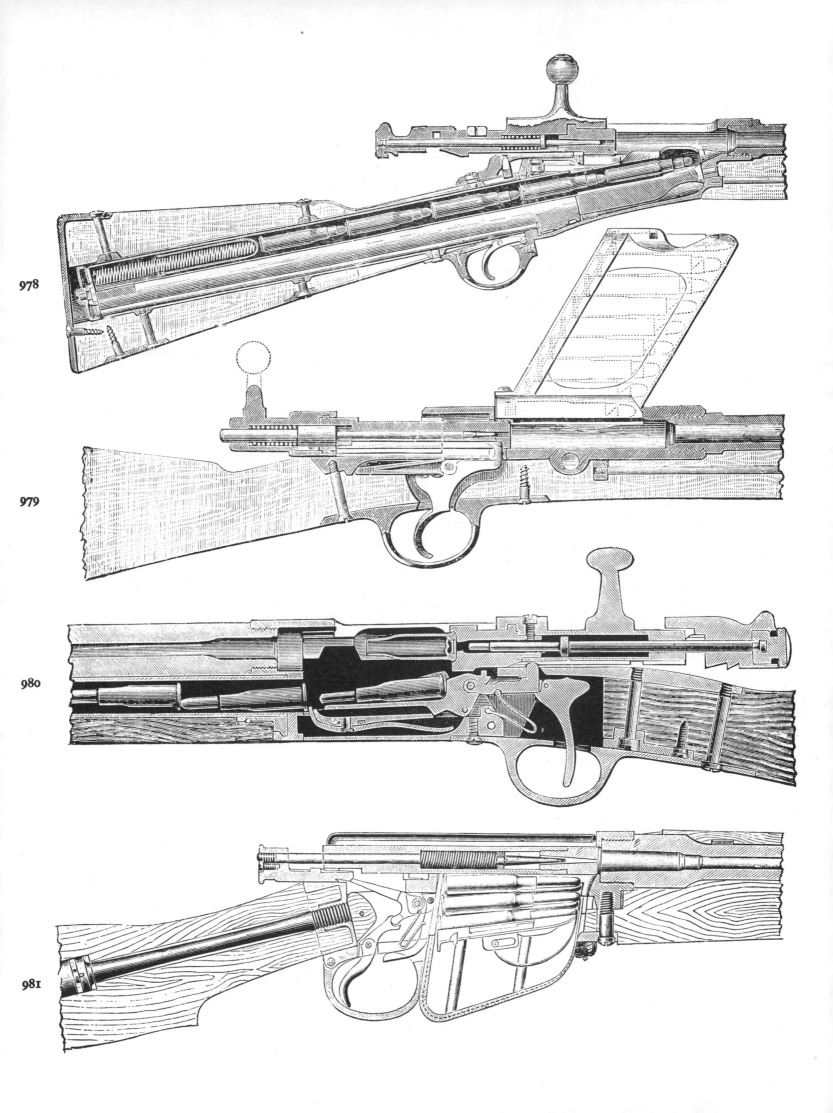

978

979

980

981

CARTRIDGES

For Separate Primers

982 Wrapped paper. For flintlock muzzleloaders. 17–18th century.

983 Wrapped paper. For British Enfield rifle, expanding bullet, 1859.

984 Cylindrical paper, reinforced base. Jean Ardouin, 1830 (*French Pat.*).

985 Cylindrical paper, soft metal base. Casimir Lefaucheux, 1834 (*French Pat.*).

986 Combustible linen. Used in American Sharps's rifle, *c.* 1860.

987 Hollow lead bullet, perforated metal base. Used in Hunt's 'Volitional Repeater'. 1847 (*English Pat.*).

988 Powder mixed with shellac, pressed into cartridge shape and coated with collodion for waterproofing. R. Bartholow, 1861 (*American Pat.*).

989 Paper with wadding base. For Westley Richards', Terry's or Greene's breechloaders. *c.* 1865.

990 Gut, spirally wound. J. Hotchkiss, 1862 (*American Pat.*).

991 All brass with perforated base (powder protected by disc of waxed paper). Edward Maynard, 1856 (*American Pat.*).

992 Black rubber. Gilbert Smith, 1857 (*American Pat.*).

993 Brass tapering case. A. E. Burnside, 1856. Large grease ridge added by P. Foster, 1860 (*American Pats.*).

994 Straight brass case with 'flop-ear' extension for extractor (another model has a cord extractor with percussion cap tied to other end). Edward Maynard, 1863 (*American Pat.*).

Percussion Primers

995 Pills.

996 Discs and patches. *Left* Sharps's disc.

997 Tubes. Right-hand one is that patented by Westley Richards in 1831.

998 Tapes. *Left* Maynard paper. *Right* Heurteloup metal.

999 Joseph Manton's wooden plug, 1834.

1000 Caps. Right-hand one is special shallow type pushed into side slot of nipple patented by William Needham in London, 1843.

Nipple Cartridges (for use with percussion caps)

1001 Paper case, screw-in metal base. Clement Pottet, 1829 (*French Pat.*).

1002 All-metal cartridge. Béatus Béringer, 1834 (*French Pat.*).

1003 Reloadable iron cartridge. Joseph Jarre, 1840 (*French Pat.*).

1004 Metal. For use in breechloader with diagonal striker. Bourcier, 1847 (*French Pat.*).

1005 Iron reloadable case. For use with repeating gun patented by S. H. Roper, 1866.

1006 Paper case secured to metal base by nipple screwed through to internal washer. T. Cullen, 1868 (*American Pat.*).

Pin-fire

1007 Paper case, brass base. Casimir Lefaucheux, 1835 (*French Pat.*).

1008 Improved seating of primer. Houllier, 1846–50 (*French Pat.*).

1009 All-metal. Devoir-Leclerq, 1853 (*French Pat.*).

1010 Pin passes through base and acts as extractor. Chaleyer, 1859 (*French Pat.*).

1011 Primer in middle of charge. William Greener, 1864 (*English Pat.*).

1012 Brass case with Minié bullet, interior pin. Gallager and Gladding, 1859 (*American Pat.*).

Rim-fire

1013 Metal base. Robert, 1831–5 (*French Pat.*).

1014 All-metal. Houllier, 1850 (*French Pat.*).

1015 Fulminate covers whole of base. Flobert, 1849 (*French Pat.*).

1016 Bottle-necked copper case, for Spencer repeating rifle. Based on American Pat. of Smith & Wesson, 1860.

1017 Front-loading copper case with cup base primer. Ellis & White, 1859 (*American Pat.*).

1018 Copper case with annular rim containing priming. S. Crispin, 1865 (*American and English Pats.*). Used in special Smith carbine.

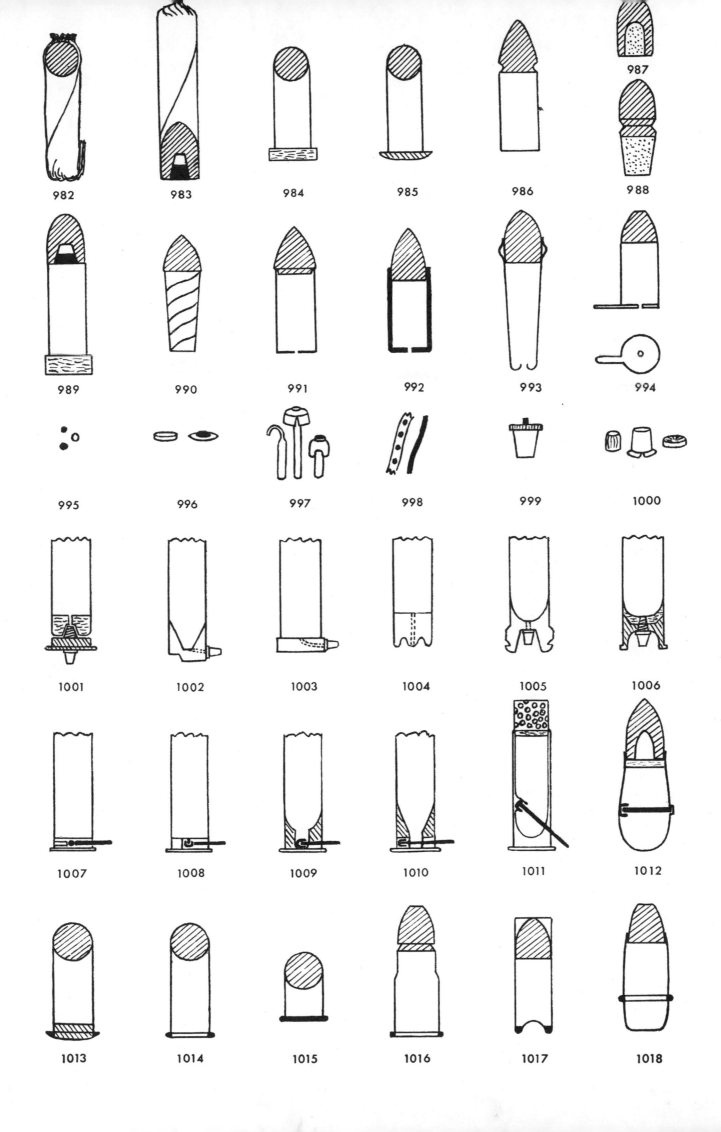

982 983 984 985 986 987 988

989 990 991 992 993 994

995 996 997 998 999 1000

1001 1002 1003 1004 1005 1006

1007 1008 1009 1010 1011 1012

1013 1014 1015 1016 1017 1018

CARTRIDGES

Teat and Lip

1019–20 Tube primer inserted in side and centre of wooden base. H. & P. Le Page, 1832 (*French Pat.*).

1021 A. H. Renette, 1835 (*French Pat.*).

1022 Heurteloup, 1835–7 (*French Pat.*).

1023 Houllier, 1846–50 (*French Pat.*).

1024 Combustible paper or cloth case tipped with fulminate. John Mollett, 1847 (*English Pat.*).

1025 Waterproof copper case with lip containing fulminate. E. Allen, 1860 (*American Pat.*).

1026 Copper case with flange at mouth and fulminated teat at base. D. Williamson, 1864 (*American Pat.*).

Needle-fire

1027 Wad and bullet for muzzleloader with powder chamber *à tige*. Needle passes through spigot. A. A. Moser, 1831 (*English Pat.*).

1028 Paper case for muzzleloader. B. F. Smith, 1839 (*American Pat.*).

1029 German Army cartridge for breechloader. 1847.

1030 Primer set in base wad. Needle does not penetrate powder. Spangenberg and Sauer, c. 1850.

1031 Needle fixed in case. Acts as extractor. A. L. Lenoir, 1849 (*French Pat.*), 1855 (*English Pat.*).

1032 German Army model 1872 with reinforced base.

Centre-fire

1033 Paper case. Brass base with fulminate 'rosette'. Pauly, 1816 (*English Pat.*).

1034 Parchment, leather or copper case. Cavity in base filled with fulminate, covered with waterproof paper. A. Galy-Cazalat, 1826–7 (*French Pat.*).

1035 Paper case, screw-in metal base. Clement Pottet, 1829 (*French Pat.*).

1036 Convex base with central fulminate. Montigny, 1833 (After *Thierbach*).

1037–8 Cylindro-conoidal bullet filled with mixture of fulminate and gunpowder, or spherical bullet cemented to charge box. W. Golden and J. Hanson, 1841 (*English Pat.*).

1039 Cup-shaped central primer for diagonal striker. Lefaucheux, 1847 (*French Pat.*).

1040 Cardboard case made in spiral coil for expansion. Joseph Needham, 1852 (*English Pat.*).

1041 Hollow conical bullet filled with gunpowder. Cork disc with fulminate covers base, left behind after discharge. Palmer, 1854 (*English and French Pats.*).

1042 Similar bullet. Priming in copper cup with steel disc anvil in base. Smith & Wesson, 1856 (*American Pat.*).

1043 Spigot from bullets acts as anvil for primer. L. Wells, 1857 (*American Pat.*).

1044 Metallic base-disc with primer and separate anvil. C. Pottet, 1855 (*French Pat.*).

1045 Metal case has pronged anvil soldered inside. G. W. Morse, 1858 (*American Pat.*).

1046 Paper case tied to bullet. Metal-strengthened base. M. Chassepot, 1866 (*French Pat.*)

1047 Expanding coiled brass case. Lubricated lead bullet with wood nose-plug and baked-clay base-plug. Iron base disc. English Boxer cartridge Mk. V, 1867.

Bullets

1048 Belted ball for British Brunswick rifle, 1837.

1049 Oval expanding bullet with plug. William Greener, 1836.

1050 'Balle cylindro-conique évidée'. Gustave Delvigne, 1841 (*French Pat.*).

1051 Expanding bullet with plug. C. E. Minié, 1849 (*French Pat.*).

1052 Self-expanding bullet for superimposed charges. John Macintosh, 1852 (*English and French Pats.*).

1053 Explosive shell studded for four-groove rifling. Copper detonator in nose. John Jacob, 1856.

1054 'Balle-obus' (explosive shell). Expanded by rammer. G. Delvigne, 1840 (*French Pat.*).

1055 Grooved lead ball with wooden nose and tail. C. Gillham, 1823 (*P.R.O., London, WO* 44/540).

1056 Hexagonal. Joseph Whitworth, 1860.

1057 Heller-Krnka tubular bullet. Separates from cardboard sabot after leaving muzzle. c. 1890.

1058 Dr. Macleod's self-rotating cylindrical bullet. Bored with four spiral holes. Conical cavity in base. Used with india-rubber wad. 1877.

1059 Modern lead bullet with nickel covering.

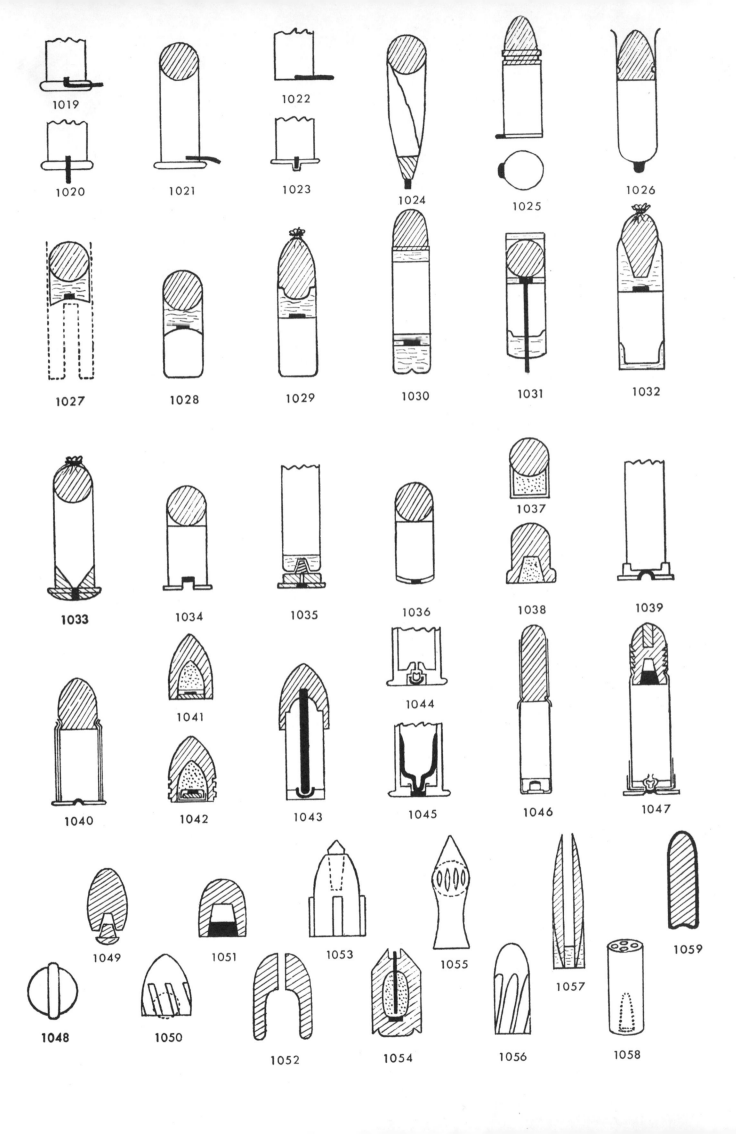

1019

1020

1021

1022

1023

1024

1025

1026

1027

1028

1029

1030

1031

1032

1033

1034

1035

1036

1037

1038

1039

1040

1041

1042

1043

1044

1045

1046

1047

1048

1049

1050

1051

1052

1053

1054

1055

1056

1057

1058

1059

SELECT BIBLIOGRAPHY

For complete bibliographies of works on firearms and related subjects, the reader is referred to those of Wirt Gerrare (1894), Maurice Cockle (1900), and Ray Riling (1951). Extensive lists are also appended to Sir James Mann's Catalogues of the European Arms and Armour in the Wallace Collection, London.

Alm, J., *Eldhandvapen*, 2 vols., Stockholm, 1933–4.

Angelucci, A., *Documenti inediti para la storia dell'armi a foco italiano*, 1850–69.

Ayalon, D., *Gunpowder and Firearms in the Mamluk Kingdom*, London, 1956.

Baker, E., *Remarks on Rifle Guns*, 11th edn., London, 1835.

Blackmore, H. L., *British Military Firearms, 1650–1850*, London, 1961.

Blair, C., *European & American Arms*, London, 1962.

Blanch, H. J., *A Century of Guns*, London, 1909.

Bottet, M., *Monographies de l'Arme Blanche (1789–1870) et de l'Arme à Feu Portative (1718–1900) des Armées Françaises de Terre et de Mer*, Paris, 1959.

Boudriot, J., *Armes à Feu Françaises Modèles Réglementaires*, 1re série, Paris, 1961; 2e série, Paris, 1963.

Carey, A. M., *English, Irish, and Scottish Firearms Makers*, New York, 1954. Reprinted, London, 1960.

Clephan, R. C., *An Outline of the History and Development of Hand Firearms*, London and Felling-on-Tyne, 1906.

Deane's *Manual of the History and Science of Fire-arms*, London, 1858.

Dillin, J. G., *The Kentucky Rifle*, 4th edn., New York, 1959.

Drummond, J., and Anderson, J., *Ancient Scottish Weapons*, London and Edinburgh, 1881.

Duchartre, P.-L., *Histoire des Armes de Chasse*, Paris, 1955.

Eckardt, W., and Morawietz, O., *Die Handwaffen des brandenburgisch-preussisch-deutschen Heeres 1640–1945*, Hamburg, 1957.

Edwards, W. B., *The Story of Colt's Revolver*, Harrisburg, Pa., 1953.
Civil War Guns, Harrisburg, Pa., 1962.

Egerton, Lord, of Tatton, *A Description of Indian and Oriental Armour*, London, 1896.

Fremantle, T. F., *The Book of the Rifle*, London, 1901.

Fuller, C. E., *Springfield Muzzleloading Shoulder Arms*, New York, 1930.
The Whitney Firearms, Huntington, W. Va., 1946.

Gardner, R. E., *Small Arms Makers*, New York, 1963.

George, J. N., *English Guns and Rifles*, Plantersville, S. Carolina, 1947.

Gluckman, A., *United States Muskets, Rifles and Carbines*, Buffalo, N. Y., 1948.

Gooding, S. J., *The Canadian Gunsmiths 1608 to 1900*, Ontario, 1962.

Grancsay, S. V., *American Engraved Powder Horns*, New York, 1945.

Grant, J. J., *Single-Shot Rifles*, New York, 1947.
More Single-Shot Rifles, New York, 1959.

Greener, William, *The Science of Gunnery*, London, 1841.

Greener, W. W., *The Gun and its Development*, 9th edn., London, 1910.

Hanson, C. E., *The Northwest Gun*, Lincoln, Nebraska, 1955.

Hatch, A., *Remington Arms in American History*, New York and Toronto, 1956.

Haven, C. T., and Belden, F. A., *A History of the Colt Revolver*, New York, 1940.

Hayward, J. F., *The Art of the Gunmaker*, Vol. I, London, 1962; Vol. II, London, 1963.

Held, R., *The Age of Firearms*, New York, 1957.

Hicks, J. E., *Ordnance Correspondence*, Mount Vernon, N.Y., 1940.
U.S. Firearms 1776–1956, Beverly Hills, Calif., 1957.

Hoff, A., *Aeldre Dansk Bøssemageri isaer i 1600-tallet*, 2 vols., Copenhagen, 1951.

Kauffmann, H. J., *Early American Gunsmiths 1650–1850*, Harrisburg, Pa., 1952.
The Pennsylvania-Kentucky Rifle, Harrisburg, Pa., 1960.

Lavin, J. D., *A History of Spanish Firearms*, London, 1965.

Lenk, T., *Flintlåset dess uppkomst och utveckling*, Stockholm, 1939.

Lewis, B. R., *Small Arms and Ammunition in the United States Service*, Washington, D.C., 1956.

Logan, H. C., *Cartridges*, Huntington, W. Va., 1948.
  Underhammer Guns, Harrisburg, Pa., 1960.

Madis, G., *The Winchester Book*, Dallas, Texas, 1961.

Malatesta, E., *Armi ed Armaioli d'Italia*, Rome, 1946.

Margerand, J., *Armement et Equipement de l'Infanterie Française du XVIᵉ au XXᵉ Siècle*, Paris, 1945.

Mattenheimer, A., *Die Rückladungs-Gewehr*, Darmstadt and Leipzig, 1876.

Meyerson, Å., *Stockholms Bössmakare*, Stockholm, 1936.

Moller, T., *Gamle Danske Militaervåben* (Old Danish Military Weapons), Copenhagen, 1963 (with English translation).

Neal, W. K., *Spanish Guns and Pistols*, London, 1955.

Parsons, J. E., *The First Winchester*, New York, 1955.

Partington, J. R., *A History of Greek Fire and Gunpowder*, Cambridge, 1960.

Peterson, H. L., *Arms and Armor in Colonial America, 1526–1783*, Harrisburg, Pa., 1956.
  The Treasury of the Gun, New York, 1962. English edition (*The Book of the Gun*), London, 1963.
  (editor) *Encyclopedia of Firearms*, London and New York, 1964.

Pollard, H. B. C., *A History of Firearms*, London, 1930.

Rathgen, B., *Das Aufkommen der Pulverwaffe*, Munich, 1925.
  Das Geschütz im Mittelalter, Berlin, 1928.

Rensselaer, S. van, *American Firearms*, Watkins Glen, N.Y., 1947.

Reynolds, E. G. B., *The Lee-Enfield Rifle*, London, 1960.

Riling, R., *The Powder Flask Book*, New Hope, Pa., 1953.

Roads, C. H., *The British Soldier's Firearm, 1850–1864*, London, 1964.

Sawyer, C. W., *Firearms in American History*, 3 vols., Boston, U.S.A., 1910–20.

Schedelmann, H., *Die Wiener Büchsenmacher und Büchsenschäfter*, Berlin, 1944.

Serven, J. E., *Colt Firearms, 1836–1958*, Santa Ana, Calif, 1959.

Smith, W. H. B., *Mannlicher Rifles and Pistols*, Harrisburg, Pa., 1947.
  Mauser Rifles and Pistols, Harrisburg, Pa., 3rd edn., 1950.
  Gas, Air and Spring Guns of the World, Harrisburg, Pa., 1957.

Smith. W. O., *The Sharps Rifle*, New York, 1943.

Støckel, J. F., *Haandskydevaabens Bedømmelse*, 2 vols., Copenhagen, 1938–43.

Stone, G. C., *A Glossary of the Construction, Decoration and Use of Arms and Armor in all Countries and in all Times*, Portland, Maine, 1934.

Stonehenge (pseud. of J. H. Walsh, *q.v.*), *The Shot-gun and Sporting Rifle*, London, 1859.

Thierbach, M., *Die geschichtliche Entwickelung der Handfeuerwaffen*, Dresden, 1886–7.

Tout, T. F., 'Firearms in England in the Fourteenth Century', *English Historical Review*, Vol. XXVI (London, 1911), pp. 666–702. Reprinted in *The Collected Papers of Thomas Frederick Tout*, Vol. II, Manchester, 1934, pp. 233–75.

Walsh, J. H., *The Modern Sportsman's Gun and Rifle*, 2 vols., London, 1882–4.

Werner, E. T. C., *Chinese Weapons*, Shanghai, 1932.

Wesley, L., *Air-guns and Air-pistols*, London, 1955.

Whitelaw, C. E., 'A Treatise on Scottish Hand Firearms'. Part of *European Hand Firearms of the 16th, 17th and 18th Centuries*, by H. J. Jackson (London, 1923).

Williamson, H. F., *Winchester—The Gun That Won The West*, Washington, D.C., 1952.
  Pepperbox Firearms, New York, 1952.

Winant, L., *Firearms Curiosa*, New York, 1955. Reprinted, London, 1961.
  Early Percussion Firearms, New York, 1959. English edition, London, 1961.

Wolff, E. G., *Air Guns*, Milwaukee Public Museum Publications in History No. 1, Milwaukee, 1958.

INDEX